THE NIV
APPLICATION
COMMENTARY

From biblical text . . . to contemporary life

THE NIV APPLICATION COMMENTARY SERIES

THE NIV APPLICATION COMMENTARY

From biblical text . . . to contemporary life

JAMES BRUCKNER

ZONDERVAN®

GRAND RAPIDS, MICHIGAN 49530 USA

ZONDERVAN.COM/
AUTHOR**TRACKER**

Dedication

To Kristine Anne
embraced by the LORD
light of Christ
God's treasured dove and comfort

ZONDERVAN®

The NIV Application Commentary: Jonah, Nahum, Habakkuk, Zephaniah
Copyright © 2004 by James Bruckner

Requests for information should be addressed to:

Zondervan, *Grand Rapids, Michigan 49530*

Library of Congress Cataloging-in-Publication Data

Bruckner, James K.
  Jonah, Nahum, Habakkuk, Zephaniah / James K. Bruckner.—1st ed.
    p. cm.—(NIV application commentary)
  Includes bibliographical references and indexes.
  ISBN-10: 0–310–20637–5
  ISBN-13: 978-0-310-20637-8
    1. Bible. O.T. Jonah—Commentaries. 2. Bible. O.T. Nahum—Commentaries.
  3. Bible. O.T. Habakkuk—Commentaries. 4. Bible. O.T. Zephaniah—Commentaries.
  I. Title. II. Series.
  BS1605.53 .B78 2004
  224'.9077—dc22   2003022095
                                                                    CIP

This edition printed on acid-free paper.

Printed in the United States of America

---

10 11 12 • 12 11 10 9 8 7

Contents

7
Series Introduction

11
General Editor's Preface

13
Author Preface

15
Abbreviations

17
Introduction to Jonah

35
Outline of Jonah

36
Select Bibliography on Jonah

39
Text and Commentary on Jonah

133
Introduction to Nahum

140
Outline of Nahum

141
Select Bibliography on Nahum

143
Text and Commentary on Nahum

197
Introduction to Habakkuk

204
Outline of Habakkuk

205
Select Bibliography on Habakkuk

207
Text and Commentary on Habakkuk

271
Introduction to Zephaniah

278
Outline of Zephaniah

279
Select Bibliography on Zephaniah

281
Text and Commentary on Zephaniah

345
Scripture Index

353
Subject Index

The NIV Application Commentary Series

When complete, the NIV Application Commentary
will include the following volumes:

Old Testament Volumes

Genesis, John H. Walton

Exodus, Peter Enns

Leviticus/Numbers, Roy Gane

Deuteronomy, Daniel I. Block

Joshua, Robert L. Hubbard Jr.

Judges/Ruth, K. Lawson Younger

1-2 Samuel, Bill T. Arnold

1-2 Kings, Gus Konkel

1-2 Chronicles, Andrew E. Hill

Ezra/Nehemiah, Douglas J. Green

Esther, Karen H. Jobes

Job, Dennis R. Magary

Psalms Volume 1, Gerald H. Wilson

Psalms Volume 2, Jamie A. Grant

Proverbs, Paul Koptak

Ecclesiastes/Song of Songs, Iain Provan

Isaiah, John N. Oswalt

Jeremiah/Lamentations, J. Andrew Dearman

Ezekiel, Iain M. Duguid

Daniel, Tremper Longman III

Hosea/Amos/Micah, Gary V. Smith

Jonah/Nahum/Habakkuk/Zephaniah,
    James Bruckner

Joel/Obadiah/Malachi, David W. Baker

Haggai/Zechariah, Mark J. Boda

New Testament Volumes

Matthew, Michael J. Wilkins

Mark, David E. Garland

Luke, Darrell L. Bock

John, Gary M. Burge

Acts, Ajith Fernando

Romans, Douglas J. Moo

1 Corinthians, Craig Blomberg

2 Corinthians, Scott Hafemann

Galatians, Scot McKnight

Ephesians, Klyne Snodgrass

Philippians, Frank Thielman

Colossians/Philemon, David E. Garland

1-2 Thessalonians, Michael W. Holmes

1-2 Timothy/Titus, Walter L. Liefeld

Hebrews, George H. Guthrie

James, David P. Nystrom

1 Peter, Scot McKnight

2 Peter/Jude, Douglas J. Moo

Letters of John, Gary M. Burge

Revelation, Craig S. Keener

To see which titles are available,
visit our web site at www.zondervan.com

NIV Application Commentary
Series Introduction

THE NIV APPLICATION COMMENTARY SERIES is unique. Most commentaries help us make the journey from our world back to the world of the Bible. They enable us to cross the barriers of time, culture, language, and geography that separate us from the biblical world. Yet they only offer a one-way ticket to the past and assume that we can somehow make the return journey on our own. Once they have explained the *original meaning* of a book or passage, these commentaries give us little or no help in exploring its *contemporary significance*. The information they offer is valuable, but the job is only half done.

Recently, a few commentaries have included some contemporary application as *one* of their goals. Yet that application is often sketchy or moralistic, and some volumes sound more like printed sermons than commentaries.

The primary goal of the NIV Application Commentary Series is to help you with the difficult but vital task of bringing an ancient message into a modern context. The series not only focuses on application as a finished product but also helps you think through the *process* of moving from the original meaning of a passage to its contemporary significance. These are commentaries, not popular expositions. They are works of reference, not devotional literature.

The format of the series is designed to achieve the goals of the series. Each passage is treated in three sections: *Original Meaning, Bridging Contexts,* and *Contemporary Significance.*

THIS SECTION HELPS you understand the meaning of the biblical text in its original context. All of the elements of traditional exegesis—in concise form—are discussed here. These include the historical, literary, and cultural context of the passage. The authors discuss matters related to grammar and syntax and the meaning of biblical words.[1] They also seek to explore the main ideas of the passage and how the biblical author develops those ideas.

---

1. Please note that in general, when the authors discuss words in the original biblical languages, the series uses a general rather than a scholarly method of transliteration.

After reading this section, you will understand the problems, questions, and concerns of the *original audience* and how the biblical author addressed those issues. This understanding is foundational to any legitimate application of the text today.

THIS SECTION BUILDS a bridge between the world of the Bible and the world of today, between the original context and the contemporary context, by focusing on both the timely and timeless aspects of the text.

God's Word is *timely*. The authors of Scripture spoke to specific situations, problems, and questions. The author of Joshua encouraged the faith of his original readers by narrating the destruction of Jericho, a seemingly impregnable city, at the hands of an angry warrior God (Josh. 6). Paul warned the Galatians about the consequences of circumcision and the dangers of trying to be justified by law (Gal. 5:2–5). The author of Hebrews tried to convince his readers that Christ is superior to Moses, the Aaronic priests, and the Old Testament sacrifices. John urged his readers to "test the spirits" of those who taught a form of incipient Gnosticism (1 John 4:1–6). In each of these cases, the timely nature of Scripture enables us to hear God's Word in situations that were *concrete* rather than abstract.

Yet the timely nature of Scripture also creates problems. Our situations, difficulties, and questions are not always directly related to those faced by the people in the Bible. Therefore, God's word to them does not always seem relevant to us. For example, when was the last time someone urged you to be circumcised, claiming that it was a necessary part of justification? How many people today care whether Christ is superior to the Aaronic priests? And how can a "test" designed to expose incipient Gnosticism be of any value in a modern culture?

Fortunately, Scripture is not only timely but *timeless*. Just as God spoke to the original audience, so he still speaks to us through the pages of Scripture. Because we share a common humanity with the people of the Bible, we discover a *universal dimension* in the problems they faced and the solutions God gave them. The timeless nature of Scripture enables it to speak with power in every time and in every culture.

Those who fail to recognize that Scripture is both timely and timeless run into a host of problems. For example, those who are intimidated by timely books such as Hebrews, Galatians, or Deuteronomy might avoid reading them because they seem meaningless today. At the other extreme, those who are convinced of the timeless nature of Scripture, but who fail to discern its timely element, may "wax eloquent" about the Melchizedekian priest-hood to a sleeping congregation, or worse still, try to apply the holy wars of the Old Testament in a physical way to God's enemies today.

The purpose of this section, therefore, is to help you discern what is timeless in the timely pages of the Bible—and what is not. For example, how do the holy wars of the Old Testament relate to the spiritual warfare of the New? If Paul's primary concern is not circumcision (as he tells us in Gal. 5:6), what *is* he concerned about? If discussions about the Aaronic priesthood or Melchizedek seem irrelevant today, what is of abiding value in these passages? If people try to "test the spirits" today with a test designed for a specific first-century heresy, what other biblical test might be more appropriate?

Yet this section does not merely uncover that which is timeless in a pas-sage but also helps you to see *how* it is uncovered. The authors of the com-mentaries seek to take what is implicit in the text and make it explicit, to take a process that normally is intuitive and explain it in a logical, orderly fash-ion. How do we know that circumcision is not Paul's primary concern? What clues in the text or its context help us realize that Paul's real concern is at a deeper level?

Of course, those passages in which the historical distance between us and the original readers is greatest require a longer treatment. Conversely, those passages in which the historical distance is smaller or seemingly nonex-istent require less attention.

One final clarification. Because this section prepares the way for dis-cussing the contemporary significance of the passage, there is not always a sharp distinction or a clear break between this section and the one that fol-lows. Yet when both sections are read together, you should have a strong sense of moving from the world of the Bible to the world of today.

THIS SECTION ALLOWS the biblical message to speak with as much power today as it did when it was first written. How can you apply what you learned about Jerusalem, Ephesus, or Corinth to our present-day needs in Chicago, Los Angeles, or London? How can you take a message originally spoken in Greek, Hebrew, and Aramaic and com-municate it clearly in our own language? How can you take the eternal truths originally spoken in a different time and culture and apply them to the sim-ilar-yet-different needs of our culture?

In order to achieve these goals, this section gives you help in several key areas.

(1) It helps you identify contemporary situations, problems, or questions that are truly comparable to those faced by the original audience. Because contemporary situations are seldom identical to those faced by the original audience, you must seek situations that are analogous if your applications are to be relevant.

(2) This section explores a variety of contexts in which the passage might be applied today. You will look at personal applications, but you will also be encouraged to think beyond private concerns to the society and culture at large.

(3) This section will alert you to any problems or difficulties you might encounter in seeking to apply the passage. And if there are several legitimate ways to apply a passage (areas in which Christians disagree), the author will bring these to your attention and help you think through the issues involved.

In seeking to achieve these goals, the contributors to this series attempt to avoid two extremes. They avoid making such specific applications that the commentary might quickly become dated. They also avoid discussing the significance of the passage in such a general way that it fails to engage contemporary life and culture.

Above all, contributors to this series have made a diligent effort not to sound moralistic or preachy. The NIV Application Commentary Series does not seek to provide ready-made sermon materials but rather tools, ideas, and insights that will help you communicate God's Word with power. If we help you to achieve that goal, then we have fulfilled the purpose for this series.

The Editors

General Editor's Preface

THE STORY OF JONAH IS SIMPLE, but with the help of James Bruckner's excellent commentary, each component of the story line teaches us an important lesson.

God asks Jonah to do something. What God asks Jonah to do is precisely stated in Jonah 1:2: "Go to the great city of Nineveh and preach against it, because its wickedness has come up before me." This is a dangerous task. God is asking Jonah to be a prophet, to bring the word of the Lord, an unwelcome message, to a people who are not living up to God's standards.

Jonah refuses. We are not used to this in the Old Testament. The other major and minor prophets all accept the challenge and do what God requests. (Nahum, in fact, seems to do precisely what God wants in presenting oracles of judgment against Nineveh.) Jonah, by contrast, is a kind of anti-prophet, a man who refuses God's call in the first place and then, when he finally acquiesces, is disappointed in the way God handles things.

Jonah not only refuses, he flees. In this incident we find much about his character. By running to Joppa to seek a ship to Tarshish, Jonah betrays his belief, his conscience, and a certain naïveté. He *believes* in God and God's request and has enough faith to hear God's voice. His *conscience* tells him that he is doing wrong by refusing God—why else would he flee? And he is *naïve* to think that he can escape the consequences of his refusal by changing his physical locale.

God punishes Jonah. The punishment—the ocean storm, being thrown overboard, being swallowed by a fish, being spit up on a beach after three days—is the usual focal point of the story in our imaginations.

Jonah complies with God's request. In the moralistic way the story is often told, the effectiveness and imaginativeness of the punishment is reinforced in our minds because Jonah's reluctance melts away (and whose wouldn't?). By all accounts, he gives the Ninevites God's message straight: "Forty days and Nineveh will be overturned" (3:4).

Jonah gets angry with God for his resolution of the story. When the Ninevites repent, God doesn't carry out Jonah's threat of destruction in forty days. Jonah is peeved. His prophetic integrity is on the line.

But the moralistic way the story is often told, emphasizing Jonah's disobedience and God's surreal punishment, can mask some of the other important dimensions of the story. Jonah as anti-prophet is far closer to our modern experience of vocation, perhaps, than we sometimes realize. We don't hear

God's call so clearly—we have to take classes on finding God's will for our life. We think of our religion as a religion of thinking right rather than doing good.

Another equally valuable way to read the story of Jonah is to focus on the first and last parts rather than the middle three sections. God makes an extravagant request of Jonah. It is a dangerous task, a mission impossible. Yet the message of Jonah is that this kind of request is not the exception but the rule. What is exceptional about Jonah is that he refuses God's call. The story of Jonah teaches us that we are all required to serve God, to act based on the graceful salvation God gives us. Moreover, Jonah teaches us that some of us, sometimes, meet the challenge and some of us, sometimes, don't. What is universal is that God calls us all.

So what does this reading lead us to do? (1) We should expect to be summoned by God to do something for the kingdom, and we should seek it and embrace it when we find it. This is not a burden; rather, it is an affirmation of who we are. We are the called ones. Followers of Christ are not just groupies but members of the road team. Mature Christians hear the calls of God—and there will be many in our lifetimes—and our hearing leads seamlessly to action.

(2) We should not be overly concerned if our actions don't lead to the outcomes we expect. Jonah wanted results that he felt vindicated his message of punishment. God had a wider grace to apply to the Ninevites. Once we have understood God's call—with the church's help, of course—and have faithfully acted in ways consistent with that call and the gifts God has given us, we must trust God to bring about a resolution. That is God's business, not ours. Others may plant the seeds, we may water and tend, but God gives the growth.

Terry C. Muck

Author Preface

CONSIDER WHAT IT MEANS TO BE FAITHFUL to God when violent enemies press hard upon you. The prophets Jonah, Nahum, Habakkuk, and Zephaniah offer God's hope and resources in the midst of personal and societal crises. They still speak to people who struggle to deal with violence. Jonah's struggle was with Nineveh, Assyria. The others struggled with the new power of Babylon, which destroyed Nineveh (Nahum) and would later destroy Judah (Habakkuk/Zephaniah). In each case God gave them words that are still timely. How should we think about the successes of terror in our world? How might we live with integrity in the midst of its threat? These prophets lived through situations in which God provided a word to sustain and strengthen his people.

I am grateful to my students, many who are now pastors and teachers, who read these texts with me in Hebrew classes. They provided an opportunity to read patiently and to soak in the rich prophetic language. I am thankful for the dedication and insights of my teachers, who are too many to be comprehensively named. Most may be found listed in the bibliography. I am especially grateful to Fredrick Carlson Holmgren and Terence E. Fretheim for their friendship and for demonstrating their care for and delight in the biblical text. Special thanks are also due to Bob Hubbard for his counsel, as well as to Andrew Dearman and Verlyn Verbrugge, who read the manuscript and improved it for the reader. I am thankful to all the people at Zondervan for the opportunity to deepen my appreciation for these biblical books and write about them.

I am indebted to those who gave me support during the labor of writing: North Park University and the Seminary administration provided a sabbatical for my research; the Oxford Center for Hebrew and Jewish Studies provided kind hospitality; the seminary faculty and staff encouraged me; librarians Ann Briody and Norma Sutton lent their expert help; student assistants Liang-Her Wu, Andrew Fortuine, and Karl Freeberg found what I needed when I needed it; my teaching assistant Paul Corner proofread the manuscript and created the indexes.

Whatever help you find in this volume for living a life of integrity before God in difficult circumstances is due, in part, to my father, the late Rev. Donald J. Bruckner. Every week he inquired about this book in detail. He encouraged me, raised hermeneutical questions, and laughed long with joy at any insight uncovered. My three sons also deserve credit. They gave me permission to write in the evenings (and sometimes on Saturdays) by their smiles and genuine words.

I dedicate this volume to my wife Kris. She not only encouraged and sustained me, but she listened long and often to new ways of expressing the meaning of these four books. Her patience and incisive questions lightened the burden. She was the first reader and her writing expertise makes this a better commentary.

James K. Bruckner
North Park Theological Seminary
February 2004

Abbreviations

AB	Anchor Bible
ABD	*Anchor Bible Dictionary*
BAR	*Biblical Archaeology Review*
BDB	F. Brown, S. R. Driver, C. A. Briggs, *A Hebrew and English Lexicon of the Old Testament* (Oxford: Clarendon, 1951)
BO	Berit Olam
HCOT	Historical Commentary on the Old Testament
ICC	International Critical Commentary
ITC	International Theological Commentary
LXX	Septuagint (Greek translation of the Old Testament)
NIB	*New Interpreter's Bible*
NIBC	New International Biblical Commentary
NICOT	New International Commentary on the Old Testament
NIV	New International Version
OTG	Old Testament Guides
OTL	Old Testament Library
TOTC	Tyndale Old Testament Commentary
WBC	Word Biblical Commentary
WEC	Wycliffe Exegetical Commentary

Introduction to Jonah

JONAH, NAHUM, HABAKKUK, AND ZEPHANIAH are four of the minor prophets. Although they are "minor" in length (each is about fifty verses), they are a crucial portion of God's revelation to his people. Originally, they were part of one scroll called "The Book of the Twelve," which included Hosea, Joel, Amos, Obadiah, *Jonah*, Micah, *Nahum, Habakkuk, Zephaniah*, Haggai, Zechariah, and Malachi. These twelve cover approximately three hundred significant years (750 B.C. to 450 B.C.) of Israel's prophetic tradition. Their canonical order is based on biblical references to the prophets' political activity. The first five prophets (Hosea to Jonah) were active sometime during the reign of Jeroboam II (d. 746 B.C.), king of the ten northern tribes. Micah was active just after that time (Micah 1:1), probably until 701 B.C., when Jerusalem almost fell to the Assyrians (see Isa. 36–39).

After a period of seventy years, Nahum, Habakkuk, and Zephaniah speak, during the new crisis of the rise of Babylon, which destroyed Nineveh (Nahum's prophecy) and would later destroy Judah (Habakkuk's and Zephaniah's prophecies). Jeremiah was a contemporary of these prophets. None of the minor prophets prophesied during the seventy-year Babylonian exile. The last three (Haggai, Zechariah, and Malachi) coincide with the return from exile and the rebuilding of Jerusalem and the temple. The four books covered in this commentary are at the center of "The Book of the Twelve."[1] They call God's people to consider what it means to be faithful when violent enemies press upon them.

Jonah's Content and Messages

THE BOOK OF Jonah contains only fifty-eight verses, but those few verses include a storm at sea, the conversion of sailors, a miraculous rescue, a song of praise, the repentance of Israel's archenemy, and an intensely honest dialogue between the Yahweh and Israel's most reluctant prophet. They reveal the nature of Yahweh's relationship to the Gentile sailors, to Israel's enemy Nineveh, to nonhuman creation (the wind, a fish, vine, worm, and cattle), as well as to his messenger Jonah. The book is, in many ways, a microcosm of God's relationship to his whole creation in history. Although the narrative is sometimes melodramatic, it covers serious subject matter. It provides an

---

1. Micah is too long to be included in this volume.

occasion for discussion of what no one really wants to talk about: God's role in the persistence of evil in the world. Jonah is engaged in an earnest protest (his running away from Nineveh) and discussion (in ch. 4) with God about the violent Ninevites.

The theme of life and death is developed in all four chapters, as the narrative explores life in relationship to Yahweh. The text considers the Ninevites' evil and their repentance, Jonah's response to God's difficult call, and the sailors' trust in and worship of the true God. Chapter 1 is about the threatened death and saved life of the sailors and Jonah. Chapter 2 concerns Jonah's death and life within Yahweh's great fish. Chapter 3 is about the death and life of the Ninevites and their animals. Chapter 4 focuses on the life and death of the vine as God's object lesson for the Ninevites' and Jonah's life in the presence of the Creator.

The book is also about the struggle of all peoples to come to terms with God's reputation. Jonah was reluctant to go and preach against Nineveh (1:1–4) because of their legendary violence and terror. He knew that if they should repent, God would likely relent from his fierce anger. His preference was that they should be destroyed. As Jonah said, "I knew that you are a gracious and compassionate God, slow to anger and abounding in love, a God who relents from sending calamity" (4:2b).

Jonah runs from Yahweh's presence (in Israel) by boarding a ship for Tarshish, and Yahweh "hurls" a great wind to slow him down. The storm causes the sailors, whose lives are on the line (1:5–12), to cry out to their own gods, lighten the ship, and cast lots to discover whose sin caused such a violent storm. They interrogate Jonah, hear his witness, and are terrified, since his god is Yahweh, who "made the sea and the land." Finally, they ask Yahweh's prophet what to do. He acknowledges his guilt and offers himself as a sacrifice for their safety.

The sailors' relationship to Yahweh then moves to the foreground (1:13–16). With charity toward Jonah, they attempt to row out of their difficulty, but the sea grows "even wilder than before," and they cry out to Yahweh for mercy. When they throw Jonah overboard, the sea stands still, and the sailors believe, offer sacrifices, and make vows to the God of heaven, sea, and earth. With the sailors worshiping onboard, the text's attention turns to Jonah in the water. Yahweh's great fish swallows him, and Jonah, like the sailors, prays a prayer of thanksgiving (1:17, 2:1–10).

In chapter 2 Jonah gives thanks for his life, from within the belly of the great fish. It begins with a summary of his "distress and cry" and continues with four more stanzas (verses) that describe Jonah's distress in the water before he was swallowed (2:3–6). The waves at the surface swept over him, and he longed for the temple, sunk to the seaweed on the bottom, and finally to the ocean floor (2:6). The song of thanks concludes with Jonah's refrain, and he declares that "salvation comes from the LORD." Yahweh's fish then vomits Jonah onto dry land (2:7–10).

Jonah 3 concerns the Ninevites' (and their animals') relationship to the Creator. When Yahweh's word comes to Jonah "a second time," he obeys immediately, and he completes the mission on the first day: "The Ninevites believed God" (3:1–5). The king hears how the city has been overturned in repentance. He, too, responds in belief and in hope that God will "with compassion turn from his fierce anger." God does (3:6–10).

Chapter 4 returns to Jonah's relationship with God and highlights Jonah's anger and God's abiding love. Jonah has fulfilled his calling to Nineveh only under the threat of his own death (see ch. 2). Now his anger with Yahweh's way is made fully manifest (4:1–5). In an attempt to demonstrate his compassion and make his point, Yahweh sends a vine to shade him, then a worm to destroy the shade, and finally a scorching wind (4:6–8). The book concludes as Yahweh reasons with Jonah, declaring his concern for all he has created, including 120,000 Ninevites as well as their cattle (4:9–11).

Interpretations

THROUGH THE CENTURIES Christians have held many diverse and wide-ranging interpretations of the primary message of Jonah. The narrative's rich imagery and plentiful themes help explain this diversity. Commentaries have, unfortunately, often focused on one salient message or another as if it were the message of the whole. Four general messages have been developed through the centuries of interpretation that continue to influence our understanding of Jonah today, although each limits the book in its own way.[2]

The Sovereignty of God and a Moral Tale: John Calvin and Disney's Pinocchio

THIS TRADITION OF interpretation presents Jonah as a negative example. Calvin suggests that Jonah wrote this account in order to teach us the futility of fleeing from God. Jonah is severely chastised by Calvin for his "disgraceful obstinacy" in fleeing his duty for the pleasures of Tarshish.[3] In a secular twist on this view, Walt Disney's movie *Pinocchio* (which rewrote the original book

---

2. See Yvonne Sherwood, *A Biblical Text and Its Afterlives: The Survival of Jonah in Western Culture* (Cambridge: Cambridge Univ. Press, 2000) for a fine history of interpretation.

3. Cited, with an extensive summary of this theme in ibid., 32–42.

with Jonah-like themes) portrays a rebellious puppet who is swallowed by a whale. The moral fairy tale of "the sufferings of the disobedient" plays out a warning similar to Calvin's reading of Jonah.[4] The characters of both Jonah and Pinocchio are portrayed as negative moral examples, whose behavior and attitudes we are to avoid in order to thwart suffering. The purpose of Jonah is to make us obedient through the fear of Yahweh.

A related vein of interpretation has been to see Jonah as an allegory for the church's responsibility to missionary outreach. When one is called to ministry or mission, resistance is futile. This approach does not take into account the vibrant biblical tradition of vigorous conversation and even protest that God invites (with Abraham, Jacob, Moses, and many of the prophets). Neither does it consider Jesus' positive assessment of Jonah as an example in relation to himself (Matt. 12:39–41; Luke 11:29–32).

Repentance and Forgiveness of the Ninevites

THE AMAZINGLY SWIFT repentance and deliverance of the Ninevites is a strong message in chapter 3. The miracle of their repentance from evil is in many ways as astounding as the fish that swallows Jonah. There are several lessons in this theme. Sometimes God's grace breaks in unexpectedly, people turn to him, and God forgives. If the Ninevites can repent, anyone can. Their model of repentance has been presented as the main theme of Jonah in the history of interpretation by both Christian and Jewish commentators.[5] Jonah is an antihero in this tradition of interpretation. He is opposed to the repentance (and even the survival!) of Israel's violent enemy, the Ninevites. According to this view, the purpose of Jonah is, therefore, to demonstrate the love of God for all people and to bring us to repentance before a gracious and merciful God. This God will not condemn anyone who seeks him.

The limitation of this theme is its relative absence in chapters 1, 2, and 4. The sailors in chapter 1, for instance, simply cry out to their gods and to God to be saved from the storm (not necessarily for repentance). Jonah does not repent in his prayer in chapter 2 but simply gives thanks for his unexpected deliverance. Jonah once again does not repent in chapter 4 (though we may wish he would) but remains angry and defiant before God. In addition, Yahweh's rationale (in ch. 4) for pardon is not that the Ninevites should be accepted because of their repentance (even though that is necessary). He argues, rather, that they are to be pitied as his ignorant creation (4:11). Certainly repentance is an important theme, but it does not carry the weight of all four chapters.

---

4. See ibid., 60–61.
5. See full discussion of the theme of repentance in the Bridging Contexts section of ch. 3.

Jonah Is Submitted to Scientific Proofs

POPULARIZED BY REV. E. PUSEY'S 1860 commentary, this relatively recent tradition focuses on the size and species of the fish/whale, the size of the fish's larynx and stomach, the availability of breathable air, and so on.[6] In this view Jonah is a litmus test of one's belief in science as a means of proving the veracity of the Bible. This approach limits the message of Jonah to two verses and a specific nineteenth-century view of reality (1:17: "But the LORD provided a great fish to swallow Jonah, and Jonah was inside the fish three days and three nights"; 2:10: "And the LORD commanded the fish, and it vomited Jonah onto dry land.").

Preoccupation with the big fish (the Heb. has "big fish," not "whale") has had both a positive and negative effect on the interpretation of Jonah in communities of faith. Positively, the great fish has kindled imagination and interest in Jonah as a book. Negatively, however, the great fish has so dominated this interpretation that the discussion of the book has been limited to this question: "Was Jonah really swallowed by that whale?" This question has served as a distraction from God's Word. For some, it is a test of literary sophistication, and to answer "yes" excludes you from the company of the supposedly well-read. Answer "no," and many will assume that you do not believe in miracles, or worse, in the authority of Scripture. When this litmus test is over, many assume that everything important about Jonah has been settled.

As to the question whether Jonah was really swallowed by the "whale," people of faith offer two possibilities: Either it really happened, or this is a literary device in a parable, telling a wonderful story of instruction. Some Christian interpreters have used this second approach in an attempt to rescue the book of Jonah for people of faith. Their motivation was to save the message (*kerygma*) of biblical books by demythologizing texts like Jonah.

I personally have no difficulty believing that the prophet was actually engulfed, housed, and vomited by a great fish. This miracle is easier to believe than the greater miracle of the Ninevites' immediate repentance. But the actuality of the fish is not an article of Christian faith. Many people of faith believe the bodily resurrection of Jesus and all his miracles, yet regard Jonah as similar to Jesus' story of the good Samaritan (Luke 10:29–37). It is even possible to hold to the doctrine of the inerrancy of the original manuscripts of Scripture and regard Jonah as a unique parable about a real prophet (2 Kings 14:25). In any case, no other prophetic book is so focused on the prophet and filled with such parable-like writing.

As much as I believe the events described in the book, we should resist the use of the "whale" question as a litmus test for orthodoxy. Such a question

---

6. Sherwood, *A Biblical Text*, 42–47.

obfuscates the Word of God in Jonah and preempts a reader's discovering God's message for today. That message must not be eclipsed by our modern preoccupations with physical phenomena. The powerful messages of reconciliation with God, his creating power, and his persistent call for his people to speak to unbelievers concerning the Lord of all creation are essential themes of Jonah. How does the miracle of the big fish serve the message of the book? This unanticipated deliverance was a surprise to Jonah, who expected to die in the water. His own miraculous physical deliverance, when all hope was lost, caused him to rethink his views on God's way with evil men.

Jonah and Typologies: Like a Reluctant Israel or Like Christ?

IN A FOURTH interpretation, Jonah has been reshaped as a type or example of a prideful and haughty Jew (or Israel). Especially at the end of the Middle Ages in Europe this anti-Semitic typology began to take hold in sermons and commentary.[7] Jonah becomes a stingy prophet who refuses to share the word of Yahweh with the non-Jew. This view goads believers not to be narrow-minded in relation to God's forgiveness and grace. Unfortunately, this interpretive method often succumbs to the implication "narrow-minded, *like the Jews*" and leads to human judgment and disdain (anti-Semitism), the inversion of the forgiveness and grace of God. Such a typology with its inherent anti-Semitism deconstructs its own purpose and ought to be avoided.

The Jewish holocaust of the twentieth century requires a fresh assessment of Christian interpretation. The biblical facts of the Jonah text simply do not support the split Jew-Gentile reading. No judgment is given in Jonah against the (Gentile pagan) sailors who pray to their own gods, nor for their subsequent sacrifice to Yahweh that takes place on the *ship*, rather than in Jerusalem. "Gentiles" (*goyim*) are never mentioned or even alluded to as Jonah's problem. Jonah's issue with Nineveh is its violence and wickedness (see comments on 1:2; 3:8, 10). These problems pertain to Israel as well, as we see in the other prophetic books.

Another typology has its origin in the New Testament. Jesus compared himself to Jonah in a positive light. The early church fathers followed this interpretation of Jonah as a sign (or type) of Jesus' own ministry, death, and resurrection (Matt. 12:39–41; Luke 11:29–32). Jonah—in the ship, in the water, in the fish, and back on dry land (chs. 1 and 2)—is compared to Jesus' incarnation, suffering, death, and resurrection. Jonah's success in his preaching in Nineveh and its people, resulting in salvation through repentance (chs. 3 and 4), is compared to Jesus' success in preaching and saving human-

---

7. For a catalogue of this widespread tendency see ibid., 21–31, 65–87.

ity. The limitations of any typology apply to this reading as well. If Jonah is read Christologically, it is no longer read as Jonah. Yet, Jesus has pointed out a positive lens through which the prophet ought to be (but almost never is) viewed. The positive application of this theme will be explored in the Contemporary Significance section of chapter 1.

It is presently in fashion to claim that since Jonah does not state a purpose or single theme, since it contains so many theological themes and possibilities, and since it has such a long and diverse history of interpretation, determining a single theme is imprudent. The complexities and diverse wonders of the text should all be faithfully considered.[8] Jonah certainly is rich in text and in interpretation. This commentary attempts to reflect some of that great inheritance. At the same time, limitations of space and the commitment to edify the church require at least some general proposal of theme.

The Rehabilitation of Jonah's Reputation in Our Eyes

UNDERSTANDING JONAH AS a true prophet of God, in its original biblical context, is a challenge for evangelical readers. As long as we insist that Jonah is an example of a "bad" prophet, we will never understand why Jesus used him as a twofold "good" example. Jesus' favorable view of the prophet invites us to remove our modern theological lenses and examine Jonah's biblical roots and the context of other faithful prophets. Jesus' positive appraisal of Jonah leads us to consider him as a faithful example of preaching (ch. 3) and challenges our preconceptions of the prophet's motivations for fleeing to Tarshish.

Jonah was a faithful prophet because God was deeply involved in his life at every stage. Jonah's frailty in running from God's call is not hidden from view, but Jesus neither vilifies nor blames him for it. His reputation as a true prophet is not tarnished. Few biblical figures are iron-clad in their faithfulness (perhaps Joseph or Daniel comes the closest). Most of them confirmed God's call on their lives first by resisting it. This pattern of "call—resistance—call confirmed with a sign" is repeated in the lives of many people whom God called to difficult tasks, including Abraham, Sarah, Moses, Jeremiah, Jonah, and even the apostle Peter.

God visited Abraham four times with the promise that he would make him a great nation (Gen. 12:1–3; 15:1–6; 17:1–21; 18:1–15). After Yahweh's first call (Gen. 12), Abram went forth from Haran, but in Egypt he relied on trickery to save himself, thereby jeopardizing Sarai in Pharaoh's harem (12:10–20). Called a second time (Gen. 15), Abram argued with God and

8. Cf. Phyllis Trible, "The Book of Jonah," in *The New Interpreter's Bible* (Nashville: Abingdon, 1996), 7:490.

suggested that Eliezer of Damascus be his heir. God, unperturbed, simply repeated to Abram the promise of a son and gave him a terrifying dream to confirm it (15:12–20). Called a third time, Abraham (by this time God had changed his and Sarah's names) fell down laughing and pleaded that God bless Ishmael, the son of his concubine, instead of persisting in blessing the nations through Sarah's son (17:17–18). Again, Abraham was not chastised for his differing viewpoint; God accepted and understood his perspective, while insisting on his own.

In Genesis 18 Abraham negotiated with God over the fate of Sodom, asking nine questions (18:23–33). God welcomed Abraham's participation, which he had initiated (18:17–21). Finally, before Isaac was conceived, Abraham and Sarah again jeopardized God's calling when Abraham lied and Sarah moved into Abimelech's tent (20:1–18). All wombs were closed and an epidemic broke out. After Sarah was restored to Abraham, she conceived and bore Isaac (21:1–3).

A similar summary can be written for the call of Moses, who resisted God's call with many arguments until God became angry with him (Ex. 3:11–4:17). Later he passively resisted God by not circumcising his son. Without the intervention of his wife, Zipporah, he would have been killed (4:24–26). Nonetheless, Moses was not considered a bad example for his resistance. It is a necessary part of the narrative and is a biblical view of the relationship between God and the people he calls. God's call comes with abundant grace to strengthen the frail of heart. Jonah's story is in many ways similar.

The prophet Jeremiah struggled to the point of death with his call and messages from Yahweh:

> O LORD, you deceived me, and I was deceived;
> you overpowered me and prevailed.
> I am ridiculed all day long;
> everyone mocks me.
> Whenever I speak, I cry out
> proclaiming violence and destruction.
> So the word of the LORD has brought me
> insult and reproach all day long.
> But if I say, "I will not mention him
> or speak any more in his name,"
> his word is in my heart like a fire,
> a fire shut up in my bones.
> I am weary of holding it in;
> indeed, I cannot. (Jer. 20:7–9)

Jeremiah resisted Yahweh to the point that he cried out for his own death (Jer. 20:14–18), much like Jonah (Jonah 1:12; 4:3, 8, 9). This is an integral part of the life of prophets who are called to the most difficult tasks. Jonah's flight from Israel was not moral rebellion as it is sometimes described. It was prophetic resistance, in the classical Old Testament tradition, to an extremely difficult word from Yahweh (forgiveness of the terror-mongers of Nineveh). God honored Jonah's resistance, as he honored the resistance of Abram, Moses, and Jeremiah. Yahweh confirmed his call by facing him and delivering him from death.[9]

If we return Jonah to his Old Testament context, our modern "iron-clad" view of him and of prophets in general may be rehabilitated. In Scripture God does not work with automatons but with people of intelligence and integrity, whose authentic humanity is part of his difficult work in the world. Jonah's protest in running was both a genuine protest and a theological rebellion (sin). Nonetheless, God is not surprised (as we are) that those whom he calls struggle with that call. If we rehabilitate our view of Jonah, we may also find ourselves and our own hidden protests against God rehabilitated as well. We may find hope for our struggles against the persistence and longevity of violent persons and nations who inflict terror on civilian populations. When we consider that God's plan is that even these people come to repentance and be forgiven, we may have a new appreciation for Jonah's flight.

Historical Context

THE PROPHET JONAH, son of Amittai, is mentioned twice in the Old Testament (2 Kings 14:25; Jonah 1:1). In 2 Kings 14:23–27 he is described as a true prophet:

> In the fifteenth year of Amaziah son of Joash king of Judah, Jeroboam son of Jehoash king of Israel became king in Samaria, and he reigned forty-one years. He did evil in the eyes of the LORD and did not turn away from any of the sins of Jeroboam son of Nebat, which he had caused Israel to commit. He was the one who restored the boundaries of Israel from Lebo Hamath to the Sea of the Arabah, in accordance with the word of the LORD, the God of Israel, spoken through his servant *Jonah son of Amittai*, the prophet from Gath Hepher.

---

9. A New Testament case could also be made for this "call—resistance—call confirmed with a sign" pattern from the lives of apostles Peter and Paul. Paul even boasts about his human weakness (1 Cor. 2:3; 15:43; 2 Cor. 11:30). His early zealous resistance to the gospel in the name of God, which in turn prepared him for his uniquely effective apostleship, is well known.

> The LORD had seen how bitterly everyone in Israel, whether slave or free, was suffering; there was no one to help them. And since the LORD had not said he would blot out the name of Israel from under heaven, he saved them by the hand of Jeroboam son of Jehoash.

Dating Jonah

COGENT ARGUMENTS AND warrants have been given by scholars for dates in each of the centuries between the eighth and the fourth centuries B.C. The dating of the final form of the composition of Jonah is widely disputed and includes a vast array of suggestions.[10] Mainstream scholarship argues for the fifth-fourth century range. Arguments for this later dating include Jonah's familiarity with Jeremiah (seventh-century B.C.) and Aramaic spellings, words, and grammatical constructions common to postexilic writing (after 538 B.C.). Further, Persian influences (538–333 B.C.) are seen in two descriptions of Ninevite practice: the decree given "by the decree of the king and his nobles" (3:7) and "but let man and beast be covered with sackcloth" (3:8a). This commentary does not seek to summarize those arguments or to offer a new suggestion for the writer's or the editor's correct quarter century.

Jonah's disagreement with Yahweh concerning the forgiveness of violent enemies was an enduring theological dialogue that could have been discussed in Israel as early as Jonah's lifetime (770 B.C.). Forward from this time the manuscript could have been edited and preserved through the centuries of Assyria's power and fall (612), still being relevant in the time of the Babylonian exile (587–538) and in the subsequent struggle of reconstruction under the Persians (538–333). The messages of the book continued to be relevant while the Jews were under the thumb of the Greeks (333–163) and the Romans (163 B.C.–A.D. 70) until it found its present place in the Hebrew canon (about A.D. 90).

The dispute in Jonah concerning the forgiveness of the violent Ninevites would have been more readily accepted at a time after Assyria was no longer a threat to Israel (after 612 B.C.). It is no surprise that after the destruction of Nineveh, Jonah's perspective in his dispute with Yahweh was taken seriously by Israel (that Nineveh should have been destroyed). Nineveh's evil did, in fact, outlast its repentance, as it was overturned in destruction by the Babylonian-Mede alliance in 612 B.C. Scholarly agreement on a date for Jonah is less important (and less possible) than awareness of the historical suffering of Israel at the hands of the Assyrians and their overzealous violence. The inspiration of this book enabled Israel to consider the same question of forgiveness with each of its subsequent oppressors (Babylon, Persia, Greece, Rome, etc.).

---

10. See James Limburg, *Jonah: A Commentary* (Louisville: John Knox, 1993), 28–29.

The layers of history may echo the same enduring question, regardless of date: "If the violent repent, should God forgive them without consequence for their actions?" Jonah's objection is always relevant.

Time Chart: Historical Events and the Canonical Order of the Twelve Minor Prophets

THE CANONICAL SETTING of the book is essential for understanding why Jonah ran from Yahweh's call to Nineveh. The narrative of Jonah is set (by the biblical canon) in the eighth century B.C. during the days of Jeroboam II (786–746 B.C.). "Jonah son of Amittai" is the prophet of 2 Kings 14:25, and the style and content of Jonah easily fit following the Elijah and Elisha narratives of 1 Kings 17–2 Kings 13. Jonah follows Hosea and Amos, his contemporaries, who also prophesied during the reign of Jeroboam II. Micah follows Jonah since Micah prophesied after the death of Jeroboam II (Mic. 1:1).

Regardless of when Jonah reached its final form, it is presented in the Book of the Twelve as a book to be understood and interpreted in an eighth-century context. In the eighth century Assyria had already established a hundred-year-old reputation throughout the ancient Near East as a cruel enemy. Near the end of Jonah's life Assyria was rising to its greatest height of power and terror. The following chart demonstrates Jonah's canonical (biblical) context.

Event	Date B.C.
Death of Ashurnasirpal II (Assyria), who boasted of his violence and torture	859
Battle of Qarqar: Shalmanezer III* (Assyria) defeats King Ahab (Israel)	853
Death of Jeroboam II**	746
Beginning of Assyrian domination of ancient Near East	745
Israel pillaged by Tiglath-Pileser III (Assyria) (2 Kings 15)	734–732
Building of Nineveh into a "great city" by Tiglath-Pileser III	727
Israel's northern ten tribes are destroyed/enslaved by Shalmanezer V	722
Prophet **Micah**'s arrival in Jerusalem (after Jeroboam)	before 701
Sennacherib of Assyria besieges (but does not capture) Jerusalem and sacks Judean cities (2 Kings 18–19)	701
Josiah (Judah) reforms Jerusalem in the ways of Yahweh (2 Kings 22–23)	621
Nahum active in Jerusalem, prophesies Assyria's (Nineveh's) fall	615
Nineveh's fall to Babylonians and Medes	612

Habakkuk prophesies the fall of Judah to Babylon	605
Zephaniah prophesies of Judah's judgment and surviving remnant***	622
Babylonians capture Jerusalem and first exiles deported	597
Jerusalem falls again after rebellion; major deportation	586
Babylon falls to Cyrus (Persian); exiles begin to return to the land	539
Haggai and **Zechariah** prophesy during reign of Darius I (Persia)	520
Malachi prophesies during the Ezra–Nehemiah mission	460–430

*According to Shalmanezer III, Ahab lost 2000 chariots and 10,000 men; Israel paid tribute to Assyria.

Prophets **Hosea, Joel, Amos, and **Obadiah** (with Isaiah) were active during some part of the reign of Jeroboam II (Israel). **Jonah** prophesied correctly during this reign that Jeroboam II would restore Israel's borders (2 Kings 14:25–27).

***Placed out of sequence in the biblical canon probably because the remnant had hope in his prophecy.

The Terror-Mongers of Nineveh, Assyria

THE ASSYRIAN KINGS were proud of their cruel and terrible reputation and went to great trouble and expense to record their exploits for posterity.[11] Archaeologists have uncovered many reliefs (large stone wall panels with carved depictions) of grisly post-battle scenes, which were erected in palaces so that they could be seen daily. In addition, written descriptions of post-battle tortures of prisoners were preserved on obelisks and cylindrical pillars. Discovered in these pictorial and written displays are gruesome details and horrific boasting. "It is as gory and bloodcurdling a history as we know."[12]

Assyrians boasted of their cruelty to captured peoples following the siege of their town or city, and their victims were not limited to combatants. (Warning: What follows is rated "R" for gore and violence.) Records brag of live dismemberment, often leaving one hand attached so they could shake it before the person died. They made parades of heads, requiring friends of the deceased to carry them elevated on poles. They boasted of their practice of stretching live prisoners with ropes so they could be skinned alive. The human skins were then displayed on city walls and on poles. They commissioned pictures of their

11. For a modern cultural analogy we might think of the slaughters of the Khmer Rouge killing fields of Cambodia, the million machete deaths in Rwanda, Hitler's eleven million, Stalin's twenty-five million lives taken, or Saddam Hussein's mass graves.

12. Erika Bleibtreu, "Grisly Assyrian Record of Torture and Death," *BAR* (Jan/Feb 1991): 52–61. I am indebted to Erika Bleibtreu for her compilation of these descriptions.

post-battle tortures where piles of heads, hands, and feet, and heads impaled on poles—eight heads to a stake—were displayed. They pulled out the tongues and testicles of live victims and burned the young alive.

Those who survived the sack of their city were tied in long lines of enslavement and deported to Assyrian cities to labor on building projects. Tens of thousands in hundreds of cities suffered this fate over the two hundred and fifty years of the Assyrians' reign of terror (c. 883–612). Two Assyrian kings distinguished themselves in boasting of cruelty before the time of the prophet Jonah son of Amittai. Ashurnasirpal II (883–859 B.C.) wrote, for example:

> I flayed [the skin from] as many nobles as had rebelled against me [and] draped their skins over the pile [of corpses]. . . . I cut off the heads of their fighters [and] built [with them] a tower before their city. I burnt their adolescent boys [and] girls. . . . I captured many troops alive: I cut off of some their arms [and] hands; I cut off of others their noses, ears, [and] extremities. I gouged out the eyes of many troops. I made one pile of the living [and] one of the heads. I hung their heads on trees around the city.[13]

Ashurnasirpal's son, Shalmaneser III (858–824 B.C.), is famous for his pictorial depictions of cruelty in large stone relief wall panels. A description of one panel is enough:

> We see an Assyrian soldier grasping the hand and arm of a [living] captured enemy whose other hand and both feet have already been cut off. Dismembered hands and feet fly through the scene. Severed enemy heads hang from the conquered city's walls.[14]

This cultural tradition of boasting of torture continued in Assyrian records in the eighth century, as Assyria expanded its empire. Tiglath-Pileser III (744–727 B.C.) threatened Israel, capturing and deporting some of the population (2 Kings 15:29). Shalmaneser V (726–722 B.C.) sacked Samaria (2 Kings 18:10). Sargon II (722–705 B.C.) finished the job in 722, leading to what we now call the "ten lost tribes of Israel." He enslaved 27,290 Israelites according to his record. Sennacherib (705–681 B.C.), who moved the capital of Assyria to Nineveh, besieged the people of Jerusalem. Yahweh delivered them miraculously (at the time of King Hezekiah and Isaiah), although the surrounding towns and villages fell and were plundered (2 Kings 19).[15]

---

13. Quoted in ibid., 57–58.

14. Ibid., 58.

15. Jerusalem later survived by paying tribute, but it was destroyed by the Babylonians 114 years later.

Given this historical context, the prophet Jonah was in a difficult situation. Yahweh asked him to go to his cultural enemies and proclaim judgment in the capital city ("Forty more days and Nineveh will be overturned," 3:4). He was asked to risk his life preaching and had no guarantees that he would not, like other unwelcomed prophets, be killed. Yet if he succeeded in his mission and they repented, he would not be welcome in Israel. No one, including God's chosen prophet, desired the possibility and threat of their enduring existence. He was caught between a rock and a hard place. In this situation, many would, like Jonah, act on the third possibility, that of flight.

Literary Elements and Meaning

JONAH IS AN imaginative and superlative narrative. Most of the places, emotions, and events are called "great." The Hebrew root *gdl* is used fifteen times in the book in the following ways: 1:2 ("great city of Nineveh"); 1:4 ("great wind" and "such a violent [lit., great] storm"); 1:10 ("this *terrified* them"; lit., "they feared a great fear"); 1:12 ("great storm"); 1:16 ("greatly feared the LORD"); 1:17 ("great fish"); 3:2 ("great city of Nineveh"); 3:3 ("a *very important* city"; lit., "a great city to God"); 3:5 ("from the greatest [person] to the least"); 3:7 ("*nobles*"; lit., "great ones"); 4:1 ("greatly displeased"; lit., "great calamity"); 4:6 ("*very* happy"; lit., "greatly joyful"); 4:10 ("make it *grow*"; lit., "make it great"); 4:11 ("great city").

This "greatness" gives the story of Jonah timeless appeal to teachers and students. Some have interpreted these unusual superlatives as indicating the fantastical quality of the story, that is, that no one would mistake this "over the top" story for a historical narrative. (Something similar is sometimes argued for the creation story in Genesis 1.) Given the creational subject matter of Jonah, the claim to true "greatness" should not be so easily quarantined. It claims no less than a radical shift in Israel's orientation toward her enemies. It declares a new ethic in religious and political alignment. It calls Jonah to make God's word available to the most evil of Israel's antagonists, at his own peril. This is a story in which the superlatives linguistically undergird its assertion and have perpetuated its telling.

Jonah the Prophet: Lessons of Irony

THE BOOK OF Jonah is in a class by itself. It is not like other books of prophecy, and Jonah does not act like other prophets. Nor is this book filled with the prophet's poetic oracles. He speaks only a few words of formal prophecy (3:4b: "Forty more days and Nineveh will be overturned."). The book is written about Jonah in the past tense, and the book never refers to him as a prophet. It is sometimes called a parable or a satire. It looks like a historical narrative that belongs in 2 Kings, but it is in the "book of the prophets."

Jonah is most like the book of Job: a dialogue between God and a pious man who does not agree with God's way in the world. It is a didactic story of the wisdom tradition (included among prophets, because Jonah is a prophet in 2 Kings 14:25). This form of piety is common in the Old Testament, though it is not common in many Christian communities of faith. God invites his people into conversation, and even disputes, concerning his way in the world.

Jonah's argument with God is not unique, but Jonah runs away in refusal of his call. Ironically, when he is "convinced" to accept it, he is unbelievably successful. The whole city repents without an argument after only one day of a three-day mission. Rather than rejoicing, however, Jonah becomes suicidal, despairing of his own prophetic success.

The book is full of ironies. He is a true prophet who at first refuses to prophesy. Jonah says, "I worship the LORD, the God of heaven, who made the sea and the land" (1:9b), but he runs from God on the sea, to another land (see Bridging Contexts on 1:9). He refuses (ch. 1) and is reluctant (ch. 3) to prophesy, yet the sailors and the Ninevites all turn to Yahweh. He leads the sailors and the Ninevites to the brink of death, but Yahweh saves them all. Pagans (sailors and Ninevites) turn to Yahweh in crisis (1:14; 3:5). Jonah runs (1:3) and walks away (4:5).

All this irony has a purpose for the reader and the message of the book. Things are not as simple as they seem. Jonah's protest and dialogue with Yahweh raises complex questions about God's relationship to the wicked of the world. His ironic responses draw the reader in to take a second look at the prophet who says more by his protestations and conversations than by the few words of his formal prophecy. Jonah reveals God's identity and way in the world through his conversations, arguments, and whole life of protest and response. He is an atypical prophet, but he is true to his calling, even in protest.

Structure

JONAH HAS A simple parallel structure, with two parallel stories.

- Jonah is with the pagan sailors/pagan Ninevites (chs. 1, 3).
- Jonah speaks to Yahweh (chs. 2, 4).

Seven scenes are established by divisions in the ancient manuscript.[16] This commentary further subdivides these seven scenes by rhetorical signs

---

16. Our Hebrew Bible is the Masoretic Text from the Leningrad codex, 1008 A.D. Its authenticity is confirmed by the Dead Seas Scroll of Jonah, discovered in 1955; it was hidden in Cave 4 near the Dead Sea around A.D. 90.

in the text. These traditional scene divisions guide the reader and demonstrate further the two parallel panels (1–3 and 4–6). Comparisons between scene 3 and scene 6 have carried the most significance for commentators (see Bridging Contexts section on 4:1–5).

1. Jonah's call and reaction (1:1–3)
2. In the storm at sea (1:4–16)
3. Prayer in the fish (1:17–2:10)
4. Jonah's second call and reaction (3:1–3a)
5. In Nineveh (3:3b–10)
6. Prayer in Nineveh (4:1–5)[17]
7. God's questions outside Nineveh (4:6–11)

Theology: Jonah and God's Way in the World

JONAH HAS A variety of responses to God's call on his life. The conversation between God and Jonah begins and ends with what ought to be done about wicked and ignorant people in the "great city" of Nineveh (1:1; 4:11). Jonah's perspective on strict justice versus God's desire to forgive even the most heinous sinners is the subject of debate. Jonah's last substantive argument summarizes his perspective: "That is why I was so quick to flee to Tarshish. I knew that you are a gracious and compassionate God, slow to anger and abounding in love, a God who relents from sending calamity" (4:2b). Jonah doesn't like it. God insists on it (see Bridging Contexts section of ch. 4).

As noted above, the Assyrians prided themselves on cruel means of torture and killing. Commonsense logic prevails in Jonah's perspective—a logic widely shared in his day and commonplace yet today. "What goes around comes around" expresses the view of *strict justice*. When the perpetrator of a heinous crime says, "I'm sorry, I'll never do it again," proponents of this view are not impressed. Most people still believe that the wicked should pay consequences for their crimes, not have the consequences removed through forgiveness. As long as a violent threat exists, it constitutes a present danger.

Jonah learned through a series of personal experiences that God's compassion and clemency were not weaknesses in God's justice, but were *better justice* than human justice. Jonah personally felt the weight of God's judgment in the storm at sea. He experienced his own false moral superiority (above God's!) in being willing to die for his position while sinking beneath the waves. His unanticipated rescue by God's fish caused him to pray and to begin rethinking his adamant position on strict justice. He realized the value of God's *better justice* when it was directed toward him. By Jonah's own stan-

---

17. The end of scene six is debated by scholars. It ends at 4:3 in the Masoretic Text, at 4:4 by setting shift, at 4:5 by thematic structure. See David A. Dorsey, *The Literary Structure of the Old Testament* (Grand Rapids: Baker, 1999), 290.

dards, he knew he deserved to drown for his rebellion. He was taught that his own purposeful rebellion as well as Nineveh's ignorant rebellion both required God's intervention.

Jonah became angry again (ch. 4) at the Ninevites' escape from death. In realizing the needs and longings of his own humanity, Jonah points out all creation's basic reliance on God's forgiveness to temper strict justice and grant undeserved deliverance. Jonah's special contribution to the canon is in God's question: "Should *I* not be concerned. . . ?" (4:11). God's concern is for the part of his creation that is ignorant of his ways and yet responsible for their actions (see Bridging Contexts section of ch. 4).

The Good News of Jonah

THE PROPHETIC GOOD news of Jonah is found in learning how God thinks. God reveals how he thinks about the ignorant wicked, repentance as a means of salvation, and the discomfort of his disagreeable chosen prophet. Interpreters have divided opinions about the prophet's theological contribution. Is the good news of Jonah found only in God's viewpoint (everyone gets second chances, the repentant wicked are forgiven, and God is patiently logical with his disgruntled prophet)? Is Jonah only a flat figure who is disgruntled, disobedient, and angry? Some see him as a comic figure who, among other things, thinks he can successfully run away from God. In this view, he is not a proper prophet who speaks on behalf of God. Most of his words and actions are rebellious.

Nevertheless (and this is the minority opinion, supported in this commentary), Jonah is a mouthpiece for God's word in the midst of his dispute with God. He is disobedient, runs away from God, and is angry about God's clemency for the violent Ninevites. But his rebellion is grounded in God's Word as he has learned it and as it is proclaimed in the Bible. The wicked will perish. High-handed rebellion will not be pardoned, even in repentance (Num. 15:27–31). Jonah's opinion concerning Nineveh, far from being rebellious, represents a major opinion that is a necessary part of any dialogue with God about wickedness in the world. Until Jonah's dialogue with God, the prophet's opinion about the wicked was known as God's way in the world.

Jonah is a true prophet voicing a true theology. In this sense he is not rebellious. Jonah is being faithful to what he knows to be God's word (strict justice) when God asks him to contravene that word with a new word. God's new word is a controversial word (even among believers today). Jonah's questions and actions in reaction to this new word are faithful to the word from Yahweh that he previously received. Jonah the prophet and Jonah the book faithfully struggle with this difficult question: "What should be done about the violently wicked who repent?" This is an even more difficult question than the early church's struggle to understand how righteous Gentiles (like Cornelius in Acts 10) could receive God's grace and Holy Spirit.

Jonah is a faithful prophet because he is true to speaking God's word (of justice) as he has known it, even to God. When he is convinced by his unexpected deliverance from the sea that God is determined to extend his forgiveness to the previously unforgivable, he goes and preaches this word to Nineveh. He is faithful to protest to God (like Abraham, Moses, and Jeremiah) in chapter 4 when the continuance of the repentant wicked seems likely. He demonstrates his integrity in representing traditional justice and by preaching to Nineveh. Jonah's protest provides an occasion for God's revelation of a better justice (4:10–11) in the context of the life of a true and honest man. The good news is that Jonah's struggle is accepted by God as a legitimate human struggle to understand the continuance of wickedness in the world.

Outline of Jonah

I. **Death and Life** (1:1–17)
  A. A Reluctant Prophet and Yahweh (1:1–3)
  B. The Sailors and the Reluctant Prophet in Yahweh's Storm
     (1:4–12)
     1. Jonah's Indifference (1:5–7)
     2. Sailors Question Jonah (1:8–10)
     3. Jonah's Confession (1:11–12)
  C. The Sailors and Yahweh (1:13–16)
  D. God's Fish (1:17)
II. **Jonah Gives Thanks for Yahweh's Great Fish** (2:1–10)
  A. The Five Stanzas of Jonah's Distress (2:1–6)
  B. The Refrain of Jonah's Deliverance (2:7–10)
III. **Preaching, Repentance, and Compassion** (3:1–10)
  A. Jonah Proclaims and the Ninevites Believe God (3:1–5)
  B. The King Responds in Hope (3:6–10)
IV. **The Creator's Love and Jonah's Anger** (4:1–11)
  A. Jonah's Anger with Yahweh (4:1–5)
  B. Vine, Worm, and Wind (4:6–8)
  C. Yahweh Reasons with Jonah (4:9–11)

Select Bibliography on Jonah

Achtemeier, Elizabeth. *Minor Prophets I*. NIBC. Peabody, Mass.: Hendrickson, 1996.

Alexander, T. Desmond. *Jonah: An Introduction and Commentary*. TOTC. Downers Grove, Ill.: InterVarsity Press, 1988.

Allen, Leslie C. *The Books of Joel, Obadiah, Jonah, and Micah*. NICOT. Grand Rapids: Eerdmans, 1976.

Baldwin, Joyce. "Jonah." Pages 543–90 in *The Minor Prophets*, vol. 2. Ed. Thomas McComisky. Grand Rapids: Baker, 1993.

Brown, William P. *Obadiah Through Malachi*. Westminster Bible Companion. Louisville: Westminster John Knox, 1996.

Craig, Kenneth M. *A Poetics of Jonah—Art in the Service of Ideology*. 2d ed. Macon, Ga.: Mercer Univ. Press, 1997.

Fretheim, Terence E. *The Message of Jonah: A Theological Commentary*. Minneapolis: Augsburg, 1977.

Kohlenberger, John R. III. *Jonah and Nahum*. Chicago: Moody, 1984.

Limburg, James. *Jonah: A Commentary*. Louisville: John Knox, 1993.

Salters, Robert B. *Jonah & Lamentations*. Sheffield: JSOT Press, 1994.

Sasson, Jack M. *Jonah: A New Translation with Introduction, Commentary, and Interpretation*. AB. New York: Doubleday, 1990.

Sherwood, Yvonne. *A Biblical Text and Its Afterlives: The Survival of Jonah in Western Culture*. Cambridge: Cambridge Univ. Press, 2000.

Simon, Uriel. *Jonah: The Traditional Hebrew Text*. Trans. L. J. Schramm. Philadelphia: Jewish Publication Society, 1999.

Stuart, Douglas K. *Hosea-Jonah*. WBC. Dallas: Word, 1989.

Sweeney, Marvin A. *The Twelve Prophets*. Collegeville, Minn.: Liturgical, 2000.

Trible, Phyllis. *Rhetorical Criticism—Context, Method and the Book of Jonah*. Minneapolis: Fortress, 1994.

_____. "The Book of Jonah." Pages 463–529 in *The New Interpreter's Bible*, vol. 7. Nashville: Abingdon, 1996.

Walton, John H. *Jonah*. Bible Study Commentary. Grand Rapids: Zondervan, 1982.

Watts, John D. W. *The Books of Joel, Obadiah, Jonah, Nahum, Habakkuk, and Zephaniah*. New York: Cambridge Univ. Press, 1975.

Wolff, Hans Walter. *Obadiah and Jonah: A Commentary*. Trans. Margaret Kohl. Minneapolis: Augsburg, 1986.

Zlotowitz, Meir. *Jonah: A New Translation with a Commentary Anthologized from Talmudic, Midrashic, and Rabbinic Sources*. Trans. Meir Zlotowitz. New York: Mesorah, 1978.

Jonah 1

T HE WORD OF THE LORD came to Jonah son of Amittai: 2"Go to the great city of Nineveh and preach against it, because its wickedness has come up before me."
3But Jonah ran away from the LORD and headed for Tarshish. He went down to Joppa, where he found a ship bound for that port. After paying the fare, he went aboard and sailed for Tarshish to flee from the LORD.

4Then the LORD sent a great wind on the sea, and such a violent storm arose that the ship threatened to break up. 5All the sailors were afraid and each cried out to his own god. And they threw the cargo into the sea to lighten the ship.

But Jonah had gone below deck, where he lay down and fell into a deep sleep. 6The captain went to him and said, "How can you sleep? Get up and call on your god! Maybe he will take notice of us, and we will not perish."

7Then the sailors said to each other, "Come, let us cast lots to find out who is responsible for this calamity." They cast lots and the lot fell on Jonah.

8So they asked him, "Tell us, who is responsible for making all this trouble for us? What do you do? Where do you come from? What is your country? From what people are you?"

9He answered, "I am a Hebrew and I worship the LORD, the God of heaven, who made the sea and the land."

10This terrified them and they asked, "What have you done?" (They knew he was running away from the LORD, because he had already told them so.)

11The sea was getting rougher and rougher. So they asked him, "What should we do to you to make the sea calm down for us?"

12"Pick me up and throw me into the sea," he replied, "and it will become calm. I know that it is my fault that this great storm has come upon you."

13Instead, the men did their best to row back to land. But they could not, for the sea grew even wilder than before.
14Then they cried to the LORD, "O LORD, please do not let us die for taking this man's life. Do not hold us accountable for killing an innocent man, for you, O LORD, have done as you

pleased." ¹⁵Then they took Jonah and threw him overboard, and the raging sea grew calm. ¹⁶At this the men greatly feared the LORD, and they offered a sacrifice to the LORD and made vows to him.

¹⁷But the LORD provided a great fish to swallow Jonah, and Jonah was inside the fish three days and three nights.

JONAH WAS A GALILEAN prophet to Jeroboam II, who reigned over the ten northern tribes from 786–746 B.C., before their enslavement and dispersion at the hands of the Assyrians in 722. Jonah successfully counseled him against the Syrian threat and prophesied his expansion of Israel to its former borders (see 2 Kings 14:25). He was from Gath Hepher (lit., "winepress" and "well") in Zebulun (about fifteen miles west of the Sea of Galilee).

Jonah 1 introduces the larger theme of death and life. It addresses the life and death of the wicked Ninevites, against whom Jonah is sent to preach, and the life and death of the pagan sailors, whose "ship threatened to break up" in the storm. At its center is the matter of the life and death of Jonah, who is thrown into a raging sea and is swallowed by a great fish. Jonah's struggle for life before God will be partially resolved in his prayer of thanksgiving (in ch. 2) and, later, in his dialogue with Yahweh (in ch. 4). The resolution of the Ninevites' struggle is resolved by Jonah's preaching, their repentance, and Yahweh's compassion (in ch. 3).

Chapter 1 resolves only the life and death struggle of the sailors. The sailors' terror in the midst of the storm has them frantically searching for a way to survive. Jonah's reluctant confession to them in the midst of their distress and his willingness to be tossed into the sea eventually result in the calming of the storm. His words also inadvertently result in the sailors' conversion to the worship of Yahweh (1:15–16). Even in reluctance and in the face of his certain death by drowning, Jonah fulfills Yahweh's call on his life by his witness to faith (see 1:9). Jonah testifies that God is the source of life, and he later states that to be separated from God's presence equals death (1:10–12; 2:4–5).

A Reluctant Prophet and Yahweh (1:1–3)

THESE THREE VERSES are full of detailed action, drawing us into the story. The word of Yahweh comes to Jonah in verse 1 (and will come to him a second time in 3:1). Yahweh tells him to preach against the wicked city of Nineveh, but Jonah runs in the opposite direction, heading for Tarshish. He goes down to Joppa, finds a ship, pays the fare, goes aboard, and sets sail. The detail gives readers the sense of being on board with him when Yahweh's great windstorm hits and threatens to break the ship apart.

"The word of the LORD came to . . ." (1:1) is a formulaic phrase used when Yahweh speaks directly to a prophet or to someone asked to participate in Yahweh's mission in a special way. When the phrase is used again in 3:1, Yahweh repeats his instructions in more detail.[1]

"Jonah" means "dove." In Genesis 8:10–11 the dove Noah sent out from the ark returned with the branch of an olive tree—an enduring symbol of peace and compassion. Thus, the "dove" may symbolically imply Yahweh's attempt to rescue Nineveh from destruction and judgment through forgiveness and mercy. The "Dove" (Jonah) of peace will be his agent.

In the Old Testament doves also moan and lament (Isa. 38:14; 59:11) as Jonah does in chapter 4. Furthermore, they are birds of sacrifice (Lev. 5:7, 11), just as Jonah is in chapter 1 to save the sailors. Finally, the psalmist longs to be a dove ("a *jonah*") to flee from the terrors of death (Ps. 55:4–8).[2] Jonah flees like a dove in chapter 1 from the terror of Nineveh.

Jonah's command is to preach in Nineveh, a "great" city as well as a wicked one. In fact, the phrase "great city" occurs three other times in the book: 3:2, 3; 4:11.[3] The implication is that such a "great," important, and large city (albeit wicked) is worth Yahweh's trouble to save.[4]

Nineveh was on the east bank of the Tigris River (near Al Mawsil or Mosul), about 550 miles northeast of Jerusalem (220 miles north of Baghdad). It was not a great city until the reign of Tiglath-Pileser III (745–727 B.C.). In 701 B.C. Sennacherib (705–681 B.C.) made it the capital of Assyria and the most powerful city in the ancient Near East, with an urban perimeter of seven and one-half miles. In the same year he attacked Jerusalem. Nineveh fell to the Babylonians and Medes dramatically in 612 B.C. Its overwhelming greatness lasted about 150 years.

Jonah's word from Yahweh regarding Nineveh is to "preach against it, because [of] its wickedness" (1:2). The following is a summary of the references to Nineveh's character as demonstrated in the text, preceded by the name of the speaker.

---

1. "The word of the LORD" (*wyhy dbr-yhwh*) in this exact form occurs 83 times, primarily in Jeremiah (21 times), Ezekiel (41 times), and Zechariah (6 times).

2. See Sherwood, *A Biblical Text and Its Afterlives*, 241–42, for a discussion of proposals for the meaning of "dove."

3. The NIV translation in 3:3 is "important city."

4. For Nineveh's wickedness, see the introduction.

> God: "Preach against it, because *its wickedness* has come up before me" (1:2).
>
> God: "Go to the great city of Nineveh and proclaim to it *the message I give you*" (3:2).
>
> Jonah: "Forty more days and *Nineveh will be overturned*" (3:4b).
>
> Assyrian king: "Let everyone call urgently on God. Let them give *up their evil ways and their violence*" (3:8b).
>
> Narrator: When God saw what they did and how they turned from *their evil ways, he had compassion* (3:10a).

Jonah, however, chooses to flee in the opposite direction (1:3). The first words of the phrase "Jonah ran away" and the first words in 1:2 ("Go") echo each other in Hebrew (lit., "rise and go"/Jonah "rose and fled"). The original language, in other words, more sharply contrasts what Yahweh asks Jonah to do with what he does immediately. Jonah knows that this call from Yahweh will not simply go away. He immediately grasps the radical and pressing nature of the call (4:2, "that is why I was so quick to flee") and thinks that only radical and immediate action will save him from God's call on his life.[5]

The reasons for Jonah's running are not explained until 4:2 and cannot be understood without historical background. Nineveh, the capital city of Assyria, was Israel's worst enemy and the bane of the ancient world. They were a powerful and well-developed civilization, known for their brutal and grisly treatment of their enemies. Jonah's response to Yahweh's directive can be understood as fear, rebellion, or moral opposition to Yahweh's mercy (as Jonah alludes to in 4:2). Jonah is not interested in participating in the redemption of this particular enemy.

It is, of course, impossible to run away from Yahweh. The expression in 1:3 means "away from the presence [*millipne*] of the LORD [in the temple]" (see 2:4, 7)—an expression used twice in this verse for emphasis. It is a common experience among people of faith to physically leave a place that reminds them of Yahweh in order to avoid the message they have heard in that place.

Verse 3 gives rise to two common questions: "Why Tarshish?" and "Why is Tarshish mentioned three times in one verse?" ("headed for Tarshish ... that port ... sailed for Tarshish").[6] Tarshish was a Phoenician city in southern Spain, just west of Gibraltar.[7] Tyre (north of Israel's coast) depended on the large merchant ships of Tarshish for shipments of silver, iron, tin, and lead

---

5. Hendiadys of *qum lek* (1:2) should be translated "go immediately."

6. The word the NIV translates as "that port" is lit. "Tarshish."

7. Not to be confused with Paul's hometown, Tarsus, of Asia Minor. For a discussion of various viewpoints on the location of Jonah's Tarshish, see David W. Baker, "Tarshish (Place)," *ABD*, 6:331–33.

(Isa. 23:1–14; Ezek. 27:12, 25). It was known as the westernmost place in the Mediterranean world (Ps. 72:10; Isa. 60:9; 66:19; Ezek. 38:13).[8]

Interestingly, the narrative includes that Jonah "paid the fare." This is detailed and economic story-telling, which moves the action along. The description of Jonah's energy and action in fleeing, especially in verse 3, masterfully takes the reader for a ride with Jonah. It conveys more than information. By the time the sailors cry out, the reader has a sense of being on the ship with them, wondering what will happen next.

The Sailors and the Reluctant Prophet in Yahweh's Storm (1:4–12)

VERSE 4 TURNS our attention to the sailors and captain of the storm-bound ship and their situation in relation to Yahweh and Jonah. They are afraid because of the storm and cry out to their gods, and they then proceed to throw their cargo overboard (a radical action for freight haulers). The captain wakes Jonah to enlist him to pray, and the men cast lots and discover Jonah's sin.

They interrogate him, hear his witness to Yahweh, and become even more terrified, since Jonah's God is "the God of heaven, who made the sea and the land." They chastise him for his foolishness in trying to run away from Yahweh ("What have you done?" 1:10). The pagan sailors seem to know the rules of relationship to gods better than Jonah. It is on account of this fleeing prophet that Yahweh is making the sea "rougher and rougher."

In the end the sailors desperately ask Jonah what they should do to him "to make the sea calm down for us." The sailors' questioning and the urgency of Yahweh's storm finally pry from Jonah a confession of guilt (v. 12), just as they had pried a confession of faith. He has, albeit under duress, fulfilled his calling as a true prophet of Yahweh by witnessing to the God of heaven, confessing his sin, and instructing the sailors to act. He has also taken a vital step toward his specific and difficult calling in that he offers himself as a sure sacrifice for their safety.

In verse 4, one can almost hear the creaking timbers as the stress of the pounding on the hull increases. The root *twl* ("hurl, send, throw") is first used in this verse and three additional times in chapter 1, increasing the sense of power and danger in the situation:

1:4: Yahweh *sent* a great wind on the sea.
1:5: [The sailors] *threw* the cargo into the sea.
1:12: "*Throw* me into the sea," he replied.
1:15: [The sailors] *threw* him overboard.

---

8. For further references see Limburg, *Jonah: A Commentary*, 43.

Jonah is passive in verses 5–7. Exhausted from his struggle and decision to flee, he sleeps. He has temporarily escaped the pressure of God's word, but by fleeing he has also turned from the possibility of calling on his God.

The captain is puzzled how Jonah can sleep through the storm (1:6). All of those on board are searching for every possible means to end their deadly predicament, including the expectation that each one must call on his gods. Jonah's decision to run from God is now a matter of life and death for the sailors and their captain. His action has endangered them. This web of inter-relationships is one of the lessons of the book. All of life is related before the Lord of life (who made the sea and the land). The prophet of Israel, pagan sailors, Ninevites, and in later verses, a fish, vine, worm, and cattle are all inter-connected under God's caring purposes.

Jonah's deep sleep in the recesses of the ship reveals his indifference to his own life and the lives of others. To see such callousness so early in the development of the narrative distances many readers from Jonah. Jonah's aversion to the evil Ninevites is understandable, but his indifference to the life of his shipmates seems callous. The pagan captain speaks of their agitation: "How can you sleep? Get up and call on your god!" (1:6). Telling the story in this way converts even the pious reader to the perspective of the impious captain.

Jonah's deep sleep is the bottom of a quick slide from "a prophet in the presence of the LORD in Israel" to "deadly indifference in the hull of a sinking ship." The Hebrew uses the same word root to describe how Jonah "went down to Joppa" (1:3, *yarad*), "went aboard [the ship]" (1:3, *yarad*), and "had gone below deck" (1:5, *yarad*). When he falls into a "deep sleep" (1:5, *yeradam*), the Hebrew words are a play on similar sounds (*yarad/yeradam*). The second root (*radam*) is repeated by the captain, who says, "How can you sleep [*nireddam*]?" Jonah's sleeping is the bottom of his flight from Yahweh (see further comments at 2:7). The captain tells Jonah to "Get up!"—in essence, to reverse his direction from "down" to "up." The captain uses the same word (*qum*) that Yahweh spoke to Jonah at the beginning (1:2; lit., "Get up and go").

Everyone in this book eventually calls on God: the sailors, Jonah, and the Ninevites. The Hebrew *qara²* is translated as both "call" and "cry out":

1:6: The captain went to him and said, "How can you sleep? Get up and *call on* your god! Maybe he will take notice of us, and we will not perish."

1:14: Then they *cried to* the LORD, "O LORD, please do not let us die for taking this man's life."

2:2: He said: "In my distress I *called to* the LORD, and he answered me."

3:8: But let man and beast be covered with sackcloth. Let everyone *call* urgently on God. Let them give up their evil ways and their violence.

The captain hopes what Jonah already knows, that his God is compassionate (see Bridging Contexts section of ch. 4). In the sailors' circumstance, they are not in a position to be particular. For them, one god is as good as another as long as it is a god that saves. The captain's request for Jonah to pray to his god is an incredible opportunity for Jonah to give witness to and demonstrate the power of the Lord of life, but he remains silent.

The captain implies a preliminary understanding of the existence of Jonah's God when he says, "Maybe he will take notice of us." The contrast is more striking in Hebrew because a more literal rendition is: "It may be that *haelohim*[9] will take notice." The verb "will take notice" is singular (as the NIV translates correctly); what is lost in translation is the plural subject *haelohim* (NIV simply "he"). The captain acknowledges the possibility that Jonah's God, the God of the Hebrews (*haelohim*), is the true God.

The sailors continue to take charge of the situation by casting lots to find the source of their calamity (1:7). As Yahweh has used the storm, he uses the lot-casting to expose Jonah to the sailors and bring him to face his calling as a prophet. The wind, the sailors, and the lots are each the agents of God for this purpose (see further comments at 1:17).

Although it is not seen in English, the interplay of Hebrew and Aramaic in the conversation shows that the sailors and Jonah are doing the best they can to communicate with each other. When speaking to each other, the sailors use an Aramaic expression: "Then the sailors said to each other, 'Come, let us cast lots to find out *who is responsible for [bešellemi]* this calamity.' They cast lots and the lot fell on Jonah." But when the sailors speak to Jonah, they say the same thing in full Hebrew: "So they asked him, 'Tell us, *who is responsible for [baʾašer lemi]* making all this trouble for us?'" (1:8a). When Jonah uses the same expression to admit his fault, he uses the sailors' Aramaic: "I know that *it is my fault [bešelli]* that this great storm has come upon you" (1:12b).

When Jonah tells them who his God is (1:9), the sailors are terrified. Immediately they understand the cause of the storm and ask the equivalent of "Are you crazy?" ("What have you done?"). The tremendous storm is the primary evidence that Jonah's God is powerful. When he says that "the LORD [is] God of heaven, who made *the sea* and the land," they know they are in trouble. Who runs away from the God of the sea *on a ship?*

The sailors' five rapid-fire questions (1:8) continue the energy of their desperate work against the storm (praying to gods, jettisoned cargo, lots cast). They have discovered Jonah by lot and now need to know more, quickly. They seek a confession and confirmation, but Jonah doesn't give them a confession yet. He ignores this part, although he knows he is cornered.

---

9. *haelohim* can be translated either "the true God" or "the gods."

Next they ask, "What do you do?" The question about occupation means, "Whom do you represent?"[10] Knowing this should help them know whom to appease. The following three questions: "Where do you come from?" "What is your country?" and "From what people are you?" Jonah can answer in a single phrase: "I am a Hebrew."

The second question is the most difficult question for Jonah. Is he a messenger of God? It is this question that has driven him to this ship. It is the question that he doesn't want to answer. When Yahweh called him to Nineveh, he didn't want to be a prophet any longer. Now the sailors want to know. In the midst of this storm, what are his commitments? What are his allegiances?

The irony of Jonah's decision is that he will die in either case. If he says nothing, the storm will kill them all. If he confesses, he knows he alone will die. God has reduced his decision to the question, "Will your life/death save the lives of others, or will it be an ordinary death at sea in a storm with pagan sailors?" This is the essence of his call to be a prophet. In the case of Nineveh, Jonah's decision was for a meaningless life and death that he could, nonetheless, choose. Now the decision is put to him again, so close that Jonah cannot fail to see the difference.

Jonah's answer to the second and vital question implies his decision (in 1:12) to have a meaningful death: "I worship the LORD, the God of heaven, who made the sea and the land" (1:9b). His "worship" (*yara*ʾ, "fear") is meaningful in fulfilling his calling. This confession itself is a fulfillment of his calling as prophet. He witnesses to the reality of Yahweh, declaring that he is the Creator, the God of heaven, sea, and land. Jonah is in the center of a traditional faith, also expressed in Psalm 95:5: "The sea is his, for he made it, and his hands formed the dry land."[11]

The question in 1:10 ("What have you done?") also implies, "What have you done *to us*?" Jonah now has to consider his guilt in the potential death of the sailors in the storm. He faces a call to put himself at risk for the sake of unbelievers for the second time, now in an intense situation. He ran from his call to the Ninevites, but now he is face to face with pagan sailors. What will he do? The sailors want to know. His witness will come only in his willingness to die as he says, "Pick me up and throw me into the sea" (1:12). In this verse Jonah turns a bit further toward Yahweh (cf. 1:9 for the first turning).

---

10. "Occupation" is the feminine noun *melaʾkah*; "messenger" or "representative" is the masculine noun from the same root, *malʾak*.

11. The parenthetical comment at 1:10b, "They knew he was running away from the LORD because he had already told them so," is not a later editor's hand. An editor would have added it at the end of verse 9 as a quotation ("I am running away from the LORD"). It is a true afterthought of the original hand, added to explain the sailors' quick understanding and rhetorical question, "What have you done?"

The sailors' question in 1:11 ("What should we do to you?") probably assumes that some ritual punishment is necessary and that they must do something to Jonah, who has not been obedient to Yahweh. Again we see the sailors' correct perception. Jonah doesn't have the will to jump himself but asks them to "pick him up" in order to "throw him" into the sea.

The tension is now heightened by the graphic language: "The sea was getting rougher and rougher" (lit., "the sea walked and raged"). In 1:11–12 the sailors and Jonah both use the Aramaic expression "to make the sea calm down," using the Aramaic word *šataq*. Jonah uses a second Aramaic expression ("it is my fault") in this exchange as well (see comments on 1:5–7). The continued use of Aramaic implies a desire to communicate.

In verse 12, Jonah prophesies correctly for the second time in the book (that the sea will become calm; cf. 1:15). His first "prophecy" (declaration of the truth of God) was in 1:9b, when he said he worships Yahweh, the God of heaven who made the sea and the land.

Jonah does not seem to be capable of simple repentance. He could have sought forgiveness during the storm (as the Ninevites do later) and committed himself to go to Nineveh. But perhaps he believes that too much "water had passed under his ship" by this time. Perhaps he is not sure that his repentance would bring forgiveness. He prefers to believe (wants to believe?!) in a God who only judges and does not forgive. He would rather die in the sea than suggest to the sailors that they turn around and return him to Joppa to complete Yahweh's call to Nineveh.

Yet Jonah does have compassion on the innocent sailors and does not want *them* to die. He will accept death for them, not in obedience to God but, nonetheless, in their place. It was a heroism born of his desperate situation. Although he is disobeying God, he still believes in Yahweh's power and in acting justly toward others. (His repentance comes in chapter 2.)

The Sailors and Yahweh (1:13–16)

THE SAILORS DO not want to kill Yahweh's prophet, so they attempt to row back to land. But as 1:14 shows, this is more than a squeamish aversion. They know Jonah is a serious problem, but they do not want to be held responsible for killing the prophet of such a powerful god. In the cosmology of the ancient Near East, one did not have to be responsible for a situation to order to incur the consequence of someone else's guilt. It was an ancient version of being "in the wrong place at the wrong time" (cf. Gen. 20).

"[Dry] land" (*bašab*) is mentioned three times in the book (1:9, 13; 2:10). Dry land is where the sailors want to be. Just as Jonah thought he could *run* from the conflict at Nineveh, the sailors think they can row out of the storm to dry land. The lesson is not subtle. Yahweh is God of *both*, as Jonah has told them: "I worship the LORD, the God of heaven, who made the sea and *the land*" (1:9b), and "the LORD commanded the fish, and it vomited Jonah onto *dry land*" (2:10).

But Yahweh will not allow an easy ending here. Each time his storm is mentioned, the sailors move closer to the truth. At first they do what one would expect from sailors in a violent storm: "All the sailors were afraid and each *cried out to his own god*. And they *threw the cargo* into the sea" (1:5a). The second time, they asked Yahweh's prophet what to do (1:11a). Now the third time that Yahweh's storm heightens, they cry out "to the LORD" (1:13b–14a). "Even wilder than before" (1:13b) is more personal and direct in Hebrew: (lit.) "The seas grew and raged *against them*." The storm raged primarily because of Jonah, but in its midst, the sailors have become personally involved.

The sailors have a specific request as they cry out to Yahweh, saying, "Please" (*annah*): "O LORD, please do not let us die for taking this man's life" (1:14). They do not want to die simply because they have taken on a passenger with a pursuing God. They have run out of other options. They tried calling on other gods, lightening the ship, asking Jonah to pray, casting lots, interrogating Jonah, and rowing. Their fear is that they will die for doing something they really don't want to do: participating in God's judgment on Jonah. It is a horrible situation for them, and they say so: "Do not hold us accountable for killing an innocent man."[12]

They know Jonah is not "innocent" in relationship to God, but in relation to them he is innocent. He has jeopardized their lives by boarding their ship, but did so unwittingly (for a comparative legal situation, see Gen. 20). That is not a capital crime. Nonetheless, the prophet (who clearly has heavenly connections) has suggested the only remaining option to losing their ship and drowning. They can only take this word from Yahweh and act on it. In this (outrageous) obedience, they become believers (1:15–16).

Yahweh declared Jonah guilty in the casting of lots. He confirmed his guilt in the words of his prophet to the sailors and by increasing the raging of the storm. The sailors, as they declare their innocence, choose to bear the possible peril of Yahweh rather than the peril of certain death in the storm. They will, in contrast to Jonah, bear the situation given to them. Jonah will also bear his situation by going over the gunwale, but he bears it in guilt. The sailors, by contrast, act innocently and obediently, which Yahweh honors. "Then they took Jonah and threw him overboard, and the raging sea grew

---

12. On "do not let us die," see 4:10 on "perish" (*abad*), which occurs at 1:6, 14; 3:9; 4:10.

---

calm" (1:15). Again, the Hebrew is more graphic: "Then they lifted Jonah up and they hurled him into the sea and the sea stood down from its raging" (see comments on "hurl" [*twl*] at 1:5).

In 1:16 we read an amazing statement: "At this the men greatly *feared* the LORD." The progression of the sailors' "conversion" to Yahweh can be seen in the Hebrew word *yara²*, which has the basic meaning "fear" (as in "the fear of the LORD is the beginning of wisdom," Ps. 111:10) or "reverence." The sailors have three kinds of "fear" (*yara²*) in this chapter. In 1:5 they *fear* dying in the storm, and each relies on his own god. In 1:9 they hear that Jonah *worships* ("fears") a God they do not know, the very God who has sent the storm. Then they are *terrified* because they realize that their circumstance is as desperate as it could be. After the raging sea grows calm, they "greatly fear the LORD" and worship him (1:16).

The text does not tell us whether this new appreciation for the Lord of heaven, land, and sea is lasting (i.e., whether they keep their "vows," 1:16). Nonetheless, 1:16 describes something new for the sailors in relationship to Yahweh, Jonah's God. They "greatly fear" ("revere") because they have witnessed Yahweh's power over creation and because he has honored their prayer for deliverance. They offer the fundamental confessions of followers of Yahweh and confess him as Creator and Deliverer. They also act on their belief by offering "a sacrifice to the LORD." A sacrifice was a public expression of dependence and worship.

The sailors make vows to Yahweh. Vows were a public expression of the intent to continue in faithful worship. The actions of sacrifice and vows are precisely the actions of worship later declared by Jonah for *his* deliverance: "But I, with a song of thanksgiving, will sacrifice to you. What I have vowed I will make good. Salvation comes from the LORD" (2:9). The change in the sailors' relationship to Yahweh evident in 1:16 is later paralleled in the Ninevites' repentance in chapter 3. Even in Jonah's disobedience, Yahweh has made him effective in his calling as a prophet, bringing people to faith in Yahweh.

God's Fish (1:17)

JONAH'S RESCUE FROM drowning via a "great fish" is an unbelievable development, at which even an ancient reader might have stopped and made an assessment concerning whether this was a legend or a miraculous account. Jonah's initial call from Yahweh to preach to his enemies was "unbelievable," as was their ready repentance. But the great fish that swallows, houses, and vomits Jonah is a "supranatural" miracle of reversal. Fish don't routinely swallow people whole. Jonah's residence in the fish for three days is unnatural, that is, a reversal of the natural. If a person were indeed swallowed by a fish, death would be inevitable. Yet the safety of Jonah is assumed in the narrative. He does not die within the fish but somehow survives.[13]

The One who has "provided" (*manah*, "assign, number, appoint") this fish is Yahweh. This verb is used in the intensive Piel form, with the meaning "special assignment" or "ordain" (see 4:6, 7, 8). This word is used of all the nonhuman agents provided by God to bring Jonah back to his calling. Jonah is swallowed, which usually means death and entering the underworld of Sheol (Num. 16:30; Prov. 1:12). But Jonah is delivered from Sheol (2:2, 6) because the fish has been appointed for an extraordinary deliverance.[14] The fish saves Jonah from drowning by swallowing or engulfing (*bala*ᶜ) him.

In the Hebrew text, 1:17 is the first verse of chapter 2, introducing Jonah's prayer from the belly of the fish. The "three days and three nights" is discussed in the Bridging Contexts section about the miraculous sign of the big fish.

THE DIVERSE AND rich tradition in the interpretation of Jonah 1:1–17 has offered many timeless themes, including: "The Lord is God of all creation"; "running away from Yahweh is foolish"; and "God calls his people to preach to those of distant cultures" (sailors, Ninevites). Modern readers have sometimes seen a theme informed by a single verse (1:17): "God *can* make a large fish, in which a man can survive" (i.e., God can do miracles).

For an interpretation to endure with integrity, it should reflect the whole chapter (in the context of the book) and not simply a portion. The evidence in chapter 1 points to the centrality of Yahweh's pursuing love in the storm and the unanticipated deliverance of Jonah and the sailors. God's astoundingly persistent and unrelenting grace pursues the fleeing prophet, unexpectedly delivers him from drowning, and returns him to the dry land of his calling. (It also causes the conversion of the sailors and will redirect Jonah to his original mission to Nineveh.) These actions declare God's tenacious commitment to reconciliation with humanity. The concluding warrants for this interpretation are found in Jesus' own words concerning Jonah.

Why Jonah ran. A common theme for teaching and preaching on Jonah 1 is that he ran because of his personal depravity, in spite of his knowledge

---

13. The distinction between "whale" and "fish" makes little difference for understanding the action in the text. The point is that "the LORD provided" in a "supernatural" way for Jonah's deliverance from drowning. A whale would have done as well. Ancient peoples did not distinguish fish from mammals in the same way that we do.

14. The original storm wind was "hurled" and not "provided," but it functions in a similar way.

of God's sovereignty. He is described as "going down" and "bottoming out," as he slides down a "slippery slope" of sin. Jonah's flight is certainly an example of the larger biblical theme of running from God. "Going down" is the refrain by which the life of anyone fleeing from God may be interpreted. In the case of Jonah, it is also important to ask why he ran and what he learned along the way.

"Going down" is indeed a metaphor used in each of Jonah's actions as well as in the inevitable consequences of "going down" that he cannot escape. He goes *down* to Joppa, *down* to the port, *down below* the deck of the ship, and lying *down*, falls into a *deep* sleep. But Yahweh "sent a great wind . . . a violent storm . . . the ship threatened to break up." Yahweh will bring him down even further, and even the pagan sailors know he is in trouble. He needs to "*get up*"! Finally, thrown overboard, he goes *down* into the water.

This downward slide of Jonah's decisions and circumstances are marked in the Hebrew by the verbs *yarad* and *radam* (see comments on 1:3–5). This same downward motion in Jonah's sinking continues in chapter 2 in his description of sinking in the sea: "From the depths of the grave I called for help. . . . You hurled me into the deep, into the very heart of the seas . . . the deep surrounded me. . . . To the roots of the mountains I sank down. . . . But you brought my life up from the pit" (2:2–6).

When Jonah's "going down" in his flight from Yahweh is preached, the good news is that God pursues him. God does not let him go but finds him out in order to rescue him. But from what kind of depravity is God rescuing Jonah? It is true that God rescues humanity from depravity by seeking our salvation in all times and places. Chapter 1 presents an occasion to teach this truth, but is it reflected by the whole text? Jonah is certainly in rebellion against God's call to him. He does sink to the depths. Yet in spite of his rebellion, his firm faith and integrity are demonstrated in three ways: He is a true prophet of God (2 Kings 14:25); Yahweh entrusts him with an extremely difficult assignment (1:2, which is surely a sign of God's favor); and he boldly confesses his faith to the sailors (1:9, "I am a Hebrew and I worship the LORD, the God of heaven, who made the sea and the land.").

Jonah maintains his integrity in confessing his sin to the sailors and is willing to die so that they may live (1:12). His brief rebellion is between his being entrusted with the assignment and his confessing his faith to the sailors. If this truth is expounded, it must resonate with the themes that follow: He believes, confesses his sin, submits to going overboard for the sake of the sailors' lives, and is then "rescued" by the grace of God by residing in the belly of the fish. Jonah's integrity and faith, when faced with God's judgment (the drowning) and grace (in the belly of the fish), nuance the truth of the text beyond rebellion and repentance.

Why did Jonah run? Jonah's running was a refusal to obey God's call to "go to Nineveh," but it was more than simple disobedience. His running demonstrates his basic disagreement with God's way of dealing with people in the world. Jonah runs because he does not want to go to Nineveh and preach God's message of repentance (see Bridging Contexts section of ch. 3). Why not? A variety of creative answers are given as to the reason for this dislike, some with more basis in the text than others.

(1) Jonah ran because the Ninevites were not Jews. But the distinction between Gentiles and Jews is never indicated in any way either in this text or in New Testament references to Jonah. The distinction is between violent wickedness and repentance of evil (1:2; 3:8, 10), not Jonah's cultural selfishness with God's forgiveness. This "Semitic" reason has been used historically to fuel the isolation of Jewish people, without textual warrant.

(2) Jonah ran because he did not want to be known as a false prophet. Jonah does say that "he knew" the Ninevites would repent (4:2). Commentators also point to the "test" of a prophet in Deuteronomy 18:22a: "If what a prophet proclaims in the name of the LORD does not take place or come true, that is a message the LORD has not spoken." But this "career" reason has no support in the text. It misses the important historical reality that prophecies of doom always contained the possibility of repentance because of God's reputation for forgiving (Ex. 34:7a).

(3) Jonah ran because he feared the wicked Ninevites. That they *were* wicked is supported in the text by God (1:2) and by the king himself (3:8). It appears, however, that Jonah was not afraid to die. He does not seem to fear the storm and readily offers himself to be tossed overboard (1:12).

(4) Jonah *ran from his call in protest against God's move toward the violently wicked.* This is the true reason for Jonah's running. It is a theological reason. He wants God to be consistent: to destroy those who are violently wicked and to prosper the righteous. He believes God is making an inconsistent and dangerous theological move by offering to forgive the Ninevites (see 4:2). God's action to save the wicked redefines what *God* means. It is a new move to convert and rehabilitate habitual and flagrant perpetrators of heinous crimes. To Jonah, God is taking an unbelievable risk in sparing the Ninevites, a risk that is bad for the victims of the world and for God's reputation. He wants nothing to do with such a strategy (see Bridging Contexts of ch. 4).

"Go to Nineveh" declares a primary theme and timeless call of the book of Jonah. God's call to Jonah to "go" establishes an enduring revelation and problem for all believers: God wants his prophet to go to his heinous enemies with a message of doom, but one that also includes (as Jonah knows, see 4:2) the possibility of forgiveness. The Old Testament has another narrative that suggests this possibility. In 2 Kings 5 the commander of the oppressing

Syrian army brought a troop into Israel seeking healing from Elisha. Yahweh led the prophet to heal him and send him home in peace (2 Kings 5:19). He did this in spite of the fact that Naaman had routinely raided Israel for loot and slaves. Again in 2 Kings 6:20–23 Elisha demonstrated compassion toward the Syrian enemies whom he healed, fed, and released when they were in his power.

Jonah is running from the visions of God he received in the temple (the typical place of Jonah's prophetic work; see 2:4, 7). Jonah is not fleeing the God of heaven, sea, and dry land; he knows that this is impossible (1:9; see below). He is running from God's specific call on his life to preach to his enemies. He heads for Tarshish and away from the temple, where he was accustomed to hearing the word of Yahweh. He hopes, at least, that God will stop calling him to speak if he can separate himself from that place of hearing God's voice.

What is timeless? God still calls believers to participate in the risky task of preaching repentance and forgiveness. This double-edged theme of God's active mercy toward enemies and the call for God's people to trust God enough to proclaim this (sometimes offensive) mercy has its beginning in Jonah.

This theme comes to full blossom in the ministry of Jesus. Jesus crosses all the social boundaries, reaching out to violent outcasts (e.g., the demoniac in the graveyard), even a zealot (Simon, who was called "the zealot," Acts 1:13), Roman centurions, and the thief on the cross. The ministry of the Holy Spirit in the early church was plainly extended to outsiders and enemies (e.g., Cornelius and the Ethiopian). Jesus calls his disciples to love their enemies and to pray for those who persecute them (Matt. 5:44). "Jonah" means "dove." His name represents God's mission of peace to all people of the world, even God's chosen people's enemies.

Where is God in Jonah? (The sovereignty of God). In the last two centuries, interpreters have tended to see Jonah 1 as a treatise on the sovereignty of God. This theme is often summarized in sermons that expound the theme: "You cannot run from God." P. Kleinert's early development of this theme is representative of the tradition.

> *There is no escape from Almighty God.* For: 1) He has so arranged the world that the work of every individual is counted upon; and his work is not allowed to stand still, but must be accomplished (Verses 1, 2). 2) Distance is no protection against Him; for to Him belong heaven and earth, the sea and the dry land (Verses 3ff, 9). 3) To Him the winds and waves are subject; for he has made all things (Verses 4, 9). 4) To Him also are subject every where, in involuntary fear, the erring hearts of men (Verses 5, 6); whoever, then, expects to find in them a

refuge against God, is deceived. 5) Even things seemingly accidental must obey Him, whenever He intends to carry out his purpose (Verse 7). 6) Everything, however far from, or near to Him it may be, must finally become an instrument in his hand (Verses 11–15), and cooperate for the glorifying of his name (Verse 16).[15]

That God is almighty is a timeless truth of Jonah. Certainly the futility of Jonah's running from the God of the sea *upon the sea* represents this truth. Jonah is a convenient occasion for this theme. Is this sovereignty of God, a theme that is found, to some degree, in every book of the Scripture, the main theme of the chapter? Does Jonah 1:1–17 present a more specific truth? Jonah knew God was the sovereign of the land and sea (1:9) and ran *in spite of that fact.*

Jonah flees from Yahweh. What does it mean that Jonah flees "from the LORD"? (1:3, lit., "from the LORD's presence"). The prophet's main perspective is the one he has inherited by faith: that Yahweh's presence is, at least most powerfully and assuredly, in the temple (2:4, 7). Technically to "flee from the presence of the LORD" means to flee from the temple. In the temple he stood before Yahweh to listen for a word (2:4). The mistake of the concept that "the presence of the LORD" is only in formal places of worship or limited by them, however, is evident as early as 1:4: "The LORD sent a great wind on the sea." If Yahweh's residence is in the temple, he is certainly not limited by it. Where is God in Jonah? He acts in the wind (1:4), the casting of lots (1:7), the fish (1:17; 2:10), the vine (4:6), the worm (4:7), and the temple (2:4). In each case, he is present, and his intentions are revealed in the nonhuman creation.

Jonah is not ignorant of the presence of Yahweh in the whole creation. His confession of faith to the sailors includes Yahweh, "who made the sea and the land" (1:9). As a good temple prophet he would have known Psalm 139:7–10.

> Where can I go from your Spirit?
>> Where can I flee from your presence?
> If I go up to the heavens, you are there;
>> if I make my bed in the depths, you are there.
> If I rise on the wings of the dawn,
>> if I settle on the far side of the sea,
> even there your hand will guide me,
>> your right hand will hold me fast.

---

15. Paul Kleinert, *Jonah,* trans. by Charles Elliott in *Lange's Commentary on the Holy Scriptures: Minor Prophets* (1874; rprt. Grand Rapids, Zondervan, n.d.), 20.

He also likely knows the more ominous warning of Amos 9:2–3. "Though they dig down to the depths of the grave, from there my hand will take them.... Though they hide from me at the bottom of the sea, there I will command the serpent to bite them."[16] So what is Jonah doing "fleeing" from Yahweh, who is known to be present everywhere? He is fleeing to Tarshish. What is Tarshish, and what difference can that make to someone seeking to escape Yahweh? Tarshish is the farthest point west known in his day, where Yahweh is not honored or known. Jonah knows he cannot really escape the God of the universe, but he can try to forget him in the midst of another culture. Jonah, however, does not receive an opportunity to see whether this strategy will work.

More specifically than the general sovereignty of God, this chapter shows the specific concern of a sovereign God for the whole creation. God is God of all creation, and he loves and works in and through what he has created (see Bridging Contexts section of ch. 4).

The sailors and Jonah. When Jonah first meets the sailors, they do not know Yahweh. They are in the midst of a storm that threatens to kill them, yet they are positive examples in their responses to Jonah and to Yahweh. They are open toward Jonah's God, asking him to pray for their deliverance (1:6). When they discover by lots that Jonah is responsible for the storm, they are eager to learn about him and his God (1:8). Jonah's confession of faith (1:9, "the God of heaven, who made the sea and the land") is in itself noteworthy. In the midst of a storm at sea, however, Jonah's faith appears murky and his God, fearsome. It is not a strong witness, but it is a faithful one.

Jonah's witness (and the end of the storm) leads the sailors to faith in Yahweh. When Jonah suggests that they throw him overboard, they resist killing him and row harder. Finally out of options, they pray to Yahweh for forgiveness before tossing him in the water. When the storm is over, they offer thanks to Yahweh for their deliverance and make vows to be faithful to him. Their strong character and open faith demonstrate to Jonah (as well as to the reader) that the world is not necessarily closed to the witness of faith, even a weak witness. Especially in crisis, the world that God loves is open to hearing a witness of the truth. The sailors are not looking for this witness or for the God of the sea and dry land. Through Jonah's willingness to be thrown overboard, however, they encounter Yahweh and his unanticipated deliverance from the storm.

The miraculous sign of the big fish. The first Jonah text that has a direct reference to the miracle of the fish is Jonah 1:17: "But the LORD provided a great fish to swallow Jonah, and Jonah was inside the fish three days and three

---

16. E. Achtemeier drew my attention to this warning.

nights." It is mentioned again at the end of chapter 2: "And the LORD commanded the fish, and it vomited Jonah onto dry land" (2:10). This part of Jonah is echoed in the New Testament in three places.

> Then some of the Pharisees and teachers of the law said to him, "Teacher, we want to see a miraculous sign from you."
> He answered, "A wicked and adulterous generation asks for *a miraculous sign!* But none will be given it except *the sign of the prophet Jonah.* For as *Jonah was three days and three nights* in the belly of a huge fish, so the Son of Man will be *three days and three nights* in the heart of the earth." (Matt. 12:38–40; cf. Luke 11:29–32)

> "A wicked and adulterous generation looks for *a miraculous sign,* but none will be given it except *the sign of Jonah.*" Jesus then left them and went away. (Matt. 16:4)

> ... that he was buried, that *he was raised on the third day,* according to the Scriptures." (1 Cor. 15:4, italics added in all passages)

The miracle of the big fish is threefold: Jonah is rescued from drowning in the sea (esp. ch. 2); Jonah is inside the fish (1:17); and Jonah is vomited onto dry land to be called again to his mission (2:10; chs. 3–4). The point of the miracle is twofold: to rescue Jonah from drowning and to call him again to his mission. Jonah's survival inside the fish for three days (mentioned only in 1:17b) has unfortunately become the modern trademark of the story.[17]

The significance of the big fish is that the reader is asked to believe the "unbelievable." What is unbelievable? For many modern readers the answer stops with: "the physical impossibility of the fish swallowing Jonah." The text, however, offers another answer to the question (the physical possibility is *not* an issue in the biblical text). The "big fish" swallowing the rebellious and drowning prophet is a sign of Yahweh's pursuing and extraordinary mercy. Jonah's prayer of thanks in chapter 2 develops this meaning.

Even more, the fish represents Yahweh's forgiveness of Jonah's rebellion against his call to the Ninevites. The fish's swallowing Jonah is a sign that Yahweh will not be dissuaded from his intention to present the possibility of repentance and forgiveness to Israel's enemy. It demonstrates the astounding lengths to which God will go to reconcile Jonah *and the violent Ninevites* to himself through Jonah. The fish represents an "unbelievable" theology: Yahweh wants to save the rebellious and the violent. Through the agency of

---

17. See the introduction and the comments on Walt Disney's version of the Pinocchio story.

the big fish, Jonah is forgiven and saved. Also unbelievable, the storm is stilled and the sailors worship the true God, and the Ninevites receive the message from Jonah, repent, and are saved. In this way the bigness of the unbelievable fish is finally about God's saving way in the world. The big fish makes a specific point of God's extravagant, unrelenting, pursuing, and saving love.

When Jesus responds in his typically cryptic way to the Pharisees' request for a miraculous sign, he speaks of the "belly of the huge fish." This reference to his descent to death ("three days and three nights in heart of the earth") is an allusion to the miracle of his resurrection. The sign of Jonah is not the belly of the fish but the rescue from death in the process of the fish's swallowing and vomiting. The miraculous sign is his deliverance from death, not his residence in the fish. This may seem like a too subtle point, but in teaching and preaching, the shift in emphasis may be catastrophic.

The common distraction. Modern readers are so fascinated with Jonah in the belly of the fish that the fish is often referred to as a whale (which apparently makes it more likely, although less of a miracle).[18] The scientific possibility of a man surviving in a whale has refocused interpretation of the miracle in such a way that we miss the point of the text and of Jesus' meaning. Rather than focusing on the miracle of Jonah's forgiveness and deliverance by the action of God (the content of chs. 1–2), too many today have focused on the *swallowing* and Jonah's *wallowing* in the "pit" of the fish's belly.

More recent interpreters (from the nineteenth century to the present) have aggravated this situation by making the "truth" of the account a litmus test for Christian faith. Using belief in Jonah's residence in the belly of a fish (or whale) as a test for a general faith in miracles tends to silence the message of God in the book itself. When the subject of Jonah is raised in conversation, the first and often only question concerning the text is: "Could the prophet really have been swallowed by a whale?" In this way the book of Jonah is reduced to a single question, and its amazing message of God's pursuing love is muted. For many, once the question of miracle/no miracle is answered, the conversation about Jonah is over. Consider, however, a legacy that begins with the question, "What does Jonah's expulsion from the fish mean?"

What miracle made all the difference to Jonah? It is not the amazing dimensions of the fish. Rather, it is Jonah's rescue from drowning (ch. 2) and later, the dry land. What miracle makes all the difference to Christians? Is it the dimensions of the grave? No, it is our deliverance from death through

---

18. A whale captain's report in the latter nineteenth century that a sailor survived such an experience lends fuel to this fire. A. J. Wilson, "The Sign of the Prophet Jonah and Its Modern Confirmations," *Princeton Theological Review* 25 (1927): 630–42.

Jesus' death. It is Jesus' being raised by the Father in a victory over sin, death, and the devil. It is our hope secured through his resurrection. The important miraculous sign of Jonah is that he is raised from the depths, not that he survives in the air sac or the wide pharynx of a whale. As a parallel, Jesus' time in the grave is not the focus of our wonder, but the empty tomb is. Jesus' mention of Jonah's three days was to quiet the Pharisees with a cryptic reference. It was not an elevation of that part of the miracle.

The timeless truth of Jonah 1 is that the inclination of every person (even a true prophet of God) is to flee from the radical grace of God. The idea that God loves and seeks reconciliation with the violent people of Nineveh puts Jonah and anyone who understands what God is suggesting, initially, to flight.

WHEN JONAH RUNS to Tarshish, it is the beginning of a serious theological argument with God. God's word commands Jonah to preach against the wicked Ninevites, and Jonah suspects (as he states in ch. 4) that Yahweh wants to save Israel's archenemy and to reconcile them to himself. Although Jonah believes God is serious, he cannot swallow this theology. Yahweh, in a countermove, decides that Jonah should be swallowed by it.

Jonah runs in the same two ways we run from God's message of forgiveness. We run from God's forgiveness for us and from our participation in proclaiming that message of forgiveness to others. Jonah, a "prophet of doom," is sent to bear a message that may result in forgiveness for Nineveh. His own rescue is a by-product of God's pursuit of his obedience. We are not prophets of doom but Christians with a call to accept for ourselves and to proclaim a similar message. In Christ, God offers an enduring call to repentance and forgiveness to the unlikeliest of people. This call begins with our own salvation. The tendency of all persons in our lost world is to run from this call, attempting to lead self-authenticating lives. God must seek after each one of us. We also run from the call to proclaim repentance and reconciliation with God to our families and friends, let alone those we do not like, or our mortal enemies.

In Jonah the difficult mercy of Yahweh finds Jonah in a dramatic storm. It also finds sailors, not looking for trouble, whose lives are imminently threatened. Hearing Jonah's witness, and receiving his self-sacrifice, they are delivered and turn to his Lord in prayer, commitment (vows), and worship.

Running to Tarshish. Jonah runs by sea toward Tarshish in spite of his knowledge that Yahweh is the God of all the sea and dry land. He runs to avoid the two places associated with Yahweh's word to him: the temple (where he heard it) and Nineveh. He heads to Tarshish, hoping to escape the sound of Yahweh's voice. He knows Yahweh is present everywhere, but he flees to a place he hopes will drown out the sound of God's word to him.

Jonah seeks a culture where he will not hear about God's faithfulness to his people, God's commandments, or any reference to God. He wants a *sui generis* ("self-referring") existence. Many people attempt a similar flight into the "culture" of secularity. They hope that if they are preoccupied with other values and commitments, they can forget God's Word. They hope that if they are surrounded by a crowd that has not heard the instruction, prophets, wisdom, or the gospel of the Lord, they too may be able to ignore it. They also believe, superseding belief in the Great Commission, that we can live *sui generis* lives.[19]

"Self-referring" lives can be sinful in two general ways.[20] (1) We may pretend not to be limited and overestimate our capacities as fallen creatures of a Creator. In this case, we do not refer to God in praise or worship because we assume we don't need him. We are self-sufficient. (2) We may pretend not to be created creatures in God's creation. We may curve inward toward the created world, underestimating our capacities in relation to God, or we may lose ourselves in some aspect of the creation that controls our lives in various idolatries. Both of these sinful postures are forms of running from God.

We should not run from God, but we do. Even our piety, as in Jonah's righteous indignation with God's mercy, can cause us to run. Until we admit we are on the run, we are lost. But when, with Jonah, we admit our true situation (1:10), we have real hope. God in his mercy does more than call us back to himself. Yahweh pursues us as he pursued Jonah, with a storm, sailors' questions, and the great fish of death. This pursuit is our only hope. Apart from it, we are still running from God and from the message of Jonah. Note Paul's question in Romans 7:

> For in my inner being I delight in God's law; but I see another law at work in the members of my body, waging war against the law of my mind and making me a prisoner of the law of sin at work within my members. What a wretched man I am! Who will rescue me from this body of death? Thanks be to God—through Jesus Christ our Lord!
>
> So then, I myself in my mind am a slave to God's law, but in the sinful nature a slave to the law of sin. (Rom. 7:22–26)

Running from the call to witness to the ends of the earth. God's call to be a witness of grace to our enemies is also something we share with Jonah. Jonah's

---

19. See Stanley Hauerwas, *The Peaceable Kingdom: A Primer in Christian Ethics* (Notre Dame, Ind.: Univ. of Notre Dame Press, 1983), ch. 2, for an expansion of the term *sui generis*.

20. See R. Niebuhr, quoted in Hauerwas, ibid., 32.

running is not ordinary running from God. It is a protest against the call to be a witness to his enemies. He runs from the temple (to avoid Yahweh's voice) and from Nineveh. Jonah believes the sovereignty of God in this calling, he simply does not want to obey it. In a similar way, we claim to believe Jesus' words: "Love your enemies and pray for those who persecute you" (Matt. 5:44), but we find it difficult to practice them. We also believe the Great Commission and Jesus' parting words that include our enemies, near and far: "You will be my witnesses in Jerusalem, and in all Judea and Samaria, and to the ends of the earth" (Acts 1:8b). Still, believers often avoid bearing witness.

As armchair prophets, we judge Jonah harshly, yet Jonah was a true and faithful prophet of God (2 Kings 14:25). He was chosen by Yahweh above all the other prophets of his day for a difficult task. Yahweh did not ask the great prophets Isaiah, Amos, or Hosea to go to the Assyrians. He called Jonah, not only to speak against Israel's enemy Assyria (like Nahum) but to go into the mouth of the Assyrian lion. Daniel is later captured with his friends and deported to Babylon and its lions' den, but Jonah is told to go on his own. He is not afraid to die when he runs from God's command. He is ready to die ("Throw me into the sea," 1:12). Rather, in his real-life struggle, Jonah concludes that God has gone too far with grace, and he doesn't care to participate in this foolishness (see 4:2). He would have preferred Nahum's assignment, to speak an irrevocable judgment of exacting retribution for Nineveh's crimes:

An oracle concerning Nineveh. . . .

> The LORD is a jealous and avenging God;
> the LORD takes vengeance and is filled with wrath.
> The LORD takes vengeance on his foes
> and maintains his wrath against his enemies. (Nah. 1:1a, 2)

There are many ways to run from God's call to be a witness of grace to our enemies. We may not physically run, but we negotiate our participation in the gospel. We may prefer Nahum's commission of condemnation to Jesus' Great Commission: "Therefore go and make disciples of all nations" (Matt 28:19a). Mission to the unreached is the first and essential command of the risen Christ ("Go and tell"). Without mission, Christianity has no commission. In spite of this, many congregations struggle to support missionaries and evangelism. At the beginning of the twenty-first century more than 144 million persons in 815 ethnic people groups have virtually no access to the gospel message.[21]

---

21. T. M. Johnson and P. F. Crossing, "Which Peoples Need Priority Attention: Those with the Least Christian Resources," *Mission Frontiers* (Jan-Feb 2002): 16–23.

In spite of these facts, the most affluent churches in the world often dedicate only small parts of their budget to mission projects outside of their locality. The judgment of Jonah is that those who resist participation in proclaiming the gospel of repentance and forgiveness have only one real hope. Those who do not go or give support, as well as those who actively or passively resist their own calls locally, regionally, and globally, can only hope to suffer the same severe mercy as Jonah.[22] They may hope that the miracle of deliverance becomes so personal that they can no longer withhold the message of rescue and life from others. To many it sounds inefficient or even foolish to send missionaries. It is as foolish as sending one prophet from Israel to preach in the Assyrian capital of Nineveh, or as sending a baby to occupied Palestine to bring good news to the world. It is the foolishness of the cross (1 Cor. 1:18–25).

Even in his reluctance, Jonah eventually does go to Nineveh. The book tells the truth about what the most difficult mission assignments are like for missionaries. In order to have integrity, a constant conversation with Yahweh must ensue, in which all the fears, disputes, and anxieties of the calling can be spoken to Yahweh. Jonah is an inspiration to anyone who has embarked on such a calling. Protest is a human reality of struggling with a call to one's enemies. The crucial question is whether or not the ambassador of Yahweh finally is given the grace to go. Jonah goes and speaks the word he is given, and thousands are saved. His first flight to Tarshish is a significant protest. But even there his calling from God is confirmed when he speaks the word of witness and the sailors are converted. Jonah is, despite his rebellious protest, a faithful witness, used by God.

A caution against anti-Semitism. Jonah must not be typecast as a faithless representative of a stingy Israel. Jonah is a person called to a seemingly impossible task, with whom Jesus identifies (Matt. 12:39–41; see below). Within the last hundred years, some Christian interpreters have controverted and flattened the message of the book of Jonah in an irresponsible and anti-Semitic explanation of its meaning. Jonah has been called "a salutary lesson to the Jews . . . renowned for their stubbornness and lack of faith."[23]

Jonah is said to be a "type of the narrow, blind, prejudiced, and fanatic Jews."[24] The transference of the prophet's struggle with a difficult word from

---

22. See the Contemporary Significance section of ch. 3

23. "Jonah," in J. D. Douglas, ed., *The New Bible Dictionary* (Leicester: Intervarsity Press, 1962), 652–54.

24. J. A. Bewer, *Critical and Exegetical Commentary on Jonah* (ICC; Edinburgh: T. & T. Clark, 1912), 64. Another commentator calls Jonah a type of "flinty-hearted Judaism" demonstrating "jealousy sunk into itself." A. Peake, "Jonah," in *Peake's Commentary on the Bible* (London: Nelson and Sons, 1919), 556.

Yahweh to the Jewish people in general has no warrant in the text. Such references are indeed a current and ongoing concern as anti-Semitism continues to rear its ugly head.[25] Anti-Semitic assertions subvert the text of Scripture by ignoring Jonah's historical setting and by failing to understand the actual life-experience of those called to such prophetic tasks.[26]

How can we hold out hope that anyone will call on the name of the Lord if they are the object of anti-Semitic hate? The apostle Paul develops an argument for Christian humility in relation to Judaism. "I ask then: Did God reject his people? By no means! I am an Israelite myself, a descendant of Abraham, from the tribe of Benjamin. God did not reject his people, whom he foreknew" (Rom. 11:1–2a). He continues, "If some of the branches have been broken off, and you, though a wild olive shoot, have been grafted in among the others and now share in the nourishing sap from the olive root, do not boast over those branches. If you do, consider this: You do not support the root, but the root supports you" (Rom. 11:17–18).

If the root of Judaism supports the branch of Christianity, on what basis does a Christian interpreter stand and strike the root? Paul issues a stern warning "Do not be arrogant, but be afraid" (Rom. 11:20b). As he draws his argument to a close, he states the case unmistakably. "But as far as election is concerned, they are loved on account of the patriarchs, for God's gifts and his call are irrevocable" (Rom. 11:28b–29).

The "Jonah as reluctant Israel" typology is unfaithful to Paul's struggle in Romans 9–11 with God's promises to the chosen people and the reality of Jesus' call for his followers to be a witness to all people. In light of the Christian record in Europe in the last century, any reading that maintains this kind of interpretation wittingly or unwittingly participates in a hateful error. At the very least, Christians are called to love and bear witness, not to hate.

Jonah as a Christ figure. In biblical typology Jonah is a Christ figure, not as an antithesis of Christ. Jesus himself is the source of this typology, developed by the teaching of the early church fathers. Jesus' positive appraisal of the meaning of Jonah is solid ground for interpreting the prophet in a favorable light. Jesus held Jonah up as a sign of his own willingness to be "buried" for three days to save others (see above, Bridging Contexts). Jesus also lifted Jonah up as a sign of a faithful preaching prophet (Luke 11:29–32; Matt. 12:41) similar to himself, though not as great. Jesus' own identification with Jonah is a positive one. When Jesus gives Simon the name Peter, at his great

---

25. For a comprehensive survey of the anti-Semitic readings of Jonah, see Sherwood, *A Biblical Text and Its Afterlives*, 64–67.

26. How would Jesus' message and salvific work have any context or audience if the Jews had not struggled to keep the faith for the hundreds of years between Jonah and Jesus? If they had failed to be faithful, to what people would the Lord have come?

confession of Jesus as the Christ, he calls him by his surname "Simon son of Jonah" (Matt. 16:17). This reference, in the same chapter as his reference to Jonah's three days, may be more than coincidental, considering Peter's later effective preaching for repentance and forgiveness in Jerusalem (Acts 2:14–42).

The church fathers favored Jonah in their sermons and anti-Marcionite tracts. Following in Jesus' interpretive footsteps, they revered Jonah as a positive example of effective preaching and victory over death and the devil. Jerome even considered Jonah's flight from Jerusalem to be like Jesus' "flight" from heaven in the Incarnation. Both fled, not in rebellion but as an attempt to save Israel. Jonah's flight would save Israel by ensuring its enemy Nineveh's destruction. Jesus' flight to earth would save the world by his death and resurrection. Like Jonah, Jesus fled the heavens for Tarshish, which is "the sea of this world."[27]

Jonah and Jesus can be compared favorably in many ways: Jesus did perfectly what Jonah also (if temporarily) accomplished; both were from Galilee; Jonah struggled with his call to preach, Jesus struggled to do the will of the Father (in the desert, at Gethsemane); both preached God's message of judgment and reconciliation to the marginalized and to sinners; both chose death willingly when the time came, for the sake of others; both went to death forsaken by others; both bore and removed the consequences of sin from others; both caused the storm to cease after sleeping through it (Jonah through repentance, Jesus through his divinity); Jonah entered the jaws of the fish, Jesus entered the jaws of the grave; both were kept for three days; both were raised up again by the Father; Jonah's obedience in preaching led to the conversion of a great city, and Jesus' obedience led to the conversion of many cultures of the world.

The ultimate victory over death is the most enduring comparison of Jonah and Jesus. The stained glass of the cathedral in Cologne, Germany, depicts Jonah emerging from the mouth of the fish/serpent with a sign of blessing mirrored by Jesus, who does the same, emerging from the tomb. If any typology is to be applied to Jonah in Christian interpretation, let us follow in the faithful footsteps of the early church, which relied on Jesus' words about the enduring meaning of Jonah for his followers. Jonah is, despite himself, a faithful witness.

As Jonah does to the sailors, we should be ready in season and out of season (2 Tim. 4:2) to give a witness concerning Yahweh to the world. We should pray for and support missionaries in difficult places. Yet, who can

---

27. Sherwood, *A Biblical Text and Its Afterlives*, 14. The most accessible discussion of Jerome is in ibid., 14–19.

love their enemy, or even their neighbor, enough to go to them with the word of life? Who will interrupt their life and their schedule to support mission work? We do not do what we ought or as much as we could. But God in his mercy calls us back from our self-centered flight. He calls us back to the center of our calling by delivering us again from our patterns of escape, our shallow excuses, and our thin arrogance of busyness. He delivers us from ourselves to be ambassadors of God. Even when our witness is hollow-sounding, like Jonah's in the storm at sea, God honors us with faithfulness to his Word and delivers us all by it. In the end we are all Jonah, resisting the grace of God, even to ourselves. We are in need of deliverance and rescue.

Rowing and the surrender of the sailors. The sailors anxiously worked to fix the problem of the storm. They had not been in the presence of Yahweh's speaking in the temple and were not on the way to witness in Nineveh, but they were making their way by their knowledge, intelligence, strength, and wits. What they did in the midst of their fear of the storm was admirable: They prayed to their gods. When their gods proved helpless, the sailors jettisoned cargo to lighten the load. They assessed all their assets, including the sleeping Jonah. Discovering his culpability in the trouble, they researched his history, actions, and role to discover the best damage control strategy. The sailors' questions for Jonah are still relevant and incisive for us today. They are motivated by fear and are desperate to solve the danger they face.

As the sailors urgently ask, with the ship pitching to and fro on the violent waves, we are drawn into the narrative. How might we answer in a similar situation, as we or those around us are about to perish "in the storm"? Jonah's faithful response establishes a bond of sympathy with the reader who is a believer in Yahweh. He confesses his identity and faith, and the sailors believe him.

> Sailors: "How can you sleep?" . . . "What do you do? Where do you come from? What is your country? From what people are you?" (1:6, 8).
>
> Jonah: "I am a Hebrew and I worship the LORD, the God of heaven, who made the sea and the land" (1:9).
>
> Terrified Sailors: "What have you done? . . . What should we do to you to make the sea calm down for us?" (1:10a, 11b).
>
> Jonah: "Pick me up and throw me into the sea and it will become calm. I know that it is my fault that this great storm has come upon you" (1:12).

Jonah is the key player, the one on whose account their present danger exists, and the sailors ask his advice. He suggests that they must toss him into the sea, and yet the risk and downside of tossing him over with the cargo seems too steep. Perhaps it will only anger Jonah's God. Or perhaps they are unwilling to toss Jonah overboard, even to save themselves. So first of all, they row. Only when that fails do they reluctantly follow Jonah's direction.

The sailors provide us an excellent example by their readiness to acknowledge their helplessness, hear Jonah's witness, act on it, and worship the true God. They hear Jonah's witness to Yahweh and believe his witness. They, like Jonah, run from the difficult action required of them (throwing Jonah overboard) but realize the futility of rowing against Yahweh's storm. They surrender, believing a seemingly impossible word from Yahweh, that Yahweh's appointed man will die for their salvation. They believe and worship Yahweh.

Who can surrender to such difficult demands in faith? We cannot. But God in his mercy calls us by his Holy Spirit. Martin Luther's explanation of the third article of the Apostles' Creed states: "I believe that I cannot, by my own understanding or effort, believe in Jesus Christ my Lord or come to him. But the Holy Spirit has called me by the gospel, enlightened me with his gifts, sanctified and kept me in the true faith. . . ."[28]

Jonah's integrity, a positive example. Jesus' celebration of Jonah as a positive example of death and resurrection works for Christian preaching precisely when it deconstructs the spirituality of the hearer. Jonah's integrity is his admission that he can neither remain standing in God's presence nor do what God requires. He flees in protest. He does not *deserve* God's mercy. Even though he knows God is merciful (4:2), he cannot claim it, because he cannot fulfill God's command. His fleeing has integrity because he recognizes his situation. If Jonah is to be saved, only God can deliver him.

By contrast, many "good" Christians cultivate their spirituality in order to establish that they are basically good people, deserving of God's favor. Whether their project is based on comparison ("I am better than those sinners") or on accomplishment ("I have committed myself to this good work") or on the absence of evil ("I have never really hurt anyone"), it is a kind of "constructed spirituality." This kind of thinking denies the truth that only God can deliver us and that our righteousness is, in fact, "alien." Righteousness projects are present in everyone who thinks of God. They are the most elaborate in the most religious Christians, lay and clergy (author included) alike. Jesus' celebration of Jonah as a positive example of his own death and resurrection works to deconstruct our projects and truly turn us to Yahweh when both Jonah's integrity and his fault in fleeing are recognized.

Jesus compares Jonah to himself. Jesus does not deserve human judgment or death. Even though he knows his innocence, he does not claim it. Only God the Father can deliver him. Jonah and Jesus represent two sides of the

---

28. Martin Luther, *Luther's Smaller Catechism* (1531), personal trans.

same coin of judgment/grace. Jonah's integrity is in knowing he is not right-eous. Jesus' integrity is that he does not claim his own righteousness as the basis of his deliverance. God the Father brings both back to life. Both are pos-itive models of hope for our own deliverance from death.

We cannot match Jesus' righteousness or his complete reliance on the Father. We can only confess our need of Jonah's integrity by fleeing from our spirituality projects and righteous arguments. Jesus calls us to the example of the sign of Jonah: to flee from the presence of our false holiness into God's storm, to his questioning sailors, and into the mouth of the great fish. In the celebration of Jonah, Jesus calls us to be transformed by his unexpected deliv-erance and grace.[29] Only then may we know the absolute mercy of our sal-vation and the pure gift of dry land. Only then may we be prepared with integrity to do what God calls us to do. Only then will we know our need to run from a self-constructed righteousness and turn toward God and his dif-ficult calling.

God's mercy. The storm is God's severe mercy for Jonah and the sailors; it is necessary in order to deliver them from their *sui generis* lives. It is the wind of the Spirit that shakes the ship's beams and opens our ears and hearts to the words of God. The sailors' conversion is God's faithfulness to his word of witness, even in the form of a weak witness from Jonah. As in Christ's death, God turns our condemnation (the crowds' betrayal, Jonah's sinking) into our salvation (resurrection/great fish).

God's mercy toward our enemies and the call for God's people to trust him enough to proclaim this mercy from the double theme of Jonah. God's mercy pursues Jonah. God called his prophet to speak to a people who were about to be destroyed for their violent crimes against humanity. He sent Jonah so that they might repent and be saved. God does not let Jonah go or leave him to wallow in his rebellion, but he quickly brings him to repentance. He pur-sues him through the storm and gives him an opportunity to fulfill his prophetic calling before the sailors, to good effect. God assigns a fish to res-cue Jonah from drowning, saving both Jonah and his aborted mission. In spite of his rebellion, Jonah is "God's dear child."[30]

Jonah begins in protest by running away from God's call. His faith in God, however, is a real-life example and source of hope for believers. His honest faith, in spite of his failing trust of his calling, may serve as an encour-agement to those who are called to ministry. All who are called to difficult

29. The early church father Irenaeus said that Jonah's unanticipated fish-deliverance is like our unanticipated deliverance from death through the unanticipated resurrection of Jesus (*Against Heresies*, 3.21.1).

30. M. Luther, cited in Limburg, *Jonah*, 51.

work struggle with trust in God (including the apostle Paul). While the storm rages, Jonah declares his faith boldly to the sailors. He calmly confesses his guilt and offers himself as the means of their deliverance from the storm. This example of renewal of faith and trust in God is an example for all who would welcome God's mercy in the midst of trouble, even when we are, ourselves, the source of the trouble.[31]

---

31. Cf. John Calvin, *Commentaries on the Minor Prophets*, trans. J. Owen (Grand Rapids: Baker, 1979), 54. For another deliverance from a storm and struggle with faith, see Mark 4:35–41.

Jonah 2

FROM INSIDE THE fish, Jonah prayed to the LORD his God. ²He said:

"In my distress I called to the LORD,
  and he answered me.
From the depths of the grave I called for help,
  and you listened to my cry.
³You hurled me into the deep,
  into the very heart of the seas,
  and the currents swirled about me;
all your waves and breakers
  swept over me.
⁴I said, 'I have been banished
  from your sight;
yet I will look again
  toward your holy temple.'
⁵The engulfing waters threatened me,
  the deep surrounded me;
  seaweed was wrapped around my head.
⁶To the roots of the mountains I sank down;
  the earth beneath barred me in forever.
But you brought my life up from the pit,
  O LORD my God.

⁷When my life was ebbing away,
  I remembered you, LORD,
and my prayer rose to you,
  to your holy temple.

⁸Those who cling to worthless idols
  forfeit the grace that could be theirs.
⁹But I, with a song of thanksgiving,
  will sacrifice to you.
What I have vowed I will make good.
  Salvation comes from the LORD."

¹⁰And the LORD commanded the fish, and it vomited Jonah onto dry land.

JONAH 2 IS Jonah's psalm of thanks from within the belly of the fish. The song primarily recounts Jonah's distress in the water and gives thanks for his rescue. It begins with a summary of his cry for help (2:2) and continues with four more stanzas describing Jonah's sinking in the water before he is swallowed by the fish (2:3–6). In the refrain (2:7–9) Jonah summarizes his cry for rescue and declares Yahweh as the true source of salvation. Then, the narrator tells us, Yahweh talked to the fish, and "it vomited Jonah onto dry land" (2:10).

The amazing context of this poetic prayer is Jonah's gratitude *while inside* the fish. He fully expected to die in the water. His thanksgiving within the belly of a fish is a proclamation of joy, with the realization that God has delivered him in spite of his running. Though he is not yet on dry land, his faith reaches a new dimension of understanding. He seems to have no doubt that, as he was delivered from drowning, he will also eventually be delivered safely to the shore.

Readers of narratives are sometimes tempted to move too quickly through poetry. This song, however, is critical to the interpretation of the book and may be the theologically richest part. Its content helps us to understand Jonah's point of view, as he speaks in the first person. The poem also offers a window into the nature and circumstances of true gratitude (see Contemporary Significance).

Inside the Fish (2:1)

IN CHAPTER 1, the captain of the sailors asked Jonah to pray to his god, and Jonah ignored him (1:6). Here for the first time Jonah speaks directly to Yahweh in response to his physical and unusual deliverance.[1] This is the prophet at his best, giving thanks for deliverance *before he is on dry land*. Surprisingly, perhaps, he does not mention the small problem of his residency in the fish. He demonstrates his comprehension of the miracle of deliverance and his full dependence on the mercy and compassion of Yahweh. He is grateful to be in Yahweh's keeping, even as he remains in the fish's belly.

The Hebrew text raises the question of whether the fish is male or female. In 1:17 noun "fish" is a masculine noun (*dag*) while in 2:1 "fish" is a feminine noun (*dagah*). It is possible that the anomaly is a scribal error (in 2:10, "the fish" is male again.). However, interpreters have attributed various meanings

---

1. Note that later (4:4–5), he again walks away without responding to Yahweh's question.

to the change.[2] The most obvious reason for the shift to the "female" fish is found in the immediate context of Jonah's prayer. The female capacities of the fish are echoed poetically in two birthing words in 2:2. The female word sets up the poetic concept of Jonah's "death" (male fish eats him) and rebirth (female fish carries and delivers him). "Inside" in 1:17b and 2:1 is a general Hebrew term for the "inward parts" (*me*c*eh*), which is a synonym of "womb" (*rehem*).[3]

In 2:2 Jonah uses two other birthing words that develop this poetical image of his deliverance. (1) When he says "in my distress" (*sarah*, 2:2a), he uses a word that is specifically used of the "travail" of childbirth. It signifies being bound up or being tied in a tight place.[4] Jonah is alluding to the distress of a child about to be born (see Bridging Contexts section for further comments). (2) When he says, "from the depths [*beten*] of the grave" (2:2b), he literally says, "from the womb [belly] of Sheol" (Sheol is the place of the dead in the Old Testament).[5] This Hebrew phrase "womb of Sheol" is the only time "womb/belly" is used with "Sheol" in Scripture. It continues the image of Jonah's birthing. He is as good as dead but may be reborn.

The Five Stanzas of Jonah's Distress (2:2–6)

THE PRAYER IS in the form of a psalm with five stanzas and a refrain.[6] The five stanzas begin with 2:2 and proceed, one verse at a time, through 2:6. In the first stanza, Jonah summarizes the basic situation (2:2): "I called . . . and you heard my voice." In the second through the fifth stanzas, Jonah describes his progressive descent into his watery grave. In stanza 2 he is *on the surface of the water* (2:3). Jonah is hurled overboard, pulled by currents, and battered by breaking waves on the surface of the sea. In stanza 3 he is *in the midst of the seas* (2:4). While sinking, he feels banished from Yahweh, yet looks toward his presence. In stanza 4 Jonah is *near the bottom* (2:5). He is engulfed and surrounded by water, sinking to the seaweed at the bottom. By the last stanza

---

2. Is it a male or female fish? Rabbi Izkakais said that Jonah didn't pray in the male fish (1:17), which was larger, so it vomited him in the water and a female fish swallowed him. In this smaller place Jonah began to pray.

3. BDB, 589; see Isa. 63:15 and Jer. 31:20.

4. BDB, 865.

5. "Sheol" is a synonym of "the pit" and refers to the place of the dead where people are cut off from memory (Ps. 88:11–12), from knowledge (Eccl. 9:10), from return (Job 7:9; 10:22), and from the presence of God (Ps. 88:5, 10–12; 115:17; Isa. 38:18). Sheol is not, however, beyond God's power (Amos 9:2; Prov. 15:11; Ps. 139:8).

6. Many different organizational patterns have been proposed for this psalm. For a summary of seven of them, see Dorsey, *The Literary Structure*, 239.

he is *drowning* (2:6). The sands (bars) of the floor of the sea will be his grave, but Yahweh brings him up (by a fish).

The major theme of "going down" and being "brought up" by Yahweh as seen in chapter 1 is also present in chapter 2. Jonah calls from the *depths* of the grave (2:2). He is "hurled . . . into the *deep*" (2:3). He is banished from the temple (*mount*) in 2:4. "The *deep* surrounded" him (2:5). He "sank *down*" to the "*roots* of the mountains," but Yahweh brings his "life *up* from the *pit*" (2:6). In the refrain (2:7–9), Jonah's "prayer *rose*" to Yahweh in the temple ("temple" can mean "God's heavenly dwelling place," as in Ps. 11:4). Finally, Jonah leaves the depths and is *vomited up*, out of the depths of the sea, out of the depths of the fish, "onto dry land" (2:10).

An interesting and common Old Testament structure, called a *chiasmus*,[7] is present in this prayer. In the midst of Jonah's going "deeper and deeper," this structure demonstrates the "center" of Jonah's faith. A chiasm often follows the pattern A B C B' A'. The "parallels" (A B/B' A') are created by the repetition of words or themes (see words in italics, below).[8] The center (C) is created by its isolation between the parallels. This center is often not only the structural center but also the interpretive (and theological) center of the rhetorical unit.

A (2:2) In my distress I called to *the* LORD, and he answered me.
   From the depths of the grave I called for help, and you listened to my cry.
   B (2:3) You hurled me into *the deep*, into the very heart of the seas,
      and the currents swirled about me; all your waves and breakers
      swept over me.
      C (2:4) I said, "I have been banished from your sight;
         yet I will look again toward your holy temple."
   B' (2:5) The engulfing waters threatened me, *the deep* surrounded me;
      seaweed was wrapped around my head.
A' (2:6) To the roots of the mountains I sank down; the earth beneath
   barred me in forever.
   But you brought *my life up from the pit*, O LORD my God.

In the first stanza (2:2 [A]), the phrases "in my distress" and "depths of the grave" refer to Jonah's drowning in the sea as he is sinking. (He confirms his experience of drowning in 2:7). "He answered me" and "You listened to my

---

7. The best source for studying Old and New Testament chiasms is Nils W. Lund, *Chiasmus in the New Testament: A Study in the Form and Function of Chiastic Structures* (Peabody, Mass.: Hendrickson, 1992).

8. Sometimes the repetition is only recognized in the original Hebrew, since English translations vary.

cry" refer to Yahweh's fish that rescued Jonah from drowning. Note that Jonah begins by referring to God in the third person ("*he* answered me"), but immediately shifts to the more personal second person ("you"), which he uses until the refrain (2:7–9) at the end of the prayer. The first and second half of verse 2 are parallel, with the second half echoing the first ("In my distress I called"/"From the depths of the grave I called," and "He answered me"/"You listened to my cry"). This is typical for introductory summaries in psalms.[9]

Stanza 2 (2:3 [B]) begins a sensate description of Jonah's descent. The reader who has been adrift may feel the vertigo of Jonah's experience: "hurled . . . into the deep . . . currents swirled . . . waves and breakers swept over me." Jonah was thrown overboard by the sailors, but Jonah knows that Yahweh has done it, and thus he says, "You hurled me," implying that the sailors were innocent (as they prayed in 1:14).

Yahweh hurled him "into *the deep*," which his original listeners would have recognized. There was underlying anxiety and fear of chaos represented by deep (and potentially turbulent) water, as it was over *the deep* that the Spirit hovered at the creation. "Now the earth was formless [*tohu*] and empty, darkness was over the surface of the deep [*tehom*], and the Spirit of God was hovering over the waters" (Gen. 1:2). The *deep* (*mesulah*) and its synonym *depths* or *deep waters* (*tehom*) are words that refer to the "chaos" of deep water. Note the following passages:

> Pharaoh's chariots and his army
> > he has hurled into the sea.
> The best of Pharaoh's officers
> > are drowned in the Red Sea.
> The *deep waters* [*tehomot*] have covered them;
> > they sank *to the depths* [*mesolot*] like a stone. (Ex. 15:4–5)

> He makes *the depths* [*mesulah*] churn like a boiling cauldron
> > and stirs up the sea like a pot of ointment.
> Behind him he leaves a glistening wake;
> > one would think *the deep* [*tehom*] had white hair. (Job 41:31–32)

> They saw the works of the LORD,
> > his wonderful deeds in *the deep* [*mesulah*].

---

9. Cf. Ps. 18:6:

> In my distress I called to the LORD;
> > I cried to my God for help.
> From his temple he heard my voice;
> > my cry came before him, into his ears.

For he spoke and stirred up a tempest
　　that lifted high the waves.
They mounted up to the heavens
　　and went down to *the depths [tehomot]*;
　　in their peril their courage melted away. (Ps. 107:24–26)

The NIV translates the second "chaos" word (*tehom*) as "deep" in Jonah 2:5 as well. Jonah continues describing the experience of the deep: "into the very heart of the sea, and the currents swirled about me." "Waves" in 2:3b is, literally, "rollers"—from the same root (*gal*) as the name "Gilgal" (based on its rolling hill country.) A whisper of hope is seen in the adjective "your," as even the deep belongs to and is an agent of Yahweh.

Stanza 3 is the centerpiece of the five stanzas (2:4 [C]). It is set apart by Jonah's quoting himself ("I said") so that the listener/reader cannot miss the central point. It is the first indication that Jonah regrets leaving his place in the presence of Yahweh in the temple. It is the turning point. In 1:3 he "ran away from the LORD and headed for Tarshish." Here he turns for the first time to look back ("Yet I will look again toward").

Jonah remembers his own words: "I said, 'I have been banished.'" When Jonah says "banished" (*garaš*), it means he feels he has *no option of return*. Jonah was not banished from Yahweh's sight when he ran to Joppa's port; he ran of his own volition. He was not banished in the storm or through his inspired word to the sailors that the storm would become calm if they threw him overboard. Jonah experienced the banishment when he was lifted up and hurled over the gunwale, and then hit the water. The word *garaš* means "thrown out." At the moment he was physically "hurled" or "cast out" of the ship, he realized, apparently for the first time, that he could no longer keep his options open. The physical reality resounded in the disconsolate cry: "I have been banished."[10] He could no longer choose to go back.

"Yet I will look again toward your holy temple" (2:4b). This turning and looking is Jonah's hope. His offense was fleeing from the "presence of the LORD" (i.e., his place of employment in the temple). Here Jonah demonstrates his understanding of the power of simply turning again toward the presence of Yahweh! Even when he is "banished" (with no option of return), he can look to Yahweh. He cannot return, but he can turn and "look . . . toward." The same word (*nabat*) is used when the Exodus people were dying from snakebite in the desert: "So Moses made a bronze snake and put it up on a pole. Then when anyone was bitten by a snake and *looked at [nabat]* the bronze snake, he lived" (Num. 21:9).

---

10. His cry is set apart rhetorically as Jonah quotes himself in the words "I said."

Stanza 4 returns to the descriptive narrative of Jonah's drowning (2:5 [B']). He is "engulfed" and "surrounded" by "waters" and "the deep" ("surrounded" is the same word as "swirled" in 2:3). He nears the bottom of the sea, with seaweed wrapped around his head. He is in deep trouble. This stanza repeats the idea of the second stanza, but now "the deep" (*tehom* here; *mesulah* in 2:3) threatens with seaweed instead of rolling and breaking waves. In 2:5 the expression "the engulfing waters threatened me" is, literally, "waters closed in on me, over life."

Stanza 5 takes Jonah to the ocean floor, "to the roots of the mountains" that are below the sea (2:6 [A']). The earth "barred me in." The word "bar" has two different meanings in English, even as in Hebrew. In both languages it means "bars" as those on a prison cell (as the grave was considered in the ancient Near East). It also denotes a "river bar" or "sand bar." Both meanings are relevant to Jonah's distress. He is about to be *imprisoned* forever in a grave of *sand*.

The chiasmus parallel is maintained in the name of Yahweh. "O LORD" in 2:6 echoes "to the LORD" (2:2). The parallel is also carried in reference to death. "Up from the pit" (2:6) mirrors the first stanza "from the depths of the grave" (2:2), using the synonyms "pit" (*šahat*) and "grave" (*še'ol*; cf. Ps. 103:2–4).[11]

The Refrain of Jonah's Deliverance (2:7–10)

THE SONG OF thanks concludes with Jonah's refrain, declaring that "salvation comes from the LORD." When his song is complete, Yahweh's fish vomits Jonah onto dry land (2:10). One contemporary singer-songwriter has captured the heart of this refrain by repeating the line "Salvation belongs to the LORD" after each line.[12]

[2:7]When my life was ebbing away, I remembered you, LORD
   Salvation belongs to the LORD.
and my prayer rose to you, to your holy temple.
   Salvation belongs to the LORD.
[2:8]Those who cling to worthless idols
   Salvation belongs to the LORD.
forfeit the grace that could be theirs.
   Salvation belongs to the LORD.

---

11. Sheol is the place of the dead under the earth, so "grave" is a good translation. See Gen. 37:35; Num. 16:30; Ps. 88:3–7; Isa. 38:17.

12. See Andrew Thompson, "Salvation Belongs to the Lord." © 2002. Used by permission. This song puts Jonah's entire second chapter psalm to music, using the biblical structure. You may listen to this song on the author's web page: http://www.personal.northpark.edu/jbruckner

[2:9]But I, with a song of thanksgiving, will sacrifice to you.
    Salvation belongs to the LORD.
What I have vowed I will make good.
    Salvation belongs to the LORD.

In the first line (2:7a) Jonah recalls that he came as close as possible to death before turning in helplessness to Yahweh. "When my life was *ebbing away [ʿaṭap]*" appropriately uses tidal language to communicate Jonah's fainting and feeble situation. When Jonah says, "I remembered you, LORD," this is more than simply recalling something to mind. In the Old Testament remembering has theological connotations. Remembering Yahweh is Israel's foremost responsibility, but Jonah did not remember Yahweh until his life was almost gone. Moses warned Israel to "remember the LORD your God, for it is he who gives you the ability to produce wealth, and so confirms his covenant, which he swore to your forefathers, as it is today" (Deut. 8:18; cf. Ex. 20:2). They failed and "did not remember the LORD their God, who had rescued them from the hands of all their enemies on every side" (Judg. 8:34).

"Your holy temple" is a central theme of the second line (2:7b). Yahweh is everywhere in the book of Jonah, but Jonah's specific references are always toward the temple (1:3; 2:4, 7). This is sometimes seen as Jonah's foolishness, especially since Yahweh comes to him in the storm, lots, and especially the fish (and later in the vine, worm, and wind). When Yahweh converses with Jonah about Nineveh (in ch. 4), he does not express great surprise that Yahweh is present on a hillside east of Nineveh. The presence of Yahweh in the "holy temple" cannot be a reference to Jonah's view of Yahweh's singular location. Rather, Yahweh's presence in the temple is a sign of the necessary gathering of the worshiping community (see Bridging Contexts section). Jonah never loses sight of the historically revealed Lord.

The third line (2:8a) about clinging to "worthless idols" is like a cannonball, given the context of Jonah. To whom is it referring? It introduces previously unidentified idols, worshiped by someone. The sailors have already worshiped Yahweh. Jonah is not confessing that he has been worshiping idols. The unidentified idol worshipers must be those who hear or read Jonah's witness and prayer. It may also allude to the sailors, who called upon their gods (idols?) for salvation from the storm, to no avail.

Idolatry in Israel was a constant problem (Hos. 4:12; Amos 5:26; cf. Deut. 32:21). The original language synonyms for the word "worthless" (*šawe'*) are "lies, deceit, futility," and it is used especially to refer to "false" prophets. Coming from Jonah, such a reference may sound undeservedly smug. Jonah, however, is preaching to his later readers. Clinging to "worthless idols" is one thing he has not done in his protest. Even in his fleeing he has not turned to false gods and forfeited grace. He has received a severe form of grace for his flight from Yahweh's presence, but it is grace that has pursued him.

The fourth line (2:8b) warns and invites the reader at the same time. Those who cling to idols "forfeit the grace that could be theirs." This can mean forsaking "a righteous life."[13] Usually this kind of grace (*ḥesed*) means "God's pursuing love" for his people. The NIV appropriately translates "their *ḥesed*" as "grace that could be theirs." It is God's *ḥesed* that they lose (understanding "their" as possession of God's gifted grace rather than a pouring forth of their own piety toward God). "They deprive themselves of the steadfast love of God, which manifests itself in God's gracious acts."[14] They deprive themselves like someone who abandons a faithful and loving spouse.[15] Jonah probably knows the Psalm 31, which has the same expressions for "cling to worthless idols" and "love" (*ḥesed*): "I hate those who cling to *worthless idols;* I trust in the LORD. I will be glad and rejoice in your *love* (*ḥesed*), for you saw my affliction and knew the anguish of my soul" (Ps. 31:6–7).

In the fifth line (2:9a) Jonah makes a promise. *"But I, with a song of thanksgiving, will sacrifice to you."* "But I" (*wa'ani*) is a common emphatic expression in many psalms (Ps. 5:7; 13:5; 31:14; 55:16; 59:16; 109:4; ten times in Ps. 119). This expression is usually followed by a declaration of trust or righteousness; it is always preceded by contrasting the wickedness of the masses or lack of trust. Jonah is willing to return to his prophetic post at the temple. Like the sailors, he wants to offer sacrifices to Yahweh. The thanksgiving sacrifice was a celebration and meal at the temple, where individuals delivered by God gave public testimony to Yahweh's act of deliverance (see Bridging Contexts section).

In the last line of the refrain (2:9b) Jonah promises to keep his vows: "What I have vowed I will make good." The expression "make good" is from the original root *šalom*, which has the sense of "make complete." He ends with the apex of the refrain, which is a confession of faith, "Salvation comes from the LORD." This is an echo of Psalm 3:8: "From the LORD comes deliverance." "Deliverance" and "salvation" are the same word in Hebrew, from the root *yaša'* (see Bridging Contexts section). The preposition "from" can also be translated "Salvation *belongs to* the LORD." Jonah's declaration is the one slight reference in this chapter to his disagreement with Yahweh concerning Nineveh. His complaint (expanded in ch. 4) is that he knows better than God

---

13. Isa. 57:1; Jer. 2:2; Hos. 6:4, 6.

14. Elizabeth Achtemeier, *Minor Prophets I* (NIBC; Peabody, Mass.: Hendrickson; 1996), 272.

15. Limburg, *Jonah*, 72. Hosea develops this theme of Israel forsaking God's *ḥesed*.

what ought to be done about Nineveh. Here he concedes that he knows that ultimately Yahweh is not bound by human rules of strict judgment/deliverance. Jonah has just learned this firsthand, since he did not expect to be rescued from drowning.

The chapter closes with Jonah's return to dry land (2:10; see comments on "dry land" at 1:13). Yahweh speaks (*'amar*) to the fish. This word is almost always translated "commanded" when God is the subject. When nonhuman creation is the hearer of God's speech, there is no resistance to his word. Only human beings need, in contrast, to be "commanded" by God. A simple word from the Creator is enough for the rest of the creation.

Jonah's regurgitation by the fish onto the land is not a happy transport, but it is his salvation. In the Old Testament, vomiting is usually a metaphor of judgment. As a biblical metaphor in Leviticus 18:25, 28; 20:22, the residents are spewed out of land, by the land, for disobedience to Yahweh. In contrast here, Jonah is spewed *in spite of* his disobedience. In Isaiah 28:4 Ephraim (northern Israel), is "swallowed" in judgment like a ripe fig. In Jeremiah 51:34, Jerusalem is swallowed, digested, and vomited out by Babylon. In Jonah, the metaphor of being swallowed and vomited is turned on its head. Both the swallowing and the vomiting are Jonah's salvation and deliverance.

Bridging Contexts

TWO MAIN POINTS should be made concerning this section of Jonah. On the one hand, the prayer/thanksgiving/psalm of Jonah from the belly of the fish is a classic Old Testament psalm. Commentators have traditionally interpreted Jonah's prayer in the context of biblical praise. It is in the standard form of some psalms of thanks. Verse 6 encapsulates his gratitude. He declares that he was dying, but Yahweh rescued him.

On the other hand, interpreters have tried to resolve the tensions of the psalm with the realities of the narrative. Jonah is not yet out of danger (he is still at sea, in a fish), but he nonetheless gives thanks for his deliverance. He claims piety in relation to God but has not repented of his flight from God. He claims piety in relation to "idolaters" (sailors, Ninevites, and Israelite listeners/readers), but his actions in chapter 1 (and 4) betray him.

A range of strategies for resolving the tensions between the psalm and the action of the narrative have been proposed. Interpreters have chosen to deny the tension, ignore it for the truth of the piety, castigate Jonah for his shallowness, or label his piety as ironic. These options will be described more fully. None of them succeeds in removing the tension, and the enduring truth of the tension remains.

Recognition of Jonah's true response is the first and necessary step in understanding this chapter. The formal elements of Jonah's heartfelt thanks for deliverance from the "drink" provide additional explanation.

Jonah's song of thanksgiving. This psalm contains the traditional elements of an individual's declarative narrative of praise to God for deliverance.[16] These are often called "psalms of thanksgiving" (*todah*). This kind of thanksgiving was accompanied by a sacrifice (a thank offering, a type of peace offering) to Yahweh that was expected when someone was rescued from death (from illness, accident, or a dangerous situation; see Lev. 3:6–11; 7:11–18; 22:18–30). The delivered person brought a meat offering that was cooked (with only the fat consumed by fire) and shared with the congregation.[17] Narrative *todah* psalms usually contain the following elements: (1) an introduction, including a summons to praise Yahweh and a summary of the theme; (2) a call to the congregation to praise Yahweh; (3) narrative account, including the crisis in retrospect and the rescue, often using "I cried," "you heard," and "you intervened"; and (4) a vow to praise.

Jonah 2 contains all of these elements, though (as in other psalms) not exactly in this order. Elements (1) and (2) are found at the end of the psalm in the refrain (2:7–9). The body of the prayer is the narrative account, including the crisis (2:2a) and the elements of the rescue (2:2b–6). This psalm was probably sung, with the refrain sung first (2:7–9) as the introduction. The refrain also doubles in this way as the concluding vow and praise (2:9).

Tensions between the song and the narrative. It has surprised readers through the centuries that Jonah prays a prayer of thanksgiving while he is still in mortal danger. He is giving thanks for his safety while he remains in the belly of a fish. Jonah has been rescued from the breakers, rollers, seaweed, and the sandy grave at the bottom of the sea. He is not, however, anywhere near dry land. He is still in motion, at sea, isolated, uncertain, and at great risk of death. Yahweh has said nothing to him, and Jonah has not repented of his running. Nonetheless, Jonah offers up a song of pure praise and thanksgiving to Yahweh. He declares his own piety and Yahweh's faithfulness. He is still in the depths of the sea but he is full of praise. These two juxtaposed truths of the text create an unresolved tension for the reader.

In order to resolve this tension (and other tensions in the chapter), some commentators have argued that chapter 2 was not part of the original book of Jonah. Historical critics suggest that this psalm was written and added at a later date than the narrative, or that the author simply borrowed it from an existing collection of psalms because of its water images. Some have sug-

---

16. For other examples of this type of psalm of praise, see Ps. 18, 30, 32, 92, 118, 138.
17. For a fuller description of the *todah* offering, see Limburg, *Jonah*, 67, 70.

gested that it was written in the safety of Jerusalem. Whatever the circumstances of its writing or origin, the song-prayer in the text is presented between two notices: Jonah was swallowed, then gave a prayer, after which he was vomited on dry land. It ought to be interpreted within this narrative sequence.

For an interpreter who seeks the meaning of the whole text of Jonah as we have received it in the canon, there is no compelling purpose for focusing on the history of the composition of book. The psalm/prayer is an integral part of the narrative development.[18] It expresses Jonah's deep gratitude for his unexpected deliverance. He is not fully delivered, but the unbelievable fish has turned Jonah's face back to Yahweh. The fish's appearance and swallowing of the prophet are powerful signs, which establish *some* anticipation of the possibility of his full deliverance to dry land. Jonah's prayer of thanks is the essential *beginning* of his experiential transformation (continued in the vine, worm, and wind encounters). The complete confidence of the prayer of thanks is not explicitly explained in the text. If one could read Jonah's mind (which we cannot), one might think that he would be pondering how to get out of the fish alive.[19] How Jonah expresses his gratitude in the psalm from the belly of the fish raises several other tensions.

Jonah claims piety in relation to "idolaters" (sailors and Ninevites). Jonah says, "Those who cling to worthless idols forfeit the grace that could be theirs. But I, with a song of thanksgiving, will sacrifice to you" (2:8–9a). This claim creates a tension because of Jonah's rebellious actions in chapter 1 and his angry conversation with God in chapter 4. Tension is also created by the abrupt reference to idolatry from a man with kelp wrapped around his head (2:5). Yes, Jonah is truly grateful for his deliverance and promises to complete the public service of thanksgiving in the temple. He expresses it, however, by contrasting himself to "idolaters."

The sailors are the only idolaters we have encountered, at a time when they had to cajole Jonah to pray to his God, something he never does in the narrative. While what Jonah says is true (idolaters forfeit grace, and their prayers to their gods *are* futile), it is spurious for Jonah to critique the sailors in relation to himself. His God is true, but his piety seems less faithful than theirs. In the storm, Jonah had little to be proud of in relation to the mariners. Both truths of the text (his gratitude for a true God and his expression of pride in relation to the sailors) create an unresolved tension for the reader.

---

18. Ibid., 33.

19. Keil thought Jonah regarded the fish as a convincing "pledge of his future complete deliverance." The text says nothing about this complete mature faith. Noted in Kleinert, *Jonah*, 26.

This tension is dealt with in a variety of ways by interpreters. On one end of the spectrum, Jonah may be a changed man. His repentance can be implied and his piety simple and genuine. This assumes a lot, however, since his attitude toward Nineveh is fundamentally the same in chapter 4. It may also be an expression of "counterfeit piety from a loquacious Jonah."[20] This implies, however, that his gratitude for his deliverance is not genuine. It could be instructively ironic, since Jonah declares the foolishness of those who "forfeit the grace that could be theirs" (2:8b) when he has himself turned his back on the presence of Yahweh, responds to Yahweh's call, and is safely back on dry land (Nineveh).

In contrast, the sailors turned toward Yahweh, sought God's direction, and were in fact saved. Now that the belly-ensconced Jonah recognizes Yahweh's grace, he is *not* in the temple, able to fulfill his calling, or in safety (see "Two truths," below.) Jonah is genuinely thankful and will fulfill his vow, but his language sounds like a late and "pious cover-up" for the fact that he still has not repented of his evasion of his call.

Jonah's self-centeredness. This theme, begun in chapter 1, continues in the midst of his praise in chapter 2. If this were only a matter of the formal construction of an independent psalm, it could be explained away.[21] The narrative context *and* the psalm reveal the prophet's self-centered viewpoint. Jonah's self-focused orientation is seen in his repetition of the pronoun "I" ten times in eight verses (2:2–9). In these verses he also says "my" seven times (not all occurrences shown).

> Verse 2: In *my* distress *I* called to the LORD.... From the depths of the grave *I* called for help.
>
> Verse 3: You hurled *me* into the deep.
>
> Verse 4: *I* said, "*I* have been banished from your sight; yet *I* will look again toward your holy temple."
>
> Verse 6: To the roots of the mountains *I* sank down.
>
> Verse 7: When *my* life was ebbing away, *I* remembered you, LORD.
>
> Verse 9: But *I*, with a song of thanksgiving, will sacrifice to you. What *I* have vowed *I* will make good.

Jonah's perception of reality seems to be distorted.[22] His self-centered declarations and tone proclaim what his situation and his previous actions deny. Yes, Jonah is truly grateful, but his description of an unwavering and

---

20. Phyllis Trible, "The Book of Jonah" (*NIB*; Nashville: Abingdon, 1996), 7:507.

21. Luther explained that Jonah must have written this later, at home, since its formality does not fit Jonah's messy situation in the belly of the fish. The text, however, offers no explanation of the kind, letting the tension ride.

22. Trible, "The Book of Jonah," 7:507.

thoroughgoing piety is hard to stomach in the context of his flight in chapter 1 and complaining in chapter 4. Jonah expresses his "conversion" here, but the problem of himself as "subject" and controller is in the grammar and the piety. He is making vows, but he is not repentant. He recalls his trust in Yahweh, yet he shows few signs of real trust. He has expressed thanks for the fact that he is still breathing, but that is all. He uses a flourish of words for his own deliverance, but has only a few reticent words for the Ninevites and sailors.

One widely accepted way of dealing with this tension is to regard Jonah's piety as an "inflated" expression of a "deflated" character, or even "grotesque" in relation to his actual actions. The story can only move on by means of a vomiting (nauseated) fish and by starting over with Yahweh's second call (3:1).[23] Perhaps in his reference to the temple and fulfilling vows there is a kind of bargaining maneuver. Whatever the case, Jonah has had a rough ride with God.

Two truths. The tension between the song and the narrative remain unresolved for a reason. The tensions remain and should not be resolved artificially because they remain in the prophet Jonah. He gives thanks from inside the fish because he is truly grateful that he is not dead yet. He does not need to wait to reach dry land to feel gratitude. Jonah has not left his fundamental beliefs about idolatry behind, despite his encounter with the exemplary sailors. Nor has he lost the deep convictions of his argument with Yahweh about Nineveh. He is grateful without repenting for running, because his basic beliefs have not changed. He still does not want Nineveh to have the opportunity to repent (see Bridging Contexts section of ch. 4).

Tension remains and must remain between the song and the narrative because Jonah is both grateful and defiant. He will go to Nineveh since Yahweh has made it clear that he *must* go. He will protest again later. For now, he will express his thanks for an unanticipated deliverance in a formal prayer.[24] The tension of his piety is not between irony and simple praise. It is not grotesque, nor should it be excluded as an editor's (misfit) addition. Jonah prays what he is capable of praying—and not more. God accepts the prayer for what it is: a stiff but true expression of thanks for not drowning. He uses formal poetry to express himself precisely *because* he is in the slime of the belly, going back to old familiar clichés and forms of the psalms he knows by heart.

Plainly put, Jonah has looked toward God (2:4, 7). It is enough for his deliverance. God will deal with his protest/running issues later. For now they must remain in tension. God answers those who call out in distress whether

---

23. Sherwood, *A Biblical Text and Its Afterlives*, 258; Trible, "The Book of Jonah," 7:506–7.

24. Sherwood describes the psalm as Jonah's "white handkerchief" (*A Biblical Text and Its Afterlives*, 256).

their issues of protest are resolved or not. He delivers those who call out in times of trouble (2:9b). He accepts Jonah's thanks and his lack of repentance because he accepts Jonah's protest, not as sin but as a welcome dialogue.

When Jonah concludes with his (true) pious and dramatic declaration of Yahweh's salvation, he is vomited out. It is true that he seems now to be ready to go to Nineveh (even though his declaration is not repentance). Were it not for his equally dramatic protest about Yahweh's salvation of the Ninevites (ch. 4), we could assume that the "vomiting" functions simply to return him to dry land. Given his opposite dramatic expressions in both places, however, the vomiting suggests that the fish also had had enough of Jonah's tensions in his belly.

JONAH'S SONG OF thanksgiving demonstrates the power of praise and thanksgiving in any circumstance for the one who turns to Yahweh (2:4, 7). It is far more than a poetic interlude in the narrative. Although Jonah's song is not full of repentance, it is enough in this situation that he turns toward Yahweh in worship. It is the first necessary step for his journey home. He concedes God's call on his life, as part of a complex and rich inheritance of faith: "In my distress I *called* to the LORD, and he *answered* me. From the depths of the grave I *called* for help, and you *listened* to my cry" (2:2). The first two verses encapsulate the contemporary significance of chapter 2. *From inside the fish*, Jonah speaks in the *past* tense ("called," "answered," "called," and "listened"). Jonah thanks Yahweh and describes his gratitude for his salvation while still in the fish, far from his final safety.

The tension of Jonah's life. The believer's life on earth, after salvation but before its fulfillment, is somewhat like Jonah's situation. Jonah has been saved but not delivered to the ultimate safety of dry land. He has not drowned (as he expected and believed he deserved) but has been found by an unexpected grace. The inside of the belly of God's fish ought to have brought his death, but it becomes a place of (relative) safety and praise. He still suffers the difficulties and discomforts of an uncertain life (inside a fish!), but he gives unreserved thanks to Yahweh. Jonah does not repent of his protest. His thanksgiving, however, does end his fleeing. He turns to Yahweh and acknowledges his salvation even though he has not resolved his questions concerning his mission to Nineveh (cf. his discussion with Yahweh in 4:2–11).

One common conclusion concerning the tension between Jonah's genuine temple piety and his actions/attitudes toward the sailors and Ninevites is that Jonah's faith simply doesn't wear very well in the world. He is good with pious language and formal poetic prayers, but he cannot bring himself to have compassion on the "outsiders" in Nineveh. This could be true if Jonah's primary issue was the insider/outsider tension between Jews and Gentiles.

The tension of Jonah's life, however, is that he loves Yahweh but has taken serious action against God's intention to offer forgiveness to the violent (as he and Yahweh discuss in ch. 4). The tension between his "temple piety" and his attitudes toward the unjust world are true to life. The tensions represents the honest struggle (and even confusion) of a person who has not resolved the incongruities of living in changing and challenging times. Jonah's song is true praise with a hint of protest.

All Jonah can do is express his faith and thanks in the midst of the tensions of his life. We miss the ongoing point of the text if we seek to resolve or remove tensions that readers have noticed for centuries. We should not smooth them out in order to make ourselves more comfortable; rather, we should recognize our own struggle in them. Faith meets the incongruity of experience in the world in chapter 2. This meeting invites us to recognize the same struggle in ourselves. It is exactly this incongruity from which interpreters across the liberal-conservative spectrum have run in attempting to resolve the tension.

Jonah's praise and (barely) hidden protest in chapter 2 are matched best by Job's open protest and (almost) hidden praise for the breath in his nostrils in Job 27:1–6:

And Job continued his discourse:

"As surely as God lives, who has denied me justice,
    the Almighty, who has made me taste bitterness of soul,
as long as I have life within me,
    the breath of God in my nostrils,
my lips will not speak wickedness,
    and my tongue will utter no deceit.
I will never admit you are in the right;
    till I die, I will not deny my integrity.
I will maintain my righteousness and never let go of it;
    my conscience will not reproach me as long as I live."

In both cases, God approves. Job is vindicated by God in the presence of his "friends" (Job 42:8), and Jonah is vomited onto dry land and called again to his mission.

The sign of Jonah. The "sign of Jonah" is the expression used by Jesus (Matt. 12:39–41) to refer to Jonah's (and his own) three days and three nights in the belly of the fish/tomb (see Matt. 12:39–40).[25] The wonder of the sign

---

25. Luke records Jesus' second interpretation of "Jonah" as a "sign" for his listeners (see Luke 11:29–30). In this passage, Jesus points to the "miracle" of the *Ninevites'* repentance.

is that *a place that ought to have been a place of death became a place of deliverance and life.*[26] No one expects a man to survive inside a fish. This reference to God's presence and life in the midst of death is taken up in Paul's description of Jesus' accomplishment in his descent: "He who descended is the very one who ascended higher than all the heavens, in order to fill the whole universe" (Eph. 4:10). This central Christian theme is also recited in the Apostles' Creed:

> He was crucified dead and buried; he descended into Hades; on the third day he rose again from the dead and ascended into heaven and sitteth on the right hand of God the Father Almighty. From thence he shall come to judge the living and the dead.

Jesus' incarnation made God visible and touchable. His descent to earth and his willing humility even to death on a cross brought redemption to all (Phil. 2:5–11). His three-day descent into death means that no place or experience is devoid of God's presence. Jonah shares in the experience of the psalmist in Psalm 139:7–12 (italics added):

> Where can I go from your Spirit?
>> Where can I flee from your presence?
> If I go up to the heavens, you are there;
>> if I make my bed in the *depths*, you are there.
> If I rise on the wings of the dawn,
>> if I settle on the *far side of the sea*,
> even there your hand will guide me,
>> your right hand will hold me fast.
> If I say, "Surely the darkness will hide me
>> and the light become night around me,"
> *even the darkness will not be dark to you;*
>> the night will shine like the day,
>> for darkness is as light to you.

Jonah's experience of God in the belly of the fish is the premiere narrative description of God's presence even in the place of the dead (Job 26:6; Ps. 139:8; Amos 9:2). Paul repeated this theme fully in Christ when he declared that nothing "will be able to separate us from the love of God that is in Christ Jesus our Lord" (Rom. 8:35–39).

The wonder is that a place of death became a place of deliverance and life was completely unexpected. When Jonah was cast over the gunwale of the ship, he did not expect to be rescued by a fish. His declaration that "salvation comes from the LORD" (2:9b) puts an exclamation point on the strange experience of sinking to the bottom of the sea and *not drowning!* When Jesus

---

26. "Swallowed" and "*šeʾol*" generally go together (see Num. 16:30).

points to the "sign of Jonah" as a sign for his own work, it includes the recognition that God is at work to save, even before those fleeing from him are aware of him. The disciples were not looking for Jesus' resurrection after his death, even though he had told them about it. Even when the women bore witness, the men didn't believe it (Luke 24:11).

The Hebrew word "salvation" is from the root *yešuʿah*. "Jesus" in Hebrew is the same: *yešuʿa*, for "he will save his people" (Matt. 1:21). When Jonah says, "Salvation comes from the LORD," he speaks the truth about God, knowing that he is still at odds with God concerning the fate of the Ninevites. Jesus' own work of salvation through his death and victory over death was done while the world was still at odds with God. God is the author of our faith, and Jonah is a key witness.

Jonah's "sign" is full of wonder. A place of death (the belly) becomes a place of deliverance. In a world that fears death, his renewed life is a primary sign of proclaiming and living the gospel. The sign of Jonah has become identified with the hope of life in Christ now, in the promise of the resurrection to come. The fear of death (usually in mid-life crises) and the denial of death (usually among the young) lead to many foolish or even death-promoting behaviors (substance abuse, thrill seeking, extramarital affairs). Jonah is a captive of the fish, but the fish is his good news. In the belly Jonah is protected from the waves and drowning. He is rescued, saved, and protected. On the other hand, he is a captive. His witness in chapter 2 is that this captivity is a captivity for which he is grateful. He never expresses the discomfort that has preoccupied some modern interpreters. His experience of the captivity is an experience of grace. Monk Thomas Merton wrote:

> Like the prophet Jonas, whom God ordered to go to Nineveh, I found myself with an almost uncontrollable desire to go in the opposite direction. God pointed one way and all my "ideals" pointed in the other. It was when Jonas was traveling as fast as he could away from Nineveh, toward Tarshish, that he was thrown overboard, and swallowed by a whale who took him where God wanted him to go.[27]

The worshiping community of faith lives in the same captive freedom—pursued and captured by the gospel of Christ. The psalm in Jonah 2 is a song of worship, written formally for worship, and it assumes a listening congregation. More than these formal facts, the fact that it is sung from the captivity of the fish is a perfect picture of believers at worship. The apostle Paul was literally a captive for the sake of the gospel. He recognized the power of the gospel in his freedom from the fear of death:

---

27. Thomas Merton, *The Sign of Jonas* (New York: Harcourt, Brace, and Co., 1953), 10–11.

Now I want you to know, brothers, that what has happened to me has really served to advance the gospel. As a result, it has become clear throughout the whole palace guard and to everyone else that I am in chains for Christ. Because of my chains, most of the brothers in the Lord have been encouraged to speak the word of God more courageously and fearlessly. (Phil. 1:12–14)

Paul elsewhere describes the wonder of being saved *now*, but expecting what has *not yet* happened, his own homegoing (2 Cor. 5:1–9). His is a description of the church in the *belly of expectation* of the Second Coming. This expectation is nowhere more relevant than in the context of worship, in which thanksgiving and praise for our deliverance is sung. The expectation in the midst of the praise, however, is that something more and better is to come.

Protest and piety. In this psalm of praise Jonah's protest is all but put aside (the protest emerges again in ch. 4). His praise is not, however, simply a pious interlude. God's relationship with believers is rich in its integration of many facets of experience. God does not expect that everyone who praises or thanks him will have resolved every doubt or question concerning the nature of the world or of existence. Jonah still disagrees with Yahweh concerning Nineveh. Yet this does not stop him from praising God or Yahweh from receiving his thanksgiving. Theirs is a rich and complex relationship. His piety is real, and so is his protest. In his thanksgiving and praise Jonah concedes God's call on his life to be his own and vows to follow that calling. He can continue to protest, but he cannot continue to run.

This tradition is well established in the Old Testament. Almost one third of the psalms contain laments. The lament psalms usually juxtapose anguish over situations of life and praise to God.[28] Laments have four basic elements: the complaint, a call for help, an affirmation of trust, and a vow to praise God. The juxtaposition of complaint and praise is seen in Psalm 13:

> How long, O LORD? Will you forget me forever?
>   How long will you hide your face from me?
> How long must I wrestle with my thoughts
>   and every day have sorrow in my heart?
>   How long will my enemy triumph over me? . . .
> But I trust in your unfailing love;
>   my heart rejoices in your salvation.
> I will sing to the LORD,
>   for he has been good to me. (Ps. 13:1–2, 5–6)

---

28. For pure lament see Ps. 88.

The book of Lamentations has five chapters of pure lament over the destruction of Jerusalem at the hands of the Babylonians, yet the center of the book contains these well-known verses of praise:

> Yet this I call to mind
>   and therefore I have hope:
> Because of the LORD's great love we are not consumed,
>   for his compassions never fail.
> They are new every morning;
>   great is your faithfulness.
> I say to myself, "The LORD is my portion;
>   therefore I will wait for him." (Lam. 3:21–24)

Faith in Yahweh is never as simple as pure obedience versus pure rebellion. Jonah helps us to see the complexity of faith. He returns to his piety and worship of the true God of heaven, sea, and dry land. At the same time he maintains his reservations of protest against God's intended way in the world with the violent Ninevites.

In the end, Jonah's prayer of thanksgiving is a witness of hope to believers. This hope has integrity and richness when his thanks are seen in the narrative context of his situation. He gives thanks in spite of the uncertainty of still being at sea. He gives thanks knowing he did not deserve rescue. He gives thanks for a haven in an unlikely place. He gives thanks in spite of deep discomfort. Jonah gives thanks in spite of his unresolved questions and issues. His is a real and hopeful faith.

In "A Sermon on Preparing to Die," Martin Luther compared the death/resurrection of a believer to the birth of a child who moves from the confines of the womb into a broad new world.

> Just as an infant is born with peril and pain from the small abode of its mother's womb into this immense heaven and hearth, that is, into this world, so man departs this life through the narrow gate of death. And although the heavens and the earth in which we dwell at present seem large and wide to us, they are nevertheless much narrower and smaller than the mother's womb in comparison with the future heaven. Therefore the death of the dear saints is called a new birth.[29]

Jonah, like all believers called by Yahweh, must be reborn by God's grace.

---

29. Martin Luther, *Luther's Works*, ed. M. O. Dietrich (Philadelphia: Fortress, 1969), 42:99.

Jonah 3

THEN THE WORD of the LORD came to Jonah a second time: ²"Go to the great city of Nineveh and proclaim to it the message I give you."

³Jonah obeyed the word of the LORD and went to Nineveh. Now Nineveh was a very important city—a visit required three days. ⁴On the first day, Jonah started into the city. He proclaimed: "Forty more days and Nineveh will be overturned." ⁵The Ninevites believed God. They declared a fast, and all of them, from the greatest to the least, put on sackcloth.

⁶When the news reached the king of Nineveh, he rose from his throne, took off his royal robes, covered himself with sackcloth and sat down in the dust. ⁷Then he issued a proclamation in Nineveh:

"By the decree of the king and his nobles:

Do not let any man or beast, herd or flock, taste anything; do not let them eat or drink. ⁸But let man and beast be covered with sackcloth. Let everyone call urgently on God. Let them give up their evil ways and their violence. ⁹Who knows? God may yet relent and with compassion turn from his fierce anger so that we will not perish."

¹⁰When God saw what they did and how they turned from their evil ways, he had compassion and did not bring upon them the destruction he had threatened.

JONAH'S PREACHING, THE Ninevites' repentance, and Yahweh's compassion comprise the primary action of chapter 3. This chapter is neatly summarized in verses 4–5, 10. Jonah threatens that the Ninevites "will be overturned," and they "believed God." In response, God sees how they have turned from evil and has compassion.

This chapter provides a convincing demonstration of God's argument with Jonah concerning what ought to be done with violent enemies: They should have an opportunity to hear from Yahweh, turn from their violent ways, and be forgiven. Chapter 3 mirrors the action of chapter 1, which begins with the first command for Jonah to go to Nineveh. The group of sailors and their leader found themselves under God's decree and acted to avoid disaster, and God delivered them, as he does here the citizens and the king.

Chapter 3 begins with Jonah's obedience in proclaiming Yahweh's message (3:1–4). His word comes to Jonah a second time and tells him to go to the great city and proclaim "the message I give you" (3:1–2). This time Jonah does immediately go to the "very important city" and begins proclaiming the "overturning" of the city within forty days. On the first day of the three-day job, the Ninevites believe (3:3–5a), and the rest of the chapter continues with the Ninevites' dramatic public repentance of evil and violence (3:5–9). The people, prior to the king's command, declare a fast and put on sackcloth (3:5b).

When the king hears, he joins in the outward signs of repentance and issues a proclamation of fasting and sackcloth, even for the animals (3:6–8). He says in humility, "Who knows? God may yet relent . . . so that we will not perish" (3:9). The chapter concludes with Yahweh's compassion and forgiveness. "God saw what they did . . . [and] had compassion and did not bring upon them the destruction he had threatened" (3:10). This is a great miracle. Even Israel's worst enemies, the most unlikely people, believe, repent, and receive God's compassion and forgiveness.

Jonah Proclaims and the Ninevites Believe God (3:1–5)

THE WORD OF Yahweh comes to Jonah "a second time." This second time harks back to the first time (1:1–2), using the same Hebrew words (in italics):

1:1–2: *The word of the* LORD *came to Jonah* son of Amittai: "*Go to the great city of Nineveh* and *preach* against it, because its wickedness has come up before me."

3:1–2: Then *the word of the* LORD *came to Jonah* a second time: "*Go to the great city of Nineveh* and *proclaim* to it the message I give you."

The prophet receives a second chance to participate in God's mission of reconciling enemies. The command "go" is expressed in Hebrew with two verbs (lit., "rising, go"). Together they mean "Go now!" or "Go immediately." In 1:1–2 Jonah rose to run away, but here Jonah has been reconciled to God's call. The mission to Nineveh can begin again, because God has called again. The content of Jonah's prophecy will not be given to him until he is actually in the city: "Go to the great city of Nineveh and proclaim to it the message I give you" (3:2). Jonah knows it will be a message against its wickedness (see 1:2: "because *its wickedness* has come up before me"; cf. also 3:8, 10).

"Jonah obeyed the word of the LORD and went to Nineveh" (3:3a). The first story of reconciliation (between Jonah and God) concludes and the second story of reconciliation (between Nineveh and God) begins. Jonah does not hesitate this time. The Hebrew expression is (lit.) "rising, Jonah went," implying his immediate departure. Why does he go this time? God has pursued him to the gates of death and brought him back. Jonah cannot escape the assignment.

The "greatness" of Nineveh (1:2; 3:2; 4:11) is explained in 3:3b (a visit required three days) and in 4:11 (120,000 people with many animals). The question of Nineveh's size can also be answered in historical terms. Tiglath-Pileser III built it into a large city by 730 B.C. Later, Sennacherib (who besieged Jerusalem in 701 B.C.) made it the capital of Assyria. Archaeologists have discovered a walled city with a total urban perimeter of seven and a half miles.

The text expresses Nineveh's importance with a significant idiom that is literally translated, "Nineveh was a great city *to God*" (NIV: "Now Nineveh was a *very* important city"). "To God" (*le'lohim*) can be an idiom for "very," but it is worth noting in this context that it reinforces a main theme of the book, namely, that Nineveh is important to God, even if not to Jonah! God has created its greatness in size and has compassion on his beloved creation (4:11).

Readers have wondered what "a visit required three days" (lit., "a three-day walk") means. Some have considered it hyperbole, in keeping with the exaggerations of the book (great fish, great city, great plant, etc.). Others have suggested that it took three days to cross the municipality or province of Nineveh (including pasture lands and towns that typically surrounded large ancient cities). Perhaps the most convincing is that it required three days to proclaim the message in all the public squares.[1] It would take three days to walk and preach in every neighborhood and to complete the proclamation to everyone in the city.

"On the first day, Jonah started into the city." Hebrew has an interesting word pair for "started" (lit., "began to go": *halal* + *labo'*). *Halal* ("began") connotes "letting loose" or "untying." It implies that Jonah "let go." The most basic form of the verb means "pierce." The implied radical nature of his "starting" into the city echoes the difficulty he has with preaching to the enemy Ninevites from the beginning of his call. For him it is not simply a matter of "getting started," but of releasing to God his (justified) reservations about this mission.

Jonah's prophecy to Nineveh is succinctly delivered in eight words (only five in Hebrew!): "Forty more days and Nineveh will be overturned [*hapak*]" (3:4b).[2]

---

1. Luther suggested the possibility that Jonah set out to walk all its streets (see *Luther's Works*, ed. H. C. Oswald [St. Louis: Concordia, 1974]), 19:84.

2. "Forty days" is the traditional length of time for reflection and purification (see Ex. 24:18; Num. 13:25; Mark 1:13).

Jonah preaches an amazing message. The Hebrew root *hapak* can mean "turn over," that is, "destroy" (as with Sodom in Gen. 19), or "turn around," meaning "bring to repentance."[3] Sherwood notes that *hapak*, therefore, refers either to "evil" (catastrophe of destruction) or to "live" (new structure of a repentant life).[4]

At first glance this message seems to be only one of gloom and doom. The Ninevites certainly understand "overturned" to mean "destroyed." Everyone in the text understands, however, that this word of destruction contains the *possibility* of Yahweh's mercy if they repent.[5] This word concept is crucial to understanding this chapter (and will be discussed in more detail in Bridging Contexts section). The double meaning of "overturned" is not lost on Jonah. He knows that Yahweh's message implies that the people may repent and God will forgive. Such a possibility is exactly why Jonah initially fled to Tarshish (see 4:2). The Ninevites also seem to understand this when they immediately repent and hear about the hope of forgiveness from the king (3:9).

It is important for the reader to see both perspectives in "Nineveh will be overturned." The conflict between the two possibilities ("destroyed" or "changed through turning to God") is the primary subject of the book of Jonah and of the argument between the prophet and God. God sends Jonah to Nineveh in hope that the Ninevites will be "overturned" through their repentance. Jonah faithfully proclaims this two-edged message but hopes (as we see in ch. 4) that "overturned" means the annihilation of the Ninevites. He understands both aspects of the word. The Ninevites, by contrast, do not fully understand it but believe it to mean "destruction." They repent in the hope that it may mean something other (and better) than their annihilation.

"The Ninevites believed God" on the first day (3:4–5). They declare a fast, and all of them, from the greatest to the least, put on sackcloth. Fasting is a means of seeking God's mercy, while sackcloth is a symbol of repentance. The Ninevites believe that Jonah's words are God's words, so the text says that they "believed God."[6] The sense is that they trust the word they have heard to be a true and reliable word for them.

---

3. The 1978 NIV version and NLT have "Nineveh will be *destroyed.*" KJV, RSV, NRSV, NASB all have "will be overthrown." The 1984 NIV version has "overturned," which is the best word for preserving both necessary possibilities of the Hebrew text.

4. This word play on the root *hapak* is similar to the English play with "evil" and "live," which is "evil" spelled backwards. Sherwood, *A Biblical Text and Its Afterlives*, 121, 236.

5. The Hebrew is a Niphal participle, which may be understood reflexively as well as passively, i.e., "will overturn *herself*" ("repent") as well as "will *be* overturned" ("destroyed").

6. "Believed *in* God" is also a possible translation (*ya'aminu be'lohim* with *bet* of transitivity; cf. Gen. 15:6).

The King Responds in Hope (3:6–10)

THE KING OF Nineveh hears how the city has responded to Jonah's preaching. Believing the word from Jonah, he leaves his throne with the traditional signs of repentance. His decree approves what the people have already done and adds the commission to pray and give up their evil ways. He hopes that God will "with compassion turn from his fierce anger" (3:9). God does (3:10).

The king takes four immediate steps in response to the prophecy of Jonah. He is "overthrown" from his throne and his dignified clothing. A small chiastic structure is commonly observed in his rising-sitting, unclothed-clothed actions.

A He *rose* from his throne
   B *took off* his royal robes
   B' *covered* himself with sackcloth
A' *sat down* in the dust

The king responds very differently than Jonah when he hears the word of Yahweh. Both believe the word of Yahweh (and "rose"), but Jonah "ran away" (1:3) while the king "rose from his throne," the first of his self-humbling actions. The king humbled himself when he *"took off* his royal robes," while Jonah was *"swept over"* by the waves. The same Hebrew verb describes both actions (ʿabar).

After the "overthrow" of the king's life before God, he takes a fifth step. He and his nobles issue a proclamation, which has five important parts:

* intensification of the general fast
* expansion of the sackcloth of repentance
* command to cry out to the God of Israel
* command to repent from evil ways and violence
* the possibility of hope and God's compassion offered

The king's proclamation (3:7–9) begins with a general fast: "Do not let any man or beast, herd or flock, taste anything" (3:7b). The people have already declared a fast, but the king intensifies it. Usually a fast includes only abstinence from food; the king adds drink to the prohibition. Moreover, the people must not even taste food, and animals must observe the fast too.

The people are already in sackcloth, but the king's decree extends the sackcloth of repentance to the animals (3:8a).[7] The radical earnestness of the decree is odd, even humorous, but it is sincere in the context. This intensification demonstrates that the nobles and king are fully convinced of their

---

7. According to the historian Herodotus, it was customary for animals to participate in mourning (see, *The Histories*, trans. R. Waterfield [Oxford: Oxford Univ. Press, 1998]), 9.24.

danger and want to ensure that the people are not lax in repentance. Not feeding the animals will jeopardize the city's economy, especially if the fast lasts forty days. The animals join in "crying out" because they are hungry. Even after one day without food the protests of twenty head of cattle can be heard from half a mile away. The bleating and bellowing would have been cacophonous.

The king adds a command for the people to "call urgently on God" for their salvation (3:8b). Like the sailors (1:14–16), the Assyrians are converted. No longer praying to their own gods, they call upon *ha'elohim*, "the true God." In the case of the Assyrians, the significant change may be from self-reliance to an acknowledgment of God (cf. the Assyrian's "I am" statement in Zeph. 2:15). This astounding turn toward God would have been shocking to the original readers. Assyria was known for its false gods and its self-worship. Now the king himself commands them to "call urgently" on Israel's God, whom have already "believed" (3:5).

Salvation is possible only through calling or "crying out" (Heb. *qara'*) to God. God told Jonah to cry out against Nineveh ("preach, proclaim," 1:2; 3:2). The ship captain told Jonah to cry out to his god ("call on," 1:6). The sailors "cried" to Yahweh (1:14). Jonah cried out to Yahweh in his distress ("called to," 2:2). Jonah cried out in Nineveh ("proclaimed," 3:4). The people believed and cried out for a general fast ("declared," 3:5). Finally the king told the people to cry out to Yahweh ("call urgently," 3:8b).

The king also commands repentance from evil ways and violence (3:8c). Religious signs of repentance (fasting, sackcloth, prayer) are accompanied by a true turning from the cause of their peril. The Hebrew here is more personal and graphic. Literally translated it says, "Let each person repent of his evil way and from the violence that is in his hands." Violence and evil toward others were widely known as Nineveh's primary point of boasting (see "The Terror Mongers" in the introduction). It is the reason God called on Jonah in the first place (1:2).

The king offers the possibility of hope and God's compassion. He does not know whether God's compassion is certain ("Who knows?"), but repentance in turning from offending a god was generally thought to be effective in averting doom. "Who knows" is an expression of humility. The believing king can rely only and humbly on the compassion of the true God for forgiveness of the violence that he has been administrating.

Jonah's mission is complete. The effect of his preaching has been stunning. The Assyrians have acknowledged the true God. They have sought him through fasting and repented of their "evil ways and their violence" (3:8). "Evil ways" refers to the way they *walk* ("foot-path") day to day. "Violence" is (lit.) "the violence that is in their *hands*." Jonah has been believed as a true prophet of God.[8] The Ninevites have been converted. In humility and repentance, they hope for compassion and deliverance (3:5, 9): "Who knows? God [*ha'elohim*] may yet relent and with compassion turn from his fierce anger."

"Down" was a major thematic word and action in chapter 1. Now chapter 3 presents the theme of "upside down." In 3:5–6 several amazing upside down actions occur. (1) The people proclaim the fast before the king. Declarations usually begin at the top and come down. This one begins in the street and reaches the king. (2) The king leaves his throne and removes the kingly robes, preparing for the possibility of the kingship of Yahweh. He joins the common people ("from the greatest to the least") in sackcloth and sits in the dust in his humility (3:6). This is an "up-ended" king. (3) The king's proclamation calls for everyone to "call urgently on [Israel's] God" (3:8). The mighty Assyrians are now, like the sailors, crying for their lives. In two short verses the Ninevites are "overturned"—not yet "destroyed" but in every other way, "turned upside down."

Jonah 3 concludes with Yahweh's compassion and forgiveness (3:10). This is a key verse in the book of Jonah. It not only saves the Ninevites, it is also the subject of Jonah's protest from chapter 1, and it will be the point of contention to the end of the book. God sees what they have done to humble themselves and how, according to the word of the king, they "turned [*šub*] from their evil ways." God sees their sincerity in repentance and has compassion.

God's move toward compassion for the violent who repent is sometimes unnecessarily confused by the use of the word "repent" as a translation for *naḥam* in 3:10.

KJV: and God *repented* of the evil, that he had said that he would do unto them.

RSV: God *repented* of the evil which he had said he would do to them.

NASB: then God *relented* concerning the calamity which He had declared He would bring upon them.

NRSV: God *changed his mind* about the calamity that he had said he would bring upon them.

NIV: he *had compassion* and did not bring upon them the destruction he had threatened.

When God is the subject of *naḥam*, it is best translated "had compassion" or "relented."[9] The basic meaning of the Hebrew word is "have compassion"

---

8. In Israel this kind of total national repentance occurs only in Josiah's reform.

9. The best discussion of the translation issue of "repent" (people) and "relent" (God) is in Kenneth Craig, *A Poetics of Jonah—Art in the Service of Ideology*, 2d ed. (Macon, Ga.: Mercer Univ. Press, 1997), 34.

or "feel sorrow." When *people* feel sorrow, the context of sin often warrants the translation "repent." The ordinary word for repent (*šub*) is also used in this text, but it carries the implication of "turning around," as in changing the way you live. *Naham* is "repentance" in the internal sense of sorrow. When *God* feels sorrow, however, the word cannot mean "repent" since God does not sin. Rather, it indicates God's sorrow for the consequences people must face as a natural result of their sin and his justice in the world order. This "sorrow" is expressed in "compassion."[10]

God's move toward compassion is what Jonah has suspected. God's compassion hidden inside his absolute judgment and Jonah's protest against it are the fulcrum of the book (see 4:2b). Jonah knows that God's judgment always implies the possibility of mercy, even when the language of judgment sounds absolute ("Forty more days . . ." 3:4). Chapter 4 is an extended conversation between God and Jonah on this and other arising issues.

JONAH 3 PRIMARILY concerns God and the Ninevites, with Jonah as God's agent. Jonah's dispute with Yahweh is not evident. He is called once again, goes to Nineveh, and preaches; the Ninevites repent, and God forgives them.[11] Jonah fulfills his calling (apparently against his own ideals) in obedience to the word of Yahweh that comes to him a second time.

This chapter may be encapsulated in three words: "overturned" (*hapak*), "repentance" (*šub*), and "compassion" (*naham*). These words represent the three major actions in the text: Jonah's preaching, the Ninevites' giving up their evil ways, and Yahweh's compassion. They also point to the enduring truth of a real relationship between sinners and Yahweh. Reconciliation with God is a threefold movement.

The three-part pattern is common in God's relationship to Israel. In 1 Samuel 7:3–11, Israel was threatened by the Philistines. They put away their Baal and Ashtoreth idols and gathered at Mizpah for repentance. They came under attack, but Yahweh delivered them with a thunderstorm. This pattern is repeated in Esther 4 in Persia, in Ezra 8:21–23 at the Ahava Canal, and in Joel 2:11–19. In each of these cases, the Israelites were under the threat of

---

10. Another context warrants the translation "vengeance" that God takes against Israel's enemies for overdoing violence. This is the sense of the name of the book Nahum, which provides "vengeance" against Nineveh for its violence and "comfort" for Israel, who lost ten tribes to Nineveh's armies and slave markets.

11. Jonah and God will return to their conversation in ch. 4. If repentance were the only message, the book could have ended with 3:10.

being "overturned" in destruction. They turned to Yahweh (in repentance) and were delivered (by God's compassion). In Jonah the same pattern is described for the Assyrian enemy. They are welcomed into the possibility of deliverance. Jeremiah 18 declares this possibility for all peoples:

> If at any time I announce that a nation or kingdom is to be uprooted, torn down and destroyed, and if that nation I warned repents of its evil, then I will relent and not inflict on it the disaster I had planned. And if at another time I announce that a nation or kingdom is to be built up and planted, and if it does evil in my sight and does not obey me, then I will reconsider the good I had intended to do for it. (Jer. 18:7–10)

Nations that are under the threat of destruction may include those who consider themselves chosen or established by God and those who do not. In Jonah, as in Jeremiah, the possibility of turning in repentance to the Creator is revealed. Hope in God's compassion is demonstrated in both cases.

Overturning. Overturning has two possibilities in this text: "destruction" (*ra'ab*) or "repentance" (*šub*). The word carries this dual meaning throughout Scripture.[12]

On the first day, Jonah starts into the city. He proclaims: "Forty more days and Nineveh will be overturned [*hapak*]." When the Ninevites hear the word *hapak*, they assume that God means "destruction." The word *ra'ab* in 3:10 is translated in various ways in English versions: "the evil" (KJV, RSV), "calamity" (NRSV, NASB), and "destruction" (NIV).

It is useful to look at several translations to see the possible range of meaning behind the NIV's "destruction" (*ra'ab*). God does not do "evil," which is a basic meaning of *ra'ab*. The verdict that something is "evil" in the Bible depends on the eye of the beholder. God called Jonah to preach because of Nineveh's *ra'ab* ("wickedness," 1:2). The sailors considered the storm a *ra'ab* ("calamity," 1:7; "trouble," 1:8). The king knew his people were engaged in ways of *ra'ab* ("evil," 3:8). God saw that they gave up their *ra'ab* ("evil ways"), and he did not bring about the *ra'ab* ("destruction") he threatened (3:10). God's "destruction" was not "evil" in the same way as the Ninevites'. Because they were engaged in evil, they experienced the possibility of their own destruction (a just judgment) as *evil* rather than *just*.

This sort of experiential verdict is an enduring reality today. Do we experience all calamities as evil or some of them as just? On what basis do God's people decide about their experiences and the experiences of others? When "calamity" falls as a just judgment on the wicked, do the people of God rejoice or hope for another kind of overturning? Jonah does not approve of

---

12. See discussion of *hapak* in the Contemporary Significance section.

a God who "relents from sending calamity [ra'ab]" to the wicked (4:2). But another kind of overturning is offered to those who recognize justice, even the justice of God's destruction. It included both repentance (šub) and God's compassion (naḥam).

The law and the gospel work together in this way. The law "kills" the self-justification of our sin by convincing us of our need to be overturned by God. The gospel resurrects us as a new creation, with a new perspective on the positive value of God's judgment toward us, even when it involves calamity. The Ninevites no longer have the same culture after their repentance. They "put away" their evil ways. A new kind of life within a transformed culture has begun.

This transformation, likened to baptism by Paul, is also like dying and rising again:

> Shall we go on sinning so that grace may increase? By no means! We died to sin; how can we live in it any longer? Or don't you know that all of us who were baptized into Christ Jesus were *baptized into his death*? We were therefore buried with him through baptism into *death* in order that, just as Christ was raised from the dead through the glory of the Father, we too may live a *new life*.
>
> If we have been united with him like this in his *death*, we will certainly also be united with him in his *resurrection*. For we know that our old self was crucified with him so that the body of sin might be done away with, that we should no longer be slaves to sin—because anyone who has died has been freed from sin. (Rom. 6:1–7, italics added)

"Overturning" is also used in Jonah 3 to describe repentance (šub): "Let everyone call urgently on God. Let them give up [šub] their evil ways and their violence" (3:8b)."When God saw what they did and how they turned [šub] from their evil ways, he had compassion" (3:10).

Repentance is repentance before Yahweh, regardless of race or culture. Jonah did not preach specifically to Gentiles but against wickedness (which included vilifying other cultures). God makes the same call to "turn from evil practices" for all of his human creation (2 Chron. 7:14; Jer. 25:5; 26:3–6). What "God saw" was not the sackcloth and fasting, but "how they turned from their evil ways" (3:10). Since about A.D. 200 the "bottom to top to bottom again" repentance of first the Ninevite people, then the king, and then the people has been the afternoon reading in synagogues celebrating the Day of Atonement (Yom Kippur). It is read as a model for the proper attitude for repentance with Isaiah's description (Isa. 58:4–7) of proper fasting.[13]

---

13. Limburg, *Jonah*, 85–87.

The observance of Yom Kippur is outlined in Leviticus 16. Once a year God's people confessed their sins, fasted for twenty-four hours, and prayed for forgiveness. After being purified through the sacrifice of a bull, the high priest entered the Most Holy Place in the tabernacle/temple to be sanctified by God for his following role. After sprinkling blood in front of the *kippur* or "cover" of the ark, he emerged, sacrificed a goat, reentered the veil, and sprinkled the blood of the goat the same way, this time for the purification of all the people. Emerging again, he put more of the goat's blood on a second goat (the scapegoat), which was led to the desert to walk off a cliff. The goat carried the symbolic sins into the desert, removing those sins from their midst of the people.[14]

The theme of repentance focuses on the transforming power of repentance and forgiveness. This yearly use and interpretation of Jonah nullifies any Christian notions that Jonah should be understood as a type of rebellious Israel in contrast to the willingly repentant pagans. Jesus refers also to the Ninevites' repentance as a witness against peoples who hear the call to repentance but do not repent (Matt. 12:41; Luke 11:32).

The reading of Jonah in the Day of Atonement service "reflects the view that this book depicts the concept of repentance so starkly and completely that it can stir hearers to repent of their ways and even modifies their conduct."[15] The Ninevites' repentance and Yahweh's forgiveness "reject the ancient view, expressed by Jonah . . . that only punishment can cleanse sin."[16] In his sovereign freedom, God accepted the Ninevites' repentance of their violent ways as a transformation. They were forgiven. The people's turning in repentance (*šub*) is mirrored by God's turning with compassion (*šub* + *naḥam*): "[God] had compassion and did not bring upon them the destruction he had threatened" (3:10b).

The combination of the two words results in an averted calamity. The turning of the Ninevites is essentially different, however, since God's turning came on his own terms whereas the people said, "Who knows?" [17] The basic difference is marked in the text by the word *naḥam* (cf. discussion above, on the translation of this word as "repent," "relent," and "have compassion").

---

14. The *kippur* is literally the "cover" of the ark, but the association is so strong that the "covering" of sins, or "atonement," is considered a second meaning of *kippur*. In the Greek Old Testament the word is *hiliasterion*, translated "mercy seat." Paul says that Jesus has become our "mercy seat" or "covering" for sin (Rom. 3:25). The apostle can say therefore, "Clothe yourselves with the Lord Jesus Christ" (Rom. 13:14).

15. Uriel Simon, *Jonah: The Traditional Hebrew Text*, trans. L. J. Schramm (Philadelphia: Jewish Publication Society, 1999), vii..

16. Yehezkel Kaufmann, *The Religion of Israel*, cited in U. Simon, *Jonah*, vii.

17. Trible, "The Book of Jonah," 7:515.

Nineveh hoped in God's *compassion*, God had *compassion*, and Jonah complained that God *relented* from sending calamity. These italicized words come from the same Hebrew word, *naham*. In Israel, to "repent" was to turn from pride to compassion. To turn toward God meant to comfort the oppressed and dispossessed (cf. Isa. 40:1). To "comfort" the widow, fatherless, and foreigner meant "repenting" of one's self-serving ways of pride. To have compassion was to turn from one's own competing ideals concerning wealth toward God and to acknowledge his agenda in the world. True repentance meant that compassion and comfort would increase in the world.

The enduring truth demonstrated in Jonah 3 is that compassion is a primary attribute of God. When it comes to justice, God is willing to sacrifice his reputation for strict constancy. He would rather be known as a God who forgives and is just. This is precisely what Jonah rails against in 4:2.

Divine "repentance" as "open to change strict judgment" keeps God's primary attribute in focus: his steadfast love and mercy. By giving attention to God's openness to change his judgment, his unchangeable attributes are brought more sharply into focus. His steadfastness is centered in his love for the world. His faithfulness is centered not in judgment but in his promises of salvation. Divine repentance enables us to place these immutable attributes in proper perspective.[18]

God's openness to change strict judgment is part of his character from the beginning of his dealings with Israel. At Sinai, during the golden calf incident, Moses pleaded with him to "relent" (*naham*) and have compassion in the midst of that calamity. God did relent, in striking similarity to his action in Nineveh. "Then the LORD relented [*naham*] and did not bring on his people the disaster he had threatened" (Ex. 32:14). In Jonah, "[God] had compassion [*naham*] and did not bring upon them the destruction he had threatened" (Jonah 3:10b; cf. also Joel 2:13).

God's will to change and save the world that he loves is immutable: "For I take no pleasure in the death of anyone, declares the Sovereign LORD. Repent and live!" (Ezek. 18:32). Scripture is not embarrassed, however, to say that God does change his mind when it comes to granting compassion even when his justice and righteousness in the world require death. The people made a golden calf and credited it, rather than God, for their deliverance from Egypt. God justly decided to destroy them (Ex. 32:7–10). In compassion, however, he changed his mind (see also Jer. 18:7–11; 26:2–3; Amos 7:3–6). He changes his mind precisely because his will to change and save the world

---

18. Terence E. Fretheim, "The Repentance of God," in *Horizons in Biblical Theology* 10 (January 1988): 63.

is unchangeable, and the world is continually turning away from him. If he did not turn in compassion, who would be saved?

God is not like us. God is free to judge the rebellious by strict justice and not forgive them when they repent. God is also free *not* to judge the rebellious by strict justice and to forgive them when they repent. This does not mean that God is capricious. When Scripture says that "God does not change his mind" (see 1 Sam. 15:28–30), it means that the wages of sin are death. The strict justice of the created order rules, and God is free to judge, but he is also free to relent.

The expression used by the king of Nineveh directs our attention to this freedom to judge according to a strict justice. He says, "Who knows?" The king knows that it is in the hand of God to judge. King David knew the same enduring truth. When his son by Bathsheba was ill as a result of his murder and adultery, he said the same thing: "While the child was still alive, I fasted and wept. I thought, 'Who knows? The LORD may be gracious to me and let the child live'" (2 Sam. 12:22). In David's case, Yahweh judged according to strict justice.

When God does change his mind, as is clear in Hosea, it is because God is not a human being. He is free to extend his primary attributes of compassion and steadfast love.[19]

> How can I give you up, Ephraim?
>   How can I hand you over, Israel?
> How can I treat you like Admah?
>   How can I make you like Zeboiim?
> My heart is changed [*hapak*] within me;
>   all my compassion is aroused.
> *I will not carry out* my fierce anger,
>   nor will I turn and devastate Ephraim.
> For I am God, and *not man*—
>   the Holy One among you.
> I will not come in wrath." (Hos. 11:8–9, italics added)

God's constancy longs for his people to return to him even when they are wicked. He is free to judge sin according to his righteousness or to forgive according to his compassion. God's change of heart stands in contrast to Jonah's consistent desire to see "justice done" and the wicked punished. This inclination is common to human experience, especially when the enemy has perpetrated terror on civilian populations and boasted of it. When it comes to forgiveness for one's own country, no one complains if God has a change of heart.

---

19. See Fretheim, "The Repentance of God," 52.

The prophet Joel employs the "Who knows" freedom refrain when Israel is starving because a "nation" of locusts continually destroys its crops:

> "Even now," declares the LORD,
>> "return to me with all your heart,
>> with fasting and weeping and mourning."
> Rend your heart
>> and not your garments.
> Return to the LORD your God,
>> for he is gracious and compassionate,
> slow to anger and abounding in love,
>> and he relents from sending calamity.
> *Who knows?* He may turn and have pity
>> and leave behind a blessing—
> grain offerings and drink offerings
>> for the LORD your God. (Joel 2:12–14, italics added)

God is free from the necessity of strict justice and can pursue a better justice in his unrelenting love for his creation. The king of Nineveh also acknowledges God's freedom with his "Who knows?" God's judgment of destruction is just, but his compassion may prevail. The fact of Jonah is that the Ninevites of that day were not punished for their wickedness. They were forgiven without punishment. They did not effectively force God's hand, however, nor were they certain of God's response. It could have justly gone the other way.

The primary foundation for understanding God's compassion is to understand our need and desperate situation. That fact leads us to humbly acknowledge, "Who knows?" Even the certainty of Christ's love and forgiveness cannot be received by the heart that reserves a suspicion of its own righteousness.[20] The fact that the hearts of the violent can be overthrown by the mere possibility of God's compassion is exactly the subject matter of Jonah's argument with God in chapter 4.

Contemporary Significance

MISSION TO THE **world in Jonah.** Assyria was a long way from Jerusalem (about 500 miles). It dominated the ancient east for about 270 years (c. 1356–1197 and 745–621 B.C.) including a harsh domination of Israel and Judah. Yet, the Old Testament records God's concern for this distant and wicked people. This surprising fact has led interpreters

---

20. John provides assurance for those of tender conscience: "If we confess our sins, he is faithful and just and will forgive us our sins and purify us from all unrighteousness" (1 John 1:9). For the callous of conscience, the freedom of God to judge justly has not been removed.

to consider the Creator's "mission to the world" as a key theme of Jonah. The Creator seeks reconciliation with the whole creation.

When God calls a person to a specific mission, the task and the journey do not always make sense. God is, nonetheless, often persistent in such calling. Moses repeatedly argued with Yahweh concerning the Exodus (Ex. 3:11–4:17). When Elijah suffered the consequences of his confrontation with Baal's prophets, Yahweh had to encourage him more than once to continue (1 Kings 19:1–18). Jeremiah struggled with Yahweh concerning his call (Jer. 20:7–9). Jonah was never convinced by Yahweh's argument about the need to transform Nineveh's wickedness.

God does not mention Nineveh's "wickedness" in his second call (Jonah 3:1–3). Like a child with a parent, Jonah is simply told to proclaim what God says ("because I said so!"). God saves his more lengthy warrant until the end of the book. We never hear Jonah's response. By ending with an open question, the book challenges to reader to examine whether God's argument is convincing (see the Original Meaning section of ch. 4). Even when Jonah obeys (3:3), he seems halfhearted in his effort, speaking the short message God gave him and walking only the first necessary day into the city. Chapter 4 demonstrates that even in obedience, Jonah is not in complete agreement with the possible outcomes of this mission.

The book of Jonah offers several opportunities to see the ready and willing response by people who are distant and ignorant of Yahweh. The pagan sailors and the Ninevites make rapid conversions (1:14–16). All of Nineveh repents after only one day of a three-day preaching tour (3:4–6). These responses to Yahweh have been interpreted as an early harbinger of God's reaching toward the Gentiles with a word of reconciliation and forgiveness.

Some have observed that the repentance of the Ninevites seems like a nonevent in the Bible as a whole. Admittedly, from a historical perspective, their repentance is momentary. Assyrian records only record their pride, never any repentance. Nahum (two books after Jonah) correctly prophesies the Ninevites' destruction for their violent and boastful ways. Their repentance does not seem believable. What does it mean for interpreting Jonah? Is the canonical message that the Ninevites' repentance wasn't worth the trouble? Jonah never says that, nor does God. Their concern was that the people *would* repent and find mercy.[21]

Theologically, the message (in the context of Nineveh's short-lived repentance) is that God in all times and in all places desires that all creation be

---

21. Assyrian Christians today readily point to their faith as inspired by God's compassion toward Nineveh in sending Jonah to them and in accepting their repentance. The text has a life beyond its original historical boundaries.

reconciled to him. Whether that preaching is unsuccessful in the long term or even unsuccessful in the short term (as in Jeremiah) is beside the point. Through the prophet Jonah, God is asking for our faithfulness in proclaiming the message he gives. This is framed twice by the lack of a message given to Jonah (1:2; 3:2). God simply says, "Go and proclaim." The message is given when he arrives (see comments on 3:2).

The repentance of Nineveh seems unbelievable in a second experiential way. When in the history of the world has such a spontaneous, thorough, and complete reversal of a violent and arrogant people ever been recorded? Jonah only "began" to go into the city, yet the whole city was converted, neighbor to neighbor. It was incredible that the Ninevites gave Jonah, a prophet from a people they dominated, any credence at all. His message was short, offensive, and vague (five Hebrew words). He never mentioned their sins or God, only their doom. It is certainly incredible that they recognized the magnitude and systemic nature of their guilt (3:8); that they were so sincere, courageous, and thorough in their repentance; that everyone in the city agreed and repented; that only one-third heard the actual word from God through Jonah but all believed; that the livestock were included in the fasting and wearing sackcloth; and that it was an intergenerational repentance (3:5). Nevertheless, the Ninevites "believed God" and radically repented to a person. It is common for commentators to be suspicious of the "never-never land" quality of Nineveh's mass repentance.[22]

Jonah himself finds that their repentance is incredible. It infuriates him to the point of self-destruction. Yet, in spite of the incredulity of readers, Jewish tradition and Jesus each lift up this incredible repentance as an example for others (Yom Kippur and Matt. 12:41; Luke 11:32). The point of the examples in each case, however, is not the greatness of the Ninevites' faith. If that were the case, their eventual return to terror certainly undermines their example. Rather, the point is the extravagant love of God that welcomes the sincerely repentant. A God who is intensely interested even in the salvation of animals (along with the wicked Ninevites) must be interested in *anyone*. A God interested in a people who will not sustain their repentance over time is an extravagant God who will welcome anyone who will turn to him. It reveals a wild and off-center God who really does love the wicked in spite of their wickedness or foolishness.

This accounts for the popularity and the canonization of Jonah long after Nineveh is destroyed by God (612 B.C.). It is not about the Ninevites' faith,

---

22. See Trible, "The Book of Jonah," 516. She cautions that we should not dismiss the claim of the text because it addresses systemic violence issues and shows the power of the body politic to turn around.

but about the unbelievably true possibility that God would care enough to overthrow their hearts. For the believing community, it stands as a reminder of the incredible love of the Creator for the creation and his radical willingness to seek out the most distant person and restore them to his grace.[23]

That Nineveh was converted to the God of Israel through Jonah's preaching remains historically unbelievable. That such an enemy should be transformed cannot be explained in ordinary human terms. This is, in fact, the portrait that the text paints for us: that this is not accomplished in ordinary human terms. It is an extraordinary, even a supernatural event. It is not based on spectacular preaching. It is a work of God and of his extravagant love. This is the hope of the book of Jonah. May God act to overthrow all of his enemies.

Jesus comes under the same scrutiny. The resurrection of the body of Christ is deemed unbelievable by most people today. The message of salvation and God's grace was then, and still is, considered foolishness.

> For Christ did not send me to baptize, but to preach the gospel—not with words of human wisdom, lest the cross of Christ be emptied of its power.
>
> For the message of the cross is foolishness to those who are perishing, but to us who are being saved it is the power of God. For it is written:
>
> > "I will destroy the wisdom of the wise,
> > the intelligence of the intelligent I will frustrate."
>
> Where is the wise man? Where is the scholar? Where is the philosopher of this age? Has not God made foolish the wisdom of the world? For since in the wisdom of God the world through its wisdom did not know him, God was pleased through the foolishness of what was preached to save those who believe. Jews demand miraculous signs and Greeks look for wisdom, but we preach Christ crucified: a stumbling block to Jews and foolishness to Gentiles, but to those whom God has called, both Jews and Greeks, Christ the power of God and the wisdom of God. For the foolishness of God is wiser than man's wisdom, and the weakness of God is stronger than man's strength. (1 Cor. 1:17–25; cf. Isa. 29:14).

Colonization and the gospel. A great barrier to missions today is the conflation of the call to missions with the Western colonialism of past centuries. No one wants to be accused of being colonial or having a colonial attitude. This

---

23. "And they believed God" describes the Ninevites as well as Abram and the children of Israel. See Gen. 15:6; Ex. 14:31; Jonah 3:5.

history often makes Christians in the West reluctant missionaries. Mission training has become more culturally sophisticated than it once was, seeking to understand cultures and peoples and respecting them as created and loved by God. It is possible to present the gospel of Jesus Christ without being an ambassador for an American way of life, with its own set of sins and corruptions.

Nonetheless, presenting the good news of the gospel and Yahweh as Creator of all the earth to an unreached people is a kind of colonization. Its goal is that the resurrected Christ will transform people and cultures by reconciling them to a relationship of love with the Creator. Christ is the colonizer of our lives, challenging values by his teaching and changing hearts with his love. The goal of missions is to "overthrow" all people and cultures, so that all the people of the world experience the blessings of knowing and being known by God.[24]

The difficult issue of the colonizing tendency of the gospel can be sorted out in part by the meanings of *hapak* and by understanding the ways Scripture uses the phrase "being overthrown by God." On the more difficult side of the word's meaning ("destroy"), Sodom and Gomorrah are the main examples (Gen. 19:21, 25, 29). God engaged Abraham in a dialogue (see Gen. 18:16–33). He was about to overthrow Sodom (like Nineveh) for its violent behaviors (Gen. 19) and wanted Abraham's participation. Abraham tried to talk him out of it, but even after he bargained with God, ten righteous men could not be found in all of Sodom. Sodom was overthrown/destroyed for its challenge to God's word in their midst.

But this is not the only possibility of being overthrown (*hapak*). The transformational meaning of *hapak* by God is seen in 1 Samuel 10. When the prophet Samuel anoints Saul as the first king over Israel, he explains to Saul how Yahweh will "overthrow" (*hapak*) him by changing him into a different person.

> "The Spirit of the LORD will come upon you in power, and you will prophesy with them; and you will be changed [*hapak*] into a different person. Once these signs are fulfilled, do whatever your hand finds to do, for God is with you.
>
> "Go down ahead of me to Gilgal. I will surely come down to you to sacrifice burnt offerings and fellowship offerings, but you must wait seven days until I come to you and tell you what you are to do."
>
> As Saul turned to leave Samuel, God changed [*hapak*] Saul's heart, and all these signs were fulfilled that day. When they arrived at Gibeah,

---

24. Cf. Charles Kraft, *Christianity in Culture: A Study in Dynamic Biblical Theologizing in Cross-Cultural Perspective* (Maryknoll, N.Y.: Orbis, 1979); Alan Neely, *Christian Mission: A Case Study Approach* (American Society of Missiology Series 21; Maryknoll, N.Y.: Orbis, 1995).

a procession of prophets met him; the Spirit of God came upon him in power, and he joined in their prophesying. (1 Sam. 10:6–10)

Saul is not "destroyed" but is "colonized" by the Spirit of God. His heart is *overthrown* ("changed"). In the Torah, Prophets, and Writings, "overthrown" is used to describe the "transformation of deliverance" rather than "destruction." All transformation involves the end of something.

- In Deuteronomy it is the end of a curse: "However, the LORD your God would not listen to Balaam but turned [*hapak*] the curse into a blessing for you, because the LORD your God loves you" (Deut. 23:5).
- In Jeremiah mourning comes to an end and becomes gladness. "For the LORD will ransom Jacob and redeem them from the hand of those stronger than they ... Then maidens will dance and be glad, young men and old as well. I will turn [*hapak*] their mourning into gladness; I will give them comfort and joy instead of sorrow" (Jer. 31:11, 13).
- In Psalm 66 the sea that was a barrier to the deliverance of the children of Israel from slavery is transformed: "Come and see what God has done, how awesome his works in man's behalf! He turned [*hapak*] the sea into dry land, they passed through the waters on foot—come, let us rejoice in him" (Ps. 66:5–6).

The four examples cited here are the substance of proclaiming the gospel in the cultures of the world. Like Saul, individual leaders will be transformed from self-serving individuals to people speaking God's word. As with Balaam, the community's curse for God's presence will be turned into a blessing. As when Israel fled slavery following Yahweh, barriers to transformation will also be transformed into pathways. Like Jeremiah people of every culture will proclaim the hope of Yahweh's transformation of the future when mourning will become gladness.

Typology and "the reluctant prophet." Jonah certainly is a reluctant prophet: "But Jonah ran away from the LORD" (1:3); "But Jonah was greatly displeased and became angry" (4:1). Why is he so reluctant?[25] Is it because the (Gentile) Ninevites are not Israelites? That issue is never mentioned in the book, but it has been a common theme among interpreters. This is referred to as the "typological" interpretation of Jonah. In it, Jonah is seen as Israel, reluctant to share the knowledge of God with the world. Nineveh (and the pagan sailors) are said to represent all Gentiles, who are simply eager to receive the knowledge of his justice and mercy.

The argument made is that the welfare of Israel is Jonah's highest value. He wants to see Nineveh destroyed and knows that they will repent and be

---

25. See "Why did Jonah run?" in ch. 1.

forgiven if he preaches. He knows the evil that their continued existence will bring on Israel. It lifts up the eagerness of the Gentiles to hear a word from Yahweh. Their simple and humble piety in repenting is easily contrasted with Jonah's complicated and apparently selfish reservations. It has also been contrasted with Israel's lack of repentance despite its many prophets. The facts of the text, however, simply do not support this symbolic reading. This interpretation has no bearing in the text, undermines its gospel word (forgiveness of the wicked), and tends to promote anti-Semitism.

The issue Jonah has with the Ninevites is not their status in relation to Israel but their wickedness (their status in relation to God). God, Jonah, and the king all recognize that wickedness, not race, is the issue: "Its wickedness has come up before me" (1:2b); "let them give up their evil ways and their violence" (3:8b); "when God saw what they did and how they turned from their evil ways, he had compassion and did not bring upon them the destruction he had threatened" (3:10a).

As Gentiles reading a Jewish Bible, we too quickly identify with the Ninevites and focus on our inclusion in God's gracious actions and his compassion. Certainly the book of Jonah is an opportunity for us to see Yahweh's love for outsiders. (See similar demonstrations toward Hagar and Ishmael in Gen. 21:17–21, Naaman in 2 Kings 5, and Hazael in 2 Kings 8:9–15). If, however, Jonah's racism is addressed by interpreters as implied in the text, care should be taken to own the accusation: The present-day Christian is in the role of Jonah, bearer of the word in the analogy, not in the place of the Ninevites.

Jonah's protest, which is against forgiving wickedness, is a legitimate concern, and to dismiss it as racism subverts the gospel message of the text. God's issue is his love for the whole creation, including the rebellious (Jonah) and the wicked (Ninevites). This is an affront to Jonah, whose theology (and common sense) tells him that the wicked deserve punishment. He was even willing to die for his rebellion. His theology of strict justice is a problem in the text that addresses the present-day reader. Racism (although also a very real modern problem) is not addressed in the historical text.

God calls Jonah a second time in the same way *because he wants the lost saved.* God has determined that his kingdom will come to the whole earth (Ezek. 18:32; John 3:16) and that it will come to Nineveh through Jonah. When God opens his eyes to see the great need in Nineveh, Jonah does not want to see it. The contemporary application of this text is in the great need of the world today. God's call does not allow for the privatization of religion. Whether at home or abroad, God reveals his mission to his people. God's call cannot be ignored by those who pray that his kingdom will not pass them by. God calls a second time because he wants the lost delivered and he wants human participation.

Jonah 4

B UT JONAH WAS greatly displeased and became angry.
²He prayed to the LORD, "O LORD, is this not what I
said when I was still at home? That is why I was so
quick to flee to Tarshish. I knew that you are a gracious and
compassionate God, slow to anger and abounding in love, a
God who relents from sending calamity. ³Now, O LORD, take
away my life, for it is better for me to die than to live."

⁴But the LORD replied, "Have you any right to be angry?"

⁵Jonah went out and sat down at a place east of the city.
There he made himself a shelter, sat in its shade and waited to
see what would happen to the city. ⁶Then the LORD God provided a vine and made it grow up over Jonah to give shade for
his head to ease his discomfort, and Jonah was very happy
about the vine. ⁷But at dawn the next day God provided a
worm, which chewed the vine so that it withered. ⁸When the
sun rose, God provided a scorching east wind, and the sun
blazed on Jonah's head so that he grew faint. He wanted to
die, and said, "It would be better for me to die than to live."

⁹But God said to Jonah, "Do you have a right to be angry
about the vine?"

"I do," he said. "I am angry enough to die."

¹⁰But the LORD said, "You have been concerned about this
vine, though you did not tend it or make it grow. It sprang up
overnight and died overnight. ¹¹But Nineveh has more than a
hundred and twenty thousand people who cannot tell their
right hand from their left, and many cattle as well. Should I
not be concerned about that great city?"

JONAH 4 AGAIN focuses on the prophet's relationship with God as they dialogue about Jonah's anger
over the ways of Yahweh. God argues his preference for compassion, even in horrible circum-
stances. God has compassion for what he has made, no matter how ignorant,
abusive, or violent the culture. Jonah is angry about God's compassion, and God
gives Jonah an object lesson in the form of a vine. He attempts to convince
Jonah (and the reader) that the basic response of compassion for living things

is more important than strict justice. God's primary argument is creational: "If you are moved to pity over the destruction of a vine you did not create, shouldn't I have pity over the destruction of people and animals I did create?" God loves all his creation, for he is "gracious and compassionate" (4:2).

Jonah's Anger with Yahweh (4:1–5)

JONAH FULFILLED HIS calling to Nineveh only under the threat of his own death. Now that his original suspicion concerning Nineveh's survival has been confirmed, Jonah fully expresses his anger with Yahweh's focused compassion (4:1–5).

The first verse uses strong language in Hebrew to express "greatly displeased." Using the words for "evil" and "calamity" (ra'ah, ra'a'), this verse can also be translated, "To Jonah it was a disaster, a great disaster. He became angry." Jonah is angry that Yahweh has had compassion on the evil Ninevites, repentance or not. For him, it is a disaster that they have averted disaster.[1] In 1:12 he demonstrated that he would rather die in the sea than suggest to the sailors that they turn around and return him to Joppa so that he can complete Yahweh's call to him. He has not wanted the Ninevites to survive in any circumstance.

Jonah is filled with burning anger. "He became angry" is expressed in Hebrew by the word *ḥarah* ("burning," as with fire); it can also be translated "was inflamed." This verb is used five times in Jonah:

> 3:9: "Who knows? God may yet relent and with compassion turn from his *fierce anger* so that we will not perish."
>
> 4:1: But Jonah was greatly displeased and became *angry*.
>
> 4:4: But the LORD replied, "Have you any right to be *angry*?"
>
> 4:9a: But God said to Jonah, "Do you have a right to be *angry* about the vine?"
>
> 4:9b: "I do," he said. "I am *angry* enough to die."

Jonah's out-of-control anger over Nineveh's repentance and God's forgiveness is best understood in reference to Nineveh's historical evil. Jonah's anger is a reflection of Yahweh's anger (3:9) over Nineveh's wickedness. But Jonah's anger also stands in contrast to Yahweh's, for he does not believe that their evil should be forgiven. He cannot accept Micah 7:18b: "You do not stay angry forever but delight to show mercy." Jonah explains his anger in Jonah 4:2:

> "O LORD, is this not what I said when I was still at home? That is why I was so quick to flee to Tarshish. I knew that you are a gracious and

---

1. See the introduction for historical background on the evil reputation of the Ninevites.

compassionate God, slow to anger and abounding in love, a God who relents from sending calamity."

This verse carries the richness of Jonah's relationship to Yahweh combined with his disputation against Yahweh. Jonah begins his prayer by crying out with the same petition form that the sailors used in 1:14 (*ʾannah*, "I plead, please, O"), perhaps indicating that Yahweh's ways are as foreign to him as to the sailors. Jonah knows that Yahweh is gracious, compassionate, slow to anger, and abounding in love; he relents from sending calamity. But Jonah does not understand why this should be shared with the evil Ninevites. He suspected that they would repent and that Yahweh would relent, but he doesn't like it and does not want to be part of this forgiveness. More than this, he does not approve of Yahweh's intent or action.

A key to understanding this verse is found in the Hebrew behind the words, "I was so quick [*qiddamti*] to flee to Tarshish." The verb *qadam* in the Piel means "I anticipated" or "I was in front" of the action. It is an advantage for a prophet to know how things will turn out! Jonah is admitting here that he understood the players and the events. His complaint against Yahweh is that he does not like the way of Yahweh's plan for Nineveh.

Jonah goes on: "I knew that you are a gracious and compassionate God, slow to anger and abounding in love, a God who relents from sending calamity." This familiar five-point description of the true God places Jonah in a long line of important Old Testament witnesses (see discussion of the other biblical witnesses in the Bridging Contexts section). (1) "Gracious" or "merciful" derives from a Hebrew word (*hannun*) that appears thirteen times in the Old Testament and is used only of God. God illustrated the meaning of the word in his law against taking collateral for a loan to a poor person[2] in Exodus 22:26–27:

> If you take your neighbor's cloak as a pledge, return it to him by sunset, because his cloak is the only covering he has for his body. What else will he sleep in? When he cries out to me, I will hear, for I am *gracious*.[3]

(2) Yahweh is also *compassionate*. The primary meaning of this word is "to be soft like a womb." It is illustrated in the soft compassion of a mother for her child in the womb. The Ninevites (like the sailors) *hoped* what Jonah has known all along: God is compassionate. The sailors and the Ninevites are a sharp critique on the prophet who selfishly guards this knowledge.

---

2. Limburg, *Jonah*, 91.

3. The NIV uses "compassionate" here.

> Sailors: *Maybe* he will take notice of us, and we will not perish (1:6b).
>
> Ninevite king: *Who knows?* God *may* yet relent and with compassion turn from his fierce anger so that we will not perish (3:9).
>
> Jonah: *I knew* that you are a gracious and compassionate God (4:2b).

(3) Yahweh is *slow to anger*. The Hebrew expression means "forbear, continue long, be patient, postpone anger, tarry long." Proverbs 16:32 translates the phrase, "Better a patient man [one slow to anger] than a warrior." Jonah disagrees that Yahweh should be patient any longer.

(4) Yahweh is *abounding in love*. This is the more intense word for love in Hebrew (ḥesed) and is best understood as God's "unrelenting love," which is God's covenant commitment to his people. With this unrelenting love he binds himself to his promises to them. It is translated in modern Hebrew as "grace" but most often in the English Bible as "steadfast love." Psalm 136 declares in each of its twenty-six verses that this *loyal love* of God "endures forever."

God gave Hosea a marriage metaphor to illustrate this kind of abounding love. Note Hosea 2:19: "I will betroth you to me forever; I will betroth you in righteousness and justice, in *love* and compassion." He tells Hosea to marry a prostitute and to be faithful to her as an example of God's faithfulness to a faithless people: "The LORD said to me, 'Go, show your love to your wife again, though she is loved by another and is an adulteress. *Love her as the LORD loves* the Israelites, though they turn to other gods and love the sacred raisin cakes'" (Hos. 3:1).

The nearest equivalent word in the New Testament is *agape*, translated "unconditional love." Both God's Old Testament "covenant" love and God's New Testament *agape* communicate God's unrelenting love for his creation and his people. Both expressions of love will unconditionally receive the repentant sinner into reconciliation with God. The unconditional love of Jesus reveals this love more fully and radically than the Old Testament (in his incarnation, death, and bodily resurrection), but it is the same love of the Father in each case.

(5) Yahweh is "a God who *relents* from sending calamity." "Relents" (naḥam) is discussed at length elsewhere (see Bridging Contexts section of ch. 3). It is one of the two kinds of God's compassion in this verse. "Compassionate God" (raḥam) is a gentle womb-like compassion of God for his good creation; naḥam is an agonizing compassion of God in relation to a sinful humanity. Jonah quotes God's reputation (see Ex. 34:6–7) for agonizing over sending calamity, even to a wicked people such as the Ninevites (cf. Jonah 3:9–10).

Jonah has had enough of Yahweh's grace, compassion, slowness to anger, love, and relenting toward the wicked. He wants no part of this dangerous game. He therefore says, "Now, O LORD, take away my life, for it is better for me to die than to live" (4:3). Jonah is distraught. He had been the agent of Yahweh's forgiveness to the enemy of his own people. Rather than seeing their just destruction, he has seen their repentance. Would anyone in Israel understand what he had done? Dying was better than living, if the enemy lived.

Jonah has believed this from the beginning (see 1:12). He repeats the refrain later (4:8–9), that he would rather die than be a party to this compassion. Typical of biblical relations with God, the prophet does not hesitate to express his deepest reservations and disagreement. He is confident enough in Yahweh's mercy to him that he is ready to die in it. He cannot live, however, with the social reality of the forgiven Ninevites living in that mercy. These simultaneous realities (his confidence in *and* his objection to God's mercy) present us with the complexity of faith in a Lord who cannot be tamed and whose mercy and forgiveness cannot be controlled. All who attempt to limit God's gracious action share Jonah's protest: Let me die now, your grace is too abundant. I want only the grace that has come *to me*.[4]

But Yahweh replies, "Have you any right to be angry?" (4:4). This question is the most important in the book of Jonah. Yahweh wants to know if Jonah's anger *results in any good*.[5] "Any right" here means "*Is it causing good [tob]* that you burn with anger?" This is a moral question more than a legal one. Jonah does not answer this question but simply walks away from the conversation. God is seeking to engage him in his distress, but Jonah is not ready to talk. (He does answer that question when it is asked again in 4:9.) Cain was asked a similar question (Gen. 4:6) about his anger. He did not answer, but instead went out and killed his brother, Abel. Jonah is at a similar point of moral decision in relation to God.

In 4:5 the reader learns that up to this point Jonah is still in Nineveh. His prayer to Yahweh and Yahweh's response (4:2–4) have been spoken in the city. This may imply that the Ninevites hear Jonah's prayer, *listening in* on the classic confession of faith concerning Yahweh's reputation in Judah. "O LORD, is this not what I said when I was still at home? That is why I was so quick to flee to Tarshish. I knew that you are a gracious and compassionate God, slow to anger and abounding in love, a God who relents from sending calamity" (4:2). Jonah's words in their hearing would have been a further

---

4. See Achtemeier, *Minor Prophets I*, 258. Note Mal. 3:14: "It is futile to serve God."
5. Hiphil of the verb *yaṭab*.

prophecy to the Ninevites in their understanding of Yahweh. They would have learned that their repentance was accepted. Jonah's prayer is the best news a prophet could deliver (compare this with Isa. 40:1–2).

Thus, "Jonah went out and sat down at a place east of the city. There he made himself a shelter, sat in its shade and waited to see what would happen to the city" (4:5). Jonah hopes that God will still destroy the city, in spite of the Ninevites' repentance. He goes to a hill east of the city to wait out the "forty days" (3:4). He waits to see whether the Ninevites' repentance and God's mercy will hold sway. God does not relieve him of his struggle of faith by taking his life as requested (4:3). In the midst of his protest, he leaves both his life and Nineveh in God's hand.

Jonah makes himself a shelter (*sukkah*). This shelter was reminiscent of shelters built in the desert by the Hebrew people as they wandered for forty years. God commanded that these shelters be built every year as a remembrance (the Feast of Booths, Tabernacles, Ingathering, or *sukkoth*) of God's provision for his people during those years of wandering (Lev. 23:39–43; see Ex. 23:16; 34:22; Deut. 16:13–15). In Zechariah 14:16 the Feast of Booths is to be the celebration for the ingathering of all nations to Jerusalem to worship God.

Thus, the presence of an Israelite prophet sitting in a temporary shelter (*sukkah*) evokes themes of the past. It also evokes the theme of Zechariah, begun here in the book of Jonah, that Yahweh is concerned about extending the blessing of his presence to all the cultures of the world and to the whole creation. Jonah waits to see the result of this attempt by Yahweh to extend that blessing to Israel's near neighbor, Nineveh.

Vine, Worm, and Wind (4:6–8)

GOD SEEKS ANOTHER entrance into the conversation with Jonah, this time through the "school" of creation. Yahweh provides an object lesson in order to demonstrate his compassion. Jonah has made a shelter for himself (4:5), but it is apparently not good enough to provide shade from the sun. God appoints "a vine" to shade Jonah, "a worm" to destroy the shade, and "a scorching east wind" to persuade Jonah to speak again. It works. In these three verses Jonah goes from his previous anger to happiness and back to anger. By then he is ready to listen to God again.

"The LORD God" (*yahweh 'elohim*) provides the shade Jonah needs. Note how at each of the crucial junctures in the book of Jonah, the whole title "LORD God" is used.[6]

---

6. In these texts "LORD" (*yahweh*) is a reminder of the personal redeeming work of God. The more general word "God" (*'elohim*) recalls the Creator.

1:9: He answered, "I am a Hebrew and I worship *the* LORD, *the God* of heaven, who made the sea and the land."

2:1: From inside the fish Jonah prayed to the LORD *his* God.

2:6: "To the roots of the mountains I sank down; the earth beneath barred me in forever. But you brought my life up from the pit, O LORD *my God.*"

4:6: Then *the* LORD God provided a vine and made it grow up over Jonah to give shade for his head to ease his discomfort, and Jonah was very happy about the vine.

When "the LORD God" provides a vine to grow up over Jonah to give shade for his head and so ease his discomfort, Jonah is happy (4:6). God ordains the nonhuman creation to call Jonah back into conversation and understanding. Ordinary things (a fish, a vine, a plant, a worm, a sultry wind) are assigned to teach Jonah. The fish protected Jonah from the water. The plant protected him from the sun. The fish returned him to his calling, on dry land. The worm dried or withered the plant, and the scorching wind brought Jonah back into conversation with God. All the nonhuman agents provided or appointed by God bring Jonah back to his calling.

Jonah's head was wrapped in weeds (2:5), shaded (4:6), and scorched by the sun (4:8). The fish was Jonah's first deliverance, and the vine was his second deliverance. The fish delivered physical safety and the vine physical ease. The vine also eased Jonah out of his evil temper and into a new hearing of God's perspective on the recent events in Nineveh. The expression "to ease his discomfort" is (lit.) "to deliver him from his calamity [ra'ah]." The Hebrew text invites a three-way comparison between Jonah's first calamity in the storm (and deliverance), Nineveh's pending calamity (and deliverance), and Jonah's trouble with the sun.

1:7: Then the sailors said to each other, "Come, let us cast lots to find out who is responsible for *this calamity [ra'ah].* They cast lots and the lot fell on Jonah.

3:10b: He had compassion and did not bring upon them *the destruction [ra'ah]* he had threatened.

4:6: Then the LORD God provided a vine and made it grow up over Jonah to give shade for his head to ease his *discomfort [ra'ah],* and Jonah was very happy about the vine.

Jonah was very happy about his first deliverance from "calamity" in the sea (2:9). He was also very happy about his deliverance from the "discomfort" (4:6) of the sun. He was not at all happy, however, about the Ninevites' deliverance from their "destruction" (4:1–3). Yahweh uses this contrast in his final question to Jonah (see 4:11).

A grub that God also "provides" kills the shade-giving vine that has made Jonah so joyful. The "withered" (dried up) vine is an echo (for Jonah's Hebrew audience) of the "dry land" of Jonah's early confession of faith (1:9: "I worship the LORD ... who made the sea and *the land*."). It also echoes the "dry land" toward which the sailors desperately rowed (see comments on "dry land" at 1:13) and onto which Jonah was vomited (2:10). The "withering" signals God's action toward Jonah's deliverance, just as the dry land was previously a place of deliverance.

"When the sun rose, God provided a scorching east wind, and the sun blazed on Jonah's head so that he grew faint" (4:8a). The wind, also provided by God, "blazes" hot (like Jonah's previous anger in 4:1, 4, 9) on Jonah's head (cf. 4:6) until he has a sunstroke. He wants to die (lit., "he asked his life to die," 4:8b). If Yahweh will not take his life, he hopes his life will just fail. This comment, to no one in particular, leads into the second round of the same conversation between Jonah and Yahweh in chapter 4. Jonah repeats the petulant comment that ended his previous conversation with the LORD (see italics):

4:3: "Now, O LORD, take away my life, *for it is better for me to die than to live.*"
4:4: But the LORD replied, "Have you any right to be angry?"
4:8b: He wanted to die, and said, *"It would be better for me to die than to live."*
4:9: But God said to Jonah, "Do you have a right to be angry about the vine?" "I do," he said. "I am angry enough *to die.*"

Jonah has been presented with the "school of creation" and has not learned anything. Yahweh now proceeds to explain things to him (4:9–11). This time Jonah does not walk away but responds to Yahweh.

Yahweh Reasons with Jonah Concerning Anger (4:9–11)

THE BOOK CONCLUDES with a question for Jonah concerning Yahweh's motivation. In 4:9 Yahweh reasons with Jonah and declares a Creator's love for all he has made regardless of its intelligence (vine, Ninevites, and animals). God's statement in 4:9 echoes their earlier conversation in 4:4 ("Have you any right to be angry?") and again raises the question of Jonah's narrow perspective on the Ninevites and God's forgiveness.

This conversation is, on the surface, about the death of the vine. Its life/death has not only caused him joy but also brought on his sunstroke. Jonah's anger over the continuation of Nineveh's existence remains just beneath the surface. In 4:8 Jonah speaks at first to no one in particular (cf. 4:3). But Yahweh listens and engages him with his previous question, focusing this time on the vine rather than Nineveh. Jonah responds verbally to Yahweh this time rather than just walking away, as he did in 4:5. For the first time he admits his anger to God.

Jonah doesn't want to consider an alternative to his anger. God, however, offers him a new perspective (4:10) as an opportunity for Jonah to be transformed. We are not told whether Jonah accepts it. The vine is an object lesson that, like parables in the New Testament, takes an unexpected turn. God describes the importance of the vine in much different terms than Jonah. It is this difference that sets up the key contrast for us between Jonah's and God's perspectives.

Jonah is concerned about the vine as a protection and comfort to him. God, however, takes Jonah's concern over the vine and turns his attention to its intrinsic value as something he has created. Jonah's concern (anger) over the death of the vine is "right," but for the wrong reason. God reminds Jonah of the Creator-created relationship ("You did not tend it or make it grow," 4:10b). Jonah has overlooked the role of the Creator in his concern for his own protection and comfort. The Creator's concern is precisely the perspective Jonah lacks concerning Nineveh. That perspective on the creation turns the chosen prophet "inside-out."

Jonah's concern for the life/death of the vine is also God's concern, but God's concern extends to "more than a hundred and twenty thousand people who cannot tell their right hand from their left, and many cattle as well" (4:11a). Having elicited some concern from Jonah over a living thing, God asks Jonah to understand his extension of concern for an ignorant population: "Should I not be concerned [*ḥus*][7] about that great city?" (4:11b).[8] To paraphrase God's concern, "If you feel compassionate about the destruction of a vine you did not create, shouldn't I be concerned about the destruction of people and animals I did create?"

God presents his warrants for his compassion and pity on Nineveh (which Jonah cannot understand) by appealing to feelings of compassion Jonah has just experienced in the destruction of the fibrous vine. God's argument does not take Nineveh's evil reputation into account at all, since they have repented and turned away from their violent ways. (Jonah cannot forgive so easily.) God invites Jonah to see the tender heart of a Creator, desperate to be reconciled to the creation he has tended and made to grow. He also invites Jonah to share in this mission of reconciliation of enemies and to share his logic and pity (*ḥus*).

It is impossible to tell whether Yahweh is using humor to jostle Jonah's cantankerous attitude, or whether Yahweh's concern extends equally to the cattle

---

7. This word means "having tears in one's eyes" (cf. Jesus' tears over Jerusalem in Luke 19:41); see Limburg, *Jonah*, 97.

8. See Bridging Contexts for a discussion of the expression "people who cannot tell their right hand from their left."

of Nineveh.[9] In either case, God's concern for cattle is the last statement of the Hebrew text. It leaves Jonah with the image he has seen in Nineveh of the king's decree: sackcloth on animals (3:8). The image seems to express humor and ignorance at the same time (cows can't repent). Yahweh's question invites Jonah to consider the pity on Nineveh from another (creational) perspective.

God also pushes the implied contrast between Jonah's deliverance from "discomfort" (*ra^{c}ah* in 4:6) and Nineveh's deliverance from "destruction" (*ra^{c}ah* in 3:10). Yahweh could well have mentioned Jonah's deliverance from the "calamity" (*ra^{c}ah* in 1:7) at sea. On a scale of trouble, the death of 120,000 people would seem to outweigh the loss of a shade vine (or even a ship at sea).

The last verse confronts the reader again with the Ninevites, who have repented of their evil ways and turned to God. It is a "great city" to God.[10] It confronts the reader with the unanswered question posed to Jonah, "Should I not be concerned?" (4:11b).

Why does God raise the issue of the Ninevites' ignorance ("people who cannot tell their right hand from their left")? God offers another warrant of pity for Jonah to consider. If they are so ignorant, how many of them could be responsible parties in the Assyrian war machine? Many were ignorant of any other way of being human and were pulled along by a ruthless government. God asks Jonah to look more deeply into the causes behind their reprehensible history against Israel and to seek those causes in pity. Prophetic judgment and the repentance of the wicked were both God's way of reforming the enemy of his chosen people.

The opposite of ignorance is not education in general. One might assume that the Ninevites simply need to be educated about what is right and wrong and the results of right and wrong action. The words of the king to the people demonstrate that knowledge of good and evil is not the problem (3:8b, "Let them give up their evil ways and their violence"). Their ignorance is of Yahweh, Creator of heaven and earth, who seeks just relationships within the creation. The opposite of ignorance in Jonah is worship and justice.

The book ends with an open question about God's way in the world. The question's importance is heightened when the narrative ends without either a concluding statement about the fate of the city or Jonah's response. We already know from 3:10 that the city will not be destroyed. Jonah, however, is left sitting on the hillside. He must simply sit and ponder God's logic: "I made them, so I pity them. Can't you see that?"

---

9. A third interpretive possibility is the poetic rendering, who are "as dumb as their cows"; see D. R. Slavitt, *The Book of the Twelve Prophets* (Oxford: Oxford Univ. Press, 2000), 68.

10. Cf. 1:2; 3:2, 3; 4:11. Archaeology has confirmed the possibility of a city of 120,000 people.

The book of Jonah forced Israel and Judah to consider that their Deliverer and Lord was not theirs alone, but the Creator of a wide creation that included other peoples. This wideness included their enemies as well as the nonhuman creation. At a time when other prophets preached about a "faithful remnant" in Judah, Jonah proclaimed a Creator whose concern for his remnant people did not preclude his concern and action on behalf of other peoples. The inclusion of the book of Jonah in the Hebrew Bible was a brilliant faithfulness to the broad vision given to Abraham in Genesis 12:3b, "All peoples on earth will be blessed through you" (see Isa. 42:6–7; 49:6). The book's viewpoint pushed the chosen people's range of vision extravagantly wider at a time when the national consciousness (both before and after the Exile) threatened to narrow.

THE CENTER OF the debate in chapter 4 pits Jonah's perspective on strict justice against God's compassion for even the most heinous sinners. Jonah's last substantive statement in this chapter summarizes his perspective: "That is why I was so quick to flee to Tarshish. I knew that you are a gracious and compassionate God, slow to anger and abounding in love, a God who relents from sending calamity" (4:2b).

Commonsense logic prevails in Jonah's perspective. The wicked should pay for their crimes, not be forgiven. Jonah's issue with God is an enduring issue. The Assyrians deserved punishment for their war crimes. This logic was widely shared then and is still commonplace among those who have suffered the sort of terror that Israel suffered at the hands of the Ninevites. When agents of terror apologize or even repent of their wrongdoing, victims and witnesses are not usually impressed. God does not suggest that justice should not or will not eventually be done. He simply argues that he would rather forgive and take the risks of letting evil persist in the world. This is a difficult dilemma for all people of faith.

The parallel themes in chapters 2 and 4 help us understand the enduring problem of trusting/not trusting God for the future. God sends the fish (in ch. 2) and the vine (ch. 4) to rescue/comfort Jonah, and he is grateful in both cases. God's forgiveness saves Nineveh from destruction, but Jonah thinks of Nineveh's rescue as a threat, more like the worm and the wind that oppress him. He gives thanks for his own rescue but is angry over Nineveh's deliverance. He does not want to rely on God for the future, in spite of the evidence that God's grace is wide enough to continue to care for him *and the Ninevites*.

The missing response is Jonah's *thanks* for Nineveh's repentance. He could have been thankful that Yahweh let him participate in this work of salvation.

As with the fish, he could have been grateful that he was "engulfed" and overwhelmed by Nineveh's unusual response. He would then have given thanks that he could be included in the surprising grace of the enemy's reconciliation to God. A true parallel between the chapters would include Jonah's recognition of God's grace in the midst of trouble (the belly of the fish and Nineveh's continuance as a world power). He cannot give that witness, but his failure invites us to consider whether we can.

A witness for God. The anchor of faith expressed in 4:2 is an enduring witness to Jonah's God. Seven places in the Old Testament use the creed: "You are a gracious and compassionate God, slow to anger and abounding in love." These attributes of Yahweh's character are used together in a variety of circumstances to build up the believer. Consider the following witnesses to what has been called an Old Testament confession of faith or creed concerning God.[11]

(1) The first use of this revelation of God is Yahweh's self-description to Moses after he forgave the people for the worship of the golden calf. They have been redeemed by God's decision to declare his unchanging reputation before them and the world:

> And [the LORD] passed in front of Moses, proclaiming, "The LORD, the LORD, the compassionate and gracious God, slow to anger, abounding in love and faithfulness, maintaining love to thousands, and forgiving wickedness, rebellion and sin. Yet he does not leave the guilty unpunished." (Ex. 34:6–7a)

(2) The prophet Joel warns of the coming judgment but reminds the people that it is not too late to *repent*, because of God's reputation. "Rend your heart and not your garments. Return to the LORD your God, for he is gracious and compassionate, slow to anger and abounding in love, and he relents from sending calamity" (Joel 2:13).

(3) David expresses his joy at Yahweh's forgiveness of his sin, declaring that "as far as the east is from the west, so far has he removed our transgressions from us" (Ps. 103:12). He knows this because of God's historic reputation: "The LORD is compassionate and gracious, slow to anger, abounding in love" (Ps. 103:8).

(4) Likewise, in Psalm 145 David declares pure praise to the Creator and Redeemer for his works and salvation. After introducing this theme, he begins his description of Yahweh's great gifts with this creed: "The LORD is gracious and compassionate, slow to anger and rich in love" (Ps. 145:8).

---

11. See Achtemeier, *Minor Prophets I*, 279. Portions of this ancient creed can also be found in Num. 14:18; 2 Chron. 30:9; Ps. 111:4; Micah 7:18; and Nahum 1:3.

(5) After the people returned from exile in Babylon and rebuilt the wall of Jerusalem, they gathered to rededicate themselves in confession to live faithfully before God. Ezra the priest reminded them of the many ways their forbears had rebelled and suffered the severe consequences of sin, yet God had not abandoned them. He reminded them of the more than thousand-year history of Yahweh's faithfulness to them, even in judgment. Their confidence that God would receive their repentance and renew his covenant that day was based on the creed: "But you are a forgiving God, gracious and compassionate, slow to anger and abounding in love. Therefore you did not desert them" (Neh. 9:17b).

(6) The psalmist too knew that though the arrogant were attacking him for his failings, Yahweh would still receive him. "But you, O Lord, are a compassionate and gracious God, slow to anger, abounding in love and faithfulness" (Ps. 86:15).

(7) Finally, Jonah recites this reputation to God as the primary reason for his discontent. He is not faithless in doing so. Rather, he invites the reader to consider the radical implications of such a God. It means that *evil will endure longer* on the earth, for God is slow to anger. It means that God's grace, love, and compassion will be extended to the rebellious, wayward, and even the violent in the world.

God does not respond to Jonah by declaring that the wicked will meet their just reward (as they will). Rather, he affirms his reputation by assuring Jonah of his care for the ignorant wicked, even for the cattle! Jonah's complaint helps us to consider the full burden of believing and serving such a God. It means that the world will be a place where the potential for great evil will remain, precisely because God hopes for the salvation of the wicked. This is a complex faith that challenges even the true prophet of God, and it continues to challenge believers to trust God more completely for the future.[12]

A timeless attitude: "I am angry enough to die." "Now, O LORD, take away my life, for it is better for me to die than to live" (4:3). Jonah looks to death three times as a way out of his disagreement with Yahweh. He never attempts to take his own life, but he does ask the sailors (1:12) and Yahweh (twice) to take it (4:3, 9). Why does Jonah despair so completely? Even with God as his counselor, his attitude toward life seems resolutely despondent.

Jonah has good reasons for this attitude. The order of the world as he knows it is coming apart. All the foundational convictions of his world view are being challenged. Fundamentally, his theology *about* God is crumbling through his experience and conversation *with* God. His depressive attitude

---

12. See 2 Peter 3:3–9, which takes up the same challenging issue.

settles like sediment. He does not want to let go of his formulations about the character of God. If even a true prophet of God lived with illusions about who God is, how much more cautious might we be in our formulations about how God should act. Jonah's disposition is based on at least six related perspectives.

1. *God* should not be the kind of God who forgives violently evil people, even if they repent. Evil should be punished, not forgiven.
2. *Justice*, to be just, requires that people suffer the full consequences of their actions, whether they are repentant or not. Nineveh has to be destroyed in order for justice to prevail.
3. *Nineveh* has been too evil to effect a true repentance and receive forgiveness. Nineveh cannot be truly repentant. Even if they could be, forgiveness cannot effectively begin a new life for them.
4. *People* need to be able to trust in a consistent, God-given, cosmic order. Trust in an ultimate structure of the moral universe is necessary for faith in God and ethical living.
5. *Living faithfully* loses its positive value if evil people are forgiven through simple repentance. Struggling daily to obey God's law looks foolish when forgiveness is given freely.
6. *The triumph of evil living* is flaunted if the evil escape judgment in the last days (they were given forty days) through repentance. This flaunting is too much for the victims of evil actions and those who are weary of those who are evil escaping punishment.

Jonah's perspectives on God's actions have some merit. God was "slow to anger" with him and engaged his concerns from God's perspective. God did not judge Jonah's attitude harshly but worked toward maintaining the relationship. He attempted to help him out of his theology and into God's dilemma: God loves all his creation, even what has become wicked.

Is Jonah a foolish prophet or in serious distress? Scholars have argued a wide range of interpretations of Jonah the prophet along this spectrum:

Anti-prophet: Some argue that Jonah represents the *end of prophecy* in Israel. Prophecy did, of course, come to an end in the fifth century B.C. This interpretation sees Jonah's struggle to speak a word as a representing the cessation of the direct speech of God to Israel and her neighbors.

Foolish prophet: Jonah is sometimes held up to ridicule as a foolish prophet. The reader looks at his actions from above and sees the irony of his running from the God of the sea, on the sea. He thanks God from within the slime of a fish's belly. He complains about grace. Finally he is absurd in wanting to die over a withered plant, while oddly not caring about the 120,000 lives in Nineveh. He seems foolish and pathetic.

Comic figure: Jonah can make us laugh. He is comic in the classical Greek fifth century B.C. sense.[13] Jonah seems comic. He is more than funny. By his dramatic responses he entertains but also invites the reader to a deeper level of understanding. This designation may not be helpful to those living in an entertainment-oriented society. Comedy in Western societies generally has deteriorated into amusement only. If "Jonah, the comedy" is only amusing, the joke is unfortunately on the uninformed reader, not on Jonah.

True prophet: Jonah acts the way he does for reasons that are given, but they are not expanded in the text. His actions are related to the social and political circumstances of his historical setting. He seems like an *anti-prophet*, yet he stands firmly in the prophetic tradition (protest, conversation with God, struggles with the content of the revelation). He seems *foolish* because he is caught in a life-and-death struggle, is a witness to atrocities, and is deeply convicted of his religious views on justice. When the reader does not share these kinds of experiences, Jonah and his perspective can be incomprehensible; he seems *comic*, but only in the classical sense of the satirical, political, and social comic who must grapple with how to respond to the violently wicked. Jonah is a *true prophet*. He is involved in a true struggle, a struggle we would rather not admit, since it is our unresolved struggle as well. It is a struggle to participate in the dialogue, to own up to the fact that there is a true struggle in God and in us.

Yahweh does make some progress with Jonah by refocusing his emotions. At the beginning of chapter 4, Jonah is angry that *someone* (Ninevites) didn't die. At the end he is angry that *something* (the vine) *did* die. This tiny window is the opening that Yahweh creates in Jonah's emotions to help him understand the Creator's perspective.

God has often used nonhuman agents to "provide" a way of understanding for people of the Bible. God communicated his intent by or through various birds, fish, and mammals. Balaam's donkey spoke to him (Num. 22:22–33). In the Elijah/Elisha narratives, ravens (1 Kings 17:4–6), lions (1 Kings 20:35–36), and two bears (2 Kings 2:23–25) were all used to reveal God's will. A dove landed on Jesus and remained there after his baptism by John (Matt. 3:16; Mark 1:10; Luke 3:22; John 1:32). A storm did Jesus' bidding to teach the disciples on the Sea of Galilee (Matt. 8:26–27; Mark 4:39–41). A fish carried a coin for Jesus' and Peter's Roman tax (Matt. 17:25–27). Jonah's vine, worm, and "scorching east wind" likewise teach. Each of these incidents is in

---

13. "The Old Comedy . . . consisted chiefly of political and social satire commonly directed at contemporary men and issues"; see "comedy" in *Webster's New International Dictionary Unabridged*, 2d ed. (Springfield, Mass.: G. S. C. Merriam Co., 1947).

the tradition of God's use of the nonhuman creation to accomplish or to teach his intent in the world.[14]

People who cannot tell their right hand from their left. The key to Jonah's special contribution to the canon is found in God's question about the people of Nineveh: "But Nineveh has more than a hundred and twenty thousand people *who cannot tell their right hand from their left*, and many cattle as well. *Should I not be concerned* about that great city?" (4:11).

Commentators do not agree on the object of God's concern. Who are the people "who cannot tell their right from their left"? Some have suggested that this means young children who have literally not yet learned the difference between their two hands (as in Deut. 1:39).[15] Others suggest that the figure of speech means that the Ninevites lack a developed ethical discernment, or they lack knowledge of God's law and therefore are not responsible for their actions; they are "virtual children."[16] Certainly the Ninevites are helpless in their ignorance (cf. the Israelites in Amos 7:2, 5).[17] But in Jonah they are also rational people, who are responsible for their actions and are quick to repent. We miss the point of God's question if we limit the expression "right hand from their left" to helplessness. The expression means all of the Ninevites who are *ignorant, but still responsible.*

God's point is that they are capable and responsible, but are ignorant *in their culture of sin.* This is why repentance, not education, is necessary. They don't know their right from their left because they have a developed and rational culture of violence. Commentators forget that Hitler's Germany was the product of the great philosophical traditions of the West. It was rational and "responsible"—and entirely ignorant of the reality of God at the same time. The expression "right from left" does not mean "innocent," "children," or "ignorant" of rational and moral reasoning. It means "ignorant of God in their culture of violence." Their crisis, in God's eyes, is that they are both ignorant and responsible.

If Jonah is taken seriously *as a prophet of God*, then his opinion and perspective must be taken seriously.[18] Jonah's anger is about embarking on the mission to the Ninevites at all, even to warn them about destruction. Warning gives them the opportunity to enter into a protective relationship with God, which Jonah believes they cannot possibly keep. He fears they will

---

14. Job 12:7–12 offers an interesting commentary on the concept of nature teaching us.

15. Simon, *Jonah*, 47.

16. See Joyce Baldwin, "Jonah," in *The Minor Prophets*, ed. Thomas McComisky (Grand Rapids: Baker, 1993), 2:590; Leslie C. Allen, *The Books of Joel, Obadiah, Jonah, and Micah* (NICOT; Grand Rapids: Eerdmans, 1976), 234.

17. Limburg, *Jonah*, 97.

18. Sherwood, *A Biblical Text and Its Afterlives*, 273.

remain a threat. A lasting repentance is rarely possible when a culture is permeated by violent structures. A radical transformation of the culture is necessary. Jonah knows it can't last.

Moreover, when the scribes included this book in the scroll of the twelve minor prophets, they knew it hadn't lasted. *The canonical original meaning assumes that we know that.* If we know that their repentance did not hold, then Jonah's prophetic dialogue with Yahweh must be taken seriously. God wants to know whether we understand that the risks of reaching the rebellious are worth the possibility of transforming a culture and an enemy into friends of God.

 APPLICATIONS. We can make many significant applications of Jonah 4. (1) God's love for the whole creation is placed in front of the reader in the final question of the book ("Should I not be concerned . . . ?"). A city distant from Israel, filled with ignorant people (and all its cattle), is placed before us as a primary object of God's concern and love. The answer to God's question is left open for us, but the answer God seeks from Jonah and from us is clearly, "Yes." God's intention is for all to know his love, insider and outsider alike. We are called to affirm his intention and to participate in the communication of his concern and love.[19]

(2) Another significant application is our common human experience of protection and exposure in relation to God.[20] So many of our actions to protect or shield ourselves from life are vain attempts to ward off catastrophe or trouble. Only God can save. Jonah seeks safety in the belly of a ship but finds it only in God's fish. He seeks protection by building a shelter, but God's plant gives him true shade. When the plant is killed, he will finally talk with God about his anger and listens to God's concern for the protection and salvation of all creation.

Seeking protection apart from God leads to false security because life is fragile and unpredictable. Jonah constantly searches for shelter, and each shelter (ship, fish, hut, plant) fails him in the end, even when provided by God.[21] Jonah even seeks shelter inside his narrow worldview and narrow theology, both of which God deconstructs for him. We all rightly seek security and salvation in life and protection from death. Only when we fully rely on the God of Scripture and do not substitute his provisions (or our own provision) for the source of our security will we integrate this message of Jonah

---

19. See ibid., 98, for this theme.
20. Thanks to Sherwood, *A Biblical Text and Its Afterlives*, 279–80, for developing this significance.
21. Ibid., 280.

in our lives. Only then will we be able to live securely between the false protection of "very happy" (4:6) and "angry enough to die" (4:9).

(3) Jonah 4 also serves as a primer on human anger.[22] Jonah becomes
angry (4:1), God is "slow" to anger (4:2), and God asks twice whether it is
good for Jonah to be angry (cf. comments on translating "good" instead of
"Is it right" at 4:4). God asks questions about anger, but he does not condemn
it. He provides a model for counseling angry people and for dealing with
personal issues of anger. God invites a conversation about the value of anger.
Jonah knows that his anger leads to death, but he cannot let it go (see comments on the "psychophysical language" of the Hebrew "burning of the
nostrils").[23]

God does not insist that Jonah let his anger go; he simply raises the question. Then he offers the opportunity to work through the issues in a conversation about the plant, worm, and vine. He leads him to see his capacity
for compassion (for the plant) as an avenue beyond his anger. This gives
Jonah the option of moving beyond his self-absorption and self-justification
by inviting him on a journey of faith in God. Even God turns from destroying Nineveh to have compassion on them (3:9–10).[24] The discussion is not
resolved, but it remains open for Jonah and for the reader to participate in
answering the final question. God's love for the whole creation is a better context for understanding our own salvation as well.

(4) Jonah's "concern" is the opening God takes to teach about God's own
motivations (cf. references to God's being "concerned" in 4:10 and 11). His
invitation is for us to understand and act in accord with his way in the world.
"Concern" means "to take action with tears flowing down the cheeks" (see
comments on 4:10–11). This kind of "concern" is "suffering action."

Here God takes upon *himself* the evil of Nineveh. He bears the weight of
its violence, the pain of a thousand plundered cities, including Israel's. God
chooses to suffer in place of Nineveh. His tears flow instead of theirs. Someday he may even choose to die.[25]

Nowhere in the Old Testament is God's struggle with concern or pity for
the repentant wicked more transparent. But note how Hosea 11:5–9 also
dramatically demonstrates Yahweh's struggle with punishment and forgiveness of his wayward people. The same theme is echoed in Jesus' words over
Jerusalem in Matthew 23:37–39 (cf. Luke 13:34–35):

---

22. Trible, "The Book of Jonah," 524–25, develops this theme.
23. This is Trible's apt expression (ibid., 524).
24. Ibid., 525.
25. Terence Fretheim, *The Message of Jonah: A Theological Commentary* (Minneapolis: Augsburg, 1997), 130.

O Jerusalem, Jerusalem, you who kill the prophets and stone those sent to you, how often I have longed to gather your children together, as a hen gathers her chicks under her wings, but you were not willing. Look, your house is left to you desolate. For I tell you, you will not see me again until you say, "Blessed is he who comes in the name of the Lord."

Jesus preached repentance from sin and returning to God during his ministry and struggled when people would not believe (Matt. 4:17; 11:20). His cry to Jerusalem does not end in despair but declares that they will say, "Blessed is he...." Peter and Paul also carried a message of repentance and faith to the Jews and the Gentiles with mixed success (Acts 2:38; 20; 21). The significance of Jonah 4 is how it elucidates, in a real historical context, our struggle with the wicked who repent. The wicked who repent are often not converted for long. God's mercy to them seems extravagant and ultimately wasted. God works with Jonah (and us) to help us understand his way in the world and the extent of his love for the whole creation.

Human communities, including most world religious communities, are governed by means of a consistent application of well-defined rules of obligation and responsibility and consequential rewards and punishments. Biblical writers acknowledge the order and "grain of the universe" and its ordering by a just Judge of all the earth.[26] Jonah the prophet shares this tradition. His word is to be taken seriously as part and parcel of the divine revelation of the book. His opinions about justice echo a long and strong biblical tradition (cf. Ex. 21:23–25; Lev. 24:17–21; Ps. 92:6–9).

Jonah's view of strict justice is not nullified by the book. It is upheld, particularly when we consider that the prophet was right. Nineveh was destroyed. The Ninevites' repentance did not hold very long. By the time the book made it into its final form (fifth century B.C.) and into the final biblical canon (A.D. 90), Nineveh was a distant memory (destroyed early in the seventh century B.C.).

God's argument for a more compassionate justice, based in a love for his wayward and ignorant creation (4:11), is not a refutation of the creational order of reward and punishment but an additional revelation concerning God's ways in the world. God does not abandon his word of judgment on the wicked or his word of blessing for the obedient. He simply demonstrates that the blessing for the obedient is *founded on* his unrelenting love. The obedient are already recipients of the grace of his law and the blessings and power that accompany keeping and guarding that law in life. That same grace is demon-

---

26. Cf. Stanley Hauerwas, *With the Grain of the Universe: The Church's Witness and Natural Theology* (Gifford Lectures; Grand Rapids: Brazos, 2001).

strated in a new and outrageous way toward the ignorant and violent rebels of Nineveh.

The extension of grace to the rebellious is not a repudiation of cosmic justice but the freedom of God to deliver unpredictably the unlikely creature. This radical grace is the hope of all cultures that turn in arrogance from the Creator. It is also the hope of the faithful law-keeper who is ignorant that God's grace and mercy undergird every law's intent, every righteous action, every inherited tradition, and every life that is open to its Creator. The grace is the same though its shape is different.

God's openness to all who repent is seen in the Jewish tradition of the Afternoon Service on the Day of Atonement (Yom Kippur). After the reading of the book of Jonah, the service supplies a response to Yahweh's final question ("Should I not pity Nineveh"), using the words of the prophet Micah in Micah 7:18–20:[27]

> Who is a God like you,
>> who pardons sin and forgives the transgression
>> of the remnant of his inheritance?
> You do not stay angry forever
>> but delight to show mercy.
> You will again have compassion on us;
>> you will tread our sins underfoot
>> and hurl all our iniquities into the depths of the sea.
> You will be true to Jacob,
>> and show mercy to Abraham,
> as you pledged on oath to our fathers
>> in days long ago.

With these words the congregation acknowledges that they, Jonah, and the Ninevites are all in the same basic relationship to Yahweh. All must accept Yahweh's forgiveness and compassion, recognizing that they also need it. All should turn and praise God for the lightening of iniquity's heavy burden of guilt.

Endings. In Christian readings, the book of Jonah ends with an open question (4:11). The rhetorical force of such an ending is comparable to the original ending of the gospel Mark: "They said nothing to anyone because they were afraid" (Mark 16:8). In each case the reader is confronted with the possibility that this *may be* the end. But the open endings hook the reader with their disequilibrium. The Gospel does not end with "no one" hearing. Two millennia later *we* have heard.[28] As we know from the other Gospels, someone

---

27. Simon, *Jonah*, xiii.

28. See Donald Juel, *Mark* (Augsburg Commentary on the New Testament; Minneapolis: Augsburg, 1990), 229–35.

told somebody! Mark's ending challenges us with the fact that for the resurrection of Jesus to transform the world, the news must be spoken. *We* cannot be silent. So with Jonah, the open question is not the end of the story. We are challenged to consider that God's concern must also be our concern.

If the theme in chapter 1 is *down* (1:3, 5), and for chapter 3 is *upside down* (3:4), the theme in chapter 4 is *inside out*. Jonah, God's chosen prophet, is at odds with Yahweh, while the evil Ninevites have received Yahweh's approval for their repentance. From Jonah's perspective, grace is being turned inside out. The alternative to his anger is for him to be turned inside out. His anger echoes Cain's anger with Abel over his favor with Yahweh. Genesis 4 and Jonah 4 have a similar vocabulary. In each text God asks Cain/Jonah a question about their anger (*harah;* Gen. 4:6–7; Jonah 4:4). God asks them to consider "right" (*tob*) from God's perspective (Gen. 4:7; Jonah 4:4). In each case "he went out ... and lived/sat ... east" (Gen. 4:16; Jonah 4:5).

These similarities invite a comparison of themes. Cain did not like Yahweh's decision to favor his brother. God asked Cain the question, "Why are you angry? ... If you do what is right, will you not be accepted?" (Gen. 4:6–7). Cain, like Jonah, was so angry he wanted to see the favored one(s) die (Gen. 4:8). Since Jonah cannot annihilate the Ninevites himself, he wants death for himself, and says so three times (4:3, 8, 9). At stake in both cases is the deep-seated human desire to limit and control God's favor for one's own political or economic advantage. Jonah mirrors Cain's murder in another twisted form, that is, in the desire for his own death.

Commonsense justice. The commonsense view of (strict) justice is more deeply ingrained in us than we care to admit. Jesus makes it the subject of his parable on the workers in the field and their compensation (Matt. 20:1–16). "No fair" is a typical response of children to benefits given to another at an adult's discretion. More weightily, many reject God or the idea of a beneficent God precisely because he allows evil people to work their abuses and crimes on humanity without just recompense or punishment. The typical statement is, "I cannot believe in a God who would allow...." Common sense tells us that in an ordered and good creation, those guilty of abuse and violence should be brought to strict justice.

Wickedness thrives in the world exactly because the Judge of all the earth does not execute the full weight of the law on them. If the Judge judged justly, *only* those who lived well, in peace with their neighbors, in honesty in their relationships, and in the fear of Yahweh, would thrive and know salvation. Yet the wicked not only thrive, but God also forgives them when they turn to him. This is a double insult to commonsense justice. Common sense argues that God risks weakening the authority of the law by diminishing the consequences of unjust living and the fear of sin. Second, common sense argues that God's delay in punishing the wicked weakens the positive incentive for living a good life, since mercy is freely given.

These problems are ancient and are not "solved." Malachi faced the same issues in his opponents' hard questions[29]:

> You have *wearied* the LORD with your words.
> "How have we *wearied* him?" you ask.
> By saying, "All who do evil are good in the eyes of the LORD, and he is pleased with them" or "Where is the God of justice?" (Mal. 2:17)

> "You have said *harsh* things against me," says the LORD.
> "Yet you ask, 'What have we said against you?'
> "You have said, 'It is futile to serve God. What did we gain by carrying out his requirements and going about like mourners before the LORD Almighty? But now we call the arrogant blessed. Certainly the evildoers prosper, and even those who challenge God escape.'" (Mal. 3:13–15; italics added in both quotes)

God's random reversals, long-suffering (slowness to anger), delay of the final judgment, freedom and the mystery of forgiveness in setting sinners free, and mysterious wedding of mercy and justice elude the lost. The alternative to strict justice that God offers Nineveh (and to which Jonah objects) is not only compassion. It is certainly not weakness. It is the preaching of judgment, followed by repentance (not simply confession), and it results in God's compassion.

This concept of forgiveness is deemed ridiculous by other religions. A Hindu professor of European history once impartially presented the Reformers' preaching of salvation by grace through faith in Jesus Christ in Romans. Then he offered his opinion on the matter of salvation by faith in anything. "It is ridiculous and absurd. This is meaningless. Faith is nothing. Salvation comes by how you live." Islam carries the same conviction. Repentance is possible, but the final judgment is based on weighing the good in one's life against the bad. If the good weighs more, one enters paradise.[30]

These religious views of salvation are extensions of human common sense about the way the world should be and how God should judge. God's message to Jonah invites him into a new understanding of God in relation to the world. According to "common sense," God errs on the side of compassion toward those who are furthest from him and his intent for his creation.

---

29. For an excellent discussion of these issues see James L. Crenshaw, "Theodicy in the Book of the Twelve," *Society of Biblical Literature 2001 Seminar Papers* (Atlanta: Society of Biblical Literature, 2001), 1–18.

30. See the Qur'an 101:6–9; 23:62; 45:29.

Why God allows wickedness. What is the timeless truth of Jonah's dialogue with Yahweh? It is Yahweh's answer to the timeless question, "Why does God allow wickedness and violence to persist in the world?" *God goes to great lengths and trouble to allow for the unlikely and random possibility of the reversal of the violent through repentance.* This truth is not presented simply or abstractly but through Jonah's great struggle in a real and difficult historical setting. Four observations help to demonstrate the weight and import of this struggle.

(1) The power of violent terror is a real threat. Like modern states that sponsor terrorism, Nineveh reigned by terrorizing vulnerable noncombatants and innocents. Nineveh's intentional terror campaign included public displays of human body parts, active slave marketing, and a public pride in their torture techniques. The power of violent terror is not an abstract wickedness. The legitimacy of Jonah's argument with God is that Nineveh's salvation from destruction (through his preaching) will result in *more terrorism* in the towns and cities of Israel.

Jonah prefers that Nineveh be destroyed for two reasons: He does not think that they can sustain their repentance (i.e., they will return to their evil ways), and he does not think that such people should be forgiven, even if they do repent. Jonah has good arguments that are grounded in biblical tradition and sustained by the actual historical results. It is God's previous policy to protect the innocent, especially his chosen, and to destroy the oppressor (the whole of the pentateuchal narrative and early prophets maintain this tradition).

Jonah is also correct in his fear that Nineveh's repentance will not hold. Nahum's oracle of the fall of Nineveh follows close on the heels of Jonah's protest. Nineveh returns, at least within one generation, to its culture of violent terror. That the book of Jonah was kept in the canon is a testimony to the integrity and cogency of his argument as a prophet in dialogue with God. Jonah is correct: If God allows the Ninevites to survive, they will terrorize the earth again. Jonah does not want to participate in this kind of certain future. His only recourse is to protest against God's course of action by running. His journey on the sea is a prophetic protest against what is, from a human perspective, God's deeply flawed policy. God allows violent cultures to persist in the world. Jonah does not think this is just.

(2) God's side of the dialogue is not about what is just. God does not deny that the Ninevites are violent and deserve destruction. He sends Jonah to announce their judgment and doom. Strict justice remains the standard even when it is delayed or unevenly applied in time. The unrepentant wrong will receive their due consequences and wages. Later (612 B.C.) God does send Babylon to destroy Nineveh for their return to grievous violence against his people.

God does not argue with Jonah about redefining the terms of human justice. God's argument in the case of Nineveh as well as in the world is that he allows for the seemingly random possibility of human reversal through repentance. Repentance is the open door for the reversal of lives of wicked and ignorant violence. God cites his love for his creation (4:11) as his primary warrant for this seemingly random and unlikely possibility.

(3) We are not God, and the text is not about the ethics of human justice. Forceful human action is never an option in Jonah and is never discussed. God is the subject of the timeless truth. Without a doubt, Israel would have destroyed Nineveh to protect its boundaries with force (as it did in the days of David and Solomon). The question concerns whether God should execute strict justice or risk the possibility of the violent repenting. In either case, God has numbered the days of Nineveh's violence. If they do not repent, they will die a violent death. If they do repent, it will be the "death" of their culture of violence. In either case they are "overturned." The point is that God allows for *either case*. Peter echoes this truth when he writes, "The Lord is not slow in keeping his promise, as some understand slowness. He is patient with you, not wanting anyone to perish, but everyone to come to repentance" (2 Peter 3:9).

(4) We are God's emissaries of reconciliation. God insists that his prophet participate in the either-case scenario. The two cases are not collapsed into one case of forgiving without repentance. The participatory risk is to declare the possibility of forgiveness to those who do not deserve it and will, in the short or the long run, abuse it (Assyrian history does not record their encounter with Jonah or any repentance). In the midst of this call to participate in the unlikely random risk of forgiving, Jonah is allowed to voice his objections and even to run from his obligation. The timeless grace of the matter is that God brings him to participate in the wonder of God's ways in the world, even when Jonah is not sure it is a good idea.

Uriel Simon cites the following midrash that demonstrates "the measured and rationed justice inscribed in the Torah, the prophetic books, Psalms, and Proverbs on the one hand, and divine mercy, which reveals the goodness and righteousness of the living God, on the other:[31]

> They asked the Torah: "How is the sinner to be punished?" It replied, "Let him bring a sacrifice and he will be pardoned."
> They asked the prophecy: "How is the sinner to be punished?" It replied, "The person who sins . . . he shall die" (Ezek. 18:4).
> They asked the David: "How is the sinner to be punished?" He replied, "May sinners disappear from the earth and the wicked be no more" (Ps. 104:35).

---

31. Simon, *Jonah*, xiii.

They asked Wisdom: "How is the sinner to be punished?" It replied, "Misfortune pursues sinners" (Prov. 13:21).

They asked the Holy One Blessed be He: "How is the sinner to be punished?" He replied, "Let him do repentance, and I will accept it, as it is written: 'Good and upright is the LORD [therefore He shows sinners the way]'" (Ps. 25:8).

Where is the hope for those living in cultures of terror? It is not in sacrifice, or in death, or in giving up, or in misfortune. It is, according to the God of Israel, in repentance and following the way of Yahweh. Everyone will be overthrown, one way or the other.

God's perspective is pity on all the ignorant (Ninevites and Jonah). Jonah is included in the ignorant, for God must instruct him with the question, "Should not I pity Nineveh, that great city, in which there are more than a hundred and twenty thousand persons who do not know their right hand from their left, and also much cattle?" Let us pray to be overthrown according to the witness of the prophet Jeremiah:

> They will be like a well-watered garden,
>   and they will sorrow no more.
> Then maidens will dance and be glad,
>   young men and old as well.
> I *will turn* [*hapak*] their mourning into gladness;
>   I will give them comfort and joy instead of sorrow. (Jer. 31:12b–13)

May his prophecy be fulfilled in our day as we pray, "Your kingdom come, your will be done on earth as it is in heaven." We know that the prophecy and his kingdom will come with or without our prayer. We pray, however, that this prophecy will come to us and overthrow us and our presumptions, that the kingdom might be his in our midst.

> Overthrow us, O God, this day. We are like Saul in our leadership; turn us into new people with a heart for your peace. We are like the Assyrians, boastful in power; turn us to repentance of our reliance on terror. And Lord, we are like Jonah, hesitant to extend your deliverance to our enemies; speak to us as we sit on the hillside in safety, that we might learn from you for all our decisions. We are like the hardened rock; turn us into streams of living water. Overthrow us for the sake of your creation and for the sake of your gospel in the world. Amen.

Introduction to Nahum

THE BOOK OF NAHUM darkly promises Judah's release from the oppression and cruelty of Nineveh.[1] "Everyone who hears the news about you claps his hands at your fall, for who has not felt your endless cruelty?" (3:19). Nahum's prophecy celebrates the fall of the sadistic empire and is a word of judgment against it. The book of Jonah is similar in its prophecy of doom to the Assyrian empire (Jonah 3:4; Nah. 1:1–2), and both end with questions from God, one of hope and one of despair (Jonah 4:11; Nah. 3:19). Both deal with God's reputation as both a just judge and a forgiving God (as revealed in the golden calf incident in Ex. 34:5–6). Nahum focuses on judgment for the wicked and Jonah on grace to the repentant. Nahum ends without repentance, and history records Nineveh's fall.

Nahum addresses the question of God's perspective on unrestrained cruelty and evil action. Reading it aloud takes only about eight minutes, yet it is perhaps the least read book in the Old Testament. Many readers do not immediately identify with the subject matter, and it may be difficult to understand for those who have not been victims of a strong and devastating oppressor. Understanding the specific historical and psychological context of the prophecy is prerequisite for receiving instruction or encouragement from this word of God.

Nahum is primarily a book of hope and comfort to those who are being or have been victimized or oppressed. It is a book for survivors, for those who want to find hope beyond their oppression. Nahum is also a word of warning to believers who find themselves associated with oppressors. When the end comes and Yahweh's slow anger is unleashed, it is critical to know in whom you place your trust.

Nahum also provides hope to believers who live in the midst of unmitigated cruelty. Modern Assyrian Christians can point to the faithful remnant that repented in the days of Jonah and remained faithful to Yahweh in the fall of Nahum's Nineveh as their spiritual ancestors. The power and cruelty of Nineveh did not endure but, as Nahum prophesied, dried up and disappeared in the sands of time.

---

1. Nineveh was the capital city of the Assyrian Empire from 701 B.C. until its destruction in 612 B.C. by the Babylonians. I use "Nineveh" and "Assyria" interchangeably in this commentary.

Content and Message

NAHUM IS AN "oracle" (1:1). Understanding its language requires knowing something about the basic rhetorical context (e.g., who is speaking to whom) and the historical background (e.g., Nineveh's reputation). The following overview of the many shifting rhetorical contexts helps to focus the book and oracle as a whole.

Form and Content

THE ORACLE IS divided into three chapters that methodically walk through Yahweh's wrath against cruelty (ch. 1), the destruction of the destroyers (ch. 2), and the end of Nineveh's long-running cruelty (ch. 3). These three chapters contain seven rhetorical sections. (1) Chapter 1 has two rhetorical parts, beginning with a description of the power of Yahweh's wrath against cruelty (1:1–10) and ending with words of reversal for Judah and for Nineveh (1:11–15).

(2) Chapter 2 has two parts, beginning with a vivid description of the final battle inside Nineveh (2:1–10) and ending with a mock lament over the end of Nineveh's "lions' den" (a metaphor for the city as a safe haven for its violent military "lions," 2:11–13).

(3) Chapter 3 has three parts. It begins with graphic descriptions of Nineveh's cruelty and its then future destruction (3:1–7). It continues by describing its vulnerability (3:8–13) and concludes by describing vain efforts to prepare for the coming battle (against the Babylonians). It also describes the corrupt infrastructure and the joy of the surrounding nations over Nineveh's fall (3:14–19). These seven subsections comprise the whole oracle.[2] For the purposes of this commentary, the seven sections have been further subdivided (see the outline, below).

Nahum's Name as a Message

THE NAME NAHUM (*naḥum*) means "comfort" (similar to Nehemiah, which means "Yahweh comforts"). It comes from a Hebrew word root that is translated many different ways, depending on its context.[3] Its meanings include "comfort, be sorry, be consoled, be compassionate." This "compassion" leads to the following translation in Jonah: "God *relented* concerning the calamity which He had declared He would bring upon them" (3:10 NASB).[4] On the

---

2. See David A. Dorsey, *The Literary Structure of the Old Testament* (Grand Rapids: Baker, 1999), 301 n. 1, for a summary of the scholarly discussion on the subdivisions of Nahum.

3. See Jonah 3, Bridging Contexts section, for an extended discussion of "compassion" (*naḥam*) in the broader biblical context.

4. The NIV has, "He had compassion and did not bring upon them the destruction he had threatened."

occasion of human repentance, therefore, a nuanced translation of the root *nḥm* means "relent in compassion."

God's *naḥam* also leads to the contra-intuitive translation "avenge." See, for example, Ezekiel 5:13: "Then my anger will cease and my wrath against them will subside, and I *will be avenged*" (see also Gen. 4:24; Num. 31:2; 1 Sam. 14:24; 2 Kings 9:7). When victims are rescued from the hands of a violent, oppressive enemy, therefore, the root *nḥm* contains a dual meaning—*compassion* on the victims through *vengeance* on the oppressor. In the book of Nahum, *nḥm* carries both implications.

Key Concepts

NAHUM ANSWERS THREE primary questions about God:

- Does God ever get angry enough about violence to do something? (Yes!)
- What makes God angry? ("Endless cruelty," see below)
- What happens when God shows his anger? (Two observable results: The *earth trembles* in ch. 1, and the *city falls* to a foreign power, Babylon, in ch. 2)

The following verses are central to understanding Nahum:

1:1–3: Yahweh is a jealous God, but slow to anger—the great Creator.
1:7: Yahweh is good.
1:12: I will afflict you no more (Yahweh's difficult role).
1:15: I will proclaim peace for the oppressed.
2:2: Yahweh will restore.
2:12–13: There will be no more strangling lions.
3:1: Nineveh is a city of blood.
3:4: This city is destroyed because of your slave trade.
3:7: Whom can I find to comfort you? (No one will sympathize.)
3:19b: Who has not been overwhelmed by your endless cruelty?

An even shorter list of key verses, which form interpretive statements for the whole book, is comprised by the concluding verses of each chapter (1:15; 2:13; 3:19).

The Good News of Nahum

IN WHAT WAY is the book of Nahum a "comfort" and to whom? It is certainly not a comfort to the Ninevites—see 3:7: "All who see you will flee from you and say, 'Nineveh is in ruins—who will mourn for her?' Where can I find anyone to *comfort* you?" Nahum's message provides comfort to and compassion for the *oppressed*.

The first sign of compassion is God's comfort to the violated survivors of cruelty. The primary image of this comfort is the oppressive devouring locusts resting on a cold city wall that fly away when the warm sun of God's judgment comes (3:17). In 2:13 he tells the oppressors, "I will leave you no prey" (also see 3:1, 19). God is dealing directly with the problem of evil in the world (1:2–3).

The second sign of compassion is the declaration that Yahweh is good, a refuge in times of trouble: "He cares for those who trust in him" (1:7). He sends peace, celebration, and freedom from the fear of violence (1:15). God is a powerful Creator (1:3b–6), who will bring comfort (*naham*) to his beloved creation.

Historical Context

ALMOST NOTHING IS known about the Judean prophet Nahum. He reports his vision of the fall of Nineveh about ninety-five years after the Ninevites carried the northern ten tribes of Israel and many Judean townspeople to slave markets and to death (722 B.C.). Nineveh fell to the Babylonians in 612 B.C., a few years after Nahum's prophecy. Jerusalem fell to the Babylonians about eighteen years later (594 B.C.) and was totally destroyed in 586 B.C.[5]

Nahum is a difficult and engaging poetic book, but it is written in a specific kind of historical and sociological setting. It cannot be understood without understanding that setting. Nahum is easily misunderstood if abstracted out of the reality of Assyria's heinous practices.[6]

The Audience of Nahum

TWO GROUPS OF people are directly addressed in Nahum: the oppressed of Judah (1:12–13, 15) and the oppressing Ninevites (1:11, 14; 2:1–2, 13; 3:5–19). What does this dual address teach us? The messages given to Judah are a word of comfort that their oppression will end. Most of the prophetic direct address, however, is directed toward Nineveh. They were warned in Jonah's day, and now they hear the word of judgment again. The warnings of Jonah and Nahum can be compared to those given by the allies to Hitler's Germany in the early and later parts of World War II. Eventually, the Nazis'

---

5. See "The Terror-Mongers of Nineveh, Assyria" in the introduction to Jonah for a description of the methods of torture and sadism for which that empire was notorious.

6. For examples of human cruelty in Assyria and by the Nazis who drew on Assyrian culture, see Jeffrey B. Russell, *The Devil: Perceptions of Evil from Antiquity to Primitive Christianity* (Ithaca, N.Y.: Cornell Univ. Press, 1977), 18, 19, 84–87; and idem, *Mephistopheles: The Devil in the Modern World* (Ithaca, N.Y.: Cornell Univ. Press, 1986), see index for "Nazis."

overwhelming human cruelty and the plundering of Europe's treasures left the allies no option but military confrontation.

It is also possible that the message of doom was heard by believers in Nineveh. Previously Jonah had also spoken a word, and the enemy Nineveh heard a similar prophecy of doom (also given without the obvious option of repentance!). In Nahum's day, some who still worshiped Yahweh could also have heard the prophecy and remembered the history. This time, however, the prophecy is more than one sentence ("Forty more days and Nineveh will be overturned," Jonah 3:4). Nahum's repetition of Nineveh's doom leaves no doubt that the "overturning" (*hapak*) means destruction and not repentance.

The Ninevite believers are living in the midst of a cruel people and are ruled by a cruel king. Is there any hope for them? Nahum's message gives them forewarning of the day when their country will fall under judgment. These believers are an implied minor audience of the text, whose perspective can also be applied to a reading of Nahum. Their implied hearing of the warning of Nineveh's destruction raises questions of ultimate allegiance and security (as do modern civil religion issues). Will these believers' first loyalty be to God or to their nation?

Endless Cruelty

NAHUM'S VISION COMES into the care and keeping of believing communities and does not only exist as a word against the endlessly cruel oppressor, Nineveh. The historical context (see above and Jonah's introduction) provides a general background for understanding Yahweh's compassion in Nahum's oracle of destruction. The text of Nahum provides us with additional windows into Nineveh's atrocities and cultural corruption.

Nineveh enslaved tens of thousands of people, including the northern ten tribes of Israel and many from weaker towns in Judah (1:13: "Now I will break their yoke from your neck and tear your shackles away"). They were "vile" in their practices of idol worship. The primary demands of Assyrian gods and goddesses (Assur, Bel, Ishtar, Marduk, Nabu, etc.) were spoils of war. The kings were dedicated to building temples to fill with plundered property and wealth: "The LORD has given a command concerning you, Nineveh: 'You will have no descendants to bear your name. I will destroy the carved images and cast idols that are in the temple of your gods. I will prepare your grave, for you are vile'" (1:14).

Nineveh employed a "scorched earth" policy in warfare, wreaking environmental disaster in the regions it conquered: "The LORD will restore the splendor of Jacob like the splendor of Israel, though destroyers have laid them waste and have ruined their vines" (2:2). Nineveh's supply of wealth was "endless" (when it was later plundered by the Babylonians) because it had been plundering all the nations of the ancient east for over one hundred years: "Plunder the silver! Plunder the gold! The supply is endless, the wealth from all its treasures!" (2:9).

The Ninevites were self-satisfied oppressors who preyed on their victims: "Where now is the lions' den, the place where they fed their young, where the lion and lioness went, and the cubs, with nothing to fear? The lion killed enough for his cubs and strangled the prey for his mate, filling his lairs with the kill and his dens with the prey" (2:11–12).

Nineveh is characterized as a "city of blood" (3:1). It enslaved whole cultures and peoples. It prostituted life and corrupted nature by reducing many societies to serve its national power, "all because of the wanton lust of a harlot, alluring, the mistress of sorceries, who enslaved nations by her prostitution and peoples by her witchcraft" (3:4).

Interpreting Nahum

NAHUM IS A difficult book to read, especially for Christians who take seriously Jesus' command to love your enemies (Matt. 5:44; Luke 6:27–30). Nahum's descriptions of God's judgment are violent: "'I am against you,' declares the LORD Almighty. 'I will lift your skirts over your face.' . . . Yet she was taken captive and went into exile. Her infants were dashed to pieces at the head of every street" (3:5a, 10a). It is offensive to read these verses and to accept such graphic violence as part of Scripture.

The easiest way to deal with Nahum's scandalizing words is to create distance between ourselves and his word from God. Those interpreting the book have found many ways of creating such distance.

- The prophet Nahum has been called a "representative of the old, narrow and shallow prophetism" of the "false" prophets.[7]
- Another commentator suggests that Nahum is "rather a disgrace" and "unwelcome a part" [sic] in Scripture.[8]
- We may isolate Nahum as a specific part of ancient nationalistic history or as an old war oracle that is no longer relevant today, which has the unfortunate effect of removing it as a living word from the Bible for us.

---

7. J. P. M. Smith, *Micah, Zephaniah, Nahum, Habakkuk, Obadiah and Joel* (ICC; Edinburgh: T. & T. Clark, 1912), 281.

8. R. Mason, *Book List of the SOTS* (1988), as quoted in K. Spronk, *Nahum* (HCOT; Kampen: Kok Pharos, 1997), 14. He has since modified his viewpoint in R. Mason, *Micah, Nahum, Obadiah* (OTG; Sheffield: JSOT Press, 1991), 82–83.

- We may isolate Nahum with other national "oracles against the nations" (as in Isa. 13, 15, 17, 19) as an old theological way God worked in the world (which is overturned in the "New" Testament). While this is partly true, in the New Testament nations still rise and fall at God's command (see comments on 3:3).
- We may also isolate Nahum by regarding it as a judgment against our national enemies. This keeps Yahweh's judgment at arm's length. Yet, it is important to recognize that the same kind of judgments are made against Israel (Jer. 13:14, 26; Ezek. 16:37; Hos. 2:3; 9:16; 10:14; Zech. 14:2; see Contemporary Significance section of Nah. 3).

The difficult challenge for today's readers is to hear the word of judgment as a living word against them. Only in this way will the text serve to call us to throw ourselves on God's mercy. The text also serves as a close message of hope for those who have been the victims of oppressive regimes. Nahum may function best as a comfort (*naham*) to them. It declares that God's justice will prevail against violent oppressors of nations and peoples.

Outline of Nahum

I. The Lord's Wrath Against Cruelty (1:1–15)
    A. Vengeance (1:1–3a)
    B. The Way of the Creator (1:3b–6)
    C. The Good and the Bad (1:7–10)
    D. Two Words from Yahweh (1:11–15)

II. The Destruction of the Destroyers (2:1–13)
    A. Warning and Promise (2:1–2)
    B. Futile Preparations (2:3–5)
    C. Nineveh's Fall (2:6–10)
    D. No More Strangling Lions (2:11–13)

III. An End to Nineveh's Endless Cruelty (3:1–19)
    A. Cruelty Exposed (3:1–7)
    B. Vulnerability (3:8–11)
    C. Ripe Figs and Peaceful Women (3:12–13)
    D. Corruption and Joy (3:14–19)

Select Bibliography on Nahum

Achtemeier, Elizabeth. *Nahum-Malachi*. Interpretation. Atlanta: Westminster John Knox, 1986.

_____. *Minor Prophets I*. NIBC. Peabody, Mass.: Hendrickson, 1996.

Baker, David. *Nahum, Habakkuk, and Zephaniah: An Introduction and Commentary*. Downers Grove, Ill.: InterVarsity Press, 1988.

Brown, William P. *Obadiah Through Malachi*. WBC. Louisville: Westminster John Knox, 1996.

Garcia-Treto, F. O. "The Book of Nahum." Pages 593–619 in *NIB*, vol. 7. Nashville: Abingdon, 1996.

Kohlenberger, John R. III. *Jonah and Nahum*. Chicago: Moody Press, 1984.

Longman, Tremper III. "Nahum." Pages 765–829 in *The Minor Prophets*, vol. 2. Ed. Thomas McComisky. Grand Rapids: Baker, 1993.

Mason, Rex. *Micah, Nahum, Obadiah*. OTG. Sheffield: JSOT Press, 1991.

Nysse, Richard. "Keeping Company with Nahum: Reading the Oracles Against the Nations As Scripture." *Word and World* 15 (Fall 1995): 412–19.

Patterson, Richard D. *Nahum, Habakkuk, Zephaniah*. WEC. Chicago: Moody Press, 1991.

Roberts, J. J. M. *Nahum, Habakkuk, and Zephaniah: A Commentary*. OTL. Louisville: Westminster John Knox, 1991.

Robertson, O. Palmer. *The Books of Nahum, Habakkuk, and Zephaniah*. NICOT. Grand Rapids: Eerdmans, 1990.

Smith, Ralph L. *Micah-Malachi*. WBC. Waco, Tex.: Word, 1984.

Smith, J. P. M. *Micah, Zephaniah, Nahum, Habakkuk, Obadiah and Joel*. ICC. Edinburgh: T. & T. Clark, 1912.

Spronk, Klaas. *Nahum*. HCOT. Kampen: Kok Pharos, 1997.

Sweeney, Marvin A. *The Twelve Prophets*. Collegeville: Liturgical, 2000.

Watts, John D. W. *The Books of Joel, Obadiah, Jonah, Nahum, Habakkuk, and Zephaniah*. New York: Cambridge Univ. Press, 1975.

Nahum 1

AN ORACLE CONCERNING Nineveh. The book of the vision of Nahum the Elkoshite.

² The LORD is a jealous and avenging God;
    the LORD takes vengeance and is filled with wrath.
The LORD takes vengeance on his foes
    and maintains his wrath against his enemies.
³ The LORD is slow to anger and great in power;
    the LORD will not leave the guilty unpunished.
His way is in the whirlwind and the storm,
    and clouds are the dust of his feet.
⁴ He rebukes the sea and dries it up;
    he makes all the rivers run dry.
Bashan and Carmel wither
    and the blossoms of Lebanon fade.
⁵ The mountains quake before him
    and the hills melt away.
    The earth trembles at his presence,
    the world and all who live in it.
⁶ Who can withstand his indignation?
    Who can endure his fierce anger?
His wrath is poured out like fire;
    the rocks are shattered before him.

⁷ The LORD is good,
    a refuge in times of trouble.
He cares for those who trust in him.
⁸   but with an overwhelming flood
he will make an end of Nineveh;
    he will pursue his foes into darkness.

⁹ Whatever they plot against the LORD
    he will bring to an end;
    trouble will not come a second time.
¹⁰ They will be entangled among thorns
    and drunk from their wine;
    they will be consumed like dry stubble.

¹¹ From you, ⌐O Nineveh,⌐ has one come forth
    who plots evil against the LORD
    and counsels wickedness.

¹² This is what the LORD says:

"Although they have allies and are numerous,
    they will be cut off and pass away.
Although I have afflicted you, ⌐O Judah,⌐
    I will afflict you no more.
¹³ Now I will break their yoke from your neck
    and tear your shackles away."

¹⁴ The LORD has given a command concerning you,
    ⌐Nineveh⌐:
"You will have no descendants to bear your name.
I will destroy the carved images
    and cast idols that are in the temple of your gods.
I will prepare your grave,
    for you are vile."

¹⁵ Look, there on the mountains,
    the feet of one who brings good news,
    who proclaims peace!
Celebrate your festivals, O Judah,
    and fulfill your vows.
No more will the wicked invade you;
    they will be completely destroyed.

Original Meaning

NAHUM 1:1 PROVIDES us with brief introductory information: "An oracle concerning Nineveh. The book of the vision of Nahum the Elkoshite." Nahum's home in Elkosh has been variously identified with Al-Qush near ancient Nineveh (near Mosul, Iraq), with a place in northern Galilee (Jerome's choice), Capernaum (which means, "village of Nahum"), and with Beit-Jebrin (southwest Judea). The location is not essential for understanding Nahum's message.

The "oracle" (*maśśaʾ*, lit., "something lifted up, burden") refers to Nahum's message, "lifted" before the people. Oracles were often "against the nations" that threatened Judah (Isa. 13:1; 15:1; 17:1; 19:1; 21:1; 23:1).[1] The written

---

1. See the introduction, "Content and Message."

document (the book of Nahum) communicates the "oracle" that Nahum received as a "vision."

Oracles and their abrupt forms are not familiar to most modern readers. The themes change frequently, and the subjects and objects of the sentences shift without notice. It is quite different than reading a narrative like Jonah. Knowing the basic rhetorical divisions and themes of an oracle text can help the reader understand its focus.

The theme of chapter 1 is Yahweh's wrath against cruelty. A longer section (1:1–10) and a shorter section (1:11–15) are its basic rhetorical parts. The longer part describes the strength of Yahweh's opposition to the Ninevite kingdom and serves as the introduction to the book. Three subtitles present its subject matter. "Vengeance" (1:1–3a) describes Yahweh's anger against those "guilty" of violence. "The Way of the Creator" (1:3b–6) describes Yahweh's powerful use of the creation to accomplish his purposes (in Nineveh's case, the Babylonian army is an element of the creation). "The Good and the Bad" (1:7–10) declares that Yahweh is a "good refuge" for those who trust in him but an "overwhelming flood" for those who plot against him.

The shorter rhetorical section (1:11–15) ends with a "word" concerning the reversal of Judah's situation ("I will break their yoke from your neck," 1:13a). Nineveh's reversal will be from plotting "evil" (1:11) to the "grave" (1:14).

Vengeance (1:1–3a)

"NAHUM" (*NAHUM*) MEANS "comfort."[2] Reading verse 2, where Yahweh's vengeance is mentioned three times, the reader wonders, "For whom is the comfort intended?"[3] This oracle "concerning Nineveh" is not simply for the Ninevites. It is also for Israel, who has suffered extensively at their hand.

The book begins with an acrostic wordplay, using the letters of the first half of the Hebrew alphabet in sequence to begin each half-verse. The main irregularity is that the first and second letter sequence (*aleph* and *bet*) is interrupted theologically by three half-verses (1:2a, b, 3a), which describe God. Nahum begins by declaring Yahweh's name five times, with descriptions of three of God's attributes: "the LORD is jealous" (1:2), "the LORD is slow to anger" (1:3), and "the LORD is . . . great in power" (1:3; see also 1:7, "the LORD is good").[4]

(1) Yahweh is "jealous" and "avenging." The participle "avenging" (*noqem*) describes what he does in reaction to the sins of Nineveh. These are difficult

---

2. The same root *nhm* is in 3:7, "Where can I find *comforters* for you?" (see the introduction).

3. See comments in the Bridging Contexts section.

4. The NIV translates the Hebrew of 1:2a well: "The LORD" *is* "jealous" and *responds by* "avenging."

words for many readers. Yahweh is not vengeful by nature, yet his vengeance is mentioned three times in this opening verse.[5] His vengeance is a response of his jealousy to particular circumstances. He does take vengeance, but he is not vengeful in character. His wrath is a circumstantial response to those who destroy what God loves. Three expressions provide the context of Yahweh's vengeance in this verse: "jealousy" as an attribute of Yahweh, "filled with wrath," and "against his enemies."

What is it about Yahweh's jealousy that causes him to respond to his foes with vengeance and wrath? What is it about his enemies that causes him to respond wrathfully? The word "jealous" (*qana'*) is also sometimes translated "zealous." It comes from the name or title God gives himself in Exodus 34:14, where he says he is *yahweh qana'* and *el qana'* ("jealous LORD" or "jealous God"). The context is that God has just delivered his people from Egypt by his intervention in history and nature, in order to make them a blessing to all nations. In response, however, they have given credit to the golden calf (see also Ex. 20:5; Deut. 5:9). That makes God "jealous." The human failure to acknowledge the true God is idolatry. Such idolatry reveals a God who is "jealous" of his name and his people. (For Christians the event of the golden calf would be similar to thanking our "lucky stars" that we are saved from sin and death in Christ.)

Praise for the deliverance of one's life belongs to God. Unlike a teenager's jealousy, God's jealousy has an ultimate grounding in his self. The word *qana'* also means "possession" (in its noun form). It means that God is rightly jealous because his people "belong to" him. He has "paid for" or "purchased" his people, even though they (or their enemies) pretend that they do not belong to him.

God's jealousy is thus based on two fundamental claims: God has made us, so we rightly belong to and should love our Creator; and God has purchased us with his acts of deliverance, so we rightly belong to the one who has saved us. When any enemy "steals" or oppresses Yahweh's people, God's heart is pained with a perfect jealousy. The phrase that Yahweh "maintains his wrath" (*notar*, 1:2) comes from a word related to gardening. To maintain wrath means to persist against weeds that choke a vine and against foxes that eat the grapes. God persists in this way for the sake of the Judean remnant.

The declaration of Yahweh's avenging is expanded by strong reinforcing statements that proceed from his jealous nature. These statements further our understanding of the vengeance of God. The following diagram of verse 2 demonstrates how God's jealousy (on the one side) and his response of wrath

---

5. The participle *noqem* is translated "avenging" once and "takes vengeance" twice in the NIV.

against the sin of his foes (on the other side) are the setting and context for God's avenging actions.

The LORD is a *jealous God*—>avenging

takes vengeance—>*is filled* with wrath

takes vengeance—>on his *foes*/against *enemies*

The expression "is filled with wrath" (*ba'al ḥemah*) means "one who has mastered wrath." He is not possessed by wrath but controls wrath as its master and uses it for his purposes. The phrases "on his foes" and "against his enemies" can be more graphically translated, "those who are hostile toward him" and "those who are personally antagonistic toward him." The words "foes" and "enemies" imply that Yahweh takes Nineveh's endless cruelty toward Judah as a personal attack on himself.

(2) Yahweh's second attribute is given in the predicate adjective in 1:3a: "The LORD is slow to anger." This can also be translated "patient in anger." Yahweh's slowness to anger against Nineveh seems to stand in contrast to his jealousy for Judah. We might expect his jealousy for Israel to lead him to quickness of anger. Yet formerly, when Israel was the object of Yahweh's anger, his slowness was an extension of that jealousy. He waited, without punishing, in hope that they would return to him through the pleading of the prophets.[6]

The expression "slow to anger" is an excerpted quotation from Ex. 34:6 and is paired with another from Exodus 34, that he does "not leave the guilty unpunished" (Ex. 34:7). God's slowness to anger is always in the context of his redeeming work, begun in the Exodus. An ancient reader who knew the Exodus story would immediately connect this phrase to its beginning in that story.[7]

(3) Yahweh's third attribute is also in 3a: "great in power." Nahum assures us that although God's vengeance against Nineveh has not come more quickly, his power is not in question. The nature of this power is explained in the 1:3b–6.

Three words that sound alike in Hebrew serve to encapsulate the first three verses: *naḥam* ("comfort," 1:1), *naqam* ("avenging," 1:2), and *naqah* ("unpunished," 1:3). Nahum's oracle brings *comfort* to those who have suffered untold atrocities by announcing *vengeance* on those who have been *exempt from punishment* for their crimes. The saying "It is mine to avenge; I will repay" (Deut. 32:35; cf. Rom. 12:19; Heb 10:30) is well known. Here in Nahum is an expanded oracle concerning this vengeance and the way the jealous Creator carries it out.

---

6. See Hos. 11:1–12; cf. Eccl. 7:8–9.

7. God is known for his patience in grace and mercy and by his "slowness" to anger. This is true whether the offender is Israel or Nineveh (cf. Rom. 9:22–26).

The Way of the Creator (1:3b–6)

YAHWEH IS THE Creator and Master of all creation. He works through his creation to show his power and accomplish his purposes. That is his "way." His way is "in the whirlwind and the storm." The way of Yahweh's power in the world is not in hasty intervention. His power is great, even though it may seem that he is slow to punish (1:3) those guilty of great cruelty. His way is through the wind, storm, sea, rivers, seasons, and earthquake (1:3–5).

His way is also a way of great power. The clouds, which bring the weather with its agricultural blessing or curse, are at his feet, a biblical symbol of complete control. The sea, a symbol of chaos and power, is under Yahweh's control. He turns the sea back ("rebukes") and it becomes dry, something seen daily in the tides (cf. 2:8). The rivers of the land run dry according to Yahweh's common order, as they do in the dry season. The places known for their agricultural abundance (Bashan, Carmel, Lebanon) wither and fade in his presence as they do after harvest.

"The mountains quake" because Yahweh is the Creator, and he causes them to do so. "The hills melt away" or "dissolve," as in the annual soil-carrying rains during the rainy season. Mount Carmel (in the north) may also be an allusion to the ten northern tribes, which were taken by Assyria in 722 B.C. This serves to remind the reader that God used Assyria to flatten the ten tribes. Now Assyria has gone too far in its excesses. Like the melting of the hills and the ten tribes, the "melting" of Nineveh's palace (2:6) is foreshadowed.

The "presence" of Yahweh in these verses is called a *theophany* ("God's appearing"). Nahum expresses this Presence in the land through descriptions of created objects' responses to Yahweh. God is seen through these responses, which may be observed by anyone, anytime, anywhere. His power may be seen in them continually. Verse 5b summarizes the reality of creaturely existence: "The earth trembles at his presence, the world and all who live in it." Whether it is a storm, a drought, a gray landscape, or an earthquake, the creation trembles and heaves in the Creator's presence.

This text warns, however, that God may also intervene and cause a dramatic change in his created patterns. Verse 6 marks this warning with a shift of subject in the question: "Who can withstand his indignation?" When his wrath is poured out, it comes in the form of fire, and rocks will be shattered. Shattering rock suggests two things. (1) This is not a common natural event, even though it is the work of the Creator. Rocks don't shatter as a natural matter of course; that is, Yahweh acts through unusual events in the created cycles. (2) The Hebrew words for "the rocks are shattered" can also mean that rock walls or altars are torn down.[8] This refers to the destruction coming on Nineveh. God is warning that he will also work through armies. A God who controls creation (shatters rocks) can also use men to pull down a city wall.

The Good and the Bad (1:7–10)

VERSES 7–10 CONCLUDE the introduction with more specific words about Nineveh's end. Verse 7 declares Yahweh's fundamental goodness and care, while verses 8–9 declare the certainty of Nineveh's doom. The original meaning can best be seen in the poetic alternating metaphors of destruction (1:8, 10) with historical comments (1:9, 11). Verse 11 is the most historically specific, referring to the king of Nineveh, who has plotted evil against Yahweh. These verses set the stage for Yahweh's direct addresses to Nineveh and Judah in verses 12–15.

The words used in verse 7 are a welcome reminder of the unchanging goodness of Yahweh, even in the midst of horrific judgment. This verse stands as a light in the midst of the darkness of Nahum's oracle. Preceded by "rocks are shattered before him" and followed by "with an overwhelming flood he will make an end," the goodness of Yahweh is not forgotten. This would have been a word of hope to any believers living in Nineveh as well as to Judah. The ultimate terms of relationship to the good Lord Creator are set in the sharpest contrast possible: Either he is a trust and a refuge, or he is opposed and a pursuer of those opponents.

God's goodness is declared in three phrases that have familiar uses in other biblical texts (1:7). "The LORD is good" is often used in the context of suffering or reaping consequences of rebellion against the Creator (Ps. 34:7–8; 145:8–10; Jer. 33:10–11; Lam. 3:21–26). "The LORD is a refuge in times of trouble" is used in Psalm 9:9; 46:1; 62:8; and Joel 3:16. "Refuge" often means a safe place of hiding from an enemy. "He cares for those who trust [*ḥasab*] in him"; *ḥasab* is often used to express "find[ing] *refuge* in the shadow of your wings" (Ps. 36:7; 57:1; see also 2 Sam. 22:31; Ps. 18:30; Prov. 30:5).

Verses 8–11 alternate between metaphors of destruction (1:8, 10) and historical comments (1:9, 11). Five metaphors describe Nineveh's end: "with an overwhelming flood," "into darkness," "entangled among thorns," "drunk from their wine," and "consumed like dry stubble."

"With an overwhelming [*ʿabar*] flood he will make an end of Nineveh" (1:8a). The word *ʿabar* occurs four times in Nahum, translated differently each time. It is a significant word root, especially in 3:19, where it gives the sharpest warrant for Nineveh's destruction. Why does Nahum begin with this

---

8. Jer. 1:10; 18:7; 52:14; Ezek. 26:9; cf. Ex. 34:13; Deut. 7:5; 12:3; Ezek. 16:39.

word ʿ*abar*? Because the opposite has been Judah's experience, since they have been "flooded" by Nineveh's aggression (3:19).[9]

The second metaphor (darkness) describes the kind of "end" Nineveh will experience (1:8–9): "He will pursue his foes into darkness." An ending can be good or bad, but Nineveh's will be in complete obscurity and oblivion.

The next three metaphors express the natural end of Nineveh's opposition. She is like thorns in a bramble, a drinking drunk, and a conflagration of fully dry stubble. Each metaphor of creation is not bad in itself (a thorn, wine, stubble), but is turned in on itself and comes to its own bad end: thorns to a tangle, wine to a wino, stubble in flames. The pictures form progressive images of trouble: first tangled, then in a stupor, and finally, dried to crackle crisply in consuming flames. The end will be final.

The metaphor of "consuming" (ʾ*akal*) occurs six times in Nahum:

1:10b: They *will be consumed* like dry stubble.

2:13: The sword *will devour* your young lions.

3:12: [Ripe] figs fall into the mouth of the *eater*.

3:13: Fire has *consumed* their [gates'] bars.

3:15: There the fire *will devour* you; the sword will cut you down and, like grasshoppers, *consume* you.

In 1:10, the metaphor of consuming is used ironically at first. Nineveh has been the consuming force for many years, stripping the land, eating its fruit, consuming the bars of many city gates in fire. Nineveh is the lion that has devoured the ancient Near East. The consuming practices of Nineveh as a lion and as a cloud of locusts are further developed in Nahum 2 and 3. The prophecy that Nineveh itself will be now consumed is almost unbelievable to the peoples of ancient world.

Two Words from Yahweh (1:11–15)

THE NEXT ADDRESS is even more forceful, for it is from the mouth of God. Up to now, Nahum has been speaking indirectly about the Ninevites as "they" and "them." Now God's words are spoken directly (second person singular) to Nineveh as "you."

"This is what the LORD says," Nahum announces in 1:12. All three chapters in Nahum end with quotations from Yahweh (1:11–14[10]; 2:13; 3:5–19).

---

9. The NIV translates ʿ*abar* as follows: "they will ... *pass away*" (1:12); "no more will the wicked *invade* you" (1:15b); and "who has *not felt* [*been overwhelmed by*] your endless cruelty?" (3:19).

10. Note that in the Heb. text, ch. 1 ends with v. 14. English versions follow the Greek Bible.

Verse 11 is punctuated by the first direct address, "From you, O *Nineveh*."[11] The powerful confrontation of Nahum's inspired voice, speaking the "you" against Nineveh, is repeated a remarkable twenty-two times. In the "you" one can hear both the intense human outcry against Nineveh's atrocities and Yahweh's response against its criminal oppression of the ancient Near East.

The historical comment in 1:11 (and 1:9) punctuates the metaphors (1:1–10) with the actual historical situation: "Whatever they plot against the LORD he will bring to an end." The fact of Nineveh's plotting (or "ingenious plan," *ḥošeb*) against Yahweh is repeated in verse 11. The king of Assyria (3:18) is plotting evil by planning an attack on Jerusalem (1:15b). His counsel is "wickedness" (*beliyaʿal*, also meaning "worthlessness," like a cloth that has become a rag or the rag that has completely worn out). The king's counsel is, like most wickedness, banality—the same, sad, old story of stupidity.

This is the last word of the introduction (1:1–11).[12] Nahum declares that this kind of wickedness is "worn out" and is absolutely over. Yahweh's "trouble" will not have to come to Nineveh a second time (1:9b). One siege against Nineveh will do (1:9), for she is entangled, drunk, and dried up.

The first word to Judah (1:12) has three parts. (1) Judah's enemy appears overwhelmingly strong, but they themselves "will be cut off" (like sheep that are "sheared") and overwhelmed (their strength and *šalom* will "pass away" [*ʿabar*; 1:8, 12, 15; 3:19]). (2) Yahweh takes responsibility for Judah's affliction and for its ending (cf. Isa. 40:2). This may have been the most difficult part of the word for the believer. (3) Yahweh addresses the very real situation of Assyrian enslavement. He will break the neck yokes and ankle shackles. Nineveh will fall, Yahweh will not afflict Judah any longer, and slavery will end. This is the beginning of Judah's good news and *naḥum* ("comfort").

The second "word" of Yahweh is to Nineveh (1:14). It also has three parts, given in the unusual form of a command (*sawah*). This means that God has given an order, as a general of an army. The order has the force of law. Since that law was given by God, it is established as a reality in the world. This reality includes the termination of Nineveh's descendents, the elimination of its gods, and God's preparation for its burial.

This chapter in our English Bibles concludes (1:15) with a second direct address to Judah ("O Judah"; see 1:12). Although this is not a quotation of

---

11. In Heb., 1:9 also has the more forceful direct address to the Ninevites: "whatever *you* plot." The NIV is the only translation that uses "they"; perhaps this keeps the abrupt change in pronouns from confusing the reader.

12. Note that Nah. 1:11 functions in two ways: as the end to the introduction and the beginning of the personal address to Nineveh (and Judah). This is a typical style in Hebrew prophetic oracles.

Yahweh, it continues the good news of declaration with a familiar ring.[13] It is the good news for which oppressed Judah has been praying. Nahum visualizes the runner on the mountain ridge road, carrying the news that Nineveh has fallen. He calls for the celebration of festivals in the new safety of the countryside. He calls for the people to do what they have promised in vows made while praying for deliverance. No longer will they be overwhelmed (see *ʿabar*, above) by a wicked, invading army. Peace and its security will come. Such prophecy brings hope to those who have trusted in Yahweh.

Bridging Contexts THE THEOLOGY OF Nahum is closely connected to God's crucial self-description to Moses at Sinai. The two main similarities are in italics:

Exodus 34:6–7: And he passed in front of Moses, proclaiming, "The LORD, the LORD, the compassionate and gracious God, *slow to anger*, abounding in love and faithfulness, maintaining love to thousands, and forgiving wickedness, rebellion and sin. Yet he does *not leave the guilty unpunished.*"

Nahum 1:3: The LORD is *slow to anger* and great in power; the LORD will *not leave the guilty unpunished.* His way is in the whirlwind and the storm, and clouds are the dust of his feet.

In Nahum 1:3 the prophet describes the God of the Exodus in a briefer format. He is "slow to anger," meaning he delays punishment of the wicked, hoping for their repentance. His slowness does not mean that the unrepentant guilty are acquitted. Within the broader context of God's reputation, Nahum celebrates that the consequences for Nineveh's sins will no longer be delayed. The time is up. Its hundred-year run of domination and two hundred and fifty years of arrogant violence are finally over.

The differences between the quotations above (Ex. 34 and Nah. 1) are also apparent. Nahum does not mention the compassionate and gracious God who abounds in love and faithfulness and forgives wickedness, rebellion, and sin. This does not mean, as many commentators erroneously conclude, that Nahum does not consider these as attributes. Any ancient reader would know that "slow to anger" is a kind of biblical shorthand that recalls the full Exodus text. Nahum's oracle is not, of course, about compassion for Nineveh. That compassion was extended, at God's insistence, through Jonah, who ran away precisely because he did not want Nineveh to receive it (Jonah 4:2). Nahum

---

13. See Isa. 52:7; Act 10:36; Rom. 10:15; Eph. 6:15.

mentions God's compassion ("slow to anger") briefly, not because he does not believe in it but because the consequences of sin cannot be delayed forever.

Another erroneous conclusion made by some interpreters is that God's slowness to anger and its compassion are extended to Israel, but the consequences of guilt are for the nations. The broader biblical context again does not support such a reading. The original warnings of consequences were for Israel at Sinai. The law is full of such warnings. The compassion of "slowness to anger" is also extended to Assyria and to the nations.[14]

Two audiences, two voices. Within its social and political context the message of Nahum 1 is consistent with the tradition of Exodus 34. It makes two claims about God. (1) The minor theme is for the violent who are listening. In compassion to the wicked, Yahweh is slow to anger, longing for the repentance of his human creation. God's compassion for the arrogant and violent leads him to relent from a strict swift justice against them (see comments on Jonah 3:10). God struggles with this in a classic Hosea 11 text, where he says he will destroy a wicked Israel, but is struck with anguish at the thought of their destruction.

(2) The major theme in Nahum is comfort for the threatened Israelites and the surrounding cultures, as in 3:7b: "Who will mourn for her? Where can I find anyone to comfort [*naḥam*] you?" In comfort for the violated, Yahweh will not remove the consequences of guilt from the unrepentant wicked.

These two truths are voiced throughout Nahum 1 like a duet, although the comfort in wrath is muted and relies on a wider biblical context. This minor theme is found in these texts:

> 1:3a: The LORD is slow to anger and great in power.
>
> 1:7: The LORD is good, a refuge in times of trouble. He cares for those who trust in him.
>
> 1:15a: Look, there on the mountains, the feet of one who brings good news, who proclaims peace! Celebrate your festivals, O Judah.

The major theme of comfort for the cruelly treated is seen in these verses:

> 1:3b: The LORD will not leave the guilty unpunished. His way is in the whirlwind and the storm, and clouds are the dust of his feet.
>
> 1:8–9: But with an overwhelming flood he will make an end of Nineveh; he will pursue his foes into darkness. Whatever they plot against the LORD he will bring to an end; trouble will not come a second time.
>
> 1:15b: No more will the wicked invade you; they will be completely destroyed.

---

14. Eventually, Jesus comes on behalf of "all nations," as in Matt. 11:17; 28:19; John 11:51–52; Gal. 3:8; Rev. 15:4; 22:2.

The goodness of God undergirds both themes. Elizabeth Achtemeier offers five ways in which God (a shortened form of the word "good") is declared "good" in Nahum.[15] The central verse is 1:7: "The LORD is good, a refuge in times of trouble. He cares for those who trust in him." It offers the first two ways God is good: because he is a refuge in troubled times and because he knows those who seek him. Yahweh's goodness also means that he "will not leave the guilty unpunished" (1:3). Goodness does not always entail the forgiveness of evil deeds or the removal of their consequences. God's goodness is also found in the fact that vengeance belongs to Yahweh. Because "the LORD takes vengeance" (repeated twice in 1:2), the faithful are not left responsible for it (Deut. 32:35; Rom. 12:19; Heb 10:30).

Finally, God is good in that he is "slow to anger" (1:3), seeking Nineveh's repentance through Jonah and allowing more than one hundred years of Assyria's barbarism before declaring an end. "God is exceedingly slow to anger, because he is exceedingly great: it is the little cur that yaps at every threatening noise; the lion waits and seems to doze."[16]

Reasonable objections to God's goodness as the theme of a book as violent as Nahum are raised by at least one commentator.[17] The claim that God is good in Nahum runs against modern ethical and philosophical categories as well as a basic human desire to define God according to our own impulses. This may explain in part why it is so little read today. Nahum challenges deeply held assumptions about the nature of goodness.

Three objections are commonly voiced. (1) How can God be associated with the (pagan) Babylonian army and its violence against Nineveh? Using violence against the violent cannot be "absolutely good." Human experience tells us that war and what we would call war crimes of the ancient Near East diminish the perpetrators. God is implicated by his association with the Babylonian army. As long as God is measured against human experience and against human measures of "absolute" goodness, the problem will remain. God is *in some way* implicated in every death in history, good and bad. The claim of goodness in Nahum is simply that God is good to those who trust in him. This is not a claim to absolute human goodness. "I will prepare your grave, for you are vile" (1:14), he says to Nineveh. If God is a warrior and a destroyer, the definition of absolute *human* goodness cannot apply to God. God is not a human.[18]

---

15. Elizabeth Achtemeier, *Nahum-Malachi* (Interpretation; Atlanta: Westminster John Knox, 1986), 8–14.

16. Ibid., 11.

17. F. O. Garcia-Treto, "The Book of Nahum" (*NIB*; Nashville: Abingdon, 1996), 7:596–97.

18. See comments on Jonah 3 in the Bridging Contexts section, "Overturning has two possibilities."

It should be noted that God did not "intervene" in Nineveh's fall to the Babylonians and Medes in 612 B.C. Assyria's demise was the combined result of corrupt internal government and culture and the rise of the Babylonian military might in the south. God did not take "special" action to destroy Nineveh. Nahum simply declares that God's avenging is accomplished through these events. The issue is that Yahweh claims to work through human political agency at all, since all human agency is corrupt to some degree. By "absolute goodness" (a category of philosophical ethics) standards, God can only be good by refusing to participate in the human world through human agency![19] To say that God can't be "absolutely good" by our standards is an inside-out argument in relation to a living God. Only a God that doesn't fit our philosophical categories can be a true God and not a theological construct.

(2) The second objection is that innocents (e.g., children) die in the fall of Nineveh. How can God be declared "good" and claim responsibility for the death of children? The forty-seven short verses of Nahum do not address the question of the death of the innocent (as in the Gen. 18 conversation between Abraham and God concerning the innocent in Sodom). Nor does it address God's call to his enemies for reconciliation (as in Jonah 4). Nahum is part of a Bible that does speak to these problems in both Old and New Testaments (consider Job or Christ's sufferings, or the martyrs of Revelation).

The problem of the suffering of innocent people is not answered in Nahum, but it may be raised in relation to other texts that do grapple with the issue (Psalms, Job, Ecclesiastes). Nahum does address God's commitment to bring to an end those who systematically and consistently oppress the innocent. His commitment to protect and vindicate the innocent is beyond question (see Ex. 22:21–24). God will overcome his enemies either by making them his friends or through apocalyptic judgment (Matt. 24; Mark 13). The innocent will ultimately be his responsibility.

(3) The final objection asks: Doesn't God also love the wicked (as in Jonah 4:11), since they are also his creation? How can they be reconciled to him if he destroys them? Nahum does not engage this discussion, but stands at the end of a long-suffering negotiation (1:3a; see the introduction, "Historical Context"), in which Nineveh has turned back from reconciliation (Jonah stands two books earlier in the canon). In the end, God's historical bias is toward those who are oppressed.

God's decision to identify with a human agent (Babylon) to destroy Nineveh means that he does sully his hands in history, even if he hesitates with a hundred years of "slowness to anger." He implicates himself even in the

---

19. See J. K. Bruckner, "Ethics," in *Dictionary of the Old Testament: Pentateuch*, ed. David W. Baker (Downers Grove, Ill.: InterVarsity Press, 2002).

death of infants. Some oppressors are so systemically evil that God is willing to participate in the desolation of the entire culture. Yahweh is really God in taking responsibility for these deaths. No human can claim that responsibility and maintain "goodness." Only the true God can do that and guarantee justice, even for the innocents.

Only a God who *can* make this claim, who *can* enter human history and the ambiguities of human life, can be God of all life and death. This kind of god cannot, by definition, be a god who measures up to the "absolute goodness" of human philosophical categories that are built on the certain limitation that no person could kill an innocent and be just at the same time. When God declared that he would enter into human history, he gave up the possibility of pleasing all philosophical definitions of "absolute power" of purity and goodness. That decision eventually would lead God to his *own* scandalous death. Only his "God-ness" caused that innocent death to rise above human scandal.

The divine warrior. The most common interpretation of Nahum 1 is that Nineveh is a symbol for all evil, especially in the form of extreme nationalistic arrogance (see the introduction to Jonah, "The Terror-Mongers of Nineveh, Assyria"). God's vengeance is not simply directed at Nineveh but is a prophecy for the end of time, confirming the promise of divine justice.[20] God's power and justice stretch from the beginning of time in the first chapter (1:4: "He rebukes the sea"; cf. Gen. 1:9–10) to the end of time (Nah. 1:8: "He will pursue his foes into darkness"). God's claim to ultimate victory is a call to repentance to live under his kingship in love rather than in violence.

The theme of Yahweh as a warrior for justice who judges evil and causes the cosmos to shake (1:2–8) can be traced through the Old and New Testaments.[21] The divine warrior's trajectory begins in Exodus 14 with the destruction of the Egyptian army in the sea. God's judgment is turned against Israel for priestly corruption in 1 Samuel 4. The northern ten tribes experience his wrath in their deportation in 722 B.C. Nahum's word against national evil is next with Nineveh destroyed in 612 B.C. Yahweh wars against Judah in their deportation in 586 B.C. In Zechariah 14:3–5 Yahweh comes forth to fight for his faithful people in days yet to come. In Jesus' day many expected the Messiah to be this warrior.

Jesus' warfare, however, was not nationalistic but against human bondage to sin, death, and the evil one (Matt. 11:2–6; Mark 3:20–30; Luke 4:18–21). His crucifixion and resurrection gave a new understanding and per-

---

20. See Brevard S. Childs, *Introduction to the Old Testament As Scripture* (Philadelphia: Fortress, 1979), 444–45; Achtemeier, *Nahum-Malachi*, 15; Ralph L. Smith, *Micah-Malachi* (WBC; Waco, Tex.: Word, 1984), 68. Cf. Garcia-Treto, "Nahum," 603, 606.

21. Tremper Longman III, "Nahum," in *The Minor Prophets*, ed. T. McComisky (Grand Rapids: Baker, 1993), 2:776–77.

spective on the ultimate love behind the warrior's use of force (Eph. 4:7–13; 6:10–20; Col. 2:8–15). Revelation 19:11–21 describes the final necessary battle of the Lord as warrior, triumphing over evil once and for all.

When we see Nahum 1 as part of this broader historical trajectory, its military imagery becomes a pressing call to take refuge in the cross of Christ as an expression of the warrior's love for us. Jesus is a dying warrior, for our sake and for our deliverance. To live in the world of the divine warrior means suffering defeat alone and without a reference, or suffering death with reference to Christ's dying warrior love. It means dying with him now, in defeat of our own rebellion, or without him later, in defeat of the same.

Creation and the Creator's "slowness" to anger. God's power ("slow to anger and great in power," 1:3) may be questioned by those who do not understand his way in the world. From the perspective of the believer in Judah who has felt the cruel oppression of Nineveh, perhaps through the loss of a child or a spouse to death or slavery, Yahweh's "slowness to anger" certainly raises questions of faith. Nahum declares that although Yahweh is slow to anger, he is also "great in power" and "will not leave the guilty unpunished" (1:3). He continues to explain the slowness of his power and punishment by describing the "way" of Yahweh. This "way" is the way of the Creator. He works in, with, and under what we call "forces of nature." His way, Nahum says, is through his creation: the wind, storm, and clouds (1:3); the sea, rivers, and seasons (1:4); and earthquake and torrential rains (1:5).

As the Creator, Yahweh is master of both order and what looks like disorder: storms, dry rivers, quaking earth, and terrified people. Nahum's word of hope is that God is in control, even when creation seems to be working against us. He calls us to consider whether we have caused "his indignation" (1:6) or whether we are simply seeing his power at work. In 1:6 the question "Who can withstand his indignation?" is similar to the familiar question of Malachi 3:2, "But who can endure the day of his coming? Who can stand when he appears? For he will be like a refiner's fire or a launderer's soap." Its creation themes are echoed in Revelation 6:16–17: "They called to the mountains and the rocks, 'Fall on us and hide us from the face of him who sits on the throne and from the wrath of the Lamb! For the great day of their wrath has come, and who can stand?'"

TWO COMMON RESPONSES to Yahweh's avenging are present in the opening verses of Nahum. Those who have suffered violence may find that God's vengeance brings them comfort. God's goodness in the midst of catastrophic events may strike a sympathetic chord.

Others may be horrified at God's wrath and the violence of his judgments. Life experience deeply influences how these verses are heard and interpreted.

Comfort for survivors. One response is to be surprised and comforted to hear that God becomes angry at all. Many believe that God does not care about the genocides and wars of the twentieth century, or that God does not take enough vengeance on the wicked. There are times when the wicked prosper ("Why does the way of the wicked prosper?" Jer. 12:1; cf. Ps. 94:3). Some might wish that God would act more quickly and not be so "slow to anger" (Nah. 1:3). Nahum declares that though God is slow to anger, he is full of wrath over ongoing cruelty. God's anger is not essentially punishing, but restorative. His wrath comes against everything that destroys life.

God is slow to intervene in hope that even the perpetrators of evil will repent and seek life (Jonah 3). Yet, in human society the unfortunate course of violent action is sometimes necessary. The American Civil War was a horrific event in which over 600,000 people were killed. It nonetheless ended the intolerable institution of slavery and preserved the country's unity. Today that war is both celebrated and grieved for its human cost.

This first response may be twisted to a false conclusion. The comfort of God's wrath for survivors of horrific events is Nahum's context. To extend this to all believers in opposition to "infidels," however, is a distortion of the meaning that serves only the reader and not the "good news" of God (Nah. 1:15). Nahum is not for isolated use in the teaching of the church. When it is taught, it must be read in conjunction with similar prophecies against God's people, in order to preclude the possibility of arrogance against one's enemies. Even within Nahum (1:12), Yahweh reminds Judah, "I afflicted you." The necessary awareness is that Judah does not take its own vengeance but that Yahweh uses another agent to exact justice. The same God who in the flesh said, "Love your enemies," also said, "It is mine to avenge; I will repay" (Lev. 19:18; Deut. 32:35; Matt. 5:44; Heb. 10:30).[22]

Can God still be good? The second common response is offense at the notion that God is portrayed as wrathful at all. Isn't God a God of love? How can a loving God take vengeance? Some Christians consider Nahum and other difficult Old Testament texts obsolete in light of the goodness of God revealed in Jesus Christ. They may wish to preserve God's reputation by "sanitizing" it. In order to deal with the God revealed in Scripture, it is necessary to read further and deeper into the nature of the love behind God's wrath.

---

22. God invites participation (Gen. 18) and offers choice to choose the good and suppress evil (Gen. 4). God gives us freedom and, with it, responsibility. God offers time for repentance (Jonah). Even in Nahum, the prophetic word of judgment comes before the judgment, leaving the door open, that some might turn to God in repentance for salvation.

(1) One wrong application of God's wrath is its use by adults to modify behavior in children. They have confused their own personal anger and God's agonizing love. The terrible result is that many children have come to associate God's wrath with their experience of angry adults playing "god." The truth of the matter is that God is a God of love, whose wrath is a response to evil actions that continually distort and hurt the helpless. God's wrath is directed at those systems of rule that make victims of his children. A deep and sad irony is evident in those who reject the wrath that is intended to be their deliverance.

Yahweh's goodness (1:7) is no simple or two-dimensional goodness, in which all evil is out of sight. It is set between verses 6 and 8 so that we can see that God's goodness is not tame or domesticated but is a powerful goodness that will bring justice to the world. Nor is it an abstract goodness, for it reaches to those who trust in him, providing a "refuge in times of trouble."[23]

(2) The second response may also be twisted to a false conclusion. The wrath of God in Nahum is a response to a specific problem of cruelty in Nineveh. Wrath is not an abstract attribute of God but is a response to human evil intentionally causing human suffering. The twentieth century was the most violent century in the history of the world. Genocides from Europe to Cambodia and from the former Soviet Union to Africa pock our history. God's wrath must always be understood in the context of current events. The facts and conclusions are twisted when the cruel historical realities against which God is responding in wrath are left out of the conversation. God's wrath is always delivered against the sociopolitical oppressors of the helpless.

God's love is behind his wrath (see God's inner struggle in Hosea 11). Anyone who has lived in a community where violent actions flourish unchecked or where law is not upheld knows the necessity of the exercise of power to check cycles and structures of evil (even in "good" people). God's vengeance is an exercise of power to stop the devastating conflagration of Nineveh's cruelty against which no human power in the ancient world had been able to stand.

Nahum is not for everyone. Nahum raises more questions than answers for many readers. For example, "Why does God speak so violently?" (3:4–7). But if Nineveh was so evil, why was God so slow to punish them? Why did God afflict Israel with Assyria in the first place (1:12)? In short, why does God allow and use violence in the world? Nahum does not attempt to answer

---

23. Some readers object to the wrath of God and insist on a soft love that closes its eyes to moral issues in the reader's life, but that is a sophomoric attitude that neither Old nor New Testament allows.

these questions in its forty-seven verses. The wisdom literature of Job, Psalms, and Ecclesiastes does struggle with these issues, and the New Testament offers a new possibility for God's people in dealing with violence.[24]

Nahum, however, is silent on these issues. The prophet simply describes Nineveh's cruelty and God's response of anger. He announces the end of Assyria's reign of terror in the ancient Near East. He does not hide the fact that innocents suffer in such affliction (3:10; cf. Ps. 44:17–26). The only glimmer of an answer within the book is found in the creation language of Nahum 1:3b–6: God uses natural means to accomplish his work in history. This means justice is generally done with the broad strokes of natural events, politics, and national power (see "The way of Yahweh in natural events," below). Innocents are often unjustly injured in such events. In the midst of these broad shifts Yahweh gives one personal word: "The LORD is good, a refuge in times of trouble. He cares for those who trust in him" (1:7).

Is there a double standard for violence (the use of force) in Nahum, one for us and one for God? Some readers are most troubled by the "avenging" language of Nahum, as Jesus commands believers to love their enemies and to pray for those who persecute them (Matt. 5:44). Yet it is clear that *God* will take vengeance. Not only is God described as avenging three times in 1:2, but chapter 1 is replete with references to God's destroying (1:3, 8, 9, 10, 12, 14, 15). How is it that God does not abide by the same counsel he gives?

The apostle Paul did not have any trouble with this double standard. He understood the difference between God and human beings:

> Do not take revenge, my friends, but leave room for God's wrath, for it is written: "It is mine to avenge; I will repay," says the Lord. On the contrary:
>
>> "If your enemy is hungry, feed him;
>> if he is thirsty, give him something to drink.
>> In doing this, you will heap burning coals on his head."
>
> Do not be overcome by evil, but overcome evil with good (Rom. 12:19–21; see Lev. 19:18; Prov. 25:21–22).

God takes vengeance precisely because God is God and we are not. God can be trusted, *because of his goodness*, to execute wrath and mercy justly. Without this trust in God as the real Lord of creation, the human potential for good and evil cannot be understood. If we rely on ourselves for vengeance, God knows that our imperfection will cause the fire of our wrath to consume us

---

24. See Habakkuk's dialogue with God concerning violence, described later in this volume.

as well. God has provided a way for us to escape that conflagration and realize our potential for good by taking our vengeance against others into himself. He has even taken *others'* just vengeance against us into himself. The God of Nahum is Paul's God: In both cases God takes responsibility for the violence, and his people are not involved.

In Nahum we are asked to trust that God's goodness is not altered by his use of the Babylonian army. This is, of course, a mystery that we must accept. In the New Testament we are asked to trust in the sufficiency of God's dying as an act that can save a violent world from destruction. This too is a mystery to be believed.

The way of Yahweh in natural events: creation and politics. A sage perspective is offered in Nahum that remains timelessly valid for us. This paraphrase of Nahum 1:3b–6 (especially when read aloud) draws out the perspective of awe in the way of Yahweh in nature. For Nahum, the forces of politics and nations are an extension of nature (human beings are simply a part of the creation). The destruction of Nineveh, like the rise and fall of nations today, belongs to a larger vision of God's power displayed in "natural" events.

Yahweh's *way* is known in the wind of the storm and in the tempest. Clouds are like dust on his feet. By his restraining word the sea-tide goes out. All the stream-beds become dry for lack of rain. The fruitful countryside of Carmel and Bashan fade and the blossoms of Lebanon wither in the dry season. Because of him the mountains are shaken by earthquake. Hills dissolve in heavy rains. In contemplating these *ways*, all the earth, and all who live in it, may respectfully tremble at his creating presence. If this is Yahweh's way in the earth, who will be able to stand when God is offended by arrogant actions? Who will stand up when his anger is kindled? His fury flows like fire and by him rock-walls are shattered.

Nahum invites us to share two perspectives that are not always evident today. The first is that the rise and fall of political powers (e.g., Babylon's destruction of Nineveh) can be understood in the context of a natural disaster ("rock-walls are shattered"). God does not use a supernatural means to destroy arrogant nations, but natural events. Five natural metaphors describe Nineveh's end (with an overwhelming flood, into darkness, entangled among thorns, drunk from their wine, consumed like dry stubble [1:8, 10]). In each case Nineveh's experience of the good creation is a disaster because of her opposition to the Creator and the creation.

The second perspective is that Yahweh's presence and activity in the world (his "way") may be better understood through the practice of observing and describing the environment. This is exactly what Nahum does in order to communicate his message. God's way can be seen in "natural" events so we can learn the power and glory of this presence.

Perhaps the most difficult sentence in the book is this one: "Although I have afflicted you, O Judah, I will afflict you no more" (1:12b). Yahweh takes responsibility for Judah's affliction by the Assyrian military presence. This common (but uncomfortable) Old Testament pattern is seen also in Hosea. "When I please, I will punish them; nations will be gathered against them to put them in bonds for their double sin" (10:10). Then God says, "How can I give you up, Ephraim? How can I hand you over, Israel?... My heart is changed within me; all my compassion is aroused. I will not carry out my fierce anger, nor will I turn and devastate Ephraim" (Hos. 11:8–9; cf. Ezek. 18:31–32). The prophets acknowledged God's hand in humanity's political circumstances.

Not every case of affliction or suffering in the world has a personal link to sin. (Jesus cautions the Pharisees against this perspective in John 9:1–3.) Not every case of affliction comes from Yahweh's hand. In every case of affliction, however, we speak to Yahweh that God might be glorified. Whether the case of affliction calls for repentance, protest against another's sin (through lament and a call for justice), or seeking comfort and healing for something that cannot be undone, God may be glorified.

Whatever the circumstance in history, believers have looked to God, in repentance (Jer. 14:19–20), in protest (Ps. 13:1–4; 35:15–17; 74:1–10), or for comfort. C. S. Lewis drew on this perspective when he said that pain is God's megaphone. With it he gets our attention and draws us into a conversation with himself about our specific circumstance. Poet John Donne invited Yahweh's affliction as a cure for his own arrogance: "Batter my heart, three person'd God ... That I may rise and stand, o'erthrow mee and bend / Your force to breake, blowe, burn, and make me new."[25]

When the problem is arrogance, as it was with Nineveh, we would do well to join John Donne. Donne was familiar with the New Testament tradition of Nahum 1:6, which was reframed in the wrath of the Lamb at the final judgment. His prayer is that the return of the Lamb would be good news for him.

> Who can withstand his indignation? Who can *endure* [stand] his fierce *anger*? His wrath is poured out like fire; the *rocks* are shattered before him. (Nah. 1:6)

> They called to the mountains and the *rocks*, "Fall on us and hide us from the face of him who sits on the throne and from the *wrath* of the Lamb! For the great day of their *wrath* has come, and who can *stand*?" (Rev 6:16–17)

---

25. From *The Poems of John Donne*, ed. H. J. C. Grierson (London: Oxford Univ. Press, 1933), 299.

Through belief in the death and resurrection of the Lamb, the good news of peace with God is declared to all nations. Judah is called to celebrate festivals in Nahum 1:15 ("Look, there on the mountains, the feet of one who brings good news, who proclaims peace! Celebrate your festivals, O Judah, and fulfill your vows"). Peter interprets this call in light of Jesus' resurrection and his vision at the house of Simon the tanner:

> I now realize how true it is that God does not show favoritism but accepts men from every nation who fear him and do what is right. You know the message God sent to the people of Israel, telling the good news of peace through Jesus Christ, who is Lord of all. (Acts 10:34–35)

Paul too includes those who speak to others of this good news in this celebration in Romans and Ephesians:

> And how can they preach unless they are sent? As it is written, "How beautiful are the feet of those who bring good news!" (Rom. 10:15)

> Stand firm then, with the belt of truth buckled around your waist, with the breastplate of righteousness in place, and with your feet fitted with the readiness that comes from the gospel of peace. (Eph. 6:14–15)

Nahum 2

¹ An attacker advances against you, ⌞Nineveh⌟.
     Guard the fortress,
     watch the road,
     brace yourselves,
     marshal all your strength!

² The LORD will restore the splendor of Jacob
     like the splendor of Israel,
  though destroyers have laid them waste
     and have ruined their vines.

³ The shields of his soldiers are red;
     the warriors are clad in scarlet.
  The metal on the chariots flashes
     on the day they are made ready;
     the spears of pine are brandished.
⁴ The chariots storm through the streets,
     rushing back and forth through the squares.
  They look like flaming torches;
     they dart about like lightning.

⁵ He summons his picked troops,
     yet they stumble on their way.
  They dash to the city wall;
     the protective shield is put in place.
⁶ The river gates are thrown open
     and the palace collapses.
⁷ It is decreed that ⌞the city⌟
     be exiled and carried away.
  Its slave girls moan like doves
     and beat upon their breasts.
⁸ Nineveh is like a pool,
     and its water is draining away.
  "Stop! Stop!" they cry,
     but no one turns back.
⁹ Plunder the silver!
     Plunder the gold!
  The supply is endless,
     the wealth from all its treasures!

———

¹⁰She is pillaged, plundered, stripped!
    Hearts melt, knees give way,
      bodies tremble, every face grows pale.

¹¹Where now is the lions' den,
    the place where they fed their young,
    where the lion and lioness went,
      and the cubs, with nothing to fear?
¹²The lion killed enough for his cubs
    and strangled the prey for his mate,
    filling his lairs with the kill
      and his dens with the prey.

¹³"I am against you,"
    declares the LORD Almighty.
"I will burn up your chariots in smoke,
    and the sword will devour your young lions.
  I will leave you no prey on the earth.
The voices of your messengers
    will no longer be heard."

Original Meaning

NAHUM 2 VIVIDLY describes the destruction of the destroyers. It begins with the final battle inside Nineveh (2:1–10), as Nahum paints a word picture of the coming war (in 612 B.C.). Nineveh's impressive preparations for battle are described in colorful detail, followed by its unexpected fall (2:6). The chapter concludes with a short mock lament over the end of the torturous "lions' den" (a term for Nineveh's walled city, a safe haven for its violent military "lions" and their human spoil, 2:11–12). It ends with Yahweh's direct quotation, "I am against you"; he will destroy her "chariots . . . young lions . . . prey . . . [and] messengers" (2:13).

In the Hebrew text Nahum 2 begins with the English 1:15 ("Look, there on the mountains"). In the English Bible form (which follows the LXX, the Greek Old Testament), this verse serves to bring chapter 1 to a positive conclusion. The original Hebrew form, however, demonstrates a better poetic balance. Chapter 1 ends with two quotations from Yahweh, one for Judah (1:12–13) and one for Nineveh (1:14), and chapter 2 then begins with "Look, there on the mountains," which is a direct address to Judah, followed by a direct address to Nineveh, "An attacker advances against you." This call to "look" for good news gives the listener a good rhetorical introduction to what follows in chapter 2.

The subject matter of chapter 2 is divided into four sections. A warning and a promise speak caution to the aggressor Nineveh and hope to the embattled Judah (2:1–2). "Futile preparations" (2:3–5) colorfully describes Nineveh's battle readiness. The description of Nineveh's fall (2:6–10) is followed by the promise of no more strangling "lions" (2:11–13).

Warning and Promise (2:1–2)

THIS CHAPTER BEGINS with a warning to prepare for the coming battle. The imperative warnings are for Nineveh to "guard ... watch ... brace ... [and] marshal." As they are called to prepare, the modern reader is also prepared for the present tense description of Nineveh's hurried mustering (2:3–5). By listening in on Yahweh's word to Nineveh, third parties are drawn into the action of the story.

Who is the "attacker" in verse 1?[1] Nahum is silent about who in fact will be God's agent in the destruction of Nineveh (Babylon). Yahweh is the only one mentioned as the opponent (1:12–13; 2:2, 13), for he is the One who guarantees Nineveh's fall from power.[2]

The Babylonian conquerors record that Nineveh was besieged unsuccessfully by the Medes in 614 B.C. They joined efforts in 612 with King Nabopolassar of Babylon and breached the walls after ten weeks. A Greek legend, written by the historian Diodorus in the first century B.C. (possibly influenced by Nahum's descriptions in 2:6, 8), claims that heavy rains swelled the river (he thought it was the Euphrates instead of the Tigris, which ran along the west side of the city). The Husur River, a tributary of the Tigris, ran through the city. The swelling river may have undermined thousands of yards of its eight-mile wall. It may have swelled even more because the attackers opened the floodgates of Sennacherib's freshwater reservoir above the city.[3] The Husur may also have been diverted to undermine the northern wall. Whatever the case, Nineveh's preparation (2:1) involved guarding the ramparts, watching the road, strengthening their loins ("bracing"), and marshaling their strength—all in vain.

Verse 2 is an aside directed to the people in Jerusalem and its countryside. Assyrian troops had "laid ... waste" and "ruined vines" (lit., "the emptiers emptied" the land and "their pruning disfigured" the vines), not only taking the produce of the land but also destroying Judah's vineyards and olive groves (cf. Deut. 20:19). Judah's potential for return to prosperity had been stripped.

---

1. "Shatterer" in the RSV. Hebrew probably is "the one who scatters you."
2. Nah. 2:1 and 3:11 give nebulous hints of an earthly opponent that Yahweh will use for his opposition.
3. Spronk, *Nahum*, 99.

Nonetheless, Yahweh promises to return their former splendor. He is the Creator (1:3b–6), and the destroyers of his creation will be destroyed (1:15; 2:2).

Futile Preparations (2:3–5)

THIS SECTION ABRUPTLY presents a picture of the Babylonian advance (2:3, 5b) and of the Ninevites' frenzied preparations (2:4–5a). It begins with a staccato description: red shields, scarlet soldiers, and flashing metal chariots. Inside the city of Nineveh Nahum foresees the events. Chariots storm (lit., "boast") through city squares like flaming torches and darts of lightning. Crack troops are on city wall ramparts.

An unnamed individual directs the energy (2:3a, "his soldiers"; 2:5a, "he summons"). He has been mentioned once before (1:11) as the one who plots evil against Yahweh. The "king of Assyria" is named finally in 3:18 as one who has lost all means of support. Although he is referred to these four times, the focus is on Nineveh's general policies of cruel rule.

The first indication of Nineveh's weakness is in the midst of their preparation for battle. "He summons his picked troops, yet they stumble on the way." The word for "picked troops" (*ʾaddiyr*) is repeated in 3:18 ("nobles"), where they "lie down to rest." Here they simply stumble as they dash to the city wall to protect the city.[4] Their fall is foreshadowed, even as they run in strength. The description of their hurried preparations ("storm," "rush," "dart," "dash") shows that they are surprised by the warning but remain confident of their strength.

The descriptions are in vivid color (2:3), and the confusion of the battle preparations is brought into the rhetoric of the text.[5] Red shields and scarlet clothing and flashing metal chariots probably belong to the ordered advancing Babylonian warriors (Babylonian chariot officers wore red [Ezek. 23:14–15]; Assyrians wore blue or purple [Ezek. 23:6]). The "spears of pine" are the lances of the charioteers. The scene abruptly shifts to inside Nineveh's walls (2:4–5a). Ninevite chariots rush around crazily and summoned troops stumble. Again, in 2:5b, a shift is made to the scene outside the wall, where the Babylonians rush the wall and set up the siege mantel, a protective shield against falling objects or arrows shot from the ramparts. Now the end is near.

Nineveh's Fall (2:6–10)

IN THESE VERSES of prophecy, Judah is led to imagine the incredible possibility that the plunderer, Nineveh, will be plundered. Her fall is pictured in five stages

---

4. Some believe this implies their drunkenness. It probably reflects their over-haste.

5. Commentators debate which army is being described in which verse.

of her capture, verse by verse. The gates through which the Husur River flowed are opened (by someone inside, or by an undermining flood; see 2:1–2), and the Babylonians, Medes, and Scythians enter and capture the city (2:6). As was common with cities that posed a threat to the general security, the people are exiled (2:7). The surprise that Nineveh could fall is realized too late. Some cry "Stop!" (lit., "Stand still"); they think of Nineveh as a "deep pool," full of reserves, and are confused by its draining (2:8). The conquering army shouts commands to "plunder" the silver, gold, wealth, and treasures in endless supply (2:9). The final scene is a city emptied of all but people, and they are weak in their hearts and knees; their bodies tremble and their faces are blank (2:10).

The first stage of Nineveh's fall is the breach of the walls and the fall of the palace. The "palace collapses" when the gates of the river are opened (2:6). "Collapse" echoes "melts away" in 1:5 (Heb., *mug*). The connection between Yahweh's control of the nonhuman creation in chapter 1 and the fall of Nineveh is subtly made. The palace virtually "melts away." The repetition of "river" (1:4 and 2:6) is a second related echo. Whether the river runs full (2:6) or runs dry (1:4), Yahweh is near.

The Hebrew word translated "palace" (*heykal*) in 2:6 is, in other contexts, translated "temple." Yahweh is considered the true king in Israel, so his "palace" is the temple. The residence for Judah's king is called the "house of the king."[6] Outside Israel, however, "palace" is a correct translation of *heykal*. It establishes a contrast between Jerusalem's ideal of God on the throne and Nineveh's king living in its highest place of authority, the palace.

The second stage of Nineveh's fall (2:7) is the decree of exile and the general mourning that accompanies the deportation of a city's population. In the NIV "the city" is in corner brackets because it is an implied subject of the verb "that [she] be exiled." Other translations follow a scholarly consensus that the "she" is the statue of Ishtar, Nineveh's goddess of fertility or Nineveh's queen.[7] In ancient warfare, the conquering army usually paraded a defeated city's deity out of the city (see 1 Sam. 4:1–11). The "girls" who beat their breasts and moan are possibly those who have served in Ishtar's temple in ritual acts of fertility.

In Jonah the moaning of repentance was heard across the spectrum, from the king to the animals (Jonah 3). In Nahum, the "slave girls moan like doves" (*yonim*). The name "Jonah" is formed from the same word as "dove" (see the introduction to Jonah). The ancient reader could not have missed the play on words or the echoes of Jonah's earlier encounter at Nineveh. This reference

---

6. See BDB, 228.

7. This involves an emendation that treats the participle behind "it is decreed" as a noun. See discussion in Tremper Longman III, "Nahum," 806.

adds exile to the weight of the picture, since its avoidance through repentance was possible. To the original hearer of the oracle, the possibility of repentance may have been considered. In Nineveh, however, the "moaning" is too late, and it comes from the slave girls, not the king (cf. Jonah 3:6).

In the third stage of Nineveh's fall (2:8) the nobles realize that Nineveh is actually captured: "Nineveh is like a pool." Nineveh is named (rather than implied) for the first time since 1:1 (it is named only once more, when it is completely abandoned, 3:7). This reference begins positively by comparing Nineveh to a pool.[8] Nineveh's reputation included its control of deep water reservoirs. It was protected by moats formed by the Husur and Tigris Rivers. Abruptly, however, its water is draining or running out. Nineveh's moats are running dry.

People shout "Stop," but with little effect because many are running away. No one looks back. Nineveh (like a pool) collapses as it empties. The speed and surprise of its collapse are expressed by the ineffective shouting. This is a contrast to God's voice in 1:4, where Yahweh "rebukes the sea," and it turns back immediately!

The fourth stage of Nineveh's fall (2:9) is the discovery of her seemingly endless treasury. The large amount of wealth accumulated because for years Assyria had stripped the lands around them (see 3:16). The expression "the supply is *endless*" (or "there is *no limit*") is also used in 3:3 of Nineveh's atrocities against its victims ("dead bodies *without number*") and in 3:9 of its "*boundless* strength." The expression refers to Nineveh's unrestrained hoarding practices. Even the oracle expresses astonishment at the "wealth" (lit., "glory") of all its treasures. There is no hesitation in calling for the seizing and redistribution of all this stolen gold and silver.

The last stage of Nineveh's fall (2:10) is the emptying of the people from the city. In the Hebrew the emphasis of the alliteration is striking (*buqah, mebuqah, mebulaqah*); the NIV preserves it in the words "pillaged ... plundered ... stripped." This devastation, desolation, and destruction, with its emptiness, void, and ruin, form the final word in the picture of Nineveh's coming fall. It is matched in the expression of finality in the faces of the people. The strength of every person is drained. Hearts melt, knees give way in a flash (like lightning in 2:4 and spears in 3:3), and bodies that were braced for battle (2:1) now tremble. Finally, the blood drains from the faces of all who are present. They are pale and "blank," like the vines that Nineveh stripped in Israel. Nineveh's ability to continue in cruelty is to be absolutely ended.[9]

---

8. The Heb. makes the positive intent clear with the words, "she was like a pool of water *in her day*."

9. See Deut. 24:20a: "When you beat the olives from your trees [at harvest], do not go over the branches a second time." Note how Nineveh did this in Nah. 2:2.

No More Strangling Lions (2:11–13)

CHAPTER 2 CONCLUDES with a question for Nineveh concerning its cruel practices and with Yahweh's direct declaration, "I am against you" (2:13; see also 3:5). The question in 2:11 ("Where now is the lions' den?") in its original context refers to the defeat that has not yet happened. It is raised beforehand in this oracle as an accusation against the Ninevites for their practice of hunting human prey and bringing them home in contentment. Isaiah said that Assyria was a lion that took whatever it pleased (Isa. 5:29). They bragged of driving children and women from their dead fathers and husbands into slavery.

The "lions' den" is a metaphor for the Assyrian practice of bringing captives into the city to be tortured and killed publicly (2:12b) (a practice the Romans emulated with early Christian captives). When the city of Surah (in Syria) surrendered with the promise of leniency, Ashurnasirpal burned it instead, cut off the legs of the military officers, brought the population home as slaves, and had the governor publicly flayed alive in the capital.

"The *place* where they fed their young" is more striking in the Hebrew, using a word that is commonly translated with the peaceful word "pasture." It demonstrates a normalization of violent practice. The killing and eating activity of lions described in these verses is common to lions. The indictment against Nineveh is that they are people and their victims are people, but they have been content to become lions and to act as though others are flesh to be torn (prey). The strangling lions represent a self-satisfied army and administration that enjoyed the support of the people at home. When they returned from the hunt to the "den," they had no anxiety or fear.

The lion was Assyria's symbol of empire. The palace of Ashurbanipal was decorated with wall reliefs of lion hunts. He imported lions to a royal preserve for his hunts. The imagery of Ishtar, goddess of sexuality and war, also included lion imagery. Ashurbanipal was the proud "lion" who mastered peoples and even actual lions. The image of the lion as hunter is reinforced by mentioning his "prey" three times (2:11[2x], 12).[10] In the pronunciation of the Hebrew, the growls of his "lion cubs" in the lair can be heard. They sound like *gurareyeh* (2:11b) and *gorotayw* (2:12a).

In 2:13 Yahweh declares that four types of oppression will end: no more chariots, no more lions, no more victims, no more Ninevite messengers. Yahweh will burn the chariots and devour the devouring lions with the sword. He will end their imposition of suffering on their prey. Their "messengers" will no longer plague the nations. Assyria used messengers to demand surrender to looting and paying tribute. If the "prey" would not surrender, they would be

---

10. The Heb. root translated "prey" (*trp*) occurs two more times, translated "killed" in 2:12 and "victims" in 3:1. The "lion" kills, strangles, and fills his lairs and dens with victims.

destroyed and deported (cf. Isa. 36:1–22). Messengers also returned to Nineveh with news of victory and a procession of new victims and booty for the city. They collected regular tributes from those who did not resist Nineveh's power.

Yahweh's name "Almighty" (*ṣebaʾot*) is mentioned for the first time in 2:13. Older translations use "LORD of hosts," which also conveys the might of the armies of heaven. This first declaration of "the LORD Almighty" is followed five verses later by another similar declaration (3:5–7). Between them is another brief picture (3:1–3), familiar to its victims, of Nineveh's army at work in slaughter.

The reversals of fortune in 2:11–13 mirror the ironies of this chapter. What was full will be empty. Strong fortifications (2:1) will become weak (2:10), full pools will be drained (2:6, 8), stolen splendor (2:2) will be removed (2:9), and lairs full of prey (2:12) will be cut off (2:13). The lion hunter (2:12) is now the hunted lion (2:13).

Bridging Contexts

WHY IS THERE such a graphic and extended narrative concerning the assault, siege, breach, and deportation of Nineveh? It is said that God is in the details. That is also the claim of the text (2:2, 13). Although the Medes and the Babylonians are the ones who attack, Yahweh says that he is doing the work.

The details of this record of Nineveh's fall to the Babylonian empire in 612 B.C. are important to Scripture for at least two reasons. (1) Recitation of how God delivers the oppressed is a longstanding and valuable tradition for inducing hope in oppressed and abused peoples. In hearing the story of deliverance, the abused may be carried to the first step of deliverance through hope that God fights for them. (2) The detailed description also stands in the biblical tradition as a warning to the arrogant that God is against anyone who is an oppressor.

Inducing hope. Hope is created in hopeless communities in Scripture in at least two fundamental ways. (1) The first is by remembering, accomplished through the recitation of stories of deliverance that God fought for his people through mighty acts in the past. The centrality of the Exodus story and the Passover cannot be overestimated. It was told at least once a year in the Jewish community, and its themes stand behind the Easter celebration. The precedent for this retelling is found in Scripture itself. In addition to the command to remember (Ex. 12:25–27), the psalmists found great hope in retelling the story in the midst of the congregation (Ps. 78; 105; 106).

These detailed remembrances of Yahweh's acts of deliverance helped later oppressed communities of faith to maintain hope. Nahum stands in this tradition of celebrating the defeat of a heinous enemy, for Israel and the Jews have faced many enemies in the years after Nineveh's demise (the Babylonians, Persians, Greeks, Romans, pogroms, Stalin, Hitler, etc.). Remembering God's past salvation endures in Christian communities in personal witness and through pastors preaching texts of deliverance, including the cross of Christ.

Nahum takes the reader through the details of *any* enemy's defeat by Yahweh: a warning to the enemy (2:1) and a promise of deliverance to the oppressed (2:2), an agent of salvation approaching in order (2:3), the enemy dashing about but stumbling (2:4, 5a), the agent attacking (2:5b) and capturing the enemy's stronghold (2:6a), the enemy moaning (2:7b) but realizing defeat and yelling "stop" (2:8), the agent plundering the wealth (2:9), the enemy being sapped of all strength (2:10), the power of the enemy's terror being recalled (2:11–12), and Yahweh declaring his opposition to the enemy and its power (2:13). Other detailed battle scenes are the one against Tyre (Ezek. 26) and the one against the Persians as God's agent against Babylon (Isa. 21:1–10; Jer. 50–51).

(2) The second fundamental way hope is created in hopeless communities is by release from bondage to anger. The recitation of the violence found in Nahum has a purifying effect when it is voiced and when God remains the subject of the sentence of vengeance. It functions in communities that seek to deal in healthy ways with the anger that comes from deep injury. Nahum stands in the tradition of the imprecatory psalms, which invoke God's vengeance on one's enemies (Ps. 35; 58; 69; 83; 109; 137). These psalms have been piously avoided in churchly practice because they are difficult to use properly. They are for communities who suffer deeply at the hand of the powerful and violent, and they are cries for God to act.

After struggling with the value of these psalms, C. S. Lewis concluded: "If we look at their railings we find they are angry not simply because these things have been done to them but because these things are manifestly wrong, are hateful to God as well as to the victim."[11] When used in this context, they release the anger that is unavoidably present and keep it from exploding in self-destructive ways. The common pattern without this voiced release of hurt and anger to God is that the oppressed become violent themselves, and the cycle of violence persists.

A warning to the arrogant. Anyone who stands against Yahweh's peace and justice is subject to Yahweh's words, "I am against you."[12] It is an error to

---

11. C. S. Lewis, *Reflections on the Psalms* (New York: Harcourt, Brace, & World, 1958), 30, as quoted in J. R. Kohlenberger III, *Jonah and Nahum* (Chicago: Moody Press, 1984).

12. Compare David Baker, *Nahum, Habakkuk, and Zephaniah: An Introduction and Commentary* (TOTC; Downers Grove, Ill.: InterVarsity Press, 1988), 23.

read Nahum nationalistically, as if anyone who stands against God's *nation* will be opposed by God. God himself declared war on his own people because of their injustice and violence against the powerless. At the time of Nahum's prophecy (615 B.C.), three years before Nineveh's fall (612 B.C.), Jerusalem was only eighteen years from being captured and twenty-nine years (586 B.C.) from being demolished by the same Babylonians who plundered the fortress at Nineveh (2 Kings 24:10–25:21).

The arrogant of Jerusalem heard the details of Nineveh's destruction at the same time they were hearing Jeremiah's preaching, warning them of their own destruction. The description would have given them food for thought and made them feel their vulnerability. Was Jerusalem more fortified against attack than Thebes and Nineveh (3:3)? Did they trust in their defenses, or did they trust in Yahweh? If they continued flouting God's law, would God let the fortress given to them through David and miraculously preserved in the Assyrian assault (2 Kings 18:13–19:35) continue to protect them? Would God send another angel of death into the enemy camp to slay its warriors by plague or sword in their sleep (Isa. 37:36–37)? Any reflective person would have felt his or her own vulnerability before Yahweh in hearing Nahum's description.

Nahum was read in the centuries that followed the catastrophic falls of Nineveh and Jerusalem to the Babylonian empire. The prophets remembered and described the arrogance of both. The detailed description of Jerusalem's fall in Lamentations reminds the attentive reader of Nahum that defeat is real and may come even to God's people when his law and protection are no longer kept. That lament is gruesome but necessary for understanding Nahum's message in context.

The people were stunned by the fall of Jerusalem (Lam. 2:13). During the siege, infants and babes died of starvation at their mother's breasts (2:11–12). Children, young people, and the elderly starved in the street, and women cannibalized their children (2:20–22). When the wall was breached, people were hunted in the streets of the ghettos and in the caves of the Judean desert (4:18–19). Those who survived were reduced to abject poverty, made to pay for water and wood (5:3–4). Virgins were raped in Zion and young men and boys were enslaved (5:11–13). Jeremiah wondered if Yahweh had rejected the people completely (5:20–22).

In the case of Lamentations, the only words of hope come in the physical center of book. Jeremiah declares his faith through clenched teeth of anguish:

> Yet this I call to mind
>   and therefore I have hope:
> Because of the LORD's great love we are not consumed,
>   for his compassions never fail.

> They are new every morning;
>> great is your faithfulness.
> I say to myself, "The LORD is my portion;
>> therefore I will wait for him." (Lam. 3:21–24)

Israel's witness (the biblical witness) to the destruction of the wicked has integrity only because they also tell the truth about the judgment of God against themselves. The difference is that the remnant turns to Yahweh in repentance and faith.

The enduring message of Nahum in the context of Scripture's full counsel is that God is against anyone and will destroy anyone who is rebelliously arrogant. Amos (who prophesied before Assyria enslaved and destroyed the northern ten tribes) made this abundantly clear by drawing the circling net of God's judgment against the lawlessness and arrogance closer and closer to home. He began with distant Damascus (Amos 1:3–5), Gaza (1:6–8), and Tyre (1:9–10). He moved closer with words against the sins of Edom (1:11–12), Ammon (1:13–15), and Moab (2:1–3). Then Yahweh spoke through Amos against Judah (2:4–5) and at length against the northern kingdom of Israel for their violence against the poor, for economic corruption, for sexual corruption, and for oppressing true faith (2:6–16). Nationalism and nationalistic interests even among God's chosen people do not protect them from the wrath and judgment of God.

Coming just before Nahum in the canon are Jonah and Micah. In Jonah, forgiveness is extended to the Ninevites when they repent. In Micah, the destruction of Jerusalem is declared for its corrupt government, people, priests, and prophets. Yahweh is against evil, no matter who is involved: Ninevite, Phoenician, pagan, Moslem, Jew, or Christian.

 ALTHOUGH FINDING A modern Christian application for the battle scene in Nahum 2 is challenging, there are several possibilities. The first is the relationship between warfare and the good news of the gospel. The second is to see how the Ninevites, once chosen by God to do his work and once forgiven of their sin through repentance, came to be enemies of God. Finally, an examination of the Ninevites' use of wealth may teach us a lesson about controlling our assets in ways that are pleasing to God.

Good news and warfare. In the preface to the battle scene in Nahum 2 (1:15 is 2:1 in the Heb. text), Nahum writes:

> Look, there on the mountains,
>> the feet of one who brings good news,
>> who proclaims peace!

> Celebrate your festivals, O Judah,
> and fulfill your vows.
> No more will the wicked invade you;
> they will be completely destroyed.

In certain times in the life of the church, images of warfare were used in thinking about the advance of the gospel. The Gospel of Mark in particular presents Jesus' confrontations with the spiritual enemy in his healing ministry. Paul describes how warfare against enemies is to be engaged in by heaping fiery coals of kindness on their heads (Rom. 12:14–21). The early church took hope in this verse as a promise of the resurrection of the martyrs in the last day—that they would experience victory over the enemies of death and the opponent of life, Satan.[13]

In spite of the misapplied historical burden of actual war-making in the Crusades, God's battle against the principalities and powers that enslave lives remains a reality of the Christian life. Paul writes that the war has already been won by the cross, resurrection, and ascension of Christ. The powers of darkness are in submission to him. He has disarmed, made a spectacle of, and triumphed over them by his death on the cross (Col. 2:13–15; cf. 1 Peter 3:22).

As a result, Christians are under attack and need the armor of God. "Put on the full armor of God so that you can take your stand against the devil's schemes. For our struggle is not against flesh and blood, but against the rulers, against the authorities, against the powers of this dark world and against the spiritual forces of evil in the heavenly realms" (Eph. 6:11–12). God's armor, given as a gift, includes truth, righteousness, the gospel of peace, faith, salvation, and the word of the Spirit. In suffering for the gospel of peace, Christians live in confidence that nothing "in all creation, will be able to separate us from the love of God that is in Christ Jesus our Lord" (Rom. 8:36–39). Like Nahum, we may live in the confidence that God has already determined the outcome of the battle. It was with this conviction that baptismal candidates were asked in the historic catechism, "Do you renounce sin, death, and the devil?" (M. Luther).

It would be a mistake to apply this battle imagery narrowly to the interior life of individual Christians. The purpose of Christ's victory and the Christian's confidence is that the gospel of peace may be proclaimed to those still living in bondage. Many people live under the authority of the same powers of evil that ruled in Nineveh. Many unbelievers are still enslaved by sin, death, and the enticements of evil. Paul uses Nahum's declaration of the battle for the "gospel of peace" to call for public witnesses:

---

13. See Spronk, *Nahum*, 17.

How, then, can they call on the one they have not believed in? And how can they believe in the one of whom they have not heard? And how can they hear without someone preaching to them? And how can they preach unless they are sent? As it is written, "How beautiful are the feet of those who bring good news!" (Rom. 10:14–15; Isa. 52:7; cf. Nah. 1:15)

The battle also calls for discipleship through teaching and explaining the gospel to those whose minds are held captive (2 Cor. 10:3–5). In all these things, the battle and the victory belong not to God's people but to God. Judah did not defeat Nineveh by itself, the Babylonians did. Whether Judah fights and wins (2 Kings 19) or someone else engages the battle against God's enemy, Yahweh is victorious and praised. The point is that God's beloved creation is set free to serve and praise him.

Friend or foe of God? "'I am against you,' declares the LORD Almighty" (2:13). When Abraham Lincoln came into office, he is reported to have said, "I am going to get rid of all my enemies. I will turn them into friends." Reconciliation is what God attempted with Nineveh in the days of Jonah, but in Nahum the time had come to "make an end" (1:8). Jacob struggled against a stranger and enemy at the River Jabbok in his struggle to return to his home and to Esau. God had attempted to befriend him years earlier when he ran (at Bethel), but Jacob was noncommittal (Gen. 28:13–22). At the river, God assaulted Jacob and turned him into a friend, giving him the name "Israel," which means "he strives with God and prevails" (Gen. 32:24–32). God also assaulted Moses after his call because of his failure to circumcise (Ex. 4:24–26).

In each case God was "against" people in order to turn them into friends. Even in the defeat of Nineveh, the possibility remained that Ninevite believers (from the time of Jonah) could rely on the friendship of God (see the introduction to Jonah). Jeremiah could profess his faith even in the horrific ruin that Yahweh brought on Jerusalem (Lam. 3, see above).

The opposition between Yahweh and people may be applied to our own situation from two perspectives. (1) God is against us, for our sake. It is not enough to ask, "Is God for us or against us?" The answer is "both." The scriptural witness is that because God is "for us," he stands against our daily tendency to rebel against him. Because of the constant temptation to live self-sufficiently, without reference to God, God confronts us and our communities with our need to confess our sin, accept his friendship, and offer praise to our Maker. God's consistent attitude toward us is friendship, even when he stands against us, until, as in Nahum, time runs out.

(2) The second application of God as foe in Nahum is in a person's or a community's opposition to Yahweh. Over a long period of time, Israel, Assyria, and finally Jerusalem itself demonstrated their opposition to God.

They were not interested in the conditions of friendship with the Almighty. They simply wanted a rubber stamp blessing. God is against those who continually demonstrate their opposition to him. He still desires their friendship but pursues it through opposition, not through invitation. Many believe, however, that their opposition to God is to their own advantage. This is the heart of the lie that Yahweh attacks. The creature cannot truly prosper by standing against the Creator. Even in standing as a foe to those who stand against him, God is for his beloved creation. Achtemeier says, "How we as nations or individuals stand in the eyes of God finally determines our death or life."[14] Only when one has known Yahweh's opposition, confessed one's sin (Matt. 12:41), and been reconciled can Paul's words have meaning for us: "If God is for us, who can be against us?" (Rom. 8:31b).

Excesses and the moderation of wealth. Chapter 2 focuses a theme that reverberates more subtly through the entire book. Nineveh is drowning in the irresponsible use of its excessive wealth. This word is not simply for the wealthy but for all who use money without reference to God.

> Nineveh is like a pool,
> and its water is draining away.
> "Stop! Stop!" they cry,
> but no one turns back.
> Plunder the silver!
> Plunder the gold!
> The supply is endless,
> the wealth from all its treasures! (2:8–9)

Other symptoms of their overconfident comfort and consuming lifestyle are found throughout the book. They are drunk from their wine, like dry stubble for burning (1:10). They are numerous and have many allies (1:12). They are full of lies and plunder (3:1), boundless in strength (3:9), and they have fortresses like a full ripe fig tree (3:12); merchants are as numerous as the stars (3:16), guards and officials are like swarms of locusts (3:17), and shepherds and nobles lie down to rest in the midst of a battle (3:18). Nineveh is full of ripe excesses.

The warning of the text to those who have wealth or who use money without moderation is that God takes that wealth away.[15] Like a pool being emptied, its water is draining away. The main image that endures for the contemporary world is the control of the flow of the water. The people yell, "Stop! Stop!" but it is too late. The floodgates (levies) are no longer in their control.

---

14. Achtemeier, *Nahum-Malachi*, 22.
15. Luther, quoted in Spronk, *Nahum*, 17.

Sennacherib had built a big reservoir to collect fresh water from the mountains. Levies controlled the water flow from this reservoir into the Husur River and into the city. The levies let the water into the city moats and canals or kept it out, thus controlling levels.[16] The outflow levies controlled the water flowing out of the city. As long as Nineveh controlled the levies, it did what it pleased. When God's agent Babylon took control, however, the draining of the reservoir into the city became a symbol for what Nineveh had been doing with its wealth and power: extravagantly gathering and flaunting at the expense of all other cultures. It was chastised because it did not control its wealth and power as it controlled its water levies. Because it did not, its water and wealth were both spilled out in unwanted ways.

No one social group within Nineveh is singled out in the book. Nahum uses the collective "you" to speak of the overripe excesses of a society. Nineveh's life of collective excess ran its course to destruction like an overflowing pool. The warning against excess is not that wealth is necessarily bad. The levy symbolizes the moderate use of wealth and a generous hand to the poor of the world. Without these, a society or a person may drown in their own wealth.

God's word on giving has many facets. God said at Sinai that a tenth of all income belonged to him for his work in the community, including sustenance for those who did not have an inheritance of land (Lev. 27:33). God also advised that when you give, it should be done freely and ungrudgingly, by opening your hand to the needy and poor (Deut. 15:10–11). Jesus raised the bar by telling the rich young ruler to give *everything* away before following him (Mark 10:21). In that light, a tithe seems like a bargain. Jesus advised us not to lay up treasures on earth, thereby neglecting heaven and our hearts (Matt. 6:19–21). The psalmist echoed the law that the offering was an integral part of worship when he said, "Ascribe to the LORD the glory due his name; bring an offering and come into his courts" (Ps. 96:8).

Jesus chastised the Pharisees for neglecting the important matters of the law: justice, mercy, and faithfulness, telling them that they should attend to them as well as to their tithe (Matt. 23:23). He advised the multitudes to "give, and it will be given to you. A good measure, pressed down, shaken together and running over, will be poured into your lap. For with the measure you use, it will be measured to you" (Luke 6:38). Using the floodgate image, God said through Malachi, "Bring the whole tithe into the storehouse, that there may be food in my house. Test me in this . . . and see if I will not throw open the floodgates of heaven and pour out so much blessing that you will not have

---

16. Spronk, ibid., 99.

room enough for it" (Mal. 3:10). Great generosity, Paul told the Corinthians, makes us rich in every way (2 Cor. 9:10–11).

By contrast, John warns that anyone who has the world's goods and closes his or her heart also closes out God's love altogether (1 John 3:17–18). Paul echoes this belief when he says that those who sow sparingly will reap sparingly (2 Cor. 9:6). He also said that we should give to support the weak, remembering the words of Jesus that "it is more blessed to give than to receive" (Acts 20:35). Those who have the ability to give much should consider it a spiritual gift and give with liberality (Rom. 12:6–8). Finally, Paul echoes the Lord's word at Sinai about giving freely when he says that God loves a cheerful giver (2 Cor. 9:7).

The total witness of Scripture on the use of wealth is more positive than Nahum's. Clearly God calls all his people to compassionate and generous giving, with at the very least the first tenth literally belonging to him. The message of Nahum on wealth and the levy is more severe: You have been given the power to control the flow of your money in moderation. If you don't, God will take control of it for redistribution.

Nahum 3

¹ Woe to the city of blood,
    full of lies,
full of plunder,
    never without victims!
² The crack of whips,
    the clatter of wheels,
galloping horses
    and jolting chariots!
³ Charging cavalry,
    flashing swords
    and glittering spears!
Many casualties,
    piles of dead,
bodies without number,
    people stumbling over the corpses—
⁴ all because of the wanton lust of a harlot,
    alluring, the mistress of sorceries,
who enslaved nations by her prostitution
    and peoples by her witchcraft.

⁵ "I am against you," declares the LORD Almighty.
    "I will lift your skirts over your face.
I will show the nations your nakedness
    and the kingdoms your shame.
⁶ I will pelt you with filth,
    I will treat you with contempt
    and make you a spectacle.
⁷ All who see you will flee from you and say,
    'Nineveh is in ruins—who will mourn for her?'
    Where can I find anyone to comfort you?"

⁸ Are you better than Thebes,
    situated on the Nile,
    with water around her?
The river was her defense,
    the waters her wall.
⁹ Cush and Egypt were her boundless strength;
    Put and Libya were among her allies.

¹⁰ Yet she was taken captive
    and went into exile.
Her infants were dashed to pieces
    at the head of every street.
Lots were cast for her nobles,
    and all her great men were put in chains.
¹¹ You too will become drunk;
    you will go into hiding
    and seek refuge from the enemy.

¹² All your fortresses are like fig trees
    with their first ripe fruit;
when they are shaken,
    the figs fall into the mouth of the eater.
¹³ Look at your troops—
    they are all women!
The gates of your land
    are wide open to your enemies;
    fire has consumed their bars.

¹⁴ Draw water for the siege,
    strengthen your defenses!
Work the clay,
    tread the mortar,
    repair the brickwork!
¹⁵ There the fire will devour you;
    the sword will cut you down
    and, like grasshoppers, consume you.
Multiply like grasshoppers,
    multiply like locusts!
¹⁶ You have increased the number of your merchants
    till they are more than the stars of the sky,
but like locusts they strip the land
    and then fly away.
¹⁷ Your guards are like locusts,
    your officials like swarms of locusts
    that settle in the walls on a cold day—
but when the sun appears they fly away,
    and no one knows where.

¹⁸ O king of Assyria, your shepherds slumber;
    your nobles lie down to rest.

Your people are scattered on the mountains
  with no one to gather them.
¹⁹ Nothing can heal your wound;
  your injury is fatal.
Everyone who hears the news about you
  claps his hands at your fall,
for who has not felt
  your endless cruelty?

THE MAIN THEME of Nahum 3 is the end of Nineveh's "endless cruelty." The graphic description of its coming woe is presented in three parts. (1) A section on Nineveh's cruelty and exposure (3:1–7) has many similarities to chapter 2. They are like panels on a wall with similar content, matching in some ways but arranged differently. It begins with a vivid description of Nineveh's bloody war-making (3:1–3; cf. 2:3–6) and with a strong sorceress metaphor for its deep offenses (3:4; cf. 2:11–12). It continues with "the LORD Almighty's" second declaration, "I am against you," and with a description of Nineveh's coming exposure (3:5–6; cf. 2:13). Human response to the judgment follows (3:7; cf. 2:7–10).

(2) A unit on Nineveh's vulnerability (3:8–13) compares Nineveh to the stronger cities of Egypt that have already fallen (3:8–11). Two metaphors taunt Nineveh's warmongers, comparing their fortresses to ripe fig trees and their troops to peace-loving women (3:12–13).

(3) The final section on Nineveh's corruption and the joy of the surrounding nations over its fall (3:14–19) mocks Nineveh's futile battle preparations and corrupt leadership. With the final metaphor of locusts (grasshoppers), Nahum indicates that Nineveh's fall will be completed through its self-serving leaders who will plunder what they can and flee (3:14–17). The last word concerning the end of Nineveh's cruelty (3:18–19) is to the king of Assyria, who will be abandoned by all his people and fearful allies. Everyone will celebrate, for who had not been overwhelmed by his oppressive actions?

Nineveh's Cruelty Exposed (3:1–7)

THE EXPOSURE OF Nineveh's cruelty is accomplished through Nahum's graphic vision of the "city of blood" (3:1–3) and by a powerful taunt metaphor for military defeat (3:4–7). It begins with a vivid description of Nineveh's war-making with a cry of "woe" (*hoy*) for all its violence. Nineveh's evil reputation and Yahweh's wrath against its details begin the chapter: "blood ... lies

... plunder ... never without victims" (3:1). The last verse of the chapter echoes this beginning with the question: "Who has not felt your endless cruelty?" (3:19).

Woe oracles were prophetic threats that had their primary context in funeral dirges (1 Kings 13:30; Jer. 22:18–19).[1] Jerusalem was the target of a similar woe oracle (Ezek. 24:6, 9) a few years after the fall of Nineveh.[2] Nineveh's woe was for four reasons: blood, lies, plunder, and victims (Nah. 3:1). Nineveh was known for shedding "blood" and often boasted of the details in art and written form (see "The Terror-Mongers of Nineveh, Assyria" in the introduction to Jonah).

Nineveh was also known for its "lies." The phrase in 3:1 can be translated, "It has perfected deceit" (see 2 Chron. 28:16, 20–21 for an example of Assyria's deceit against Israel). Its government had perfected duplicity in its treatment of other countries, making peace and then attacking (not unlike Hitler with Czechoslovakia). Such governments also practice domestic propaganda against their own citizens to create a false sense of prosperity and peace.

Nineveh had many of the spoils of its "plunder." At its height the Assyrian empire controlled the Middle East from North Africa to Iran, and the city of Nineveh received many stolen treasures. Nineveh's "merchants" were like locusts that descended on conquered cities and stripped them of all their goods (see 3:16). This city of blood was never without "victims" (2:12–13; 3:1; lit., "prey that is torn"; see 2:11–13).

This description of Nineveh and its woeful reputation is abruptly followed by a sensory vision of preparation to stage an attack (3:2), the attack itself (3:3a), and the resultant carnage (3:3b). The sounds and sensations carry the listener to the scene of preparation for battle: "crack ... clatter ... gallop ... jolt." These sounds of the mobilization of troops would be familiar to the many witnesses of Nineveh's aggressions. The sights of the attack then transport the hearer to the battle itself: "charging cavalry, flashing swords, and glittering spears." Finally, the carnage appears, its magnitude reinforced by a repetitive fourfold description: "Many casualties, piles of dead, bodies without number, people stumbling over the corpses."

Exposure of evil always requires a detailed description of what has been done; otherwise all is lost in abstraction. In three short verses Nahum summarizes Nineveh's own offensive reputation: blood, lies, plunder, victims, whips, wheels, horses, chariots, cavalry, swords, spears, casualties, dead, bodies, corpses. What is the motivation for this unparalleled aggression in the ancient world?

---

1. See Longman, "Nahum," 812, for an extended discussion of "woe."
2. For other examples of woe oracles, see Amos 5:18–20; 6:1–7; Mic. 2:1–4.

Verse 4 begins a strong metaphor with the source of Nineveh's deep offenses. All the dead bodies and slaves of Assyria's aggressions are "because of the wanton lust" (3:4a). The metaphor of a sorceress-harlot, though not familiar to modern readers, serves to name the source of Nineveh's corruptions. Nahum joins two metaphors (harlotry and sorcery) as one offense by the parallel poetic structure in 3:4: "wanton lust [blood, lies, plunder, victims] of a harlot [*zonah*] . . . mistress of sorceries [*kašap*]," followed by "enslaved nations by her prostitution [*zonah*] . . . witchcraft [*kašap*]."

With a double metaphor verse 4 presents the primary and deep offense of Nineveh's rule over the ancient Near East (3:4). The primary offense is found in the phrase "who enslaved nations . . . and peoples." Nations may be translated "cultures" or "ethnic groups"; "peoples" may be translated "families" or "clans." Enslaving them is what the Ninevites did. Nineveh captured many political and ethnic groups and forced them to submit to its control and will, sustaining a lucrative slave-based economy. The reference is not to simple prostitution, but the combination of sorcery and harlotry, which indicate the tremendous power and wealth gained.

Elsewhere the "harlotry" of ritual prostitution refers to Jerusalem or the people of Israel (Ezek. 16:14–34; 23:1–21; Hos. 1:2). A faithful marriage relationship is an important biblical metaphor for the exclusive nature of human faithfulness to Yahweh. The reference to harlotry is not a direct reference to sexual sin but an indirect metaphor from biblical law for seeking personal power by following other gods, betraying Yahweh. Worship of the gods that tempted Israel often included ritual intercourse at the temple. As a result, the most powerful metaphor for turning away from Yahweh was fornication or harlotry. When used of Israel, the metaphor means "turning to other gods."

Nineveh's offense as a sorceress-harlot was in following "gods" of greed, sexuality, and power. The focus is not on their improper sexuality but on the use of power by which Nineveh enslaved many ethnic groups, cultures, and nations. That metaphor points to the enslaving of nations, the primary offense named in 3:4.[3]

Yahweh then states directly a second time, "I am against you" (3:5; cf. 2:13). He says "I" six times in 3:5–7, giving a description of his revelation to the nations (3:5–6). He will "reveal" the truth beneath Nineveh's glitter and allure in order that the cultures of the world will "see." Yahweh's deeds come in two sets. In 3:5 the "seeing" is in the verb "I will show" or "I will cause (them) to see," which means, "I will cause them to understand" their nakedness and their shame. This is a reversal of the deception (3:5) in which all

---

3. Cf. Rev. 17:3–6.

things come to light. Yahweh will lift the metaphorical skirts to show the world the detestable truth of Nineveh's enslavements and torture. The lies of the glitter and the false glamor are stripped away, and the naked truth of the abuse is fully exposed and made helpless.[4] It is an ironic reversal of Nineveh's position, even at the time of this prophecy, when she proudly exposed the helplessness of her victims.

Yahweh will make Nineveh "a spectacle" by throwing "filth" and treating them with "contempt" (3:6). The word translated "filth" (*šiqquṣim*) is translated in other contexts as "detestable" or "abominable." It is often a reference to idols, which are "filth" to Yahweh. The image may be of God throwing Nineveh's idols back at it. "Contempt" is from the root for "fool" (*nabal*). It is an ironically appropriate description of a fool who made a pit to trap others but falls into it himself (Ps. 7:15–16). To be treated as a *nabal* means that Nineveh will receive its own violent medicine.

The human response to Yahweh's deeds of revelation follows in 3:7: They will flee and wonder, "Who will mourn for her?" (3:7). The entire area had been enslaved by Nineveh. Some were enticed, some were tricked, and some were forced, but all became its slaves. When Yahweh exposes the evil of Nineveh's actions, its corrupting of what had been created good will be obvious to everyone. All will see the festering diseases beneath its alluring beauty. No one will defend slavery and its promises of wealth, power, and prowess. Yahweh's utterance concludes with the question that echoes Nahum's name: "Where can I find anyone to comfort you?"

Nineveh's Vulnerability (3:8–13)

NAHUM NOW COMPARES Nineveh to the stronger cities of Egypt that fell fifty years before Nineveh (663 B.C.) and then compares its fortresses to ripe figs and its troops to peaceful women.

(1) The demeaning tone of Yahweh's questions to the Ninevites serves to convince them of the warnings of Nineveh's coming fall. "So, you believe it is impossible? You feel your security is sure? Are your defenses better than those of Thebes?" If some Ninevites believe the prophecy, perhaps they will repent and flee. Israelites hearing this address to Nineveh may also be convinced to hope that it is possible for the strong city to fall. This is a rhetorical question that anticipates a negative answer.

Thebes was also defended by waterworks and moats filled by the Nile River. It was one of the great and enduring cities of the ancient world (2000–663 B.C.). At the time of its defeat, Thebes controlled Egypt and Cush

---

4. If "nakedness" or "shame" is understood here as genitalia, the masculine forms in Hebrew should be taken into account with the female image of the harlot.

(ancient Ethiopia that included northern Sudan) and was allied with Put (part of present-day Libya or else Somalia) and Libya. The great irony is that Thebes was conquered by Assyrian King Ashurbanipal. It was the best-defended city ever conquered until Nineveh. The comparison would have raised a valid and haunting question among those who remembered their conquest of Thebes.

Nahum describes what Assyria did to Thebes, rhetorically adding to their offenses. Their deeds were typical of ancient warfare and will now also accompany Assyria's defeat by Babylon. Infants were dashed upon the ground (2 Kings 8:12; Isa. 13:16; Hos. 13:16), and the honored elders, wealthy, political leaders, and strong men were chained and sold into slavery.

"You too will become drunk" (3:11) is an image of despair and helplessness, a common response of those who suddenly encounter the consequences of their sins before God (Ps. 75:8; Isa. 19:14; 51:17; Rev 14:10; 16:19; 19:15). Like Thebes, Nineveh will "go into hiding" (the Heb. may also mean "swoon" or "pass out") and seek refuge from the attacking enemy.

(2) Nahum goes on to use two metaphors to provoke Nineveh's warmongers, comparing their fortresses to ripe fig trees and their troops to peace-loving women (3:12–13). A shift in verb tense brings us into the present. Nahum takes a tour of Nineveh's defenses. Its fortresses are like ripe figs, falling off the branch to be eaten.[5] Its troops "are all [like] women" who do not want to or cannot fight. Its city gates cannot be closed because they have been used as fuel in a fire. The whole impression of the tour is domestic and open. This would be greatly ironic to those under Assyria's thumb of oppression. It would also be an offensive description to the Ninevites, who consider themselves fit, war-worthy, and prepared.

Nineveh's Corruption and the Joy of the Nations (3:14–19)

THIS CHAPTER AND book conclude with a second vision of battle, a "slippery" insect metaphor, and a rejoicing dirge that ends with a question from the LORD.

Nahum ironically cautions the Ninevites to make preparations to strengthen their weak defenses (3:14). This is the second time sarcasm has been used to attract the powerful Ninevites' attention (cf. 2:1). The metaphor of locusts (3:15–17) indicates that, in the end, Nineveh's self-serving leaders will plunder the city themselves and flee.

Five general-like commands direct the repair work for the city under attack: "Draw water for the siege, strengthen your defenses! Work the clay,

---

5. The metaphor of "eating" is continued in 3:13, 15. See the summary at 1:10.

tread the mortar, repair the brickwork." These preparations, however, will come too late. Nahum prophesies that while they work, "the fire will devour you; the sword will cut you down and, like grasshoppers, consume you" (3:15). The same Hebrew word (ʾakal) that has the general meaning of "eating" is translated "devour" and "consume." Both the fire and the sword will swallow Nineveh.

In the middle of 3:15 Nahum switches to the metaphor "grasshoppers." In 3:15a the "grasshoppers" are the swords that will consume Nineveh. In 3:15b–17 Nahum pivots on the word "grasshopper" and begins to speak of the Ninevites themselves as the locusts. This literary move does more than change the subject to Nineveh. It points to the corruption of Nineveh's leaders (merchants, guards, and officials), who will continue their stripping ways in Nineveh even on the day of their fall. They, like grasshoppers and locusts, strip the land. They also, like the insects, will fly away when the sun appears. The cutters become flyers.

The inclusion of "merchants," "guards," and "officials" in this corruption taunt details the systemic evil of the culture. Everyone is complicit and involved. The burden of Assyrian rule on the land has been the officials and traders who regularly followed their conquering army. Assyria's "officials" are scribes and lawyers who redistributed the land and the wealth. Her "merchants" are traders who gathered the wealth and exported it to Nineveh's markets (see 2:9). Her "guards" are professional soldiers who have provided a military escort for the merchants and officials and caused trouble. Everyone knew or was related to somebody in this enterprise.

The final word is directed to the king of Assyria (3:18–19). It is a dirge of isolation as his people are scattered, his nobles and shepherds fall asleep, and his previously conquered neighbors celebrate, clapping their hands. "Your people are scattered" can be translated, "your troops are scattered" (cf. 3:13), or even, "your troops catch their breath."[6] In that case they are running away with "no one to gather them"; that is, the king's military officers are also gone.

The final sentences express the absolute end in three waves. "No one to gather [the people]," "nothing can heal," and "everyone . . . claps his hands." Why will everyone clap their hands? Because everyone has felt "your endless cruelty" (i.e., "your continual evil"—an echo of 1:11, "one who plots evil"). "Who has not felt [ʿabar]" can be translated "who has not been overwhelmed by." Their ending is expressed dramatically and with power.[7] Everyone rejoices to be free of this evil regime.

---

6. See Longman, "Nahum," 828, for a summary of the scholarly discussion.

7. ʿabar is a major word theme of Nahum (see 1:8, 12; 2:1; 3:19; see comments at 1:8).

THE SIGNIFICANCE OF Nahum 3 first appears as a series of difficulties or enduring problems of the text. Three themes create tension for the interpreter: the violence of God, the image of the sexual abuse of the metaphorical woman, and the related exposure of sin. Each of these is an enduring challenge for the reader today.

The violence of God. God says, "Are you better than Thebes?" and "her infants were dashed to pieces at the head of every street" (3:8a, 10b). A simple reading of the text reveals that earlier the Assyrians "dashed" infants to the ground, and the Babylonians are now dashing the Assyrian children. Most readers, however, quickly see the theological problem just beneath the surface. God implies and history shows that God commissioned the same violence in Nineveh. Infants were killed by ancient armies to annihilate hope for future restoration and to empty the arms of women marching in shackles to distant slave markets. How can we talk of a God who claims responsibility for the violent death of innocents?

A common response of interpreters is to say nothing, thereby avoiding the simmering imagery. Many commentaries dodge the problem through silence. A Bible teacher or pastor may do this also, for good reason, since resolving the problem of God's violence for students or parishioners is not easy. The Bible, however, does not afford the luxury of ignoring what everyone knows to be true in the world: Every day innocent children are killed in wars, in clinics, or in violent homes. Scripture does not hide the enduring reality of a world gone mad. Grown women and men kill children in God's world.

The tension is necessarily resolved in part by stating that sin and the will of sinful people account for these heinous crimes against children. Today, as then, rebellious people futilely seek to increase their own well-being through violence against the most powerless.[8] After all, it is the evil Assyrians and the Babylonians who actually commit the murder of the infants.

The tension may be further resolved linguistically and philosophically by noting that when speaking of God, Scripture uses the language of "accommodation." Since God is not a human being, Scripture necessarily uses anthropomorphisms to speak of his actions in the world. Often the anthropomorphisms erroneously cause us to think of God as a human being and to forget that what Yahweh does is done perfectly. In addition, God, as Creator, is behind all that is done in the universe. Any single action must be understood as part of a larger pattern that is not easily understood.

---

8. Our society, like the ancient societies, steals life from children by not carefully attending to their nurture in gestation or in the critical first three years.

The sharp edges of the text remain sharp. The problem with each of these solutions, for people who read Scripture as God's Word, is that God directly takes responsibility for the destruction of Thebes and Nineveh. To dismiss the slaughter of infants as the work of evil men, linguistically or philosophically, does not actually put it out of mind. Nor does it settle the contemporary issue of innocent suffering today. God is still the master of an awful mess. "Answers" to the mess are in short supply.

One wisdom tradition offers the "answer" that "all life is suffering." With this perspective one accepts the problem and lives into it. The story of Jesus offers another perspective that includes God. "When Herod realized that he had been outwitted by the Magi, he was furious, and he gave orders to kill all the boys in Bethlehem and its vicinity who were two years old and under, in accordance with the time he had learned from the Magi" (Matt. 2:16). God in the flesh entered into the fight against evil, not as an obvious conquering warrior but as an innocent. The infant Jesus himself was the target of the same strategy as "dashing on the rocks." God's ownership of the responsibility for the human problem did not remain philosophical but took on flesh. He became vulnerable to the violence, running (with Mary and Joseph) for his life to Egypt. He entered the "mess" and the violence, even to a torturous death as an abandoned criminal.

Against women? In the contemporary setting the label of misogyny is thought appropriate for any hint of violence against women. However, any interpretation that supports a general notion of hatred against women must be deconstructed. Anyone who uses Nahum as support to legitimize hatred of women makes an egregious interpretive error. It is obvious that the text is violent and that the object of the violence is a woman. This may be enough in our present climate of awareness of violence against women to avoid public reading of this problematic and easily misinterpreted description of God violently using a woman (3:5–6).

If we read these dangerous verses publicly, two fundamental truths ought to be clearly articulated. (1) The violence that God says Babylon will do for him is against everyone in Assyria. Anyone who uses the metaphor of violence against the sorceress-harlot may see the finger of God pointed at them. The prophecy is against all those who use power and sexuality inappropriately. To apply this text against women in particular is to use interpretive power inappropriately. The actual violence of the text is against the entire population—men, women, and children. The sorceress-harlot metaphor in particular is a reference to a nation's use of seduction and power for horrific purposes (see the Original Meaning section). We would do well to consider that Wisdom is also portrayed as a woman and to learn from her (Prov. 1–4, 7–9).

(2) God is the One who claims responsibility for the violence against everyone. If the text is applied to our situation, God's responsibility and not human agency must be clearly understood. "Vengeance is mine," says the Lord. No one can claim to do God's work of vengeance without condemning themselves. That God used the equally corrupt Babylonian army as his agent in this work is no accident. He did not use holy warriors, and the Babylonians did not see themselves as such. Those who do God's will in violence of this magnitude stand condemned by their own violence.

In the final assessment, the text remains problematic. Even with the interpretive caveats outlined above, the use of the metaphor of violence against a woman (even a powerful woman) must be approached with a deep sense of grief and interpretive warning. Violence is too much alive in the cultures of the world today to proceed in any other way.

Nakedness exposed. The image of the violent and complete exposure of Assyria tells an enduring truth about God's judgment: Everything will be revealed in God's judgment. Every life will be an open book. Jesus claimed to be the light that would expose all deeds (John 3:19–20). The early church experienced radical conversions, even of sorcerers, who confessed their evil deeds publicly (Acts 19:18–20). Paul encouraged believers to be clothed with the light of Christ and so expose their dark deeds in repentance (Rom. 13:12–14; Eph. 5:8–14). Through John, the Spirit warned the church that the Lord knew their deeds and "shameful nakedness" and counseled them to repent and be covered (Rev. 3:14–19).

The enduring truth echoed throughout the New Testament is that everyone, when exposed before God, will be found to be a shameful and diseased sorceress-harlot. It is a harsh image, but it tells the truth. Prostitutes offer what they cannot deliver: beauty and love. They sell what should not be sold and cannot be bought: intimacy and a lifetime of love, care, and commitment. The exposure of Assyria and our own exposure demonstrate that what any culture offers, believes, and promises apart from Christ is a lie. We are exposed as "sorcerers" when we trust in things that bring us power (e.g., technologies, both domestic and military). Serving created things for the power they render is a form of idolatry that attempts to stand in for the Creator. The exposure of cultures and individuals ultimately leads to a powerless death. Everyone is exposed under the harsh image of the sorceress-harlot.

Everyone is exposed before God, naked in unrighteousness and in need of being clothed. "Clothe yourself in Christ," Paul admonishes (Rom. 13:14). The word "clothe" or "cover" also means "atone" or "deliver" in Hebrew (*kapar*—as in Yom Kippur, Day of Atonement.). The *kapporet* was the "mercy seat" (the cover) of the ark of the covenant, where the blood of forgiveness was sprinkled. Paul knew that to be clothed in Christ meant that the nakedness of each person's unrighteousness was "covered" by Christ.

We don't like the violent judgment of God. We don't like the violence of the cross. We don't like the exposing light of the cross that reveals our self-centeredness before a God who is willing to give everything, even himself. His self-giving exposure on a cross exposes our selfishness, our nakedness, our shortcomings, and our corruptions. Unless we are made naked and die to ourselves, we can never be clothed in Jesus. In regard to our desperate need, we are no different than the people of Nineveh.

A NATURAL RESPONSE to the most uncomfortable parts of Nahum is to create distance between the book and our present situation. The descriptions of the abusive exposure of the harlot in 3:5 and the killing of infants in 3:10 are especially disturbing.[9] Avoiding these passages of Scripture is the most obvious way to apply our contemporary discomfort. This avoidance sometimes rests on the claim that Christ's command to love our enemies has made some texts insignificant for the Christian (Joshua and Nahum are usually at the top of the list). Yet something may be learned from this part of God's Word. At the other end of the spectrum, the book may be applied as an excuse for *human* violence against evil. This involves putting humanity in the place of God or the Babylonian army in the text, something that is commonly called "sin" (see the Original Meaning section on 1:2).[10]

Between these two extremes, Christians have used a wide range of strategies for understanding Nahum. Many have the effect of pushing the violence into a neat interpretive corner. These rationales avoid the possibility that God will afflict us and those who are dear to us. God's violence against the woman and against the infants is a warning that catastrophic violence may also come into our communities and require a response from the faithful. Those who have taken Nahum's word to heart may be prepared to speak and to act in accordance with the gospel. On that occasion Christians will have the opportunity to stand with the suffering and earn the credibility of a witness to God's power both to kill and make alive. The alternative is to

---

9. For his excellent discussion and interpretive proposals for Nahum I am indebted to Richard Nysse, "Keeping Company with Nahum: Reading the Oracles Against the Nations As Scripture," in *Word and World* 15 (Fall 1995): 412–19.

10. The lawful use of force for maintaining security in a community should not be confused with "violence."

distance oneself ideologically from the suffering (even one's own) and to lose credibility and even one's faith in a good God.

We distance ourselves in a variety of ways from the text's claim that God uses violence to accomplish his will. We can isolate such claims as the embarrassing historical nationalistic diatribes of the Judean prophet against Nineveh. This comes at the cost of removing God from the discussion. We can isolate it as a unique historical circumstance in which God acted before the time of Christ. This requires ignoring or dancing around Jesus' own words about the violence of the nations to come (Matt. 24; Mark 13; Luke 19:44; 21:18–36) and the violence of the book of Revelation. Another strategy is to point only to the positive passages of comfort in Nahum, such as: "His way is in the whirlwind" (1:3b); "the LORD is good" (1:7); "look ... the feet of one who brings good news" (1:15); and "the LORD will restore" (2:2). The quality of the poetry can also be praised.

Perhaps the most common and easily accepted move is to acknowledge violence as the necessary punishment of the enemy of God, even with its troubling murder of innocents and actual rape of Ninevite women by the Babylonians. This reading, of course, has substantial warrants in the text and is a common assumption of ancient warfare. The end result, however, is either that the text is again relegated to significance only in the *past*, or that we are left only with the option of applying it against our own enemies. There is no word in it *for us* except that God will destroy our enemies. The problem with this application is that most of the time in Scripture, the words of God against a people are against his own people.

Just as in Nahum 3:5, God uses rape-like language against the people of Jerusalem through Isaiah, Jeremiah, Ezekiel, and Zechariah. "I will pull up your skirts over your face that your shame may be seen" (Jer. 13:26), and "I will gather all the nations to Jerusalem to fight against it; the city will be captured, the houses ransacked, and the women raped" (Zech. 14:2a; see also Isa. 47:2–3; Ezek. 16:37).

Just as in Nahum 3:10, God prophesies through Jeremiah, Hosea, and Ezekiel that he will kill infants with everyone else in Jerusalem on the day of wrath. "Even if they bear children, I will slay their cherished offspring" (Hos. 9:16b), and "'I will smash them one against the other, fathers and sons alike, declares the LORD. I will allow no pity or mercy or compassion to keep me from destroying them'" (Jer. 13:14; see also Hos. 10:10–15; 13:16). God is against Nineveh (Nahum 2:13) in the same way that he is against his beloved people. Nineveh does not stand alone. The identical language ("I am against you") is used in Scripture primarily against his covenant people (Isa. 63:10; Jer. 21:5–6; Ezek. 5:8; 21:3). In this context we dare not read Nahum as if we are exempt from God's judgment or cataclysmic violence. To claim exemption is exactly what the enemies of God did. We must read "in solidarity with the judged."[11]

The challenge for Christians is to hear Nahum as a living word against us. The violence of God may be accepted as relevant Scripture for the Christian today by bringing it close. It may be brought close by considering ourselves as the Ninevites. It may also be brought close by reading similar words spoken against God's chosen people. Historically, no one escapes the violence of God. God's enemies and God's beloved all suffer from their rebellion. The difference is whether the suffering is accepted in repentance and becomes redemptive or not.

The first Christians suffered such unmerciful persecution at the hand of the Romans that John cried out "How long?" (Rev. 6:10). Their suffering drove them to rely on the cross of Christ, the memory of Jesus' sufferings (the Lamb that was slain), the warnings to the churches, and the promise of the fulfillment of his resurrection victory (themes of Revelation). Paul spoke of his sufferings that came from many sources, yet ultimately from God. Some sufferings were a direct result of his preaching, but others "just happened" (see his catalog of painful experiences in 2 Cor. 11:24–27). He also suffered a chronic physical ailment ("thorn in the flesh") that God would not remove from him in order that God's power could be perfected in him (12:7–9).

John Donne also understood the advantage and grace of being assaulted by God.

> I, like a usrupt towne, to another due,
> Labor to admit you, but Oh, to no end.
> Reason, your viceroy in mee, mee should defend
> But is captiv'd and proves weak or untrue . . .
> [I] am betroth'd unto your enemie:
> Divorce mee, untie or breake that knot againe.
> Take mee to you, imprison me, for I,
> Except you enthrall mee, never shall be free,
> Nor ever chast[e] except you ravish me.[12]

Donne invited the assault of God because it freed him from his bondage to the limitation of his own experiences. This positive view of assault as a way to experience the grace of God is not commonly used. Certainly to one who has been actually battered or raped this application may be futile and counterproductive. For them, Nahum's word of comfort through the Lord's vengeance against the wicked may suffice. But the word stands against the powerful and self-satisfied.

---

11. Nysse, "Keeping Company with Nahum," 419.

12. "Batter My Heart," a sonnet by John Donne; see Grierson, ed., *The Poems of John Donne*, 299; the poem can also be found at http://www.recmusic.org/lieder/merge.cgi?11.

Jesus echoes the harshest part of Nahum's prophecy (3:10). The word of warning is the same: "They will dash you to the ground, you and the children within your walls" (Luke 19:44a). By his presence, teaching, life, death, and resurrection, Jesus offers a new doorway to peace with God. Those who die in him will also rise with him. He does not, however, remove the reality of death or the threat of a vengeful death for those who do "not recognize the time of God's coming to you" (19:44). All who persist in rebellion against the Creator are subject to the severe warnings of Nahum and Jesus. Christians also died in Jerusalem when the Romans finally razed it in A.D. 70. The difference was that they died in hope and promise rather than in fear and judgment.

The harshest themes of Nahum's judgment are also used in the book of Revelation. There the referent city is Rome, which inherited the metaphor of the sorceress-harlot (3:4) from Assyria and Babylon (Rev. 9:20; 17:1–2; 18:23). In Revelation, the warning against the self-serving worship of created things stands, as does the promise that the sufferings of the faithful will bear fruit and be vindicated in a new creation. The two general concerns of these texts are the magic arts and false worship of immorality. In our present-day context these translate into money and sexuality. The purpose of the "magic arts" is the unbridled pursuit of prosperity and unrestrained manipulation of wealth, people, and material (see the Revelation texts noted above). Immorality is known biblically as the worship of created things. The main context is the libertine use of physical sensuality outside the created boundaries of marriage.

The same themes may be traced in the sins of our century(s). The recent history of the world has been filled with crimes against humanity and God. Most of them have manipulated populations through murder and terror to increase the wealth of the rulers in power. Much genocide is documented in our time, accounting for the murder of forty million people: the Soviet people under Stalin, Jews and others under Nazism, Armenians, Cambodians, Ugandans, Rwandans, Sudanese, Bosnians, and Iraqis. Who profited or still profits from these murders?

In earlier generations, Americans were responsible for the enslavement and deaths of many Africans. In 1860 there were as many as four million slaves in our country. We traded human lives for cheap labor and profit in order to sustain a way of life. The study of the slave trade to the Americas is instructive for considering our own history and future. Especially instructive is the attitude of repentance and acknowledgment that Abraham Lincoln presented to the American people in his second inaugural address on March 4, 1865. He publicly submitted to the possibility that whites would suffer blood for every drop of African blood that had been shed.

If we shall suppose that American slavery is one of those offenses which, in the providence of God, must needs come, but which, having continued through his appointed time, he now wills to remove, and that he gives to both North and South this terrible war, as the woe due to those by whom the offense came, shall we discern therein any departure from those divine attributes which the believers in a living God always ascribe to him? Fondly do we hope—fervently do we pray—that this mighty scourge of war may speedily pass away. Yet, if God wills that it continue until all the wealth piled by the bondsman's two hundred and fifty years of unrequited toil shall be sunk, and until every drop of blood drawn by the lash shall be paid by another drawn with the sword, as was said three thousand years ago, so still it must be said, "The judgments of the Lord are true and righteous altogether."[13]

If we take God's anger against our sin seriously as a result of reading Nahum's and Jesus' words of judgment, our response to uncovered national sin may follow the same course. The accumulation of wealth at human cost, the sacrifice of child-raising for economic gain, or the sacrifice of marriage vows in attempts at sexual "self-fulfillment" tempts every generation. These things may be, like the sorceress-harlot, alluring (3:4). They may appear desirable on the surface, but they lead to slavery. All that glitters is not gold. Each case of sin leads to someone's enslavement. Sin leads us away from God's love and his law—away from marriage, children, worship, and care for the suffering and dispossessed, for the stranger, for the unbeliever. May God assault us and break our self-serving shackles.

The Christian celebration of the Lord's Supper is a practice that invites us to regularly receive God's "assault" on our self-centered enslavements. God has offered a new wine in place of the wrath-filled cup that awaits those who maintain their rebellion against the Creator.[14] We are invited to drink from the new cup of Christ's sufferings (Mark 10:38–39). The cup of remembrance and thanksgiving (1 Cor. 10:16; 11:25) is the drink the Lord offers to those who want to be freed of the world's common enslavements and their consequential wrath. Rather than wrath, the cup is filled with the new wine of the gospel.

---

13. Abraham Lincoln, as found in *Abraham Lincoln: Speeches and Writings, 1859–1865* (New York: Literary Classics of the United States, 1989), 687.

14. Achtemeier, *Nahum-Malachi*, 27.

Introduction to Habakkuk

THE BOOK OF HABAKKUK is a dialogue between Habakkuk and Yahweh during a vision Habakkuk receives from Yahweh. It begins with Habakkuk's complaint against local corruption and leads to a prophecy that spans ninety years, as he is drawn into a progressively more difficult understanding of faith. It begins with the persistent question, "Why . . . ?" (1:3, 13) and ends with a sung prayer ("In wrath remember mercy," 3:2) and a confession of faith ("Though the fig tree does not bud . . . yet I will rejoice in the LORD," 3:17–18). How does Habakkuk move from his questioning to this expanded expression of his own faith?

As we listen in on the conversation, we hear Habakkuk wrestling with an increasingly difficult word from Yahweh as he struggles to hold on to the faith behind his question, "Why?" He believes that Yahweh is a righteous and holy God who cannot tolerate wickedness, yet he notes that evil prospers. Habakkuk is looking for an explanation or some reasoning that he can pass on to his congregation (2:1), but none is forthcoming. By the end of the conversation he realizes that he may someday run out of concrete reasons to believe. He realizes he may have to confess his faith based on the memory of what he once knew to be true. Without immediate sociological or material evidence of Yahweh's love, he will have to say, as he does in the last verses, that although there is no food anywhere, "yet I will rejoice in the LORD." Even devastated in the grief of exile, starvation, and slavery, he believes he will continue to believe.

Content

IN CHAPTER 1, Habakkuk enters into conversation with Yahweh. His first question is, "LORD, why do you tolerate wrong?" (1:1–4). Yahweh's first response (which is not precisely an answer) is, "Look . . . I am raising up the [more ruthless] Babylonians" (1:5–11). Habakkuk then rephrases the question, "LORD, why then do you tolerate the [more] treacherous?" (1:12–17).

Chapter 2 begins with Habakkuk waiting on the ramparts to see how Yahweh will answer the rephrased question. His answer includes five "woes." As Habakkuk watches for and receives the revelation, Yahweh describes two ways of waiting: puffed-up desire or faith (2:1–6a). Then, from the mouths of the Babylonian captives come five future woes for the "way of the puffed up" (2:6b–20).

1. The first woe, "[Your debtors] will ... make you tremble" (2:6b–8), rests on those who become wealthy by extortion.
2. "Stones of the wall will cry out [against you]" (2:9–11) denotes public shame for those who build their security by unjust gain.
3. Those who build profit through bloodshed and crime (2:12–14) will be overcome with exhaustion and by the knowledge of the glory of Yahweh, which will fill the earth.
4. Exposure to the terror of trees and animals (2:15–17) will come on those who entice others to drunkenness in order to take advantage of them.
5. The final woe concerns lifeless, breathless, and silent idols (2:18–20). This is the foolishness of worshiping anything created in place of the life-giving Creator.

Chapter 3 is a song Habakkuk writes to Yahweh as a response to the conversation in chapters 1 and 2 (3:1–15). The song is followed by a concluding confession of fear and faith (3:16–19). The refrain that begins the song asks Yahweh to "renew" his fame and his deeds (3:1–2). It describes the days of old when God came forth as a brilliant warrior for Israel against her enemies (3:3–8). He "uncovered [his] bow" and arrows in the storm and lightning to deliver Israel (3:9–13a). He crushed the leader of the land of wickedness when Israel was helpless (3:13b–15). The book concludes with Habakkuk's honest fear about what will come (3:16) as well as his undying faith and joy "in the LORD" (3:16–19).

The subtitle of Habakkuk could be, "Yahweh Prepares His People for a Hard Change." Anyone who experiences terrible difficulties in life will benefit from studying this book. Yahweh tells the prophet that his people will experience the end of prosperity, the end of their political autonomy, the increased success of the "more wicked," and the withdrawal of Yahweh's protection. What will remain for them? Yahweh promises it will get better after it gets worse. They can cling to their memory of Yahweh's faithfulness, as in Habakkuk's song (3:1–15). They have the benefit of a forewarning from Yahweh and the witness of a faithful and believing prophet, committed to joy (3:17–19).

Habakkuk is a microcosm of faith. Its fifty-six verses express many facets of Israel's rich heritage. The early faith of Abraham is echoed in 2:4 (cf. Gen. 15:6; Rom. 1:17). The song (Hab. 3) is full of the historical reflection on the Exodus, desert wandering, and entrance to the Promised Land. It stands in the biblical tradition of dialogue between God and the prophets (as in Gen. 18). It also reflects biblical wisdom literature in its struggle with the suffering of the righteous and the prosperity of the wicked (lamented in the Psalms and discussed in Ecclesiastes and Job). It is also a bridge to the enduring post-temple faith of a people in exile in Babylon and during the time of the second temple. The best-known verses from this book are as follows:

The righteous will live by his faith. (2:4b)

The LORD is in his holy temple; let all the earth be silent before him. (2:20)

Though the fig tree does not bud and there are no grapes on the vines, though the olive crop fails and the fields produce no food, though there are no sheep in the pen and no cattle in the stalls, yet I will rejoice in the LORD, I will be joyful in God my Savior. (3:17–18)

The Sovereign LORD is my strength; he makes my feet like the feet of a deer, he enables me to go on the heights. (3:19)

Difficult Style

LIKE MOST ORACLES, Habakkuk has a difficult style. Abrupt changes in the subject of the sentence and in the subject matter in the midst of dialogue make it difficult to follow the progression of thought. The text refers to specific political situations that span about seventy years, but it does not explain them (see "Historical Context," below). Each section that follows will fill in the necessary contexts for the dialogue and the politics.

In chapters 1 and 2, when Yahweh responds to Habakkuk's complaint about why Yahweh tolerates wrong, God doesn't answer the question directly. Rather, he says simply that things will be getting worse! Hope seems minimal. Yahweh doesn't defend his goodness in his responses but rather seems to despair *with* the people. He doesn't offer an answer to the question until 2:4b. In chapter 3 Habakkuk seems to give up on his questions and resorts to a recollection of Israel's past and Yahweh's power in the memory of Israel. His song functions in part as a lament, longing for the past days of God's more obvious presence. In the context of the questions of chapter 1, chapter 3 functions as a resource of hope, through remembering God's faithfulness in the past (see Ps. 77, which laments the present while celebrating the past).

Habakkuk (*ḥabaqquq*) means "embrace," especially as a means of keeping warm when there is no other shelter (Job 24:8 = "hug"). It is an appropriate name for this prophet who was warmed by his extended conversation with Yahweh in a vision. God embraces his questions and in doing so embraces him. His revelation to the prophet of the devastation to come on Judah was not a comfortable message. Nonetheless, Habakkuk's undying faith and joy in Yahweh ("though the fig tree does not bud," 3:17) are a shelter when it appear that every other means of shelter will be removed.[1]

Why is the book called an oracle? "Oracle" (*maśśa'*) means "burden." This oracle, revealed to the prophet Habakkuk in a vision, must be communicated to God's people in Judah (2:1). Yahweh tells him to "write down" what he is told—that the Babylonians will destroy them, which will be a heavy burden to deliver. Yet the song and the confession of faith and joy in chapter 3 are also part of the "burden." The oracle calls the people not to despair but to live by faith (2:4b) and to share in Habakkuk's joy in Yahweh.

The Good News of Habakkuk

A FEW VERSES from Habakkuk have been commonly excerpted and used by the church. While we will look closely at their meaning in the original context, Habakkuk's jumpy oracle style sets these words in bold relief. Perhaps the most often quoted is "the righteous will live by his faith" (2:4b). The center of the book expresses Yahweh's ultimate purpose in the world, "for the earth will be filled with the knowledge of the glory of the LORD, as the waters cover the sea" (2:14). The consummate expression of Habakkuk's faith concludes the book (3:17–19):

> Though the fig tree does not bud
> > and there are no grapes on the vines,
> though the olive crop fails
> > and the fields produce no food,
> though there are no sheep in the pen
> > and no cattle in the stalls,
> yet I will rejoice in the LORD,
> > I will be joyful in God my Savior.
> The Sovereign LORD is my strength;
> > he makes my feet like the feet of a deer,
> > he enables me to go on the heights.

These positive expressions of faith are set in a context of great uncertainty. Habakkuk's faith is strong enough to pursue difficult questions in direct conversation with Yahweh. Some of these key verses are timeless expressions, proverbs, questions, and observations for all people in all places.

Habakkuk's key question is, "Why do you make me look at injustice? Why do you tolerate wrong? Destruction and violence are before me; there

---

1. Many scholars consider the name Habakkuk to be an Akkadian loan word for a garden plant. See J. J. M. Roberts, *Nahum, Habakkuk, and Zephaniah: A Commentary* (OTL; Louisville: Westminster John Knox, 1991), 86.

is strife, and conflict abounds" (1:3). His main problem is that "the law is paralyzed, and justice never prevails. The wicked hem in the righteous, so that justice is perverted" (1:4b). The wicked "are a law to themselves and promote their own honor" (1:7b). They are "guilty men, whose own strength is their god" (1:11b).

Habakkuk then repeats the key question, "Why then do you tolerate the treacherous? Why are you silent while the wicked swallow up those more righteous than themselves?" (1:13b). He suggests that the world God made is a discouraging and terrible place:

> You have made men like fish in the sea,
>> like sea creatures that have no ruler.
> The wicked foe pulls all of them up with hooks,
>> he catches them in his net,
> he gathers them up in his dragnet;
>> and so he rejoices and is glad. (1:14–15)

Still, Habakkuk maintains his faith by resolving to wait for Yahweh. "I will stand at my watch and station myself on the ramparts; I will look to see what he will say to me, and what answer I am to give to this complaint" (2:1). In response, Yahweh encourages him in his waiting. "For the revelation awaits an appointed time; it speaks of the end and will not prove false. Though it linger, wait for it; it will certainly come and will not delay" (2:3). Judgment will eventually come to the wicked:

> The violence you have done to Lebanon will overwhelm you,
>> and your destruction of animals will terrify you.
> For you have shed man's blood;
>> you have destroyed lands and cities and everyone in them. (2:17)

In the meantime everyone is encouraged to be faithful in worship. "But the LORD is in his holy temple; let all the earth be silent before him" (2:20). Habakkuk is faithful, ending his book with a psalm that is grounded in Yahweh's past faithfulness and hopes for speedy recovery from judgment.

> LORD, I have heard of your fame;
>> I stand in awe of your deeds, O LORD.
> Renew them in our day,
>> in our time make them known;
>> in wrath remember mercy. (3:2)

The conversations that constitute the book are remarkable for their length and progression of thought. Habakkuk's questions, God's surprising response, Habakkuk's reaction to the response and his rephrasing the question, God's further answer, and Habakkuk's responses in his song of worship constitute a convincing human-divine dialogue. Habakkuk's faithful incredulity is common to the humanity and hopes of people of faith.

Historical Context

HABAKKUK WAS PROBABLY an official temple musician-prophet (1 Chron. 25:1; consider the mention of using his own stringed instruments to accompany the singing in 3:19b).[2] He was a contemporary of Nahum, Zephaniah, and Jeremiah.

Habakkuk prophesied the fall of Judah to Babylon in the year of the Babylonians' victory over the Egyptians at Carchemish in northern Syria (605 B.C.). The Egyptian king Neco had marched north to assist a failing Assyrian empire in 609. King Josiah (Judah's last good hope for a just government) blocked their advance and lost his life (see 2 Kings 21–23). When King Neco marched home, he established King Jehoiakim (Josiah's son) as his vassal. Four years later Neco lost to the Babylonians (King Nebuchadnezzar) at the Battle of Carchemish (605). Nebuchadnezzar kept Jehoiakim as his vassal in Judah until he rebelled four years later (601). Nebuchadnezzar then put Jehoiachin on the throne but exiled him to Babylon after three months. By 597 Jerusalem was sacked and the monarchy was ended with a third son of Josiah (Zedekiah) on the throne.[3]

Habakkuk prophesied in the midst of this violent political upheaval. The subject matter of the book covers sixty-six years (605–539) in fifty-six verses. It begins in this context of Assyria's upheaval, describes the Babylonian victory over Jerusalem (597), and prophesies Babylon's subsequent fall to Persia (539).[4]

Each section of Habakkuk is best understood in its specific historical context. In 1:1–4 Habakkuk complains about 609–601, when the corrupt Jehoiakim ruled in Jerusalem. In 1:5–17 we see references to the Babylonian attacks on Jerusalem in 597/586. In 2:1–20 Yahweh promises the defeat of the Babylonians that results in the exiles' return to the land in 538. Chapter 3 is a song that rests in God's faithfulness to act in history.

Through this extended dialogue with Yahweh, including his concluding hymn, we hear Habakkuk's vibrant faith and deep humanity, learning and

---

2. F. F. Bruce, "Habakkuk," in *The Minor Prophets,* ed. Thomas McComisky (Grand Rapids: Baker, 1993), 2:832.

3. Cf. Roberts, 83–84; Bruce, 2:833–34; Theodore Hiebert, "The Book of Habakkuk," (*NIB;* Nashville: Abingdon, 1996), 7:626.

4. See the timeline in the introduction to Jonah.

growing in relation to God. He asks healthy questions (1:2–4) and is persistent in his questioning (1:12–2:1). He is historically grounded in the memory of Israel (3:1–15). He expresses a profound faith in song (3:16–19). His humanity and joy are a model and a challenge. The result is a book that is a timeless witness to God's purposes in a world dominated by corruption and violence.

Outline of Habakkuk

I. Habakkuk's Dialogue with Yahweh (1:1–17)
   A. Yahweh, Why Do You Tolerate Wrong? (1:1–4)
   B. Look, I Am Raising Up the More Wicked Babylonians (1:5–11)
   C. Yahweh, Why Do You Tolerate the More Treacherous? (1:12–17)

II. Yahweh's Revelation (2:1–20)
   A. Watching for and Receiving a Revelation (2:1–3)
   B. Two Ways: Faith or Puffed-Up Desire (2:4–5)
   C. Five Future Woes for the Puffed Up from the Survivors (2:6–20)
      1. Your Victims Will Make You Tremble (2:6b–8).
      2. Wall-Stones and Woodwork Will Cry Out Against You (2:9–11)
      3. Exhaustion of Bloodshed and the Knowledge of Glory (2:12–14)
      4. Exposure to the Terror of Trees and Animals (2:15–17)
      5. Lifeless, Breathless, and Silent Idols (2:18–20)

III. A Song to Yahweh (3:1–19)
   A. Renew Your Fame and Your Deeds, O Yahweh (3:1–2)
   B. In Days of Old, God Came Forth (3:3–8)
   C. You Uncovered Your Bow and Arrows (3:9–13a)
   D. You Crushed the Leader of Wickedness (3:13b–15)
   E. The Fear, Faith, and Joy of Habakkuk (3:16–19)

Select Bibliography on Habakkuk

Achtemeier, Elizabeth. *Nahum-Malachi.* Interpretation. Atlanta: Westminster John Knox, 1986.

Andersen, Francis. *Habakkuk: A New Translation with Introduction and Commentary.* AB. New York: Doubleday, 2001.

Baker, David. *Nahum, Habakkuk, and Zephaniah: An Introduction and Commentary.* Downers Grove, Ill.: InterVarsity Press, 1988.

Boadt, Lawrence. *Jeremiah 26–52, Habakkuk, Zephaniah, Nahum.* Wilmington: Michael Glazier, 1982.

Brown, William P. *Obadiah Through Malachi.* Westminster Bible Commentary. Louisville: Westminster John Knox, 1996.

Bruce, F. F. "Habakkuk." Pages 831–96 in *The Minor Prophets,* vol. 2. Ed. Thomas McComisky. Grand Rapids: Baker, 1993.

Haak, Robert D. *Habakkuk.* New York: Brill, 1992.

Hiebert, Theodore. "The Book of Habakkuk." Pages 623–55 in *The New Interpreter's Bible,* vol. 7. Nashville: Abingdon, 1996.

Mason, Rex. *Zephaniah, Habakkuk, Joel.* Sheffield: JSOT Press, 1994.

Roberts, J. J. M. *Nahum, Habakkuk, and Zephaniah: A Commentary.* OTL. Louisville: Westminster John Knox, 1991.

Robertson, O. Palmer. *The Books of Nahum, Habakkuk, and Zephaniah.* NICOT. Grand Rapids: Eerdmans, 1990.

Smith, Ralph L. *Micah-Malachi.* WBC. Waco, Tex.: Word, 1984.

Sweeney, Marvin A. *The Twelve Prophets.* Collegeville, Minn.: Liturgical, 2000.

Habakkuk 1

THE ORACLE THAT Habakkuk the prophet received.

²How long, O LORD, must I call for help,
  but you do not listen?
Or cry out to you, "Violence!"
  but you do not save?
³Why do you make me look at injustice?
  Why do you tolerate wrong?
Destruction and violence are before me;
  there is strife, and conflict abounds.
⁴Therefore the law is paralyzed,
  and justice never prevails.
The wicked hem in the righteous,
  so that justice is perverted.

⁵"Look at the nations and watch—
  and be utterly amazed.
For I am going to do something in your days
  that you would not believe,
  even if you were told.
⁶I am raising up the Babylonians,
  that ruthless and impetuous people,
who sweep across the whole earth
  to seize dwelling places not their own.
⁷They are a feared and dreaded people;
  they are a law to themselves
  and promote their own honor.
⁸Their horses are swifter than leopards,
  fiercer than wolves at dusk.
Their cavalry gallops headlong;
  their horsemen come from afar.
They fly like a vulture swooping to devour;
⁹ they all come bent on violence.
Their hordes advance like a desert wind
  and gather prisoners like sand.
¹⁰They deride kings
  and scoff at rulers.

> They laugh at all fortified cities;
> > they build earthen ramps and capture them.
> ¹¹ Then they sweep past like the wind and go on—
> > guilty men, whose own strength is their god."
>
> ¹² O LORD, are you not from everlasting?
> > My God, my Holy One, we will not die.
> O LORD, you have appointed them to execute
> > judgment;
> > O Rock, you have ordained them to punish.
> ¹³ Your eyes are too pure to look on evil;
> > you cannot tolerate wrong.
> Why then do you tolerate the treacherous?
> > Why are you silent while the wicked
> > swallow up those more righteous than themselves?
> ¹⁴ You have made men like fish in the sea,
> > like sea creatures that have no ruler.
> ¹⁵ The wicked foe pulls all of them up with hooks,
> > he catches them in his net,
> he gathers them up in his dragnet;
> > and so he rejoices and is glad.
> ¹⁶ Therefore he sacrifices to his net
> > and burns incense to his dragnet,
> for by his net he lives in luxury
> > and enjoys the choicest food.
> ¹⁷ Is he to keep on emptying his net,
> > destroying nations without mercy?

THE ENTIRE BOOK of Habakkuk is an oracle given as a dialogue between Habakkuk and Yahweh. Chapter 1 records the prophet's first set of questions ("O LORD ... why do you tolerate wrong?" 1:2–4), Yahweh's first response ("Look ... I am raising up the more wicked Babylonians," 1:5–11), and the second set of questions ("O LORD ... why then do you tolerate the treacherous?" 1:12–17). Habakkuk's second set of questions rephrases, intensifies, and expands the original question in light of the new information given in Yahweh's response. The key question of the chapter (and book) is asked in both sets: "Why do you tolerate wrong?" (1:3b), and "You cannot tolerate wrong. Why then do you tolerate the treacherous?" (1:13b).

The Oracle (1:1)

"THE ORACLE THAT Habakkuk the prophet received" was given to him as a conversation with Yahweh. The inspired oracle (or "burden," see comments on Nah. 1:1) includes *both* sides of the conversation (his questions, Yahweh's response, and his concluding song). Habakkuk receives the oracle in the temple in Jerusalem, where he is a prophet-musician during a time of violent national and international upheaval (see the introduction).

Yahweh, Why Do You Tolerate Wrong? (1:2–4)

HABAKKUK'S FIRST SET of questions comes in like crashing waves. In verse 2 he wonders how long he must wait for God's help against violence. In verse 3 he wants to know why he and Yahweh must continue tolerating six problems: injustice, wrongful suffering, destruction, violence, strife, and conflict. In verse 4, these problems lead to four more: The law is paralyzed, justice never prevails, the wicked hem in the righteous; and because of these three, justice is perverted. The corruption of national politics is the historical context of his complaint.

Habakkuk asked his questions at a time when hopes for justice and righteousness had been raised and dashed again and again in Judah. King Josiah had returned the country to God's instruction for righteous living after the rediscovery of the book of Deuteronomy (622 B.C.; read 2 Kings 22–23). Josiah was killed, however, in battle with Pharaoh Neco in 609 B.C. (see the introduction). King Jehoiakim (Josiah's son) ruled corruptly (as Neco's vassal) during the time of Habakkuk's prophecy (see 2 Kings 23:35–37; Jer. 22:13–19). The corruption of Jerusalem's government under Jehoiakim is the main historical context for Habakkuk's complaint here.

In 1:2, Habakkuk wants to know how long he must call for help before Yahweh will listen and save. His cry against violence is a legal plea for justice in the Old Testament, which God promises to hear (Gen. 18:21; Ex. 2:23; 22:23). This ordinary complaint of local corruption in Judah begins like a lament common to the Psalms and in Job (see Bridging Contexts section).

The prophet addresses six problems of corruption in Judah in matched pairs in 1:3. "Injustice" (*ʾawen*) and "wrong" (*ʿamal*, "wrongful suffering") are two sides of the same coin. The injustice of the perpetrator and the wrong suffered are two parts of the same human problem. Why doesn't Yahweh intervene in this life-denying dynamic? He "tolerates" it (*nabat* has the sense of "stand by and watch," 1:3, 5, 13; 2:15).

The third and fourth problems are also a pair. "Destruction" (*šod*) and "violence" (*ḥamas*) wreak havoc on communities' life-supporting infrastructures and relationships. The last pair of problems, "strife" (*rib*) and "conflict" (*madon*), are legal terms in Hebrew. Habakkuk says they "abound," indicating that there are many lawsuits and legal quarrels in Judah's courts.

In 1:4 Habakkuk goes on to say that these six problems have led to four situations that are even more terrible, again in pairs: "The law is paralyzed, and justice never prevails," and "the wicked hem in the righteous, so that justice is perverted." In other words, the courts do not work any longer. Thus, in a few brief words, Habakkuk describes a society full of crime, violence, corruption, mock legal battles, and the defeat of the righteous. It is a ruined society, and the prophet wants to know why Yahweh tolerates the flourishing of such wickedness.

Look, I Am Raising Up the More Wicked Babylonians (1:5–11)

YAHWEH RESPONDS BY redirecting Habakkuk's attention from local issues to international issues of violence. His first response has no introduction. God simply begins speaking, but the content of his response is surprising. Is God ignoring the question? Habakkuk's question and Yahweh's answer seem unrelated. Habakkuk begins with a domestic problem, and Yahweh answers with an international issue. Habakkuk says, "Look at this!" and Yahweh replies, "Look at that!" Yet Yahweh uses the same verbs as Habakkuk used in his questions.

> Habakkuk: "Why do you make me *look at [ra'ah]* injustice? Why do you *tolerate [nabat]* wrong?" (1:3).
> Yahweh: "*Look at [ra'ah]* the nations and *watch [nabat]*" (1:5).

Yahweh responds to the question by providing a bigger version of the question. Judah is corrupt, but Babylon is worse. Just look and see.

Verse 5 prepares the prophet for this abrupt response. "You would not believe, even if you were told." The situation is going to get worse. Yahweh's response represents a kind of teaching that intensifies the conversation and shakes the student into thinking in a larger and more complex matrix of relationships. Yahweh's challenge is for Habakkuk to believe the unbelievable. He is, of course, being told, and he *does* have difficulty believing it (1:12–13). God will raise up a cruel and impetuous people, the "Babylonians."[1]

The Babylonians' reputation was terrifying (1:6). They were "ruthless" (*mar*), meaning embittering, galling, and fierce. They were also "impetuous"

---

1. Other translations have "the Chaldeans," which is a biblical name for the neo-Babylonians, esp. under Nebuchadnezzar's rule (2 Kings 25:1–13; Ezek. 23:23; Jer. 21:4). The Hebrew (*kasdim*) is a reference to a region between the mouths of the Euphrates and Tigris Rivers at the Persian Gulf. See Ralph L. Smith, *Micah-Malachi* (WBC; Waco, Tex.: Word, 1984), 101.

(*mahar*), meaning swift, quick, and hasty. These rhyming Hebrew words described an army that would rapidly change the face of political structures. They would "sweep across the whole earth to seize" Jerusalem. Yahweh judges their violent taking of "dwelling places not their own" even as he raises them to end the violence of Habakkuk's complaint.

The source of the Babylonians' ruthlessness is described in 1:7. They are "feared" and "dreaded" (terrible, shocking, and awful) because they were "a law to themselves." They are the originators of their own justice, "promoting their own honor" (majesty, dignity, and splendor). Although they are God's agent, they cannot be the permanent solution to Habakkuk's complaint. Like the Assyrians before them, they are not the source of justice for God's people.[2] They are simply God's agent in bringing the fruit of unrighteousness to Jerusalem's doorstep. Judah's rulers also had been "promoting their own honor."

Babylon's impetuous speed and swift advance to Jerusalem are described in 1:8–9 by using comparisons to wild animals: Their "horses are swifter than leopards"; they are "fiercer than wolves at dusk. Their cavalry gallops headlong ... from afar"; and they fly "like a vulture swooping to devour" (1:8). Nebuchadnezzar demonstrated his daring military speed following the Battle of Carchemish (605 B.C.), where he secured his domination of the ancient Near East by defeating the Egyptian imperial forces. Following the battle he immediately pursued the defeated army more than 150 miles to crush them completely.[3] Hearing of his father's death (Nabopolasar), he raced home, hundreds of miles, to secure his throne. With the same daring speed his "hordes," advancing "like a desert wind," would fall on Jerusalem. Its numerous inhabitants, like those of the surrounding towns, would be gathered "as prisoners like sand" and marched in long lines to Babylon.

The Babylonians' god was her self-satisfied pleasure in military strength (1:10–11). Once the Babylonians defeated the Assyrians at Nineveh (612 B.C.) and the Egyptians at Carchemish (605 B.C.), no one could stop their might. They could "deride kings and scoff at rulers" (1:10). Once they controlled the open fields and the trade routes, they could "laugh at all fortified cities," building earthen ramps to the tops of walls to enter them.

Again, Yahweh's description of what will come does not hide the fact of Babylonian guilt. "Then they sweep past like the wind and go on—guilty men, whose own strength is their god" (1:11). This verse concludes Yahweh's first response. The indictment of guilt means that they have committed some offense, namely, their worship of their own strength. Here "strength"

---

2. Roberts, *Nahum, Habakkuk, and Zephaniah*, 96.
3. Ibid., 96.

(*koḥ*) means muscle-strength or brawn. Elsewhere the word refers to Samson's might (Judg. 16:5, 9, 19), a wild ox (Job 39:11), a blacksmith (Isa. 44:12), a lone warrior (Isa. 63:1), a goat (Dan. 8:6), or a man of brute strength (Amos 2:14). Babylon has a brute force that enables them to laugh at kings and fortified cities. Not only do they have this power, they worship it. This strength is their god. Habakkuk expands on this "secular" idolatry (the strongest people win) and asks Yahweh to say more about it in his second question (1:14–17).

Yahweh, Why Do You Tolerate the [More] Treacherous? (1:12–17)

IN HIS SECOND speech (1:12–17) Habakkuk rephrases his first question by asking, in essence, "Why do you tolerate a people more treacherous than Judah?" In 1:12 he struggles to accept what he has heard. In 1:13 he rephrases the question based on the new information. In 1:14–16 he expands the question with the metaphor of a commercial fisherman, and in 1:17 Habakkuk again pushes forward the question of Yahweh's toleration of the wicked. The Lord's answers will come in chapter 2.

The historical context of Habakkuk's concern is the prospect of the "more wicked" Babylonian rule in Jerusalem. When Nebuchadnezzar defeated the Egyptians at Carchemish, he also took control of Jerusalem, retaining Jehoiakim as his vassal. When Jehoiakim rebelled, Nebuchadnezzar conquered the city and began deporting the people to Babylon (597 B.C.).

The second complaint begins abruptly (1:12). We know Habakkuk has begun to speak again only because the address begins, "O LORD." Habakkuk is making an argument against what Yahweh has just said. It sounds wrong to him, so he quotes *to* God what he knows *about* God: "Are you not from everlasting? My God, my Holy One ..." and in the same breath adds, "We will not die."[4] Habakkuk means that since his God is eternal (unlike idols), God's people must also endure and prosper. God's eternal promises to Abraham and to David were at the heart of Israel's faith (Gen. 12:1–3; 15:4–6; 17:5–8; 2 Sam. 7:13, 16; 1 Kings 2:45; 9:5).

The panic and crisis of processing the news about the coming of the Babylonians can be heard in the intensely personal, "my God, my Holy One" (1:12a). He is processing the shock of the news. We hear it also in his statement of incredulity, "We will not die!" (Do they die? See the Bridging Con-

---

4. Many versions have "You will not die," referring to God. The original word is debated, but *all* ancient manuscripts and versions have "we." For a shift in scholarly opinion see R. J. Haak, *Habakkuk* (VTSup 44; Leiden: Brill, 1992), 48. Cf. O. P. Robertson, *The Books of Nahum, Habakkuk, and Zephaniah* (NICOT; Grand Rapids: Eerdmans, 1990), 157.

texts section.) He punctuates his speech with six of God's names and attributes, which bring comfort in the midst of his distress: "LORD . . . everlasting . . . my God, my Holy One . . . LORD . . . Rock."

Immediately, however, he says that he believes Yahweh concerning the Babylonians: "You have appointed . . . you have ordained" (1:12b). In one verse Habakkuk progresses from incredulity to acknowledgment of the facts through his trust and knowledge of Yahweh. Even though Jerusalem will be captured and God's people exiled, they will survive as a people, for God is a Rock of refuge. "We will not die" becomes a cry of hope for the future.

In spite of his belief, what Habakkuk has heard about the Babylonians doesn't fit with what he knows about God, for the Babylonians are wicked (1:15) and idolatrous (1:16). Nor does he think his question has been answered by Yahweh's response. After all, the Babylonians are *more* treacherous than the wicked in Judah. Yahweh has only intensified the question. So, Habakkuk asks again, broadening the question beyond Judah to include the ancient world.

Habakkuk begins by appealing to the traditional reputation of Yahweh, repeating part of his original question in 1:3 ("Why do you tolerate wrong?") as statements of fact: "Your eyes are too pure to look on evil, you cannot tolerate wrong" (1:13a). These two statements set up the two questions that follow: "Why then do you tolerate the treacherous [Babylonians]" and "Why are you silent while the wicked swallow up those more righteous?" (1:13b). The answers to these questions (the first about the perpetrators of evil and the other about the suffering of their victims) will have to wait for chapter 2. For now, Habakkuk wants to explain his questions and objections more fully with the use of a fishing metaphor.

The joy of the wicked fisherman bothers Habakkuk (1:14–17). The heart of his objection is the apparent enjoyment and success that the wicked find in their cruel actions. The center of his description of the fisherman (1:14–16) is "so he rejoices and is glad" (1:15b). Habakkuk offers nine objections to their treacherous metaphorical activities and God's toleration of them. This wicked fisherman (the Babylonian empire) pulls the more righteous up with hooks, catches them in his net, gathers them up in his dragnet, rejoices, is glad, sacrifices to his net, burns incense to his dragnet, lives in luxury, and enjoys the choicest food. The first three objections concern the abuses of the fisherman. The fourth and fifth object to his happiness. The sixth and seventh object to his false worship (reiterating and amplifying Yahweh's observation in 1:11b). The last two wonder about his high living, in that the wicked seem to "have it all."

The objection goes even deeper. Habakkuk realizes that he doesn't like the world he sees or the world as God describes it. His implied question is twofold: (1) "Why don't you destroy the wicked?" (at least don't sanction their success!); (2) "Why do they exist at all?" This second question is implied in 1:14a by the phrase, "You *have made men [ʾadam]* like fish in the sea, like sea creatures that have no ruler." The Hebrew word translated "men" is the same word for the name Adam. It echoes the creation itself and the inherent freedom to choose who or what created thing will rule over them (see Bridging Contexts section).

After his nine-point list, Habakkuk ends the metaphor with another form of his original questions (1:3, 13), which can be paraphrased, "Are you going to keep on tolerating this? If so, how long?" (1:17). This is the prime question of the book. The answer in chapter 2 will be "Yes," and "for a while." Yahweh is aware of all these issues and will offer a lengthy perspective on justice and how it will be accomplished.

QUESTIONS AND LAMENT. Habakkuk's pressing questions and lament (1:2–4) are given to him by Yahweh in an "oracle" (1:1). This setting implies that *even this questioning* is inspired by the Spirit of Yahweh. Through the ages believers have asked similar questions of the Lord in prayer. In Habakkuk's case, asking such difficult questions is part of what "the prophet received" (1:1). Questions and lament are part of a believer's burden, and honest dialogue with God is a necessary form of relationship with him. The persistence of the questioner, the "woes" (ch. 2), and the song of remembrance (ch. 3) are each a necessary part of this rich book.

The powerful and corrupt leadership that Habakkuk faces, causing him to cry out, is an evil that persists in every age. King Jehoiakim's corrupt vassal relationship with Egypt (and later with Nebuchadnezzar) affected every area of life in Jerusalem. Habakkuk's contemporary Jeremiah documents the violence that the king perpetrated on the people.[5] He killed the innocent who opposed him and refused to pay poor laborers (Jer. 22:13–19). Under his administration the prophets and priesthood were corrupted in adultery and abuse of authority (23:1–2, 9–11). The king sent assassins who killed the prophet Uriah for prophesying (as Habakkuk and Jeremiah also did) that Jerusalem would fall (26:20–23). He burned Jeremiah's handwritten prophecy in his fireplace as a threat against him (Jer. 36). Like Habakkuk, Jeremiah said that Babylon was God's agent of discipline against his chosen people.

In the face of this situation Yahweh gave his prophet words of lament (1:2a, "How long, O LORD, must I call for help, but you do not listen?").

---

5. Bruce, "Habakkuk," 845.

Lamentation and questioning are God's gift to the believer. They provide a pathway of honest faith and faithful conversation with him in horrible times.[6] One third of the Psalms are prayers/songs of lament.[7] Habakkuk's words echo throughout the Psalter ("How long?" Ps. 6:3; 13:1–2; 79:5; 89:46; "Why do you . . . ?" Ps. 10:1; 44:23–24; 74:11). The entire books of Job and Lamentations are dedicated to expressing the confusion and pain of unbearable suffering by the faithful.

Jesus himself lamented faithfully to the Father from the cross, using the words of Psalm 22:1 (see Matt. 27:46, "My God, my God, why have you forsaken me?"). Like Habakkuk, Jesus models for us the possibility of being honest with God about our situations through lament without guilt. Habakkuk, the psalmists, and Jesus did not hesitate to bring their complaints to the Lord or to ask their questions directly. In their laments they were resolute in faithfulness, even when the Lord's response was not what they wanted to hear (see comments on 3:17–19).

Protest and lament can be faithful or unfaithful.[8] Railing against God can be unfaithful, particularly when the protest is accompanied by life-denying or death-promoting behaviors. Some will protest against God through self-destructive and abusive behaviors toward others, often those who love them. This unfaithful path of protest usually begins with a significant but subtle distinction. The faithful protest begins with an attitude that continues to address God ("God, how could you allow. . . ?"). The unfaithful protest begins with the impersonal (and judging) abstraction ("How could God allow. . . ?").

Habakkuk's questioning is similar to the faithful protest found in the book of Job. Job's faithfulness is found in his insistence that theological discussion with his so-called friends does not satisfy him. He wants to converse directly with God (Job 30:2–23; 31:6; 35). Yahweh accepts Job's protest as faithful and rejected his friends' defense of the deity (42:7–8). Habakkuk's protest is faithful and inspired because it is done out of the conviction that God is good all the time, even in death and dying. This conviction does not silence the questions and pain of the faithful in Scripture. Rather, it focuses the questions in the form of personal dialogue with a loving Creator and Redeemer, who accompanies the sufferer and will, in perfect time, bring victory, healing, and restoration. Those who long for the kingdom of God with its peace, love, and goodness may find hope on the pathway of lament and faithful protest.

---

6. For an excellent discussion of suffering and lament, see Daniel Simundson, *Where Is God in My Suffering?* (Minneapolis: Augsburg, 1983).

7. See Ps. 3–7; 13; 17; 22; 25–28; 31; 35; 39; 42–44; 51; 54–57; 59–64; 69–71; 74; 76; 77; 79; 80; 83; 86; 88; 90; 102; 109; 120; 130; 137; 140–43.

8. Rom. 9:19–24; Bruce, "Habakkuk," 844.

The struggle of faith. The timeless struggle of faith in a violent world is expressed in Habakkuk's declaration, "We will not die!" (1:12–17). After Yahweh finished telling Habakkuk in detail about the coming attack of the Babylonians on Jerusalem (1:5–11), the prophet's reaction to this horrible news is twofold, expressing protest and faith simultaneously. He cannot believe what he has heard, yet he believes it. It disturbs him terribly, yet he has faith that the people will endure through and beyond their defeat. Many people did die in the siege and fall of Jerusalem (see Lamentations). The tone of faithful protest is like that of a terminally ill patient insisting, "I will not die!" Habakkuk surrounds this protest with punctuations of God's attributes. Naming them can bring comfort in the midst of distress ("everlasting," "Holy One," "Rock").

The second part of Habakkuk's reaction resonates as hope a tone below his protest. God's people will not die but endure, because their God is the Rock. They (i.e., their children) later return to rebuild the temple and resettle the land (538 B.C.). They do not die (as a people) but survive the fire of Yahweh's purification.

Habakkuk has hope. He accepts Yahweh's word about the Babylonians' destruction of Jerusalem. "You have appointed them to execute judgment.... You have ordained them to punish" (1:12). He is a prophet of hope precisely because he is willing to face the truth of the consequences of judgment on Judah's rebellion against God. True biblical prophets "refused the easy and almost universal practice of identifying God's rule exclusively with the policies of their own country."[9] Habakkuk stands with his contemporaries Jeremiah and Isaiah, who declare quite unpatriotically that the national enemy will discipline God's people. They do not declare the Babylonians "good." To the contrary, God's judgment will later fall harder on the enemy (Hab. 2:6–20). In the meantime, Habakkuk accepts the coming discipline in hope, because he knows it is a sign of Yahweh's activity and justice for his chosen people.

Habakkuk has hope in the face of judgment because he has a history and relationship of trust with Yahweh. He knows that it is Yahweh, "my God," who is "everlasting," who speaks (1:12). His relationship with the author of eternity is personal. He has the benefit of an eternal perspective, even in face of suffering punishment for the sins of those around him. Although he cannot understand why the whole city must suffer, he knows from personal experience that Yahweh is good, addressing him as "my Holy One" (1:12). Finally, he speaks to God with the name that reaches deep into Israel's redemptive history and forward into the revelation of

---

9. Hiebert, "The Book of Habakkuk," 7:637.

Christ, "O Rock."[10] This name expresses a whole history of experiencing God's faithfulness and deliverance in the worst of times. It also reveals an expansive tradition of worship from which Habakkuk, a temple musician, can draw (cf. Hab. 3:19b).

Habakkuk's protest. Habakkuk argues against the success of the worse Babylonians. His expression of hope in the Rock is followed by protests common to all on whom judgment falls: "We are not as bad as they are!" (cf. 1:13b, "Why are you silent while the wicked swallow up those more righteous than themselves?"). This kind of comparison is a universal argument against any judgment. Adam compared himself to Eve to claim more righteous ground (Gen. 3:12, "The woman you put here with me—she gave me some fruit from the tree, and I ate it."). Eve blamed the serpent. The relative scale of righteousness is used daily as an excuse for misdeeds. One apparently repentant cocaine dealer said, "I'm not as bad as most dealers. I only sold to people who really could afford it as a luxury." He thought of himself, like the corrupt rulers of Jerusalem, as more righteous or "less bad" than others.

Why must God use the "less righteous" to chastise the "less wicked"? It is because Yahweh has no righteous people remaining to do the work. His so-called righteous people were warned by the prophets about their corruption for over 150 years. An obvious example of what God would do had been provided to them by the exile of the northern ten tribes. If chastisement from a righteous source were possible, it would have come from among God's chosen people! It is exactly these people about whom Habakkuk begins his complaint (1:2–4). In the course of world events, upon whom may God rely to execute judgment justly?

Habakkuk's objection goes even deeper. He realizes that he doesn't like the world he sees or the world as God describes it. He asks enduring and universal questions. "Why doesn't God destroy the wicked?" "Why do they exist at all?" Habakkuk complains about the creation, as Adam complained about Eve: God "made men like fish in the sea . . . that have no ruler" (1:14a). This is an emotional and dramatic conversation. "The wicked foe pulls all of them up with hooks" (1:15a). God accepts Habakkuk's protests without answering his questions. Habakkuk understands more than it seems.

Habakkuk implies that he knows God has made the world and people "like fish in the sea." The real problem is that he doesn't like it, not that he doesn't understand it. God's world gives the wicked and the violent too much freedom. This objection is common to all people of faith. Sometimes it is avoided,

---

10. Gen. 49:24; Deut. 32:4, 15–18, 30–37; 1 Sam. 2:2; 2 Sam. 22:32, 47; 23:3; Ps. 18:2, 31, 46; 19:14; 27:5; 28:1; 31:2–3; 40:2; 42:9; 61:2; 62:2–7; 71:3; 78:20, 35; 81:16; 89:26; 92:15; 94:22; 95:1; 105:41; 114:8; 144:1; Rom. 9:33; 1 Cor. 10:4; 1 Peter 2:6.

or censored, or dismissed. Its validity as a question is necessary, however, to all healthy conversation with God. It is the means by which all great people of faith have entered into partnership with God for justice, mercy, and redemption in the world. Abraham was used by God to help judge Sodom (Gen. 18:17–33). God engaged Moses to confront the murderous Pharaoh (Ex. 3). He anointed David to protect his people from the violence of the Philistines. He chose Job to suffer righteously in protest as an example to all who would protest faithfully.

God's ultimate demonstration of the depth of his compassion in the world was to come in the flesh as one of the "fish in the sea." He does not answer the question, "Why do the violent have so much freedom?" Rather, he demonstrates that their freedom extends even to killing the Son of God. For Habakkuk as well as for followers of Christ, the enduring reality and answer are that the chosen of God are called to live righteously in a violent world without giving in to violence. They are called to stand in partnership with God for a world of peace. When they fail in the calling of peace (as in Habakkuk's Jerusalem), all they can do is wait for the day of the Lord. Habakkuk begins his waiting on the ramparts of the city wall (2:1). Faith waits to see what word of hope Yahweh will sent to a failed and judged society.

We are left with the timeless question of the first chapter, "How long, O LORD?" It is the enduring cry of the one who suffers and hopes in protesting prayer. Are the violent Babylonians going "to keep on ... destroying nations without mercy" (1:17; see Rev. 6:10)? Yahweh's response and promise are "No." His direct response to this question describes the five "woes" that will befall the violent (ch. 2).

HABAKKUK IS A difficult book, especially in the modern context. Why does God give us a book with the death of Habakkuk's community as the basic plot? We are increasingly aware that such horrors are a current reality for many in the world. For anyone who has experienced or may experience the loss of a good way of life, cultural displacement, or abrupt change in cultural security, the message of Habakkuk is both relevant and timely. It does not sugarcoat reality. Within just a few years of the conversation, Jerusalem was completely destroyed.

God's message is fundamentally that soon the internal corruption that Habakkuk dislikes will give way to a much worse external enemy. Habakkuk's response gives us an opportunity to see how a believer may deal faithfully with news of impending death and destruction. Habakkuk responds like a person who has just heard that someone he loves has a cancer that will certainly kill him or her. The prophet's way of life and his life itself will soon come to an abrupt and painful end. We do not know whether Habakkuk survived the exile (as Jeremiah did).

Five stages of grief. Writing about death and dying, Elisabeth Kübler-Ross outlines five normal stages of healthy grieving.[11] *Life* magazine described it as "a profound lesson for the living." These stages are denial/isolation, anger, bargaining, depression, and acceptance. Habakkuk, whose hope is in Yahweh, has led believers through these "stages" for more than 2,500 years.

- *Isolation* is heard in his opening words: "You do not listen. . . . You do not save" (1:2).
- *Anger* bubbles up in the repeated exclamations, "Why? . . . Why? . . . Justice never prevails . . . justice is perverted" (1:3–4).
- Upon hearing the bad news, Habakkuk immediately *denies* what he has heard, "My Holy One, we will not die!" (1:12).
- He begins *bargaining* by repeating what he has heard, "You have ordained them" (1:12) and then arguing a case with "Your eyes are too pure . . . you cannot tolerate wrong" (1:13).
- Unable to understand what is happening to his community he moves toward *depression*, asking again, "Why? . . . Why?" (1:13). He dwells on the hopelessness of their situation before Yahweh: "You have made men like fish in the sea. . . . The wicked foe pulls all of them up with hooks" (1:14–17).
- Finally, Habakkuk will come to *acceptance* in a song he writes (ch. 3), but not until Yahweh speaks again (ch. 2).

Death is a certainty for God's faithful as well as for the wicked. Habakkuk gives believers a resource for dealing with that certainty in healthy and faithful ways. God tells Habakkuk about the catastrophe he will bring on Jerusalem so that he and any faithful remnant can prepare for the persecution and death that are certainly coming. As a result, some are able to accept what they cannot fully understand. They can live in hope of Yahweh's future, even in death.

God's first interest. The ruthless Babylonians are only an intermediate solution to the problem of injustice, even though they are God's agent against a corrupt Jerusalem, for the Babylonians will also be destroyed (Hab. 2:6–20). The purpose of such political cataclysms in Scripture is to turn God's people back to his ultimate purpose for his creation, namely, human faithfulness in relationships, living by the instruction of his Word, and true worship.

---

11. Elisabeth Kübler-Ross, *On Death and Dying: What the Dying Have to Teach Doctors, Nurses, Clergy and Their Own Families* (New York: Macmillan, 1969).

God's first interest is not in our prosperity or political power. He prefers to destroy us (in hope of eventually accomplishing his greater purpose) rather than to see us prosper in political security while chasing after our own whims. The lesson of the history of God's people is that God is not primarily committed to the peace, security, and prosperity of his people. Consider his first response in the Garden of Eden. Yahweh removed Adam and Eve from their security when they turned away from a trusting relationship with him. God's first concern for us is faithfulness, living by his Word, and true worship. These daily human expressions of trust in Yahweh are manifestly more important to God than fiscal prosperity. He has a much more lasting plan.

You wouldn't believe it, even if you were told. The time between Habakkuk's announcement and the fall of Jerusalem was about eight years. In the original language the "you" in 1:5 is plural and can be translated "you all" (the plural occurs six times in 1:5). God is giving Habakkuk a message to repeat to a wider audience. It is not just for him; it is for the whole society to hear. When Paul and Barnabas are in the synagogue at Antioch, the apostle quotes this passage. He applies the "you wouldn't believe it" and "be amazed" to the resurrection of Jesus from the dead, the forgiveness of sins through him, and justification through faith:

> But the one whom God raised from the dead did not see decay.
>
> Therefore, my brothers, I want you to know that through Jesus the forgiveness of sins is proclaimed to you. Through him everyone who believes is justified from everything you could not be justified from by the Law of Moses. Take care that what the prophets have said does not happen to you:
>
> > "Look, you scoffers,
> > wonder and perish,
> > for I am going to do something in your days
> > that you would never believe,
> > even if someone told you." (Acts 13:37–41)[12]

If God has died and been raised from the dead, then anyone who does not give up the ways of self-sufficiency, self-worship, or prosperity-worship to follow God's Word is lost. Even the murderous convict ("Misfit") of "A Good Man Is Hard to Find" knows this truth. As a grandmother confronts him with the name "Jesus" just before her own murder at his hands, he confesses the necessary radical response to Jesus' resurrection:

---

12. The difference in wording between this rendition and the one we read in Habakkuk exists because Paul is working with the LXX version of Habakkuk. As we know from Qumran, the authoritative text of the Hebrew Scriptures had not yet officially been established. The Heb. word for "scoffers" (*bogadim*) and "among the nations" (*baggoyim*) are similar.

Jesus was the only One that ever raised the dead ... and he shouldn't have done it. He thrown everything off balance. If He did what He said, then it's nothing for you to do but throw away everything and fol- low Him.[13]

If Christ has indeed been raised and our sins are forgiven by faith in him, amazement, wonder, and the transformation of faith are possible. We would not have believed it if we had been told in advance. But God has already accomplished the defeat of sin and death. He has sent his Spirit to call, gather, and enlighten us through his Word. This is the persistent power of the gospel to transform lives now through a salvation that has already been accomplished.

The message of Habakkuk's proclamation is that God is interested first in restoring us to a right relationship with himself as created and redeemed people. Without that reconciled relationship, earthly peace and security are a façade. God draws us into lives of faithfulness in relationships through the instruction of his Word. His Holy Spirit tutors us in true worship. The suf- fering of the Babylonian occupation is a dire example of God's radical com- mitment to these goals. Jesus' suffering on the cross is his ultimate appeal to a world bent on violence. God will stop at nothing in order to draw us near to himself and the way of peace he offers.

The source of false worship. The deeper causes of injustice in every cul- ture are uncovered in Habakkuk's response to Yahweh in 1:12–17 ("He sac- rifices to his net"). In every time and every place, cultures center their life on the most obvious source of their strength and prosperity. Seagoing cultures have sea and storm gods. Agricultural cultures have grain gods. Hunting cul- tures center on totems and spirits that control the animals. Technological soci- eties such as our own do not identify "gods" but elevate (worship) values that lead to greater control over life: wealth, information, and military tech- nology. A fisherman reveres his fishing net.

For the Babylonians the fisherman's net was a symbol of military power.[14] They worshiped the tool that was the means of their wealth, taken from other cities and towns. The Greek historian Herodotus records that the Scythians even made sacrifices to a sword.[15] They made a god of the source of their standard of living. To criticize that source was at once unpatriotic and blasphemy of the civil religion.

---

13. Flannery O'Connor, "A Good Man Is Hard to Find" in *A Good Man Is Hard to Find and Other Stories* (New York: Harcourt Brace Jovanovich, 1976), 28.

14. Roberts, *Nahum, Habakkuk, and Zephaniah,* 104.

15. See his *Histories* 4.62, cited in Lawrence Boadt, *Jeremiah 26–52, Habakkuk, Zephaniah, Nahum* (Wilmington: Michael Glazier, 1982), 178.

Christians may find that an examination of their allegiances creates internal conflict when they are part of an affluent society. Habakkuk reveals the deeper causes of violence when he points to the worship of "the net" and calls for a rigorous evaluation of any devotion to prosperity in light of our ultimate devotion to God. He shows us the problem from the side of a small country dominated by a great economic and military power.[16] His exposure of the worship of the source of prosperity is echoed by Isaiah's ridicule of the deluded man who worships what he himself makes (Isa. 44:9–20).

---

16. Hiebert, "The Book of Habakkuk," 630.

Habakkuk 2

¹ I will stand at my watch
   and station myself on the ramparts;
I will look to see what he will say to me,
   and what answer I am to give to this complaint.

²Then the LORD replied:

"Write down the revelation
   and make it plain on tablets
   so that a herald may run with it.
³ For the revelation awaits an appointed time;
   it speaks of the end
   and will not prove false.
Though it linger, wait for it;
   it will certainly come and will not delay.

⁴ "See, he is puffed up;
   his desires are not upright—
   but the righteous will live by his faith—
⁵ indeed, wine betrays him;
   he is arrogant and never at rest.
Because he is as greedy as the grave
   and like death is never satisfied,
he gathers to himself all the nations
   and takes captive all the peoples.

⁶"Will not all of them taunt him with ridicule and scorn,
saying,

"'Woe to him who piles up stolen goods
   and makes himself wealthy by extortion!
   How long must this go on?'
⁷ Will not your debtors suddenly arise?
   Will they not wake up and make you tremble?
   Then you will become their victim.
⁸ Because you have plundered many nations,
   the peoples who are left will plunder you.
For you have shed man's blood;
   you have destroyed lands and cities and everyone in
      them.

⁹"Woe to him who builds his realm by unjust gain
　　to set his nest on high,
　　to escape the clutches of ruin!
¹⁰You have plotted the ruin of many peoples,
　　shaming your own house and forfeiting your life.
¹¹The stones of the wall will cry out,
　　and the beams of the woodwork will echo it.

¹²"Woe to him who builds a city with bloodshed
　　and establishes a town by crime!
¹³Has not the LORD Almighty determined
　　that the people's labor is only fuel for the fire,
　　that the nations exhaust themselves for nothing?
¹⁴For the earth will be filled with the knowledge of the glory
　　　　of the LORD,
　　as the waters cover the sea.

¹⁵"Woe to him who gives drink to his neighbors,
　　pouring it from the wineskin till they are drunk,
　　so that he can gaze on their naked bodies.
¹⁶You will be filled with shame instead of glory.
　　Now it is your turn! Drink and be exposed!
　The cup from the LORD's right hand is coming around
　　　　to you,
　　and disgrace will cover your glory.
¹⁷The violence you have done to Lebanon will overwhelm
　　　　you,
　　and your destruction of animals will terrify you.
　For you have shed man's blood;
　　you have destroyed lands and cities and everyone
　　　　in them.

¹⁸"Of what value is an idol, since a man has carved it?
　　Or an image that teaches lies?
　For he who makes it trusts in his own creation;
　　he makes idols that cannot speak.
¹⁹Woe to him who says to wood, 'Come to life!'
　　Or to lifeless stone, 'Wake up!'
　Can it give guidance?
　　It is covered with gold and silver;
　　there is no breath in it.
²⁰But the LORD is in his holy temple;
　　let all the earth be silent before him."

HABAKKUK 2 GIVES Yahweh's revelation of the fall and the "woes" of Babylon. In 2:2 he tells the prophet to take notes (lit., "write a vision") on the future. It is a revelation within a revelation. The prophet waits on the city wall to see what answer Yahweh will give regarding his question about the wicked (2:1). God tells him to write down and publish two ways in the world: puffed-up desire and faith (2:4–6a). The way of puffed-up desire leads to five "woes" from the mouths of the Babylonians' captives (2:6b–20).

The revelation addresses the prophet's questions from chapter 1: "Why ... do you tolerate the treacherous?" (1:13b), and "Why are you silent while the wicked swallow up those more righteous than themselves?" (1:13b). The question about God's toleration is addressed succinctly in 2:4b. This half verse that may be the best known part of the book: "The righteous will live by his faith." The second question has a much more lengthy answer (2:6–20). Together these responses form Yahweh's "plain" truth for dealing with the situation and the persistence of wickedness in the world.

Several important points of God's reputation are at stake in Habakkuk's questions and in the answers given in chapter 2. As noted in 1:12–13, God is everlasting, holy, solid as a rock, and too pure to look on evil, and he cannot tolerate wrong. Three issues emerge in here. (1) How can the faithful believe if Jerusalem falls? (2) How can God's reputation stand in the world if the Babylonians (and the wicked in general) prosper? (3) How does Yahweh's reputation stand up to Babylon's idolatry? The first issue is addressed in 2:4b. The second is answered in the prophecy of Babylon's end (and the implied restoration of the people in the land; 2:7–8, 10b, 16). The third is answered between the lines in 2:11 (as creation itself will cry out against the Babylonians), in 2:14 (where the earth will be filled with the knowledge of God's glory), and in 2:20 (as the entire world is commanded to be silent before Yahweh in his temple).

Watching for and Receiving a Revelation (2:1–3)

HABAKKUK WAITS ON the ramparts to see what Yahweh will answer this time. Confident that he will respond again, the prophet watches for and receives a "revelation" (2:2; *hazon*, "vision"). He needs a detailed response to give to the complaint he has brought on behalf of his constituency (2:1b). The news about the Babylonians' onslaught will raise serious questions in Jerusalem (see 1:5b). The NIV includes a footnote for the translation "complaint," offering as an alternative, "when I am rebuked" (*yakah*). The prophecy has sounded like doom, and the people will certainly have complained or rebuked Habakkuk as a false prophet. He must try to convince them. What can he say to them? How can God allow such an evil adversary the freedom to wreak havoc against his chosen people? Habakkuk has no words of his own to offer.

At this point, the original readers recognize that they have reached the apex of the book. God is going to answer both complaints and explain why the wicked rule in Judah and the more wicked Babylonians will also rule. Yahweh is about to instruct the prophet on how to speak to his congregation, and he does not want them to miss the apex either. "Write down the revelation and make it plain on tablets so that a herald may run with it" (2:2).[1] God tells Habakkuk to publish and distribute what he is about to say. He doesn't want anyone to remain confused about his position. This is the only time in the book when Yahweh is introduced as the speaker (2:2a).

Yahweh's second introductory comment (2:3) is a strong repetitive statement not to dismiss what he is about to say. He knows that many will not like the response they hear and will dismiss his word as ineffective or false. He knows too that his way is not the way preferred by his people. Thus, with his own words he says that the revelation will "await its appointed time" and, "though it linger," they are to "wait for it" (2:3). The people will be tempted to disbelieve because of the long wait, as were the faithful in Judah who witnessed the success of local corruption. Also tempted will be the exiles in Babylon for seventy years before the return to the land. Faith requires waiting for Yahweh's justice.

Yahweh next cautions them to believe the certain words of Habakkuk, which "will certainly come and will not delay" (2:3). The people will be tempted to call the prophecy a lie or to expect Yahweh not to act. Here Yahweh agrees with the prophet, who is worried that he will be rebuked as a liar (2:1). Yahweh's own words warn the prophet's listeners and readers not to dismiss his word. He calls them to trust what they are about to hear as God's way in the world. These introductory words prepare them to hear answers to the two questions: "What about the way of the righteous?" (2:4b), and "What about the success of the wicked?" (2:6–20).

Two Ways: Faith or Puffed-Up Desire (2:4–5)

"SEE, HE IS puffed up; his desires are not upright" (2:4a). Although it is not mentioned here, "he" means the Babylonians (1:6). The abrupt shift in sub-

---

1. The meaning of the "running" of the herald (or reader) is debated. Possibilities include: (1) that even one running can read it, (2) that the one who reads will run in terror, (3) that the one who reads will live by it, or (4) that the reader's eye will run easily over it. The NIV is an appropriate translation. The point is that the message is plain so that it may be easily understood by everyone.

ject and the cryptic reference to Babylon are anticipated only by the reference to the future in 2:3a ("awaits an appointed time"). These two verses serve as an introduction to the five woes that follow (2:6–20).

"Puffed up" (ʿapal) is an odd expression that expresses well the original sense of being swollen, like the swelling of a tumor, or swollen with presumption, or badly proud (Num. 14:44). In context it refers to Yahweh's description of the Babylonians as a "law to themselves," a culture that promotes its own honor (1:7) and whose own strength is their god (1:11).

Another possibility for translating ʿapal is "to lose faith." This coincides better with Habakkuk in the LXX ("lose faith"), which is quoted in Hebrews 10:38.[2] This interpretation leads to a similar interpretation of pride, because it is *faith in the vision* of Yahweh's triumph over evil (ch. 3) that is lost. When faith in Yahweh's promise of victory is lost, human pride has free reign. People will then say, "The LORD will do nothing, either good or bad" (Zeph. 1:12; cf. Jer. 17:15; 2 Peter 3:3–4).

The next phrase, "his desires are not upright" (2:4a), is a necessary part of Yahweh's answer to Habakkuk's hearers. "Desire" (nepeš) had the potential to be good or to be used for evil. The original word means "life in relation to others." God does not lift the responsibility of life's choices from his human creation (see Gen. 4:7; Josh. 24:15). This expression ("his desires are not upright") is a fundamental part of Yahweh's response to Habakkuk's complaint. The Babylonians' "desires" could be upright or not. Yahweh will not take away the will (or desire) to choose, even from Babylon. That is why the wicked prosper.

The way of the righteous person is described in 2:4b. "The righteous will live by his faith." In context, "the righteous" (2:4b) is a synonym for "the upright" (2:4a). The Hebrew word for "faith" (ʾaman) means "fidelity" and "steadfastness" (see Bridging Contexts section). The root of the word is the same as that of "amen," meaning "confirmed." It is the ultimate expression and commitment of trust. It can be paraphrased, "those who want to live in right relationship with God and his people will live by their trust in the promises of the LORD."

For the original readers of the text, living by faith meant believing Yahweh's word given through Habakkuk. It meant singing the song Habakkuk sings and provides for them (see ch. 3). Faith means claiming the radical faith of 3:17–19 as their own, even when in exile six hundred miles from their homes and without a temple. Faith means waiting seventy years for the return to their impoverished homeland. Faith meant trust and even joy in the midst of adversity. The fullest expression of the original meaning of "the righteous will live by his faith" is found in Habakkuk 3.

---

2. Roberts, *Nahum, Habakkuk, and Zephaniah*, 106, 111.

The way of the "puffed up" is addressed again in 2:5, which adds three descriptive details. (1) The Babylonians were known for their wine and consumption of wine (see the fourth woe at 2:15–17).[3] Excessive wine "betrays" (or "is treacherous") because it deceives the drinker into feeling more important ("puffed up") than is warranted.[4] The Hebrew for "betrays" (*bagad*) comes from the root "cloak," as in "cloak and dagger." Wine is like that. It hides its danger. It is a false pride, a pride that is not "upright." This false sense is treacherous for Babylon because it will lead to its ultimate demise (539 B.C.).

(2) The second mark of the way of the "puffed up" is arrogance. Arrogance is, by definition, a false pride.

(3) The enemy is never "at rest" because he is greedy. Greed marks the way of the wicked like a gravestone. "Like death" (*šeʾol*) the Babylonians are never satisfied. They consume but are never full. They will take all the cultures of the ancient Near East captive, collect the people as possessions, and bring their treasures home, but they will still be restless.

Five Future Woes for the Puffed Up
from the Survivors (2:6–20)

THE REMAINDER OF chapter 2 contains Yahweh's words for the future survivors to speak to the "puffed up." Included are his indictments against extortion, unjust wealth, bloodshed, drunkenness and enticing to drunkenness, and trusting in created things. The taunts include being plundered by their victims, public shame, knowledge of the futility of their lives, exposure of their deeds, and knowledge of the isolation they have created by worshiping dead things. All these "woes," Yahweh says, will be spoken by the survivors to their captors. This is the true consequence of wicked living. It is not joy as the prophet and his constituencies believe and claim (1:15).

Verses 5b–6a are central to Yahweh's response to Habakkuk's questions about the wicked enduring. Yahweh insists that the only respite the righteous will receive as they wait for the fall of the wicked is what they themselves will do and say in the five following woes. The power of the oppressed to respond is also noted; "all" the cultures of the earth agree on these woes. They are the spoken woes of "all the nations ... all the peoples ... all of them" (2:5b–6a).

"Will not all of them taunt him with ridicule and scorn, saying, 'Woe ... '?" The five woes begin with this important framing by Yahweh. The context of the woes is the speaking out of "all the nations and ... all the [captive] peo-

---

3. Many English translations use the Greek/Syriac and Qumran versions, which have "wealth" (*bon*) instead of "wine" (*bayyayin*).

4. In Isa. 28:7–8 Isaiah writes of a similar problem for Israel.

ples." God himself describes these woes, but he says that they will be spoken by the survivors of the atrocities of the wicked. The voices of the captive survivors will be filled with "ridicule and scorn" (2:5–6). The word translated "scorn" (*liṣ*) refers also to a mocking poem in Hebrew. "Ridicule" (*ḥidah*) can mean "riddle," and "taunt" (*mašal*) also means "parable." These words introduce the fifteen-verse/five-woe revelation that follows.

Thus, the voices of the captive survivors speak the woes. This would have been carefully noted by the original readers. "Woes" (*hoy*) are laments for the justice that will come against the "puffed up." Yahweh establishes the laments, but they *are to be spoken* by the survivors to their captors. The laments are, at this stage in the story, ironic, since the captive survivors do not usually lament for their persecutors. Yahweh's gift to the survivors is a lament, not for themselves and their victimization; rather, it is a tool against their captors.

Lament in the scripture is the seedbed of hope. It creates survivors (i.e., people with hope) out of victims (i.e., people without hope; see Bridging Contexts section). When the captives "lament" for their captors, their saying (a "woe") is a "taunt" (2:6a). But it is not a groundless taunt. It is also prophetic, since it comes from Yahweh and will eventually happen. In this way Yahweh gives all the captive people prophetic speech, a rhetorically brilliant and sociologically complex gift, in their lament for the Babylonians.

It is clear to Habakkuk, to God, and to us that these behaviors are treacherous or "woeful," but what is the content of the "woe" for them? What does God say will happen to these treacherous about whom Habakkuk laments? It is this content that provides Yahweh's answer to Habakkuk's questions, "What about the joy and prosperity of the violent?" (1:15–17). The content of the woe is found at the end of each paragraph of woe.

The first woe (2:6b–8). The first woe of the puffed-up way is that the Babylonian plunderers will be plundered later by the survivors. This woe is given especially against those who have become "wealthy by extortion," after "piling up stolen goods" (2:6).[5] Their crimes are described more fully in 2:8b: "For you have shed man's blood; you have destroyed lands and cities and everyone in them." The crimes are not simply against individuals (shedding of blood) but also against the earth (*ḥamas ʾereṣ*; lit., "violence of earth") and against the cities that support life (2:8b). The indictment begins in the widest circle and moves inward: earth to towns to dwellers. The same indictment, naming the three kinds of victims, is repeated at 2:17, where Yahweh adds "animals" and trees ("Lebanon," see below) to the list of victims of violence.

---

5. The most common form of extortion in the ancient world was to demand tribute in exchange for not leveling a city, as in 597 B.C. Jerusalem. The Babylonians carried off the treasures of the temple and the palace.

The taunt itself may be paraphrased, "He has a wealth of debts for he has been a fool in his rule." In their extortion of nations the Babylonians have become rich in their debts. They have built up a burden of debt by wrongfully acquiring the wealth of other peoples. They thought they were taking from them. In truth, the people will say, "We were only loaning to you. You are debtors. You owe both capital and interest." The debt has come due.

This taunt will come from survivors of all the cultures that have been destroyed (2:8). The Babylonians will tremble as the nations wake up and come to collect their debts; they will plunder the plunderer. This cycle of violence and plunder is the way of power in the ancient world. The taunt given by Yahweh is a bit of wisdom, teaching the foolishness of the way of power. Unjust power that is used to create wealth will be used to undo that wealth.

The second woe (2:9–11). The second woe of the puffed-up way is shame and the knowledge of a wasted life. Public shame will come on those who have built their security by unjust profit. Babylon's crime is "the ruin of many peoples" (2:10a). Highlighted here is what seemed to be a good motive, to build his "realm" (*bayit*) or "household" security, "to set his nest on high, to escape the clutches of ruin" (2:9). These are noteworthy domestic goals. Building a family or cultural legacy by means of "unjust gain," however, will lead to woe. The metaphor of "nest" can be linked to the "vulture swooping to devour" (1:8). It is not shameful for a vulture to act as a vulture, but Yahweh declares the same behavior among people is shameful.

The consequence of this unjust means of building security is shame on the builder's household and "forfeiting your life" (2:10b). "Forfeiting" (*ḥata'*) is related to the common Hebrew word for sin and has the sense of missing the target. The implication of "forfeiting" is not just dying but a wasted life. Instead of escaping ruin, the builder's life missed the mark in shame.

The distinct sound "ts" (Heb. *ṣ*) resounds in verses 9 and 10 in the key words of the text. Taken together they sounded like a taunt with a lot of hissing: "builds gain" (*boṣea' beṣa'*), "to escape" (*lehinnaṣal*), "you have plotted" (*ya'aṣta*), "the ruin of" (*qeṣot*). Together they would have sounded (phonetically) like "bo-tsaya, be-tsa, lehin-na-tsayl, yaats-ta, qe-tsot." Verse 11 adds the final "ts" sound in the word "woodwork" (*me'eṣ*).

The accompanying taunt is that the house itself will cry out and echo the shame of the ruined builder (2:11). The stones of the wall and the woodwork are all that remain after the builder is dead. They will be standing reminders to the survivors of the shame and the sin by which they were built. The builder will find ruin and shame instead of safety for his household.

The third woe (2:12–14). The third woe of the puffed-up way is that the wicked Babylonians know they have spent their lives for nothing and have forfeited not only their lives (cf. 2:10) but also the glory of Yahweh. Human labor is fuel for the fire for those who build with bloodshed.

The crime is similar to the one named in the first two woes, but now Yahweh sharpens the point. The sin remains building (2:9, 12) with crime (2:6, 9, 12) and bloodshed (2:8, 12). For the first time, however, Yahweh is mentioned by name in the taunts: "Has not the LORD Almighty determined. . . ?" This means that Babylon's crimes are not only perpetrated against the many cultures of the ancient Near East but also against Yahweh. Up until this point, the crimes have been against humanity and the consequences in the realm of humanity (2:6–11). Now Yahweh declares that the people should declare their captors' futility against what he has determined. They will "build" and "labor . . . for nothing" (2:12).

The consequence is that the cultures who have pursued bloodshed and crime (2:12) have exchanged the knowledge of the glory of Yahweh for vain labor and effort. They have replaced it with "nothing" (*riq*). This same word is also used in Job 39:16. The ostrich "treats her young harshly, as if they were not hers; she cares not that her labor was *in vain*." The vanity of labor that is only "fuel for the fire" is not a general proverb regarding all labor. After all, those who live in the promise of Yahweh's blessing do "not toil in vain" (Isa. 65:23). The vanity of the "people's labor" here (Hab. 2:13), by contrast, is a specific reference to its context in the previous verse, "who builds a city with bloodshed" (2:12).

The five woes form two panels: The first and second woes form the first panel and the fourth and fifth form the second. These panels are divided by the third woe (2:12–14), the centerpiece of which is verse 14: "For the earth will be filled with the knowledge of the glory of the LORD, as the waters cover the sea." This declaration refers to God's intention to bless all the nations of the world through Israel by bringing the whole creation back to the Creator through Israel's history (Ex. 9:16; Num. 14:21; Isa. 11:9; see Bridging Contexts section). It is tantamount to the future captives preaching God's salvation history of Israel to their captors.

The fourth woe. The fourth woe of the puffed-up way is exposure, shame, and disgrace. Yahweh will bring these experiences on those who entice others to drunkenness in order to take advantage of them.[6] The image is meant to be shocking. The Babylonian practice of inducing drunkenness is abusive in itself as well as a symbol for the degradation and exposure of lands and cultures.[7] They amuse themselves at their captives' expense. Their crime, like

---

6. Verse 15 has a double meaning in Heb. The NIV preserves the originally intended shock value of the actual forced drunkenness. See Bridging Contexts section.

7. See v. 17. This is the second reference to wine (cf. 2:5a).

rape, is primarily a crime of violence, using sexuality as a means to expose and debase their victims. By their crimes they further demoralize a conquered community. The taunt is that Babylon's "glory" (2:16) in the power of drunkenness will be covered by shame. This "glory" stands in stark contrast to the "glory of the LORD," which will "fill the earth" (2:14).

The second mention of Yahweh in the taunt of the survivors is in 2:16. It is a warning that Yahweh will act. The "right hand" refers to his intervening power (Ex. 15:6; Ps. 17:7; 20:6; 44:3). When Yahweh says, "Now it's your turn! Drink and be exposed!" the drunkenness has a metaphorical meaning, referring to the fall of Babylon. Daniel mentions the famous Babylonian wine-drinking party, where a hand appeared and wrote on the wall (Dan. 5:1–5). That night the Babylonian king was slain and the Mede Darius began to rule. Cyrus II of Persia captured the city in 539 B.C. without a fight and allowed the exiles to return to their homeland the next year. Babylon was found exposed and shamed, both literally and metaphorically. The "cup from the LORD's right hand" was Cyrus, whom Yahweh calls his "anointed" (Isa. 44:28–45:1).

The metaphor of nakedness is even more taunting in the Hebrew. "Exposed" (2:16b) is literally a reference to the uncovering of the foreskin. The expression "you will be filled" (2:16a) is also ironic in the original, since it uses the same verb root as in 2:5, meaning never "satisfied" (śabaʿ). Now Yahweh and the people will say, "You will be satisfied [filled]," but with shame.

In 2:17 is an abrupt shift, yet one that is integral to understanding the images of drunkenness and nakedness. The Babylonian practice of making their victims drunk in order to strip them is expanded as a symbol for the denuding of the land. Especially in Lebanon, the Babylonians declared war on the ancient Near East environment. The violence done to trees, animals, lands, cities, and everyone in them is the weight of the crime. Lebanon is naked of trees, the cities are naked of people, and the land is naked of animals. All of Yahweh's beloved creation has been assaulted.

What are the consequences of this woe for the Babylonians? "The cup from the LORD's right hand" will pour the wine of "disgrace" over the Babylonians' glory (2:16). What is in the cup? Verse 17 tells us. First, the "violence you have done to Lebanon will overwhelm you." This is a cryptic reference to the destruction of the majestic cedars of Lebanon.[8] Nebuchadnezzar felled all the cedars of Lebanon. Second, their "destruction of animals will terrify"

---

8. See Isa. 14:8: The whole earth breaks forth into singing at the demise of Babylon; the cedars say, "Now that you have been laid low, no woodsman comes to cut us down" (see also Isa. 10:34; 55:12).

them. The cedars of Lebanon were used to create the extensive woodwork in Babylon, which will remain to witness against its violence (2:11).[9]

This fourth woe is the first one in the second panel. It concludes in exactly the same way as the first woe of the first panel, with the same half-verse summary of the indictment against them: "For you have shed man's blood; you have destroyed lands and cities and everyone in them" (2:8b, 17b). In the first panel the consequence is that "those you have plundered will plunder you." In the second panel the consequence is the overwhelming terror of violence to trees and animals. All creation will combine to bring justice to the destructive Babylonians.

The fifth woe (2:18–20). The fifth woe of the puffed-up way is the futility and spiritual isolation that will be experienced by those who trust in lifeless created things. The foolishness of worshiping anything in place of the life-giving Creator will become evident to the Babylonian who trusts in his own strength (1:11, 16).

This last woe begins abruptly without the customary word "Woe" (see v. 19). It is easier to see the break in the Hebrew text since there is a paragraph marker at the end of verse 17. This new theme of idolatry begins with the obvious logic against trusting in things that are made: "He who makes it trusts in his own creation." By trusting in what he has made for himself, a man ignores the Creator of all the earth. An idol is an extension of this foolishness of trusting one's own strength, for such a worker is essentially trusting in himself.

The consequence of such ignorant trust and the taunt given by Yahweh for the captives to speak to their captors is sevenfold. An idol has no value because it has been carved by a human being, teaches lies, cannot speak, cannot come to life, cannot wake up, cannot give guidance, and has no breath (i.e., is dead). The expression in 2:19b that ends the taunts has more "ridicule and scorn" (2:6a) in Hebrew than in English. It implies a person standing mockingly before an idol exclaiming, "It teaches! Look! It is gold and silver! And full of breath! Oh, there isn't any in it."

By contrast, Yahweh is present in the temple he has created, teaches truth (as in this revelation), is speaking, is alive, is awake, gives guidance, and is

---

9. In what way will these things terrify and overwhelm them? By the awful realization that they have destroyed what cannot be replaced? By the fear of haunting (probably not an ancient concept for animals!)? Not haunting but rather, a nightmare: The verb for "terrify" (*ḥatat*) also means "terror of a nightmare." The text centers on "violence" and "destruction" themselves being overwhelming and terrifying. Yahweh's cup includes the reality that acts of destruction of any kind are not lost to memory but remain with the perpetrator of the violence. Justice is done in Yahweh's creation by the reality that disgraceful deeds cannot be undone, but their shame eventually "will overwhelm" the doer.

the One who gives the breath of life. Silence is for the people and the whole earth to keep in his presence (2:20b). No one has to call out to wake him up or arouse him to teach. He is already speaking.

At the time of this prophecy, Yahweh's presence "in his holy temple" would have been understood to refer to Solomon's temple. In a few short years after the revelation (586 B.C.) when these woes would be spoken by the captives to their captors, the temple would be destroyed. Through the revelation of Isaiah Yahweh's temple was proclaimed to be in the heavens. God was said to dwell in the heavens, which meant in the observable creation (Isa. 66:1–2).

In 2:19 created wood and stone are worshiped but are silent when asked for guidance. But created wood and stone *will* speak by Yahweh's word (2:11). They will be God's witnesses against those who have trusted in them and made them with unjust profits, at the expense of the earth, towns, and others' blood (2:8).

Just as the centerpiece of the woes concludes with a declaration about Yahweh (2:14), so also does the last woe (2:20). The chapter ends abruptly: "But the LORD is in his holy temple; let all the earth be silent before him" (2:20). The word translated "be silent" can be pronounced, in Hebrew, "Hush" (*has*).

The dialogue with Yahweh is over. He has responded to, though not directly answered, Habakkuk's questions about the suffering of the righteous (1:3, 13b) and the success of the wicked (1:13, 15–17). Habakkuk accepts Yahweh's responses. The response to the first question in 2:4b ("the righteous shall live by his faith") and to the second in 2:6–20 (the wicked will reap what they sow) are accepted in 3:16–19. The only response left for Habakkuk is worship. The book does not end with the completion of the dialogue but concludes with the prophet's song of praise. Habakkuk's sung prayer of response to Yahweh's monologue struggles with a new shape to his faith in God.

THE ENDURING MESSAGE of Habakkuk is carried in the words "the righteous will live by his faith" (2:4b). These words are quoted three times in the New Testament (Rom. 1:17; Gal. 3:11; Heb. 10:38), possibly altered from the LXX ("the righteous shall live by *my* [God's] faith").[10] The original Hebrew is "the righteous will live by *his faithfulness*," or, possibly, "the righteous will live by *its faithfulness*" (referring to the word of God

---

10. See Heb. 10:38, "My righteous one will live by faith"; Rom. 1:17 and Gal. 3:11, "The righteous will live by faith."

given to Habakkuk in the "revelation," 2:2–3).[11] The righteous will believe what God is about to say and live by trust in his word and thus in Yahweh himself. The meaning of this text (and its use by people of faith through the centuries) relies on the relationships between the faith and faithfulness of the believer and the faithfulness of God.

"The righteous will live . . ." is part of Yahweh's response to Habakkuk's question, "Why do you tolerate the treacherous?" (1:13). Habakkuk asked his questions of God in a historically specific way: Why do you tolerate injustice, wrong, destruction, violence, strife, and conflict in Judah? (cf. 1:3). He also asked the question in a more general way that spans the centuries: You cannot tolerate any evil, so why do you tolerate the wicked in silence (cf. 1:13)? God answers the first historically specific question in detail: The Babylonians will be destroyed before long (2:6–20). The second Yahweh answered in 2:1–4 ("Write the revelation, make it plain, wait for it, it is true, and live by faith in it"). This is a timeless recommendation for all people. "The righteous will live . . ." addresses the reality of the condition of human existence in the world and God's role in it. It also points to a fuller response and hope developed in chapter 3.

Historically specific response. If we hear only the historically specific aspect of the question (609 B.C., Judean corruption and Babylonian atrocities), the question is far removed from us. It is only *their* question. It certainly *was* their question. When Habakkuk asked, "Why don't you do something?" Yahweh's answer was swift: "I will do something soon, by bringing the Babylonians to you. I will put an end to Jerusalem's corruption." In a simple, linear fashion one can hear the second question and answer in a similar way: What about Babylonian wickedness? Will you tolerate that? God's answer: No, they will only last for a while (seventy years); then I will destroy them, too. Reading the question and answer in this way, one can deduce that what Habakkuk needed (and received from Yahweh) was a larger and slower worldview, one that allowed for God's slow-moving justice.

It is true that God's justice moves in large, broad strokes in history. He makes the nations rise and fall. Even the simplest historical reading, however, raises the question of whether a community of justice (without corruption) was established in Judea after Babylon's fall. Were violence and corruption still a problem? It was still a problem in the postexilic community, through the Greek and Roman rule, and so on, until the destruction of the second temple in A.D. 70. God's response to the first (historical) hearing of the question is in the woes of 2:6b–20. Justice is accomplished in the natural judgments of societies against the corrupt and violent. Victims will take revenge (2:8).

---

11. Roberts, *Nahum, Habakkuk, and Zephaniah,* 105.

History will remember violence (2:11); the violent will not endure (2:13) but will be exposed (2:16). The prosperous wicked will realize their foolish isolation from their objects of worship (2:19). These forms of judgment are not swift. Like history, they take time.

A timeless recommendation. If the question "Why do you tolerate wrong?" is heard in the second way, it also becomes a present, modern question. Habakkuk wants to know why, if God cannot tolerate wrong and is too pure to look on evil (1:13), the treacherous continue to succeed. Why should corruption exist at all in Judah and Babylon? This is a question for every time and place. Can communities of justice and truth ever be established, anywhere? Under what conditions will the purity of God be manifest in a society? God does answer these questions in Habakkuk, but only in brief and indirect ways. Although indirect, these answers are not abstract. They have become the best loved and applied texts of the book:

- "The righteous will live ..." (2:4b).
- "For the earth will be filled with the knowledge of the glory of the LORD, as the waters cover the sea" (2:14).
- "The Sovereign LORD is my strength; he makes my feet like the feet of a deer, he enables me to go on the heights" (3:19).

How shall the righteous person live? How shall we understand the various biblical renditions of this verse (Hebrew, LXX, New Testament quotations)? Is there a sharp contrast in meaning between "living by faith" (Romans and Galatians), "living by faithfulness" (Hebrew), "living by [God's] faith" (or promise) concerning the future of the righteous (LXX), and "living by [God's revelation's] faithfulness" (Heb., alternate translation)? Certainly there is a difference in emphasis, but is it a sharp contrast? These revelations, taken together, form a complete picture of faith and faithfulness in relation to God.

The perceived contrast between living "by faith" and living "by faithfulness" is a false dichotomy. The original Hebrew for "faithfulness" (ʾenumah) also means "steady faith" or "trust."[12] Faithful living and trust (steady faith) are inextricably bound together. If I have faith in a bridge over a chasm to hold me but I will not cross it, I am not living by that faith. If I have faith in my spouse to be true but hire a detective to follow her, my faith claim is in jeopardy. If I have faith in marriage but am not faithful to my wife, do I keep faith or live by it? Faith is what faith does. "Living by faithfulness" is redundant because faith is *lived faith* when someone is faithful. Faith as an abstraction or as assent to a principle is not living by faith.

---

12. BDB, 53.

The one who trusts God in faith lives faithfully by his Word. Conversely, the one who is faithful to his Word also clearly trusts it and has faith in the One who gave it. The root of the Hebrew word demonstrates this natural link through the primary social context of a small child's trust in the faithfulness of a nursemaid to carry her (Isa. 60:4, NIV "carried"; Ruth 4:16, NIV "cared for" = nursed). Trust is a circle of trustworthiness, trusting, and living because of that trust. In any case, if you have faith in God or in his revealed Word (its faithfulness), you live faithfully.

The words "live by" in "the righteous will live by faith" eradicate any contrast between faith and faithfulness. Living "by faith" is an activity. It means that one "lives" according to God's Word, in relation to its promises and commands for relationships. Faith is demonstrated *as faith* in *faithful* living. Living "by faithfulness" (fidelity, integrity, steady trust) is simply the experience of "living by faith," not a contrast to it. Faith that is not a lived faithfulness or not matched by faithful living is a damaged faith. A person living a faithful life may be plagued by doubts, but that is not the ideal expressed in the words "faith/faithfulness." The complete faith/faithful life is not centered in continually "feeling trust" in God but in the permanence of long-term fidelity and loyalty to Yahweh and his promises. That permanence is based in enduring trust and deep feeling and is measured by a life, not by emotions that accompany the joys and troubles of life.

(1) In Hebrews 10:35–39 we read one of the New Testament's quotes of Habakkuk 2:4b:

> So do not throw away your confidence; it will be richly rewarded. You need to persevere so that when you have done the will of God, you will receive what he has promised. For in just a very little while,
>
> "He who is coming will come and will not delay.
> But *my righteous one will live by faith*.
> And if he shrinks back,
> I will not be pleased with him."
>
> But we are not of those who shrink back and are destroyed, but of those who believe and are saved.

Enduring in faith in difficult times is the primary context of Hebrews, as in Habakkuk. Hebrews 10:25–34 describes a congregation struggling to keep faith because it is being pulled apart by various forces. Some have given up meeting for worship while others deliberately sin, "trampling" the blood of Jesus and "insulting the Spirit of grace." They have grown weary of persecution, loss of property, and sympathy for those in prison. The author encourages them not to give up the struggle of faith but to endure in it.

The difference between the texts is the object of the faith. Habakkuk calls the people to live in the confidence of the vision (2:6–20) that the Babylonians will be destroyed and in faith of Yahweh's appearing on the earth in power (3:1–15). The combination of confidence and faith in Yahweh's power and promise is the object of Habakkuk's faith. The purpose of the Hebrews text is to give assurance of the promise of Christ to return to receive his own and judge the wicked. This eschatological hope is also in the power and promise of God. It is based on confidence in Jesus' promise (Heb. 10:23) and forgiveness (10:17–19).

These texts share a common faith in the God who has demonstrated the power of his love for his people and who promises to act on their behalf in the future. Hebrews' vision of this love and judgment, however, includes the entire world and addresses God's universal action in the first and second comings of Christ. Both texts encourage the believer to live in the confidence of what God has done, believing that God will also be faithful to his promises in the future. In both cases, to fail in faith is death, but to persevere is life in God.

(2) Romans 1:17 also quotes Habakkuk 2:4b as a universal message for all who will believe the gospel of Christ. Paul explains that he is eager to preach to non-Jews because God has, in Jesus, offered a personal relationship with him to all cultures and peoples:

> That is why I am so eager to preach the gospel also to you who are at Rome.
>
> I am not ashamed of the gospel, because it is the power of God for the salvation of everyone who believes: first for the Jew, then for the Gentile. For in the gospel a righteousness from God is revealed, a righteousness that is by faith from first to last, just as it is written: "The righteous will live by faith." (Rom. 1:15–17; cf. Gen. 15:6; Gal. 3:6; Rom. 4:3)

"The righteous will live by faith" is the heart of the gospel that Paul wants to preach to the Romans. This gospel connects the "righteous" (those who live uprightly in the community before God) and the revelation of a "righteousness from God," which is Jesus Christ (Rom. 3:21; 1 Cor. 1:30; 1 Peter 3:18; 1 John 2:1). In the Old Testament "righteous" does not mean faultless or perfect in every thought of the heart. Jesus and later Paul taught about that radical idea of a righteousness before God that is only satisfied by a completely righteous One.

"The righteous" person in the Old Testament lives an upright life in relation to God and neighbor. A person of integrity who keeps the outward commands of God is a pillar of a community and is considered a righteous person. It is in this sense that Job could rightly claim to be righteous before God. In the intertestamental period (the last four hundred years before Christ), the Jewish community engaged in a debate concerning the nature of "righteousness."

Two trajectories can be detected. On the one hand, a person is "righteous" who keeps the outward and observable forms of the commandments. In this sense, for example, keeping the command "You shall not covet" is observable by defining it as "You shall not defraud." On the other hand, the law is intensified or made more radical. This is the tradition Jesus uses when he reinterprets "You shall not murder" as "You shall not call your brother a fool" (cf. Matt. 5:21–22). Jesus upholds both traditions in his conversation with the rich young ruler in Mark 10. He asks him about the necessary outward form of the commands (which he could do and had done) and then asks him to give up everything, which he could not do.[13]

(3) Paul returns to this theme in Galatians 3:11–12, 14:

> Clearly no one is justified before God by the law, because, "The righteous will live by faith." The law is not based on faith; on the contrary, "The man who does these things will live by them." Christ ... redeemed us in order that the blessing given to Abraham might come to the Gentiles through Christ Jesus, so that by faith we might receive the promise of the Spirit.

When Paul writes that "the righteous will live by faith," he is speaking about more than the outward keeping of the law. He says that no one is justified by the law (which *can* be kept in its outward public form). Rather, Paul is speaking about the impossibility of keeping the radical interpretation of the law. You can live your whole life without defrauding anyone, and it will make your life better. You cannot, however, live a whole life without secretly coveting something that belongs to someone else. It is for this reason Christ came. He is the (radical and inward) righteousness of God that we can never attain. Paul pushes this concept to the front of the discussion when he says that the righteousness of God (Jesus) is revealed in the gospel (Rom. 1:17). Christ Jesus has become our righteousness (cf. 1 Cor. 1:30).

Paul is not setting up a dichotomy between faith as "belief" or "assent" and living a life of patient trust and endurance.[14] Paul expects Christians to assent to Christ as their righteousness by living patiently within that righteousness.

---

13. J. K. Bruckner, "On the One Hand ... On the Other Hand: The Two-Fold Meaning of the Law Against Covetousness," in *Hear and Obey: Essays in Honor of Frederick Carlson Holmgren* (Chicago: Covenant, 1997), 97–118.

14. Cf. Hiebert, "The Book of Habakkuk," 7:643.

He contrasts the two ways of living patient, faithful lives. He argues that the focal point of the faithful doing good deeds of righteousness is Christ's righteousness, not the law's mandates. Christ is the motivation for the good deeds of faith. An earned righteousness is not.

Luther insisted, in a similar way, that faith in God's forgiveness and grace in Jesus Christ form true faith. He also insisted that this experience of grace through faith will overflow into a life of good deeds toward one's neighbor. Faith flows into faithfulness as naturally as spring water flows into a streambed. There is no dichotomy between the water and the stream. Conversely, faithfulness presupposes faith as the forest stream presupposes its water. If only crude oil were to flow in the streambed, it would no longer be a forest stream. Self-promoting good works cannot pass for faithful living. They lack the essential element of faith. When Paul says that "the righteous will live by faith," it is no contrast to Habakkuk's Hebrew, "the just shall live by his faithfulness." *Faithfulness is* (by their definition) *living by faith.*

HABAKKUK 2 PROVIDES practical help for times when our foundations are shaken. When we receive bad news that someone we love will soon die, that peace and security are quickly moving toward war and destruction, or that our religious leadership is falling from grace through corruption, our personal world can be shaken to the core. In Habakkuk 2, through his complaint, the prophet is seeking a word of good news from Yahweh. He waits and is told to make the message plain in writing, so that everyone in need can understand it. Yahweh gives him words (five woes) to speak against the source of their suffering (2:6–19) and reminds them to participate in worship (2:20). God gives the woes (or taunts) as a bit of wisdom, to teach the foolishness of the way of power. Power used to create unjust wealth will also be used to undo that wealth.

Practical helps. (1) The first practical help that the prophet models is to seek Yahweh (2:1). The lamenting prophet goes up onto the city wall ramparts to look for the coming of good news. He intentionally seeks a word from Yahweh that will sustain him and the people.

In Isaiah 20:1–12, Isaiah describes in detail the experience of suffering and his climb to a wall to look for news. His experience is parallel to Habakkuk's and gives us more detail. He is filled with anguish and seized by pangs like a woman's labor. As is common in deep grief, he cannot hear or see what is around him very well, so bowed is he in his dismay (21:3). He describes being consumed by terror: "My heart falters, fear makes me tremble; the twilight I longed for has become a horror to me" (21:4). Yahweh tells him to set a watchman on the wall to look and listen for news. The prophet goes himself, for he is so consumed by grief and fear. The watchman stays awake whole nights (21:8). Then the news comes: "Babylon has fallen, has fallen!" (21:9).

In the Christian tradition Babylon and its fall have come to represent the sting of death and its defeat in the resurrection. We may, like the prophets, be racked in pain and fear, but the message on the wall is announced to all the people. Death and its oppression have been defeated. Scripture gives us the freedom to grieve with the faithful prophets when we experience severe loss. But it sends us up onto the heights to look for the word of victory from the Lord.

(2) The second practical help is to wait on Yahweh. Habakkuk waits for the revelation, and in the revelation he is told to wait on Yahweh's action (2:1, 3b). Waiting is common in biblical lamenting over great loss. In times of great trouble, waiting on Yahweh is a necessary practice for those who want to hear and see his word of deliverance (Ps. 33:16–22; 106:12–15). Psalm 62:1–8 echoes in Habakkuk's waiting. The psalmist waits (or "rests") in silence for Yahweh, who is a rock, a fortress, and a refuge. His hope rests in the mighty rock (62:5–7). Yahweh has set the appointed time for deliverance.

The Christian takes hope specifically in God's timing because of the confluence of timing in the first coming of Christ. Jesus came into history as a Jew shortly before the Jews (and Jewish Christians) were dispersed from Jerusalem around the Roman empire. It was a time when a wide area spoke Greek, the language of the New Testament. Moreover, letters (like Paul's) and missionaries could travel easily over the extensive Roman road system. It was a time of suffering, when people were hungry for the gospel of healing through Christ's suffering and the healing ministries of the church. It was the fullness of time (Gal. 4:2–5; Eph. 1:10; cf. Mark 1:15).

Our waiting for the Second Coming is grounded in the reality of Christ's first coming, governed by the promise that he will return (John 14:3) and guided by the Father, who alone knows the timing (Mark 13:32). His seeming delay in returning is not a delay but is his perfect waiting, which creates the possibility that repentance and grace may spread more widely (2 Peter 3:8–9). This is the eschatological (end-time) hope that frames the New Testament writers' quotations of Habakkuk 2:4 (Rom. 1:17; Gal. 3:11; Heb. 10:37–38; see above). The same hope for the restoration of the whole creation is expressed in Paul's patience and hope in the midst of his suffering (Rom. 8:18–25).

(3) The third practical help is to make the message plain so the people can understand it. God reveals himself most clearly through the written Word. Beginning with Moses and the people at Sinai, Yahweh commanded

the writing of his words so that they would remain clear for everyone.[15] The prophets sometimes wrote on large wooden tablets so that everyone could see their words (Isa. 8:1–4; 30:7–8). The tablets functioned like public notices in public places.[16] In Deuteronomy 27:8 Moses tells the people to write the law in plain and large letters on stones. The prophets are also commanded to write their words in books so they may be read.

From antiquity Yahweh has provided his lasting message of deliverance in writing so that people can study and understand it. The Scriptures are that plain message for us. In the worst of times the Word of God is a resource of hope, comfort, and direction for God's people. To "make it plain" sometimes requires assistance in explaining the message. Moses also made Yahweh's word "plain" to the people (see *ba'ar* in Deut. 1:5; NIV "expound"; RSV "explain"). Good preaching from the pulpit and good teaching will do the same. It will bring hope from Scripture to the hurting, without lying about the consequences of sin. It will preach the whole counsel of God, law and gospel together.

Yahweh's message through Habakkuk does not promise a quick and false solution to their suffering. He wants them to understand the reality of their future. He does not lie about the pain that must be endured (2:3). In the time of Habakkuk the lying prophet Hananiah opposed Jeremiah, promising the people a quick end to Babylon's domination (Jer. 28:10–15). Many lying prophets offered easier hope through false prophecies about the end (see Ezek. 13:6–19; Mic. 2:6–11). The message of Yahweh's deliverance is plain and truthful. It does not promise a quick solution to personal or national loss, but it does not leave the people without hope. The plain truth is that God is with them in their suffering and dying and will deliver them in time. This message can be trusted; the righteous will live by faith in it.

(4) The fourth practical help in Habakkuk 2 is in the woes or taunts that form the larger part of this chapter (2:6–19). Yahweh gives the prophet words of woe for the people to speak against the source of their suffering. He also reminds them to participate in worship, even in silence (2:20). As we read, it is tempting for us to keep a safe distance from the actions that bring the woes (extortion, bloodshed, inciting drunkenness, idolatry). The woes however, are given by God to Habakkuk as a resource for the people. They are God's response to the question, "Why do you tolerate the

---

15. Scholars disagree about the content of the revelation. Is it 2:4b only, the whole second chapter, or ch. 3? It must be all three: The righteous will live by faith (2:4–5), woe will come to the wicked (2:6–20), and Yahweh will come to judge the earth (3:1–15).

16. Smith, *Micah-Malachi*, 106.

treacherous?" God's applied wisdom is for his people to be reminded in detail, by reciting these woes, what will happen to the treacherous. They are a litany for the suffering to speak about the death of the violence done to them (2:6a).

Five woes as practical help. The context of the woes reveals their application for all times and peoples. The five woes are from God, but God says that they are for the captive peoples to speak to their captors as taunts. The puffed up (proud) cannot rest because God will, sooner or later, bring judgment. Keeping track of who is speaking in this section is complicated. Yahweh is speaking through Habakkuk's vision, saying that the captives will speak woes! The woes are given exactly as an application of a living life of faith and faithfulness in terrible times. They are words to be repeated when one has no words with which to respond to horrific circumstances. In addition, readers since Habakkuk's day have read the woes as general proverbs (see Luke 19:40; 1 Cor. 12:3).

"Woe" in the prophetic writings is not a curse. It is like saying, "Alas" (NRSV) or "How terrible for them!" It is an ironic lament for the death of the wicked. The woes list the sinful behavior and describe its consequential judgment (punishment is appropriate to the specific sin). This form is also found in Isaiah 5:8–25, where the woes are against the corrupt in Jerusalem, and their woe will be experienced at the hands of the Babylonians. The woes in Habakkuk are against the Babylonians' excesses. The woes of the excesses of the "puffed up" (Hab. 2:4a) are expressed in contrast to the righteousness of the one who lives "by faith" (2:4b).

Isaiah's and Habakkuk's woes are instructive wisdom for the believer. In each woe the lack of faith takes the form of relying on oneself instead of God. Moses warned those who prosper in a similar way.

> When you eat and are satisfied, when you build fine houses and settle down ... and all you have is multiplied, then your heart will become proud and you will forget the LORD your God, who brought you ... out of the land of slavery.... He led you through the vast and dreadful desert.... He brought you water out of hard rock. He gave you manna to eat in the desert.... You may say to yourself, "My power and the strength of my hands have produced this wealth for me." But remember the LORD your God, for it is he who gives you the ability to produce wealth ... as it is today.
>
> If you ever forget the LORD your God ... I testify against you today that you will surely be destroyed. (Deut. 8:12–19)

For our success we rely on and give credit to almost anything besides God: our intelligence, wealth, logic, strength, military might, aesthetic abilities, pride of status or birth, tenacity, or problem-solving skills.[17] All of these are gifts from God, and we too easily give ourselves the credit for them and what they enable us to accomplish. This is basic idolatry. We do not need a shrine in order to worship them. They are worshiped every time we rely on them without reference to God, every time we are proud of our accomplishments without noticing their source, every time we take credit without thanksgiving, and every time we gain wealth by taking advantage of another. The woes are to remind everyone who achieves something in life to continue to live by faith and not to enter the woes of the puffed-up life.

The woes demonstrate the foolishness of living a puffed-up life. They stand in stark contrast to living by faith. The woes are an ironic lamentation for the death of violence and the implosion of unbelief and idolatry. They are most directly applicable to governments that impoverish the wealth, dignity, and security of their citizens.[18] They also apply to any myopic pursuit of power and self-promotion (1:7b, 11b), which will never be satisfied (2:5).

The insatiable pursuit of wealth, status, or consumerism is like being drunk with wine (2:5). Its satisfaction is false and gives no true rest (2:5). Sleep experts tell us that although alcohol may initially cause one to fall asleep more quickly, it keeps a person from entering into deep restful sleep. The nightmares of the Babylonians about animals and trees expand on this idea (2:17). Babylon did not rest until it had taken all the cultures of the ancient world captive and brought their treasures home, including their songs (Ps. 137). They were proud with their own importance. Our day-to-day world remains under bondage of greed and death. Respite in this life will come from hearing the five woes spoken as a warning (2:5b–6a) and choosing personally to live by faith.

(1) The first woe is that your victims "will wake up and make you tremble" (2:6b–8). This is echoed in the conventional wisdom that "what goes round comes round." In contrast, a life of faith means living without victimizing anyone, without coveting or gaining wealth at someone else's expense. It means being honest in all monetary deals, even if you need the resources and no one seems to be watching. Debts of extortion and theft always come due. Fraud within the American corporate life and corrupt governments worldwide will end in woe for the perpetrators and their descendents.

(2) The second woe is "the stones of the wall … and … the woodwork" will cry out against you even if you try to guarantee your financial security (2:9–11; cf. Jer. 22:13–19). Recent media fascination with crime families

---

17. Elizabeth Achtemeier, *Nahum-Malachi* (Interpretation; Atlanta: Westminster John Knox, 1986), 45.

18. Hiebert, "The Book of Habakkuk," 7:647.

and Mafia films highlights the human capacity to love families tenderly but to provide for them through violent crime. The capacity for both good and evil resides in each person, simultaneously. Our fascination is that violence and love can be expressed concurrently. Yahweh calls this sin and shame (2:10) and self-deception (Obad. 3).

Wisdom remembers that violent deeds are not forgotten. We are called to live peaceable lives by faith. That means trusting God for our true security in him. We believe the word of the prophet, the psalmist, and Jesus that the meek will inherit the earth (Ps. 37:11; Zeph. 3:12; Matt. 5:5). Even the rocks know that the human goal of secure households or cultures does not justify any means. Even the woodwork knows that this kind of life will miss the mark (2:11). The woodwork especially "knows" the environmental disaster that Babylon's violence has done. It was made from the cutting of ancient trees (see the fourth woe).

(3) The third woe is the centerpiece that contains a promise. It concerns the exhaustion of "bloodshed" and "the knowledge of glory of the LORD . . . cover[ing] the earth" (2:12–14). God has a greater plan for the earth than the violence it presently suffers. God stands against anyone who builds legacies by power and bloodshed. In 2:12 he speaks specifically against Babylon, but the principle may be universally applied, since the same words are elsewhere spoken against Jerusalem, Nineveh, and others (Jer. 51:58; Mic. 3:9–12; Nah. 3:1).

The person who lives by faith trusts in the promise that one day, "as the waters cover the sea," the glory of Yahweh will fill the earth. Caleb followed God wholeheartedly, trusted the glory he had seen, and received the promise of inheriting the land (Num. 14:17–25). In a similar way Habakkuk 3:3 calls us to remember God's glory known in the past ("his glory covered the heavens and his praise filled the earth"). To live by faith is to live by the memory and promise of God's glory in the earth.

The fullest manifestation of that glory is possible in the present because of Jesus. "For God, who said, 'Let light shine out of darkness,' made his light shine in our hearts to give us the light of the knowledge of the glory of God in the face of Christ" (2 Cor. 4:6). A house, a city, or a country is built with blessing when Yahweh is involved in the project: "Unless the LORD builds the house, its builders labor in vain. Unless the LORD watches over the city, the watchmen stand guard in vain" (Ps. 127:1). The ultimate victory of Yahweh's knowledge in the new creation is described by Isaiah in Isaiah 11:5–10:

> Righteousness will be his belt
>   and faithfulness the sash around his waist.
> The wolf will live with the lamb,
>   the leopard will lie down with the goat,

> the calf and the lion and the yearling together;
>> and a little child will lead them.
> The cow will feed with the bear,
>> their young will lie down together,
>> and the lion will eat straw like the ox.
> The infant will play near the hole of the cobra,
>> and the young child put his hand into the viper's nest.
> They will neither harm nor destroy
>> on all my holy mountain,
> *for the earth will be full of the knowledge of the* LORD
>> *as the waters cover the sea.*

In that day the Root of Jesse will stand as a banner for the peoples; the nations will rally to him, and his place of rest will be glorious.

(4) The fourth woe is being "exposed" to the terror of trees and animals (2:15–17). Those who glory in exposing (dominating and shaming) others will be exposed themselves by the nonhuman creation. The strength of the shocking image may cause us to miss the point of the image of nakedness in 2:16–17. The violence done to trees, animals, lands, and people is the weight of the crime. Lebanon is naked of trees, the cities are naked of people, and the land is naked of animals. The image of drunken exposure shows the perversion in the Babylonian mind. Their practice of making their victims drunk in order to strip them is a symbol for the rape of the land. The "scorched-earth" policy of recent wars echoes the practice.

The clear-cutting of the ancient cedar forests of Lebanon demonstrates the Babylonian abusive attitude toward all life. The exposure of Babylon (lit., "exposed foreskin" in 2:16a) results in nakedness, which calls for covering of some kind. When the Babylonians look for a covering, they will find only the memory of the violence they have done to Lebanon. Yahweh is angry because he planted the ancient cedars and they belonged to him (Ps. 104:16). He is not happy they have been cut down (2 Kings 19:23; Isa. 14:8; 37:24; 40:16; 55:12; Hab. 2:17).

God's intense love for his entire creation causes great anger when that creation is abused. Those who live by faith will care for the nonhuman creation as part of a home and community that is made and loved by the Creator. They will care for it as for themselves and take hope in God's promise to renew the face of the earth in the new creation.

The violence done to the earth is a recurring biblical theme that has taken on new significance in our day (Num. 35:33–34; Hos. 4:1–3). Pollution of lakes and streams by profit-seeking industries is an obvious example of a judgment that comes back around. Fish die and drinking water is compromised when violence is done to the earth. A life of faith exercises good dominion in human and nonhuman relationships (Gen. 2:15–19). God will recreate the earth just as he will give new bodies in the resurrection. In the meantime, he expects us to protect and care for our physical bodies and the earth.

(5) The final woe is against trusting in lifeless, breathless, and silent idols (2:18–20). Worshiping anything created by God or made by another person is simply foolish, yet it is done widely in every culture. In our secular society idolatry may not seem so obvious, since the objects trusted are technically not worshiped or consulted for advice. They are, nonetheless, trusted as the most real and valuable securities. Cars, houses, investments, credit, and bank accounts lead the list of representative gods. They are the road to opportunity, but they cannot give guidance. The love of them is the root of all kinds of evil (1 Tim. 6:10).

The wisdom of the woe is that idols are dumb. "He who makes it trusts in his own creation" (2:18b). In Elijah's time, Baal was such a god of prosperity. The purpose of worship of the various Baals was fiscal success and power. If Baal failed, they believed he was "asleep" (1 Kings 18:27). People worshiped these gods in order to increase their prosperity. In any case, they controlled them (Isa. 44:9–20) even as we control our prosperity. True faith honors God in all things, even in the ability to earn money. To live by faith in the true God means worshiping and honoring him in both good and bad experiences. True worship means trusting him for all we need from day to day. Luther explained belief in God the Father in this way:

> I believe that God has created me and all that exists. He has given me and still preserves my body and soul with all their powers. He provides me with food and clothing, home and family, daily work, and all that I need from day to day. God also protects me in time of danger and guards me from every evil. All this he does out of fatherly and divine goodness and mercy, though I do not deserve it. Therefore I surely ought to thank and praise, serve and obey him.[19]

The final word in chapter 2 is that those who live by faith and by God's plan for his beloved creation will prevail. The peaceable kingdom of God will come because "the LORD is in his holy temple; let all the earth be silent before him." His temple and throne are in heaven (Ps. 11:4; the Jerusalem temple was only a copy of the heavenly temple. Even when Jerusalem was destroyed by Babylon, God was still on the throne).

---

19. Martin Luther's *Small Catechism*, from the explanation of the First Article of the Apostles' Creed.

So it is for all who worship him in any sanctuary or in any place set aside for worship. The silence of this worship is not just the silence of reverence. It is the silence of acceptance of the judgment of God against the nation for its sins. A similar silence is observed in Revelation 8:1. For one half hour heaven is silent before the seventh seal is broken and the judgment of the earth ensues (cf. Amos 8:3; Zeph. 1:7). Until that time Yahweh's gift to the survivors of abuse and violence is a lament. The lament is not for themselves and their victimization. Rather, it is a lament for and against the violent. It is a seedbed of hope in which Yahweh transforms victims into hopeful survivors.

Habakkuk 3

A PRAYER OF Habakkuk the prophet. On *shigionoth*.

² LORD, I have heard of your fame;
    I stand in awe of your deeds, O LORD.
Renew them in our day,
    in our time make them known;
    in wrath remember mercy.

³ God came from Teman,
    the Holy One from Mount Paran.   *Selah*

His glory covered the heavens
    and his praise filled the earth.
⁴ His splendor was like the sunrise;
    rays flashed from his hand,
    where his power was hidden.
⁵ Plague went before him;
    pestilence followed his steps.
⁶ He stood, and shook the earth;
    he looked, and made the nations tremble.
The ancient mountains crumbled
    and the age-old hills collapsed.
    His ways are eternal.
⁷ I saw the tents of Cushan in distress,
    the dwellings of Midian in anguish.

⁸ Were you angry with the rivers, O LORD?
    Was your wrath against the streams?
Did you rage against the sea
    when you rode with your horses
    and your victorious chariots?
⁹ You uncovered your bow,
    you called for many arrows.   *Selah*

You split the earth with rivers;
¹⁰   the mountains saw you and writhed.
Torrents of water swept by;
    the deep roared
    and lifted its waves on high.

¹¹ Sun and moon stood still in the heavens
   at the glint of your flying arrows,
   at the lightning of your flashing spear.
¹² In wrath you strode through the earth
   and in anger you threshed the nations.
¹³ You came out to deliver your people,
   to save your anointed one.
  You crushed the leader of the land of wickedness,
   you stripped him from head to foot.   *Selah*
¹⁴ With his own spear you pierced his head
   when his warriors stormed out to scatter us,
  gloating as though about to devour
   the wretched who were in hiding.
¹⁵ You trampled the sea with your horses,
   churning the great waters.

¹⁶ I heard and my heart pounded,
   my lips quivered at the sound;
  decay crept into my bones,
   and my legs trembled.
  Yet I will wait patiently for the day of calamity
   to come on the nation invading us.
¹⁷ Though the fig tree does not bud
   and there are no grapes on the vines,
  though the olive crop fails
   and the fields produce no food,
  though there are no sheep in the pen
   and no cattle in the stalls,
¹⁸ yet I will rejoice in the LORD,
   I will be joyful in God my Savior.

¹⁹ The Sovereign LORD is my strength;
   he makes my feet like the feet of a deer,
   he enables me to go on the heights.

For the director of music. On my stringed instruments.

HABAKKUK 3 IS a song to Yahweh about his power and way in the world. Some have argued that Habakkuk 3 was added to the oracle rather than being a part of the oracle.[1] True, it is different in form and content from the rest of the book. Like a psalm it has a title that sets it apart. Nevertheless, it is integral to the book. The concluding verses (3:16–19) enclose the song into the whole revelation. They refer back to Yahweh's revelation of the rise of the Babylonians and their demise (ch. 2). The song functions as a response to the revelation within the book. It continues Habakkuk's dialogue with Yahweh concerning the success of violent people. It is an integral conclusion of the entire oracle, received in a vision by Habakkuk and announced in 1:1. The words of the prophet, even those spoken *to God* in chapter 3, are a gift *from God*. This circle of inspiration is a legacy of biblical prophecy in general.

Title and Structure (3:1)

THE TITLE IN 3:1 identifies the chapter as "a prayer of Habakkuk." This prayer was sung, the last verse giving instrumental directions for the music leader (3:19). "On *Shigionoth*" is probably the tune or musical setting for singing.[2]

The formal part of the song begins in verse 2 with the refrain ("LORD, I have heard of your fame") and continues in three musical "stanzas" through 3:15. Verses 16–19 follow a freer form (like a musical "bridge"), beginning again with the verb used in 3:2, "I heard." Although the tenses are different in the NIV, the verbs in 3:2 and 3:16 are identical (*šamaʿti*).

The main themes of the song are found in the refrain (3:2): standing in awe, remembering God's acts of power, and praying for their return with mercy. The first stanza (3:3–8) describes the powerful and awesome manifestations of God's presence in creation in the past. It expresses wonder about the physical power of God's wrath in the earth. The second stanza (3:9–13a) declares the purpose of Yahweh's wrath. The motivation behind his anger is to save his chosen people and the "anointed one" (the king). The third stanza (3:13b–15) describes Yahweh's defeat of the leader of wickedness who is about to destroy God's people.[3] The final bridge (3:16–19) is

---

1. For a summary of the discussion see F. I. Andersen, *Habakkuk: A New Translation with Introduction and Commentary* (AB; New York: Doubleday, 2001), 259–60. Andersen says that the arguments that the psalm is out of place "have no weight whatsoever." So also Roberts, *Nahum, Habakkuk, and Zephaniah*, 148.

2. "Shigionoth" only occurs here and in Ps. 7:1. Its meaning is uncertain, but it comes from the root *šagah*, which means "stumbling" or "go astray" and may refer to Habakkuk's need for guidance from Yahweh.

3. Verse 16 may be part of the third stanza of the song, although it is a response and not part of the description of God's acts of power.

Habakkuk's response to his description of God's acts of power. Although he is terror-stricken, he declares his willingness to endure God's judgment of his people and to rejoice and trust in Yahweh's strength, even in starvation.

The three stanzas are introduced by half verses that serve as stanza titles. Each title is followed by the dividing word *"Selah."*[4] This pause coming at the end of the title, not at the end of the stanza, may appear at first a bit odd in an English Bible. But the original audience and choir would have seen the title as an announcement of the stanza to come. While awkward in textual form, it works well poetically and musically. If the refrain (3:2) was sung between each stanza, it would have been sung as follows:

> Refrain: "LORD, I have heard of your fame; I stand in awe of your deeds, O LORD. Renew them in our day, in our time make them known; in wrath remember mercy" (3:2).
>
> Stanza 1 title: "God came from Teman, the Holy One from Mount Paran. *Selah"* (3:3a).
>
> Lyrics continue (3:3b–8), followed by Refrain.
>
> Stanza 2 title: "You uncovered your bow, you called for many arrows. *Selah"* (3:9a).
>
> Lyrics continue (3:9b–13a), followed by Refrain.
>
> Stanza 3 title: "You crushed the leader of the land of wickedness, you stripped him from head to foot. *Selah"* (3:13b)
>
> Lyrics continue (3:14–15), followed by Refrain.
>
> Musical bridge (3:16–19).

The three stanzas of the song describe an appearance of Yahweh in the world, commonly called a "theophany" (a physical manifestation God's presence to humanity).[5] God strides forth on the earth as a warrior against crime, visible in the storm of his creation: sun, lightning, flood, plague, and earthquake. When he appears, people and the earth tremble at his power.

The Refrain (3:2)

THIS SUNG PRAYER is a response to Yahweh's long response (ch. 2) to Habakkuk's questions. Habakkuk struggles in this song with his newly forming faith and understanding of Yahweh''s way in the world. He is *not* "silent before him" (2:20) but praises him in a song that struggles to let go of the powerful images of his dearly held beliefs. The song expresses his faith in the way of Yahweh by his past deeds in contrast to his recently revealed inten-

---

4. The meaning of the word is not known, but it functions in biblical songs as a musical divider.

5. See Ex. 15:3–12; 19:16–19; Judg. 5:4–5; Ps. 18:6–19; 68:4–19.

tions (ch. 2). He looks back to a time when God's power seemed more direct and evident. He preferred that past display of visible power to the course that Judean and Babylonian history is about to take.

The song praises Yahweh for how Habakkuk would like him to act in this new situation, similar to how he acted in Israel's memory. It is a subtle form of protestation that does not stop with protest. In verse 16, when the song changes form and enters its concluding bridge, Habakkuk has accepted a new realization—the revelation that Yahweh will work in a different and unsettling way to accomplish his purpose of covering the earth "with the knowledge of the glory of the LORD" (2:14). In the end he declares his unconditional allegiance to Yahweh, no matter what the personal consequences may be for him (3:17–19).

As in all good refrains, the themes of Habakkuk's song are contained in 3:2. The first phrase addresses God as "LORD" and witnesses to the telling and retelling of his "fame" in the community. "Fame" (*šemaʿ*) means reputation or what the prophet has heard people say about Yahweh. That fame alludes to Yahweh's acts of deliverance of Israel from Egypt, their entrance to Canaan, and the later assaults of the Philistines (Josh. 9:9; Isa. 66:19).

The second phrase of the refrain is a witness to Habakkuk's faith in those dramatic deeds of deliverance: He "stands in awe." He pleads in the third and fourth phrase that Yahweh will return to this mode of operation in the world in his time (a longing, in contrast to the victory of the Babylonians and their delayed demise described in ch. 2). Finally, the prophet sings for the "mercy" that always accompanies Yahweh's wrathful response to sin.

The song's three verses speak primarily of Yahweh's coming forth in "deeds" of power. Not until the concluding bridge (3:16–19) does the prophet relinquish the plea and accept the revelation of chapter 2. Until then, he returns to the memory of the awesome presence of Yahweh in Israel's history, his famous acts of deliverance, and his displays of power in the creation. He longs for them to be "renewed" (*ḥayah* in 3:2; lit., "let them live").

In Days of Old, God Came Forth (3:3–8)

As ALREADY NOTED, the title of the song's first stanza (3:3a) is marked off by "*Selah*." This stanza declares the visible presence of God in the battles of Israel's history. He is visible in the display of his power in the sunrise, lightning, plague, earthquake, and storms on the waters. Earth, water, and sky serve the Creator, who comes forth to deliver.

"God came from Teman ... from Mount Paran" (3:3a) leaves the reader wondering where Teman is and what God is doing there. The context would be clearer to the original listener. Teman is in southern Palestine and the

Paran mountains lie further south, on the eastern edge of the Sinai Peninsula. God's formation of Israel began in this region. It is the place in which Israel found refuge from Egypt after deliverance from the Egyptian army at the sea. It is the place of Mount Sinai, where the order of the community was established under God's instructions. It is the place that God began to act in mighty ways to lead, protect, judge, and shape his people.

In Israel's memory God went forth before his people as a warrior against their oppressors, using the forces of nature as his armies. In Exodus 14–15 he used cloud, fire, darkness, and the sea to deliver them. He used an earthquake at Jericho under Joshua. In Judges 5 God used torrential rains. In 1 Samuel 7 he used a thunderstorm to rout the enemy. David consolidated his power over the Philistines in 2 Samuel 5 with Yahweh's direction and a wind in the balsam trees. In 2 Kings 18–19 a plague defeated the Assyrian army that surely would have taken Jerusalem.

Concerning those days, Habakkuk sings, "His glory covered the heavens and his praise filled the earth" (3:3b). This phrase looks back to the time that Yahweh said would come again ("the earth will be filled with the knowledge of the glory of the LORD," 2:14). The sound and sight of Yahweh's splendor were audible and visible to all. In the verses that follow Habakkuk vividly describes the visual and auditory experiences of Israel's memory.

Verses 4–6 describe the visible powerful presence of the Creator-Warrior God in the creation, warring against the wicked. His bright splendor is seen in the light of the sun at sunrise and his power in the flashing rays of lightning (3:4). In these things, however, his true power was held back ("hidden, veiled," *ḥabab*). A plague outbreak paved his way and pestilence (burning fever) followed him in his attack on the wicked (see 2 Kings 19:35–36). They were his creation and worked his purposes as he walked (3:5). When he stood still (3:6), he shook the earth with an earthquake. The mountains crumbled in an avalanche of rock and the "age-old hills collapsed."

Those age-old hills were known as the domain of the Baals and the Ashtoreth, Canaanite gods and goddesses widely worshiped (even in Israel) for the prosperity and fertility they were reputed to bring. They were household gods that had shrines on hilltops near every village. Habakkuk follows the description of these crumbling "age-old hills" with the counterpoint: "His ways are eternal" (3:6). False worship on them may be old, but the Maker is both before and after, forever. The hills themselves acknowledge his presence, bowing down. When the Creator-Warrior walks on his eternal pathway, the whole earth dramatically responds. Especially in exile, faith in the eternal Creator who "shook the earth" will be remembered (Isa. 40:12, 28; 42:5–9; 43:1, 15–21).

In 3:7–8 the distress of the people of the earth (mentioned in 3:4a) is brought into focus. The "tents of Cushan" and "dwellings of Midian" refer to the people living in the south, past whom Yahweh marched north on the way from the southern mountains of Paran. They were in anguish because of the Creator's presence with Israel (Num. 31:7; Judg. 3:10). The word translated "distress" (*ʿawan*) means distress resulting from injustice. Its second meaning, "idolatry," may be the proper context here. Cushan and Midian are in distress at the presence of the Creator-Warrior because they have been worshiping gods of their own making. Yahweh is marching north to deal with Babylon, but his presence and passing-by are terrifying to those who do not honor him.

In 3:8 Habakkuk sings three rhetorical questions. Was Yahweh's anger against the rivers, streams, and sea? Of course not! They were in tumult on behalf of the Creator-Warrior, who fought for his people. They were his arsenal against the people who opposed his rule. These three rhetorical questions are perhaps the most subtle expression of the song's theme, longing for a more dramatic and obvious display of Yahweh's power. Habakkuk and all Israel know that Yahweh can fight for them through the creation. The stopping of rivers (Jordan), the flooding of wadis (Deborah), and the tumult of the Red Sea (Exodus) were obviously not natural events of creation. They were used in the fighting for Israel because Yahweh is present and they are his creation. Habakkuk directly addresses Yahweh in these questions, remembering and longing for this kind of intervention again.

You Uncovered Your Bow and Arrows (3:9–13a)

THE SECOND STANZA continues describing the Creator-Warrior's presence, his action in the earth, water, and sky, and its effect on the peoples of the earth. The title of this stanza ("You uncovered your bow, you called for many arrows") is followed by the "*Selah.*" Yahweh arrives as a bowman (Deut. 32:23; Ezek. 5:16). No single historical event is indicated, but the usual memories of Israel are the background for the audience of this collage of musical images (the Exodus, Deborah's victory, Samuel and Israel at Ebenezer; Ps. 77:11–20).

The main part of this stanza recalls how three main elements have responded to Yahweh's actions: the "mountains … writhed" (3:10a), the ocean "deep roared and lifted its waves" (3:10b), and the "sun and moon stood still," out of the way of Yahweh's bright flashes (3:11a). Earth, water, and fire in the sky acknowledged the Creator and acted for his delivering purposes.

The cause of creation's acknowledgment of the Creator-Warrior is a powerful storm with which he fought against the nations. Torrential downpours caused flooding (3:10a; see Judg. 5:4; Ps. 77:16–18), the ocean roared with hurricane force, and lightning was hurled as spears. This storm was more than a show of nature in Israel. It represents all the times that Yahweh changed the course of history for his people by fighting for them, against the odds, with timely storms. Because their warring and delivering God is also the Creator, anything is possible (see Bridging Contexts section).

In 3:12–13, Habakkuk recalls how Yahweh "came out" in the historical storms to "thresh," "deliver," and "save." He would like Yahweh to do this in the situation with Babylon. Knowing that he will not, Habakkuk's song takes comfort in and continues to believe in the God who is still able to stride on the earth to deliver. Yahweh's simple striding is enough to "thresh" or tread on the nations who oppose him.

"He came out" (in the Heb. text of 3:13) echoes Habakkuk's complaint in chapter 1 that "justice is perverted" (1:4b: lit., "comes out crooked"). In Yahweh's appearance in days of old, he "came out to deliver" (3:13). In Habakkuk's day, by contrast, justice has come out crooked. Habakkuk longs for a return to the day when things come out right.

In the past, Yahweh came out "to deliver your people" and "to save your anointed one" (Israel). In the Old Testament "the anointed one" sometimes refers to Israel (Ex. 19:6; Ps. 28:8), sometimes to the king of Israel (anointed by the prophet to rule on behalf of Yahweh, the true king), and, in later writings, to the expected righteous King, the Messiah (*mašiaḥ*, "anointed").[6]

You Crushed the Leader of Wickedness (3:13b–15)

THIS STANZA GIVES the reason for Yahweh's personal intervention. As with the first two stanzas, this one's title is announced just before the *"Selah"*: "You crushed the leader of the land of wickedness, you stripped him from head to foot." It describes Yahweh's victory over a violent leader whose army was attacking the defeated and helpless people of Israel (3:14b). Yahweh completely defeated him with a head wound: "You crushed the leader … you pierced his head" (3:13b, 14a). This stanza ends with a reminder that the Creator-Warrior churned the sea with his horses: "You trampled the sea" (3:15).

The "crushing of the head" is also seen in Psalm 74:12–14, where the head of the chaos monster, Leviathan, is crushed and Yahweh establishes cosmic order and justice. In Psalm 89:9–10, Rahab, also a symbol of evil chaos and the force behind evil enemies, is crushed by Yahweh. Habakkuk draws on this common ancient tradition of personifying evil as Rahab and her dragon associate, Leviathan (see also Job 26:12–13; Isa. 27:1; 51:9–10).

Habakkuk's song describes a battle scene in which Israel's helpless people are about to be scattered by an attacking army that "stormed out to scat-

---

6. As the expectation of the Messiah intensified in Second Temple Judaism, texts that originally were references to the anointed king were reinterpreted as psalms of expectation of the coming King.

ter us, gloating as though about to devour the wretched who were in hiding"
(3:14b). Chaos was about to descend on God's people. God turned the tables,
defeating chaos with an actual storm. The leader of chaos was defeated as
God walked on the storm (controlling it). The original listener would have
heard this as a reference to several well-known historical events (Ex. 14;
Deut. 33; Judg. 5; 1 Sam. 7). With these biblical referents in mind, Habakkuk's
song turns toward the cosmic battle against the persistence of evil in the
world, which continually threatens to undo God's creation.

The collage of historical referents in Habakkuk 3:13b–15 is combined to
express the collective memory of Yahweh's fighting and victory for his
oppressed people. The combined memory of his intervention against evil is
the hope that holds Habakkuk and his congregation in the face of an impending devastating defeat. They believe that Yahweh will eventually do this to
Babylon as well. Until then, the song and the memories it elicits will hold
them in faith, as they believe in the Creator-Warrior of Israel. They will
need it, for soon they will be "the wretched who were in hiding" (cf. Lam.
4:18–19).

The Fear, Faith, and Joy of Habakkuk (3:16–19)

HABAKKUK FINALLY ACKNOWLEDGES that he has gotten the message about
Babylon's coming triumph (3:16). He is afraid because he believes the words
concerning Judah's demise to be true. His song has expressed hope in the earlier displays of the power of Yahweh. Nonetheless, he vows to rejoice in
spite of what may come.

As Habakkuk's song comes to its conclusion, the form and content change.
In musical terms this is called a "bridge," which introduces a new musical
theme and sometimes a change in key or tempo. The lyrics, as in Habakkuk's
song, often offer a counterpoint to the previous theme of the song. The
counterpoint cannot be more powerful than it is in Habakkuk's song. In 3:2–
15 he sang of the visible power of Yahweh. Now, in 3:16–19, he will sing of
his joy, even when the simplest sign of Yahweh's favor (food on the table) is
absent.

The musical bridge begins (3:16a) with a connection to the refrain (3:2)
in the words "I heard." Habakkuk acknowledges that he has heard what God
said about the devastation that the Babylonians will bring (chs. 1–2). He
feels the horror in every part of his body. His heart, lips, bones, and legs are
internally shaken. "Heart pounded" in Hebrew also is associated with the
involuntary trembling of a stomachache that may lead to a cry of grief. The
"decay in his bones" indicates a general weakness, and the "trembling" in the
legs is faltering or stumbling. In spite of this Habakkuk says: "I will wait

patiently for the day of calamity to fall" on Babylon. He knows Israel's devastation will be great as long as the Creator-Warrior does not intervene, but
the prophet will wait patiently. In the meantime, he will believe. No matter
what the external evidence, he believes what Yahweh has spoken. He "heard"
(3:2, 16), he "trembled" (3:16), and yet he "will rejoice" (3:18).

Habakkuk believes and trusts in this powerful "striding" God. He believes
that Yahweh will establish justice on the earth. He trusts his word and will
patiently wait, because God is the guarantor of the victory. He does not
trust first in his own perspective but in the potency of God, which enables
him to wait in faith, even when the wicked rule the earth.

This idea is reinforced in 3:17–19. God's display of power in the past
(3:2–15), which Habakkuk's congregation can sing again and again, enables
them to abide Yahweh's restraint in the present, even amidst the coming suffering. Because they have experienced and remember God's presence in the
storm, they can be sure of that presence in the silence. His presence, even
in this prophecy, has instructed them to prepare to wait ("though it linger,
wait for it," 2:3). He has left them with a promise that "it will certainly come
and will not delay" (2:3). He has also left them with five strong woes to
repeat in the midst of their suffering as they remember their promised deliverance (2:6–17).

Verse 17 should be read in the context of verse 16. "I will wait patiently
for the day of calamity to come on . . . [Babylon] though the fig tree does not
bud. . . ." Even though Habakkuk believes that Babylon will eventually fall
(ch. 2), he knows it will be a horrible wait and goes on to describe the experience of oppression and poverty that will settle on the conquered. These are
the conditions the prophet expects and anticipates overcoming in patience
(3:16b, *nuah*, "rest"). He will not be a victim. He will be a survivor. He lists all
the sources of food and agricultural commerce of the ancient world: fig trees,
grape vines, olive trees, field produce, sheep, and cattle. Under these terrible
conditions, Habakkuk resolves to be joyful, not superficially with eyes closed
to the struggle for justice or deliverance but looking truth in the face.

His emphatic assertion of faith in 3:18–19 consists of two sets of parallel statements (A, B). In the center is Habakkuk's confession of faith:

A Yet I will rejoice in the LORD,
  I will be joyful in God my Savior.
Center: The Sovereign LORD is my strength.
B He makes my feet like the feet of a deer,
  He enables me to go on the heights.

Habakkuk's joy is also typical in the Psalms but is a contrast to the usual
rejoicing over God's good gifts and protection (Ps. 5:11–12; 13:5–6; 16:5–11;

47:1–4). Habakkuk rejoices despite the lack of goods and protection. He shows he is prepared to live by faith in unseen promises, even in suffering. His joy is in contrast to the pleasure of the Babylonian, who rejoices because "he lives in luxury and enjoys the choicest food" (1:15–16).

The central expression ("The sovereign LORD is my strength") is also common in the Psalms (Ps. 28:7; 59:10, 17; 118:14; cf. Ex. 15:2; Isa. 12:2; 49:5; Jer. 16:19). In contrast, however, the typical word for "strength" (ʿoz) is absent. Its synonym (ḥayil), translated "strength" in the NIV, can mean "army." God is Habakkuk's army, standing against the Babylonians, "whose own strength is their god" (1:11b).[7] Habakkuk's faith has found its sure footing *as faith*. He does not hope or believe in what he sees but in what he has heard as promises from Yahweh. His feet are established on the path by Yahweh, even on the difficult and rocky heights.

HABAKKUK 3 CREATES and maintains hope in the face of a calamitous future and provides a lasting resource for survival following the devastation of an enemy attack. The prophet demonstrates the geography of hope in two ways: *looking back* by reciting Yahweh's victories on Israel's behalf (cf. Deut. 26:1–11; Ps. 78; Acts 7) and *looking up* at creation's wonders as a sign of the Creator's presence and power (cf. Ps. 19:1–4; Rom. 1:19–20). When Israel was suffering and lamenting under the hardship of foreign rule, remembering God's creating power and mighty acts of salvation became the substance of their hope and faith (Isa. 40:12–31; 42:5–25).

Habakkuk prefers his vision of Yahweh's manifest power in 3:2–15 (see his refrain at 3:2). At the end of his song, he begins the musical bridge (3:16a) by describing how much he doesn't like what he has learned about Israel's captivity in chapter 1. He has a physically manifested anxiety attack (trembling and quivering). In difficult times, when God's power is not obvious, the people rely on his past mighty acts and the creation's witness to the Creator. This song is a model for renewing and maintaining hope in the face of difficult circumstances.

Looking back. Looking back into Israel's history establishes a foundation of trust and hope for the faithful. Songs of Yahweh's intervention that rescued and brought victory to a helpless people are essential to remembering the past. Remembering provides the basis for their present and future hope of deliverance. Through these songs we maintain meaningful connection between God's past actions and the present reality. Many songs of

---

7. Roberts, *Nahum, Habakkuk, and Zephaniah*, 158.

deliverance were sung in Israel and are found in Scripture (see Jonah 2). They have the double function of giving praise to God for what he has done and creating hope for his deliverance in the future.

A special feature of some of these songs is the theophany, when Yahweh appears to humanity in a physical manifestation (usually in what we would call "a force of nature"). The primary avenue of hope and meaning in 3:1–15 is Yahweh as the Creator-Warrior. Using the power of creation, Yahweh appeared to (theophany), fought for, and miraculously established Israel. He saved the people from Pharaoh's army (Ex. 15:3–12). At Sinai, he appeared to establish his instructions for community and personal living (Ex. 19:16–19). He came forth to save the people in dire times (Judg. 5:4–5). The people were established in the land by Yahweh's intervention (Ps. 68:4–19). David was established as a secure king by theophany (Ps. 18:6–19).

Theophanies are dramatic because they change common perceptions of reality. They remove the illusion that God is not present. The earth convulses, and the convulsions are understood to be an act of the Creator against the nations. They are "against" the nations, because the nations do not acknowledge Yahweh as Creator. The most stable and visible mountains are affected (3:6, 10; cf. Judg. 5:5; Mic. 1:4; Hag. 2:6–7). Like Elijah at Horeb after he ran from Jezebel, Yahweh's power is seen despite the depressing political situation (1 Kings 19). God convulses the mountain with wind, earthquake, and splitting rocks. He also speaks in a still, small voice for those who wait for it.

In some circumstances, plagues were also used as a weapon. Not every plague was Yahweh's battle, but he did use plagues as a weapon against Egypt in Exodus 5:3 and 9:15, when Pharaoh would not let the people go. It was threatened against Israel (Lev. 26:25) if they were ever rebellious, and it was used against them at Baal Peor when they began joining in worship through cultic prostitution (Num. 25:3–9). It was also brought against them in the time of Jeremiah (a contemporary of Habakkuk); he was told not to pray for the people to be spared the sword, famine, or plague (Jer. 14:11–12). Plague is also the vision of the future offered in the book of Revelation. The fourth pale-horse rider of judgment is death, killing by means of sword, famine, wild beasts, and plague (Ezek. 14:21; Rev. 6:8).

The dramatic manifestations of shattering mountains and devastating plagues serve the Creator in decimating the view that the creation is centered on humanity. Anthropocentrism is deconstructed when microorganisms rain down terror or tectonic plates convulse and level cities. God uses such micro- and mega-means to reorient illusory idolatries.

Habakkuk is tapping a strong tradition of hope when he sings his general remembrance of Yahweh's "coming forth." In those days now past, Habakkuk sings, "His glory covered the heavens and his praise filled the earth" (3:3). He looks back to the time that Yahweh said would come again ("the earth will be filled with the knowledge of the glory of the LORD," 2:14). Remembering the past gives an anchor to the present while the faithful wait for the future.

Habakkuk's song about Yahweh's intervention in past battles recalls his actual victories that delivered the helpless. The purpose of Yahweh's violent interventions was to rescue his people: "You came out to deliver your people, to save your anointed one. You crushed the leader of the land of wickedness, you stripped him from head to foot. With his own spear you pierced his head when his warriors stormed out to scatter us" (3:13–14). The LXX suggests a cosmic referent: "You did smite the head of Death."[8]

This reference to death's defeat helps us to connect Habakkuk to the New Testament and to the present. It is eternal death, not physical death, that ultimately concerns Yahweh. His actual victories for Israel are the necessary background for understanding the possibility of a final cosmic defeat of evil. God delivers his people from Pharaoh, from the Assyrians, from Babylon, from the enemy of all creation through Christ, and finally, from death. Biblical songs endure, as songs to be sung by the faithful, as means to create hope of this deliverance in the present. For the Christian, no theophany is more life-changing than the Incarnation. Reading the narratives of Jesus' birth, life, death, and resurrection and singing of them are essential to the building of character, hope, and faith today.

Looking up and around. Creation is a witness to God's glory (3:3b; 2:14; see Ps. 19:1–4). The power of the created world is another avenue of hope and meaning in Habakkuk's song. When God intervened on Israel's behalf, it was often through the natural forces of water, wind, and earth. By considering the rivers, mountains, earthquakes, and floods, those who suffer are reminded of the Creator's presence, power, and love. They are reminded of the Creator who has also redeemed them by means of these things, and of the redemption gained through them.

God's rule over the basic elements of nature is demonstrated in 3:8–10. The water of the heavens, the terrestrial sea, and the subterranean rivers are each noted in Hebrew.[9] Sun, moon, lightning, and earthquake declare his glory. In all creation, above, on, and under the earth, Yahweh rules.

The Israelites saw actual storms that gave them victory in battle against stronger foes. What they saw is celebrated in their memory. As a result they knew that their Deliverer was also their Creator. They knew that anything was possible from their God. Any deliverance from a storm becomes a witness

---

8. Albright, cited in Bruce, "Habakkuk," 890.
9. Andersen, *Habakkuk*, 326.

to that deliverance. For Christians, the tree of the empty cross, and by extension any tree, can be a witness to the Creator and Christ's victory over death.

The memory of the Creator-Warrior using his creation to fight for the Israelites was a constitutive and necessary part of their faith. This is further revealed in the Incarnation and is developed in Athanasius' fourth-century writing "On the Incarnation." Why did God become human? God became incarnate because only Jesus, the one through whom everything was made (John 1:3), could save the lost creation. Like Father, like Son. If the Redeemer is also the Creator, anything is possible; even the dead can be raised and sin, death, and the devil be defeated.[10]

Yahweh "split the earth with rivers" (3:9b). This recalls the original creation as well as Yahweh's use of a flash flood to defeat Israel's enemies (Judg. 5:5). God is still creating new realities through his created world. This odd image of "splitting" or tearing the earth is echoed in Jesus' creating power demonstrated in Mark 1:10. At his baptism, "he saw heaven being torn open." The barrier of heaven was removed. At Jesus' death, the graves were opened, and the barrier of the earth and death were removed. The temple curtain was also torn as the barrier of holiness was removed. God splits the barriers that separate him from his human creation.[11]

Part of Habakkuk's refrain is "I stand in awe of your deeds, O LORD. Renew them in our day" (3:2). Asking Yahweh to renew his deeds is a cry for life to be established as God intended it. It is like the Christian praying, "Your kingdom come."[12] It will surely come without our praying for it, but we pray that it may also come to us.[13] To pray for and hope in a renewal of God's mighty acts is like Moses on Mount Pisgah looking into a promised land that the people will soon enter (Deut. 34:1–4). It is also like the disciples on the Mount of Transfiguration receiving a glimpse of Jesus' glory with Moses and Elijah (Mark 9:2–8).[14]

The observance of the Lord's Supper is a present way of publicly practicing that hope for renewal. As a foretaste of the feast to come, it is a place to "stand in awe" of the Lord's deeds on our behalf and to pray that he will "renew them" soon.

Shaken and transformed by Yahweh's response. When Yahweh begins responding to Habakkuk's questions, Habakkuk does not like what he hears

---

10. Athanasius, *On the Incarnation*, ed. and trans. by Sister P. Lawson (New York: Macmillan, 1981).

11. Donald Juel, *The Gospel of Mark* (Interpreting Biblical Texts; Nashville: Abingdon, 1999), 59, 147–48.

12. Achtemeier, *Nahum-Malachi*, 54.

13. See Luther's "Small Catechism."

14. Achtemeier, *Nahum-Malachi*, 56.

(1:13b). His song (3:2–19) is about the military power of Yahweh, recalling a kaleidoscope of history. This remembrance stands in stark contrast to the submission of Israel that God has promised will come (2:6–20) and is expected in Habakkuk's personal future (3:16b). The song in chapter 3 subtly continues Habakkuk's previous objections while accepting this hard word about Judah's future in exile.

The song has "four stupendous moments."[15] Each of them spans the centuries to connect to the modern believer. (1) The refrain (3:2) and bridge (3:16–19) are intensely personal addresses to Yahweh. Even in the midst of approaching national calamity, Yahweh speaks and listens to the individual who seeks him. (2) The opening stanza is cosmic in scope, as God's acts are remembered in the third person. (3) The prophet shifts to the personal "you" as Yahweh's might ranges from the heavens to the deeps in the middle stanza. God may be addressed directly, even in his most awesome works. (4) God is involved in human history in the final stanza.

Concluding his song of past remembrance, Habakkuk is shaken (3:16a) as he accepts Yahweh's power and the mystery of God's way in the world. He knows that they will be delivered, but only after a great national and personal experience of calamity. By the end of the song he is transformed, for he says: "Yet I will wait patiently for the calamity" (3:16b) and "Yet I will rejoice" (3:18a). Although he does not like what he has heard (his heart pounds, his lips quiver, and his legs tremble), he comes to accept and trust, not in his own preferences, but in the word of the One he has heard and believed.

A SEASONED FAITH. Believing in a Warrior-Creator has two possible outcomes. God can defeat your enemies, or he can defeat you. If we believe that God will only defeat our enemies, we may not ready be for a Messiah like Jesus. If faith is only grounded in Yahweh's defeating enemies in the way that Habakkuk describes in 3:3–15 (e.g., flashing fingertips), it will not be strong or based in reality. Habakkuk's song continues to accept Yahweh's judgment and his march against his own people, for their sake. Habakkuk's faith is made strong by remembering the power of God's deliverance. Yahweh's saving acts in the Exodus, the desert wanderings, and the settlement of the land are a necessary grounding in history that make verses 3:17–19 possible.

Yet Habakkuk accepts Yahweh's judgment against his own country and the consequences of his nation's sin. His entrance into conversation with

---

15. Andersen, *Habakkuk*, 261–62.

God is a call for a legal judgment on the sin within his own country. The ending of his conversation is an acceptance of the judgment's verdict ("I will wait patiently for the day of calamity"). This acceptance of judgment close to home is a necessary part of a double-fisted and reality-based faith. The challenge of Habakkuk 3 is whether one matures in faith from 3:3–15 to 3:16–19. Both perspectives are necessary to a full faith. Hope is surely generated by memories of deliverance (3:3–15) as well as by trust in Yahweh, regardless of immediate circumstances (3:16–19).

Its application is found in growing in the grace and the knowledge of God (1:13b and 3:16b). This chapter demonstrates the necessary process of struggling with our previously held conceptions of God as well as growing into God's revelation of his way in the world. Through the centuries, people of faith have used 3:16–19 more often than 3:1–15. The last four verses represent a more seasoned, deepened, and stalwart faith than the earlier verses. They are the necessary maturing of a lasting faith, free of illusions.

Nevertheless, 3:1–15 is not just an immature "stage" or process that must be left behind. Their strength is given by Yahweh in Habakkuk's vision as a necessary memory of God's power. They are a necessary confession of the historic deeds of God and the awe inspired by his majesty in acts of ongoing creation.

A flexible steeled faith (3:16–19). Amazing things can happen when worshiping Yahweh. Perspectives change. People change. After singing his song of his triumph (3:3–15), Habakkuk's faith finds a renewed vigor. His concluding lines are perhaps the most loved in the entire book. They illustrate a person who has begun to "live by faith" (2:4b).

Habakkuk moves from terror and deprivation (3:16–17) to satisfaction, joy, and confidence (3:18–19) in four verses. These verses give four glimpses into the prophet's heart. The first two tell the truth about his acceptance of judgment. Verse 16 describes his trembling legs as he accepts God's judgment. Verse 17 describes the experience of the loss of the common blessings in life. The second two reflect the power of faith and hope in Yahweh. Verse 18 expresses joy and satisfaction, simply "in the LORD." Verse 19 describes confident and strong legs on the heights.

These four verses summarize the shape of the whole book. Habakkuk is faithful in his questioning and worries, trembling in honest and accepting conversation with God. He recognizes the need for judgment and accepts the suffering it will bring. His faith, however, is not shaken. He perseveres in a joy that is beyond common logic. As a result, his faith is established in full confidence and sure footing.

Habakkuk is resolute in his faith, even when Yahweh's response is not the answer he prefers to hear (3:17–19). His faith is like a strong steel blade that is flexible but does not break. Habakkuk's resolution is like Job's: "I spoke ... twice but I will say no more" (Job 40:5b); "Shall we accept good from God, and not trouble?" (Job 2:10); and "Though he slay me, yet will I hope in him; I will surely defend my ways to his face" (Job 13:15). Jeremiah's collection of Lamentations is similar in his stalwart, gritty expression of faith in a loving God in spite of immediate sociological and psychological evidence to the contrary. The center of the graphic and extensive laments in Lamentations is also a confession of undying belief:

> I well remember them,
>   and my soul is downcast within me.
> Yet this I call to mind
>   and therefore I have hope:
> Because of the LORD's great love we are not consumed,
>   for his compassions never fail.
> They are new every morning;
>   great is your faithfulness.
> I say to myself, "The LORD is my portion;
>   therefore I will wait for him. (Lam. 3:20–24)

Applying Habakkuk's stalwart faith in the midst of judgment or trouble involves four movements of the heart, developed below: accepting Yahweh's judgment (3:16a), accepting scarcity as a consequence of sin (3:17), resolving to rejoice in Yahweh in all circumstances (3:18), and experiencing the gifts of confidence and hope from Yahweh (3:19).

Accepting Yahweh's judgment (3:16). When we see that we will suffer for our own sins or because someone else sinned, the normal response is fear (cf. Isa. 13:5–9; Jer. 6:23–24): "I heard and my heart pounded, my lips quivered at the sound; decay crept into my bones, and my legs trembled." Though Habakkuk does not like the answer he has heard, he is ready to say, "Yet I will wait patiently for the day of calamity to come on the nation invading us." When suffering is a path to someone's redemption, it can be endured in faith. Habakkuk's faith includes his acceptance of the Babylonian captivity of Judah (3:16).

Habakkuk's initial question about the justice of the Babylonians' invasion (1:13b) is set aside. His trembling fear remains, yet he accepts even the likelihood of his own death, having faith that Yahweh has an ultimate victory in store. For the just to live by faith means loving and serving him in one's dying as well as in one's living. As Bonhoeffer wrote in *The Cost of Discipleship*, when Christ calls us, he bids us to come and die to ourselves.[16] When Jesus

---

16. Dietrich Bonhoeffer, *The Cost of Discipleship*, trans. R. H. Fuller (New York: SCM Press, 1995), 89.

tells his disciples that he will be put to death (Mark 10:32–34; Luke 18:31–34), they are incredulous. Likewise, Habakkuk at first does not believe that God will lead his people to their deaths (1:12–17). In the end he believes that God's promise is trustworthy, even if it means the destruction of the temple and waiting for its restoration in faith. Believing leads to trembling.

Trembling is also a normal response to an experience of the presence of Yahweh (Isa. 6:5). Matthew's account of Jesus and the three disciples on the Mount of Transfiguration echoes Habakkuk's fear and trembling after seeing a vision of God's presence (3:3–15). Habakkuk's fear, however, becomes confidence because of Yahweh's comforting presence. The disciples also are "terrified" and fall on the ground, but Jesus touches them and tells them, "Don't be afraid" (Matt. 17:7). When they look, the shining of Jesus' transfiguration and the vision of Moses and Elijah are gone. They are comforted in seeing "no one except Jesus" (Matt. 17:8).

Accepting scarcity as a consequence of sin (3:17). "Though the fig tree does not bud and there are no grapes on the vines, though the olive crop fails and the fields produce no food, though there are no sheep in the pen and no cattle in the stalls. . . ." When the harvest is in, everyone is happy. God's people are expected also to give credit for their success to the Giver of the harvest and to bring a firstfruit offering (Deut. 26:1–11).

But when the harvest does not come in, who accepts the scarcity as right? William Cowper (d. 1800) draws from Habakkuk's mature faith in his well-known hymn "God Moves in a Mysterious Way."[17] He reminds Christians to "judge not the Lord by feeble sense" (by what is in the barn or bank), "but trust him for his grace. Behind a frowning providence [scarcity], He hides a smiling face." Scarcity is not always a consequence of sin; but when it is, the mature recognize and accept their difficulties as well as their blessings as God's righteousness and presence in their life. Cowper adds a verse that reflects Yahweh's advice to "wait" in faith because "it . . . will not prove false" (2:3–4). "Blind unbelief is sure to err and scan his work in vain; God is his own interpreter and he will make it plain." In another hymn Cowper also intones Habakkuk's exemplary faith in the hymn: "Sometime a Light Surprises the Child of God Who Sings." The presence of God is the bounty found in scarcity.

> Though vine nor fig tree neither their wonted fruit shall bear;
> Though all the fields should wither nor flock nor herds be there;
> Yet God, the same abiding, his praise shall tune my voice;
> For while in him confiding, I cannot but rejoice.

---

17. Many other commentators have previously noted this connection. Public domain.

Jesus claimed a similar reality in response to the tempter when he quoted, "Man does not live on bread alone, but on every word that comes from the mouth of God" (Matt. 4:4). The original text is Moses' explanation that God "humbled you and let you hunger" so that you might know the blessing of hearing him speak (Deut. 8:3). Habakkuk has learned what God taught the people in the desert and what Jesus reiterates for us. Scarcity leads us to recognize our need for a God who seeks to speak with us.

Resolving to rejoice in Yahweh in all circumstances (3:18). Only by "plumbing the depths of our deepest pains and disillusionments and lifting them up" in conversation with God can this kind of joy be known.[18] Habakkuk says, "Yet I will rejoice in the LORD, I will be joyful in God my Savior." Habakkuk has every reason *not* to rejoice. He is himself a righteous man. Yet, he and other good people he knows are going to suffer hardship and death as a part of Yahweh's judgment against the wicked. His resolution to be joyful makes the best of a bad situation, but it is more than that. He knows that despite the circumstances, life is good and God is good and worthy of praise. No matter how bad life is, God is the source of hope and joy.

Such rejoicing happens by faith. Mary was visited by the Lord and became pregnant, but only by faith did she trust that her child would be the Messiah. When Elizabeth highlighted Mary's faith and blessedness for believing the Lord's word to her and work in her, Mary rejoiced (Luke 1:45–46). Habakkuk's joy is similar. He believes that Israel will eventually be delivered from exile in Babylon, but first they must endure it. His faith that Yahweh's work will be done on earth causes him to rejoice in spite of the difficult circumstances. In each case, the subject of rejoicing is not simply individual situations but rejoicing that their faith has involved them in the greater work of God for his people and the future of blessing on the earth.

What makes the steeled faith of 3:17–19 possible? God's presence makes all the difference. It is not the content of the message that Habakkuk receives or even the promise that the Babylonian oppression will pass after a while (2:3b, "It will certainly come"; the Exile lasted seventy years). Nor is the faith and joy made possible by Habakkuk's memory of past displays of power, recalled to memory by thunderstorms (ch. 3). Each of these is necessary to his faith's foundation, but Yahweh knows that Habakkuk will not be able to believe it even if told (1:5). How, then, is he able not only to believe the prophecy of coming doom, but also to declare his joy, even if reduced to poverty? It is because *God is present to him*, speaks to him, responds to him,

---

18. William P. Brown, *Obadiah Through Malachi* (Westminster Bible Commentary; Louisville: Westminster John Knox, 1996), 97.

addresses and listens to his questions, and gives him a vision of his presence and a song to write about it.

What single event can overcome all your doubts and objections to the condition of the world? Is it not God's actual presence before you, speaking with you, addressing you, and listening in person? A living and conversant faith is a faith like Habakkuk's. The psalmist has such a resilient faith in Psalm 73. He has a determination to remain faithful even in unpromising circumstances. He is among those "who cherish divine presence above presents."[19]

Experiencing the gifts of confidence and hope from Yahweh (3:19). "The Sovereign LORD is my strength; he makes my feet like the feet of a deer, he enables me to go on the heights." The sure footing of faith in difficult times and places can be celebrated. Generations of Christians know and bear witness to the strength of daily communion with the Lord in prayer, singing, reading, and remembering Scripture. That is what leads Habakkuk to this classic celebration.

"To go on the heights" certainly describes the place of confidence and hope that Yahweh gives to those who seek him. He is faithful. "Going on the heights" also has a broader application than the habit of the "devotions" of prayer, singing, and reading. It means that the confidence and hope gained result in the ultimate victory over the enemy that seeks our defeat. It means a defeat of bondage to false gods, usually related to money, sex, fame, and power. These were the benefits sought from the Baals and Ashtoreth worshiped in the high places of Canaan (Deut. 32:12–13; 33:29). The means to this victory over bondage to the false gods in the high places is seen in David's image of the surefooted deer on the heights (2 Sam. 22:22–37; cf. Ps. 18:34). The power of purity through keeping Yahweh's commandments is an important element of this victory.

These aspects of "going on the heights" help us to understand the events and significance of the New Testament. Victory in purity, in prayer, and over bondage to false gods and values foreshadows the cosmic victory over sin, death, and the devil accomplished in the resurrection. Jesus' battle and defeat of the enemy are expressed in the phrase "with his own spear you pierced his head" (Hab. 3:14a). In the New Testament the death of the Son looks like a victory for evil to the outside observer. The enemy sought to kill the Son of righteousness, *who defeated death by dying.* The descent of the Son of God to the realm of the dead became the spear that unexpectedly defeated the attacker.

The resurrection is celebrated as a cosmic victory over death and the forces of chaos. Every Easter and every Sunday's "little Easter" worship are a cry of victory. This shout of triumph is foreshadowed in Habakkuk's victory

---

19. J. L. Crenshaw, *A Whirlpool of Torment* (Philadelphia: Fortress, 1984), 107–8.

image, "you trampled the sea with your horses" (3:15a). This is Habakkuk's ultimate hope in treading the heights (3:19). Death and chaos are defeated by Yahweh. Jesus inaugurates the restoration of justice and righteousness in the kingdom of God in fulfilling Isaiah 35:6: "Then will the lame leap like a deer, and the mute tongue shout for joy" (Matt. 11:5; Luke 7:22).

We can learn much from Habakkuk's extended dialogue with Yahweh. With him we can ask difficult questions (1:2–4) and be persistent in questioning (1:12–2:1). We can be historically grounded in God's mighty acts of deliverance (3:1–15). We are also invited to join him in his profound faith in song (3:16–19). Habakkuk's humanity and joy are a model and a challenge. May we be witnesses, like Habakkuk, to God's purposes in a world dominated by corruption. May Yahweh's kingdom come also to us.

Introduction to Zephaniah

ZEPHANIAH IS A BOOK of judgment against Judah and its capital city, Jerusalem (chs. 1 and 3). In the midst of this judgment comes God's call for a faithful remnant, who will be sheltered when Jerusalem and its enemies are destroyed. God's promise of joy returning to Jerusalem concludes the book.

Yahweh's zeal for the worship of his people is the unifying theme of this prophecy. This zeal is expressed in the devastating and jealous judgment of Yahweh against his wayward people, as well as in the promise that a remnant of worshipers will survive the "day of the LORD's jealous wrath." His people's sins are many and varied, but all point to one reality: They no longer trust in Yahweh or worship him. Rather, they worship Baal and permit idolatrous priests (1:4). They worship the starry host and swear by Yahweh *and* by Molech (1:5). They turn back from Yahweh (1:6), engage in violence and fraud (1:9), are complacent and unbelieving (1:12), trust in wealth (1:8–10, 13, 18), and do not seek Yahweh (1:6; 2:1). The unrighteous know no shame (3:5a), rejoicing in pride and haughtiness (3:11). Twelve more sins are listed at the start of chapter 3:

> Woe to the city of oppressors,
> > rebellious and defiled!
> She obeys no one,
> > she accepts no correction.
> She does not trust in the LORD,
> > she does not draw near to her God.
> Her officials are roaring lions,
> > her rulers are evening wolves,
> > who leave nothing for the morning.
> Her prophets are arrogant;
> > they are treacherous men.
> Her priests profane the sanctuary
> > and do violence to the law. (3:1–4)

Idolatry is the first problem Zephaniah mentions (1:4–6, 9), but he quickly moves to the problem behind the external idolatry: the focus of the human heart's trust and worship. They are proud and arrogant; they trust in themselves and in their wealth. Jerusalem is no different from her unbelieving neighbors, Moab and Assyria. Moab insulted and threatened Yahweh's people (2:8). Assyria was guilty of blasphemy and pride (2:15). Yahweh brought his warning and jealous fire on Israel's neighbors for these sins, and he will do so to his own people.

Content

CHAPTER 1 BEGINS darkly and rails against the corruption of worship, leadership, and wealth in Jerusalem. Zephaniah prophesies the complete and sudden end of the whole world, including animals, birds, and fish. Judah's duplicitous worship will be replaced by Yahweh's consecrated sacrifice of Jerusalem's people. The prophet continues with the punishment of the complacent wealthy who do not expect Yahweh to act. "The great day of the LORD" is described (1:14–18) in vivid detail (e.g., "blood poured out like dust"). It concludes with a reminder that the whole land (*'ereṣ*) will be consumed in the fire of his wrath.

Chapter 2 offers the first glimmer of hope and is less absolute about the destruction. The possibility of a repentant remnant surviving is introduced (2:3, 6–7, 9b, 11; see also 3:9–10, 12–13). Zephaniah makes an appeal to any in Judah who remain humble to come together to seek Yahweh in hope that they might escape the coming violent end. He continues by announcing the violent day of Yahweh against the Philistine cities (2:4), Moab and Ammon across the Jordan (2:8), Ethiopia ("Cush," 2:12), and Assyria (2:13). The humble and faithful remnant is offered additional hope in the promise that they will possess the Philistine and Transjordan lands. Abruptly the survival of the other nations is announced, further softening the harsh first chapter. Nations on every shore will worship Yahweh (2:11). Nonetheless, the violent populations of Cush and Assyria will be mocked for their prideful folly and will be destroyed.

Chapter 3 summarizes the whole book well, repeating the major themes of destruction and survival. Arrogant Jerusalem will be destroyed (3:1–4); all other nations will be annihilated (3:6). The cleansing of the whole land is announced again (3:8) because Jerusalem will not accept correction (3:7). Survivors who meekly and humbly trust in the name of Yahweh will be gathered and restored (3:9–13). Zephaniah ends with a promise from Yahweh for a future free from fear and filled with singing, honor, and restoration (3:14–20).

Zephaniah is in the Bible because it is a true prophecy of Jerusalem's fall to Babylon (597/586 B.C.). It is valuable for its description of the sins for which Jerusalem fell (1:4–6, 8–13; 3:1–4, 13). Zephaniah's call to the people to humility before God helped pave the way for King Josiah's reform (who became king in 640 B.C.). Its striking and colorful language captures the reader's attention: "foreign clothes" (1:8); "avoid stepping on the threshold" (1:9);

"search Jerusalem with lamps" and "like wine left on its dregs" (1:12); "blood will be poured out like dust and their entrails like filth" (1:17); "a place of weeds and salt pits" (2:9); "scoff and shake their fists" (2:15); "evening wolves" (3:3); "serve him shoulder to shoulder" (3:9); "haughty on my holy hill" (3:11).[1]

Beyond these literary and historical interests, Zephaniah is a warning and a call to those who believe they are God's chosen. It is a strong call to a self-absorbed culture to come back to reality. Yahweh, who made everything, calls everyone to turn to him in humility for redemption. Hope is woven together with the historical reality of judgment against arrogance. Zephaniah is a warning against false pride, trust in wealth, and false gods. It is a call for humility before Yahweh, who is their shelter (2:3). It calls us to a vision of the possibility of Yahweh's joy (3:15–20).

God's better desire for his people is expressed in the recurring call to a purified remnant of worshipers: "Gather together, gather together ... seek the LORD ... seek righteousness, seek humility" (2:1–3); "[The seacoast] will belong to the remnant" (2:7); "The nations on every shore will worship him" (2:11); "The LORD within her is righteous; he does no wrong. Morning by morning he dispenses his justice, and every new day he does not fail" (3:5); "Surely you will fear me and accept correction" (3:7); "Then will I purify the lips of the peoples, that all of them may call on the name of the LORD and serve him shoulder to shoulder" (3:9); "From beyond the rivers of Cush [Ethiopia] my worshipers, my scattered people will bring me offerings" (3:10); "But I will leave within you the meek and humble, who trust in the name of the LORD" (3:12); "Sing, O Daughter of Zion; shout aloud, O Israel!" (3:14); "The LORD, the King of Israel, is with you; never again will you fear any harm" (3:15b).

In the end, Yahweh takes responsibility for purifying and gathering the remnant himself. He makes a long series of promises in chapter 3: "Then will I purify the lips of the peoples" (3:9); "You will not be put to shame for all the wrongs you have done to me, because I will remove from this city those who rejoice in their pride" (3:11); "But I will leave within you the meek and humble, who trust in the name of the LORD" (3:12); "The LORD, the King of Israel, is with you; never again will you fear any harm" (3:15); "The LORD your God ... will take great delight in you, he will quiet you with his love, he will rejoice over you with singing" (3:17); "The sorrows for the appointed feasts I will remove from you" (3:18); "I will deal with all who oppressed you; I will rescue the lame and gather those who have been scattered. I will give them praise and honor in every land where they were put to shame" (3:19); "At that time I will gather you; at that time I will bring you home. I will give you honor and praise among all the peoples of the earth" (3:20).

---

1. Many of these phrases are noted by Adele Berlin, *Zephaniah: A New Translation with Introduction and Commentary* (AB; New York: Doubleday, 1994), 12.

These promises establish a foundation of future hope in this last prophetic book before the Babylonians destroyed Jerusalem.[2] The remnant receive a word to which they can cling.

Primary Issues

THE SWEEPING OF **the land.** The announcement of "sweeping away" everything "on the face of the earth" is shocking (1:2–3). Zephaniah's opening verses can confuse the first-time reader because the dramatic language describes the removal of all human beings, animals, fish, and birds from the face of the earth. Although this easily could be read as apocalyptic imagery of the end of time, it did not have that meaning in its original setting nor in the context of the book as a whole. The intentionally dramatic opening verses are like a warning shot across the bow of a ship.

Yahweh often spoke this way through the prophets in order to garner his people's attention. When Jonah went to Nineveh, Yahweh told him to say, "Forty more days and Nineveh will be overturned" (Jonah 3:4). In that case, both destruction and salvation were possible. The original reader of Zephaniah would understand the phrase: "I will sweep away everything from the face of the earth," just as the Ninevites understood their judgment prophecy. They believed God would destroy them *if they did not repent*, but they also knew to listen for the option of repentance. They were familiar with this kind of hyperbolic prophetic speech. God himself gives us a clue to this kind of speech by saying, "I said to the city, 'Surely you will fear me and accept correction!' Then her dwelling would not be cut off, nor all my punishments come upon her" (3:7).

The people did, of course, believe that Yahweh *could* bring great devastation on them (as he did). But they knew and believed Yahweh's reputation: "The LORD, the LORD, the compassionate and gracious God, slow to anger, abounding in love and faithfulness, maintaining love to thousands, and forgiving wickedness, rebellion and sin" (Ex. 34:6–7a). Like the people of Nineveh, they knew that repentance was a possibility. As we read further in Zephaniah, Yahweh makes that possibility abundantly clear (2:3, 7, 9b; 3:8–13, 20). He declares that nations on every shore will worship him following the destruction (2:11).

The whole world. Zephaniah's original audience would have heard the prophecy differently from a modern reader, whose "world" is now literally the whole earth. Zephaniah's "earth" or "land" was a fertile crescent, stretching

---

2. Zephaniah is the last book in the prophetic canon sequence that addresses a pre-destruction Judah.

from Cush (Ethiopia) on the southwest to northeastern Assyria, down the Tigris and Euphrates Rivers to Babylon. The "earth" meant the arable soil that sustained them daily. The "land" meant everything of value in and around Judah. Sweeping away from the "face of the earth," therefore, did not mean the destruction of the planet in that historical setting. Rather, it meant the known world at that time.

This particular destruction was accomplished in Babylon's conquest of the ancient Near East approximately fifty years after Zephaniah's prophecy (586 B.C.). Babylon is glaringly omitted from Zephaniah as part of the "whole world" to be destroyed since it is the agent by which the destruction will be accomplished by God. Nor does the translation "the whole world" mean the annihilation of everything. The world and its people will endure the consuming fire of God's anger as we see in 3:8–9: "The whole world will be consumed by the fire of my jealous anger. Then will I purify the lips of the peoples, that all of them may call on the name of the LORD and serve him shoulder to shoulder."

Eschatological interpretations of Zephaniah are common, and the text's meaning does extend beyond its historical context. The New Testament teaches of a time when all things will be tested by fire and the heaven and earth will be recreated. There, the "purification" of the world is not by "sweeping away" but by fire. Nonetheless, the cleansing references in Zephaniah have been associated with the "end of time" texts that speak of the final judgment of all things, as well as the creation of a new earth and a new heaven (2 Peter 3:10–13; Rev. 16).

Indeed, the oracle is so comprehensive in its declarations of destruction that it is natural to assume that this can only be a description of an apocalypse. Zephaniah describes two situations that still seem to be in our future: the purification of the earth (1:2–3a, 18b; 3:8b) and the blessing of the faithful remnant (3:13, 15b–16a, 19b–20). The challenge for the Christian interpreter is to understand the original meaning in context but at the same time to explain its trajectory into the New Testament and beyond.

What does Zephaniah mean, for example, when he says, "The LORD will be awesome to them when he destroys all the gods of the land. The nations on every shore will worship him, everyone in its own land" (2:11)? What lands? What nations? The key to understanding the destroyed earth/restored earth "ecology" in Zephaniah is through worship. When the people worship the Creator, the forces of destructive chaos are held back.[3] When even his chosen people turn to other gods, Yahweh releases those forces. The Creator's desire is that all created things rightly give praise and honor to

---

3. J. Levenson, *Creation and the Persistence of Evil* (San Francisco: Harper and Row, 1988), 127.

him. Zephaniah reverses the order of creation in his list of destruction: humans, animals, birds, fish (1:3; cf. Gen. 1:20–27).[4]

Whether in the past, present, or future, the health of the created world is directly connected to the rightful worship of the Creator by the human creation. When God is truly worshiped, whether then or now, worship is accompanied by the restoration of the creation. This is an integral theme of Zephaniah's prophecy of destruction and restoration. The Babylonian onslaught and captivity brought destruction. When the people returned to the land from exile (538 B.C.), the land and its animals were renewed, with pure worship in Jerusalem being restored. Yet, we still await an enduring fulfillment of the prophet's full vision. We await the day when all the nations worship him, each in their own land (2:11), and when "the meek and humble, who trust in the name of the LORD," are established in the land (3:12). That future fulfillment of pure worship and relationship will also follow a more complete cleansing by fire (2 Peter 3:10–13).

The jealousy and wrath of Yahweh. Yahweh's jealousy and wrath are described in three places in Zephaniah (1:15–18; 2:1–3; 3:6–10). Rightful worship of the Creator by the created is the key to understanding divine jealousy. God describes himself as "jealous" in the Bible in response to the recently delivered Hebrew slaves who quickly rejected the One who delivered them. At Sinai they bowed down to a golden calf and said, "These are your gods, O Israel, who brought you up out of Egypt" (Ex. 32:8). The first dimension of Yahweh's jealousy is hurt and anger over unfaithfulness to the truth. God had delivered his people, but they gave credit to an idol! This dimension of Yahweh's jealous wrath in Zephaniah is seen in his passion for his redeemed people to live in the light of truth. Since they worship (trust in) their wealth and prosperity, they live a lie and will die (1:15–18).

Yahweh's desire for his people's integrity in worship is also the issue in 2:1–3: "Seek righteousness, seek humility; perhaps you will be sheltered on the day of the LORD's anger" (2:3b). Seeking Yahweh in worship is not simply a means of protection from wrath. His flaring response precisely is intended to bring his people back to the true worship of a delivering and saving God, not to send them scurrying for cover (even under his own wings). God's intense desire is that his beloved people live in the freedom and integrity of telling the truth about who made them and redeemed them. Worshiping God in truth is not negotiable.

A second dimension of Yahweh's jealousy is that he moves faithfully and forcefully to protect his faithful possession from anyone who corrupts them

---

4. Berlin, *Zephaniah*, 81–82. She notes similar patterns in Job 3; Jer. 4:23–28; and Hos. 4:1–3.

(3:6–9). He will pursue those who jeopardize his faithful remnant. His pursuit takes the form of wrath, as a response to those who tempt his people to wrongful worship of created things. The Creator will stand up to "testify" by means of "the fire of [his] jealous anger" (3:8). He will stand against those who threaten his people by leading them away from worshiping him. The result will be a return to the rightful worship of the Creator by the created (3:9–10). Among the most surprising results of this dimension of Yahweh's jealous anger is that other nations will also worship the him (2:11). A more thorough discussion of Yahweh's jealous wrath may be found in the commentary on Nahum.[5]

Historical Context

IN 722 B.C. Israel's northern ten tribes were destroyed or enslaved by Shalmanezer V and Sargon II of Assyria. In 701, during the reign of Hezekiah, Sennacherib of Assyria besieged (but did not capture) Jerusalem and sacked many Judean cities (2 Kings 18–19). Sixty years later, Josiah (640–609) was anointed to the throne in Jerusalem. In the eighteenth year of his reign, he began to reform Jerusalem and Judah in the ways of Yahweh (2 Kings 21–23).[6] Sometime during Josiah's reign (630s) Zephaniah prophesied of Judah's coming judgment and the survival of a faithful remnant. Yahweh's indictments against the people of Jerusalem are similar to the subjects of Josiah's reform.[7] It is likely that Zephaniah's message set the stage for Josiah's reform while Josiah was still a boy-king.[8]

The reforms, however, were not enough. Twelve years after Josiah's death the Babylonians captured Jerusalem and deported the first exiles (597 B.C.), fulfilling part of Zephaniah's prophecy.

"Zephaniah" means "the LORD hides" (*ṣapan* + *yah; yah* is short for Yahweh, translated "LORD"). It can also mean that Yahweh "protects" or even "treasures" the one given this name. Zephaniah was apparently the great, great grandson of King Hezekiah, one of Judah's best kings (see comments on 1:1). His name may mean that he was "hidden" (as a person with royal blood) at the time of his birth during the violence of the evil king Manasseh (his great-uncle).[9] He was one of the true prophets prophesying during King Josiah's reign (with Jeremiah, Habakkuk, and Nahum). His message was a warning of Yahweh's wrath against false loyalties, a call to return to a loving Creator, and hope for the faithful remnant.

---

5. See the Original Meaning section of Nah. 1:1–3a.

6. The book of Chronicles has the first of Josiah's changes in the twelfth year of his reign.

7. For a good discussion of the issues of dating Zephaniah, see Berlin, *Zephaniah*, 33–42.

8. J. J. M. Roberts, *Nahum, Habakkuk, and Zephaniah: A Commentary* (OTL; Louisville: Westminster John Knox, 1991), 166.

9. Ralph L. Smith, *Micah-Malachi* (WBC; Waco, Tex.: Word, 1984), 120.

Outline of Zephaniah

I. **The Dark Day of Yahweh Against Judah** (1:1–18)
   A. "I Will Sweep Away Everything" (1:2–3)
   B. Against Judah (1:4–13)
      1. Yahweh's Hand Stretched Out Against Those in Jerusalem (1:4–6)
      2. The Day of Yahweh's Sacrifice (1:7–9)
      3. Those Who Trust in Wealth (1:10–13)
   C. A Great Day of Darkness (1:14–18)

II. **Yahweh Against the Nations, and a Remnant Sheltered** (2:1–15)
   A. Call for a Remnant to Seek Yahweh (2:1–3)
   B. Against the Philistines to the Southwest (2:4–7)
   C. Against Moab and Ammon to the East (2:8–11)
   D. Against Enemies to the North and South (2:12–15)

III. **Jerusalem's Judgment and Jerusalem's Joy** (3:1–20)
   A. The City of Arrogance and Corruption (3:1–5)
   B. Futile Warnings (3:6–8)
   C. Promises for the Remnant (3:9–13)
      1. I Will Purify (3:9–10)
      2. I Will Leave a Remnant of Israel (3:11–13)
   D. Day of Joy in Jerusalem (3:14–20)
      1. Yahweh Is with You (3:14–17)
      2. I Will Bring You Home (3:18–20)

Select Bibliography on Zephaniah

Achtemeier, Elizabeth. *Nahum–Malachi*. Interpretation. Atlanta: Westminster John Knox, 1986.

Bennett, Robert. "The Book of Zephaniah." Pages 659–704 in *The New Interpreter's Bible*, vol. 7. Nashville: Abingdon, 1996.

Berlin, Adele. *Zephaniah: A New Translation with Introduction and Commentary*. AB. New York: Doubleday, 1994.

Brown, William P. *Obadiah Through Malachi*. Westminster Bible Commentary. Louisville: Westminster John Knox, 1996.

Dorsey, David A. *The Literary Structure of the Old Testament*. Grand Rapids: Baker, 1999.

Mason, Rex. *Zephaniah, Habakkuk, Joel*. Sheffield: JSOT Press, 1994.

Motyer, J. Alec. "Zephaniah." Pages 897–962 in *The Minor Prophets*, vol. 3. Ed. Thomas McComisky. Grand Rapids: Baker, 1993.

Roberts, J. J. M. *Nahum, Habakkuk, and Zephaniah: A Commentary*. OTL. Louisville: Westminster John Knox, 1991.

Robertson, O. Palmer. *The Books of Nahum, Habakkuk, and Zephaniah*. NICOT. Grand Rapids: Eerdmans, 1990.

Smith, Ralph L. *Micah–Malachi*. WBC. Waco, Tex.: Word, 1984.

Sweeney, Marvin A. *The Twelve Prophets*. BO. Collegeville: Liturgical, 2000.

Széles, Mária Eszenyei. *Wrath and Mercy: A Commentary on the Books of Habakkuk and Zephaniah*. Trans. by G. A. F. Knight. ITC. Grand Rapids: Eerdmans, 1987.

Vlaardingerbroek, Johannes. *Zephaniah*. Leuven: Peeters, 1999.

Zephaniah 1

THE WORD OF the LORD that came to Zephaniah son of Cushi, the son of Gedaliah, the son of Amariah, the son of Hezekiah, during the reign of Josiah son of Amon king of Judah:

² "I will sweep away everything
    from the face of the earth,"
                        declares the LORD.
³ "I will sweep away both men and animals;
    I will sweep away the birds of the air
    and the fish of the sea.
The wicked will have only heaps of rubble
    when I cut off man from the face of the earth,"
                        declares the LORD.

⁴ "I will stretch out my hand against Judah
    and against all who live in Jerusalem.
I will cut off from this place every remnant of Baal,
    the names of the pagan and the idolatrous priests—
⁵ those who bow down on the roofs
    to worship the starry host,
those who bow down and swear by the LORD
    and who also swear by Molech,
⁶ those who turn back from following the LORD
    and neither seek the LORD nor inquire of him.
⁷ Be silent before the Sovereign LORD,
    for the day of the LORD is near.
The LORD has prepared a sacrifice;
    he has consecrated those he has invited.
⁸ On the day of the LORD's sacrifice
    I will punish the princes
    and the king's sons
and all those clad
    in foreign clothes.
⁹ On that day I will punish
    all who avoid stepping on the threshold,
who fill the temple of their gods
    with violence and deceit.

¹⁰"On that day," declares the LORD,
    "a cry will go up from the Fish Gate,
    wailing from the New Quarter,
    and a loud crash from the hills.
¹¹ Wail, you who live in the market district;
    all your merchants will be wiped out,
    all who trade with silver will be ruined.
¹² At that time I will search Jerusalem with lamps
    and punish those who are complacent,
    who are like wine left on its dregs,
  who think, 'The LORD will do nothing,
    either good or bad.'
¹³ Their wealth will be plundered,
    their houses demolished.
  They will build houses
    but not live in them;
  they will plant vineyards
    but not drink the wine.

¹⁴"The great day of the LORD is near—
    near and coming quickly.
  Listen! The cry on the day of the LORD will
        be bitter,
    the shouting of the warrior there.
¹⁵ That day will be a day of wrath,
    a day of distress and anguish,
  a day of trouble and ruin,
    a day of darkness and gloom,
    a day of clouds and blackness,
¹⁶ a day of trumpet and battle cry
    against the fortified cities
    and against the corner towers.
¹⁷ I will bring distress on the people
    and they will walk like blind men,
    because they have sinned against
        the LORD.
  Their blood will be poured out like dust
    and their entrails like filth.
¹⁸ Neither their silver nor their gold
    will be able to save them
    on the day of the LORD's wrath.

In the fire of his jealousy
the whole world will be consumed,
for he will make a sudden end
of all who live in the earth."

THE PROPHECY OF the dark "day of the LORD" was spoken against Yahweh's own beloved people. Chapter 1 begins and ends without compromise. God says, "I will sweep away everything" (1:2–3), and the prophet concludes, "He will make a sudden end of all who live in the land [NIV earth]" (1:18). The offenses that demand this harsh judgment are listed as indictments against the people of Judah. Corrupt worship is at the top of the list, including syncretism—the worship of Yahweh alongside the worship of many other created things (1:4–6). The wealthy leaders of corrupt worship themselves will become the consecrated sacrifice on the day of Yahweh (1:7–9). Believers who trust in commerce and wealth are also indicted, as the complacency of Jerusalem's better neighborhoods is noted and described (1:10–13). Finally, the prophet describe a "great day of darkness" and graphic death in Jerusalem.[1]

The Prophet Zephaniah (1:1)

ZEPHANIAH WAS THE "son of Cushi, the son of Gedaliah, the son of Amariah, the son of Hezekiah." He belonged to a faithful and believing family, if the naming of the children is any indication. All of his ancestors except his father had names that include the "LORD" (Cushi means "my Ethiopian"; perhaps his grandmother was from Ethiopia). Hezekiah means "the LORD is my strength." Amariah means "the LORD speaks." Gedaliah means "the LORD is great."[2] Zephaniah's name means "the LORD hides," "protects," or even "treasures." If his great, great grandfather Hezekiah was indeed *the* King Hezekiah, he may have been in danger at the time of his birth.[3]

Zephaniah prophesied during the reign of King Josiah (meaning "the LORD supports"). Josiah came to the throne as a boy after the fifty-five-year reign of evil Manasseh and the futile two-year reign of Amon (which ended in assassination by servants). Josiah's good and productive thirty-one-year

---

1. Jerusalem surrendered to the Babylonians in 597 B.C. after a year of siege and starvation. Zephaniah's warning echoed for about thirty years before that "day of darkness."

2. In each case the "iah" is transliterated from "yah," which is short for Yahweh. The tradition of treating "Yahweh" as a name too holy to be spoken (lest his name be taken in vain) is preserved in English translations by using the capitalized "LORD" in its place.

3. See "Introduction, Historical Context."

reign was guided by the discovery of the book of Deuteronomy in the eighteenth year of his reign during a remodeling of the temple (2 Kings 21:24–23:30; 2 Chron. 33:25–35:27). His reform of the corruption of wealth and worship in Jerusalem (also Zephaniah's subject matter) delayed Yahweh's judgment pronounced by Zephaniah. Hulda the prophetess confirmed Zephaniah's word that the day of Yahweh (the Babylonian onslaught) would come indeed, but it would be delayed because of Josiah's humility before God (2 Kings 22:20).

Zephaniah's words are related to that reform in some way. Perhaps his preaching preceded the reform and called people to participate: "Gather together, gather together, O shameful nation" (2:1). His words may also have been unwelcome by some in the reform movement, for his radical message of destruction did not explicitly offer a reprieve through repentance (see, e.g., 1:2–3). Reformers usually offer the hope of a better (immediate) future as an incentive to reform, but Zephaniah offers none of this. He only offers hope for a future generation ("daughter of Zion," 3:14; cf. also 3:10).

"I Will Sweep Away Everything" (1:2–3)

CHAPTER 1 IS a word of severe warning against God's chosen in Judah. The first verses (1:2–4) introduce the broader theme of a radical house cleaning ("sweeping away") of the whole known world. In Zephaniah's day that world included the civilized and politically powerful "known" world of the ancient Near East's "Fertile Crescent."

When Yahweh says, "I will sweep away everything from the face of the *earth*," the word translated "earth" (1:2, 3) is *'adamah*, which means "tilled land, earth as owned property, earth as arable soil." The sweeping away is a clearing of the human control of the agriculture, a reversal of Genesis 2:15. Sweeping the earth means cleansing the food-producing earth of people.[4]

The Fertile Crescent (of semi-arable land) stretched from Ethiopia ("Cush") in Judah's southwest to northeastern Assyria (northern Iraq). The extent of "everything" (cf. 1:2, 3, 18; 3:8) is identified in the biblical text as Judah and all who live in Jerusalem (1:4), Gaza, Ashkelon, Ashdod, Ekron (2:4), Canaan, Philistia (2:5), Moab, Ammon (2:8), Cush (2:12), and Assyria (2:13). The absence of the Babylonians in this description is interesting. Although they were known to Zephaniah, they may be missing because they were not a political factor when Zephaniah wrote, but also because

---

4. In the rest of Zephaniah, the NIV English words "earth," (1:18; 3:20), "land" (2:3, 5, 11; 3:19), and "world" (1:18; 3:8) come from the Heb. *'ereṣ*. It is translated "world" and "earth" in 1:18 but may also be translated, "In the fire of his jealousy, the whole *country* will be consumed, for he will make a sudden end to all who live in the *land*."

they were to be Yahweh's agent in the destruction of "all the earth." They are not included in the ones to be destroyed. The nations on this list of "everything" on the face of the land are conquered and ruled for about seventy years by the neo-Babylonians (612–539 B.C.). As Yahweh's agent, they "swept away" everyone in Judah to captivity and destroyed any means of surviving in the land with land-destroying policies.

Zephaniah also describes what is *not* destroyed in the cleansing of the land. That includes the gold that endures the fire of destruction and purification, the "land by the sea," "shepherds" and "sheep" (2:6–7); "the remnant," "the survivors," "their land" (2:9); "the nations on every shore" (2:11); "flocks," "herds," "creatures of every kind" (2:14); "peoples," "worshipers," "scattered people" (3:9 –10); "the meek and humble," "[those] who trust" (3:12); and "all the peoples of the earth" (3:20). It is a comprehensive list.

What should we make of this? Is the earth to be destroyed or not? Not in Zephaniah. A good summary of Zephaniah's perspective is offered in the words of 3:8b–10. "The whole world will be consumed by the fire of my jealous anger. Then will I purify the lips of the peoples.... From beyond the rivers of Cush ... my scattered people will bring me offerings." In the same paragraph Zephaniah declares the purification of the whole world through Yahweh's consuming fire and speaks of the actual scattered people and geography of his day. We can assume that the "consuming fire," then, is not for annihilation but purification. It is for the destruction of the societal structures of corruption, rebellion, and false worship.

"I will sweep away everything" is a shocking beginning to any book. Yahweh speaks directly, as throughout most of chapter 1 (1:2–6, 8–17). Zephaniah is opposed to arrogance and complacency and desires humility before Yahweh, but these opening verses have no hint of any nuances in the judgment to come. He makes no mention of a separation of the humble from the arrogant. Nor does he present an eventual return of a humble worshiping remnant. Even the animals, birds, and fish will be swept away.

The image "sweep away" refers to the wind that "sweeps" chaff away from grain during threshing. The verb is doubled in Hebrew for emphasis ("utterly sweep away"), indicating that the coming wind is no ordinary wind that will separate the grain and chaff. Rather, it is a storm wind that will "sweep away everything," the chaff mixed together with the grain.

"I will sweep away the birds of the air and the fish of the sea. The wicked will have only heaps of rubble" (1:3b). This part of the verse is difficult to translate, as the NIV indicates in a footnote. It can also be translated, "I will sweep away the birds of the air and the fish of the sea, and that rubble—the wicked." The uncertainty is whether the former verb ("sweep away") or an implied verb ("will have") should be used. In any case, the second possibility helps us to understand the meaning of the NIV translation and the point of Yahweh's devastating action: The wicked will be disposed of and swept away.

So why does Zephaniah begin with such an absolute statement as, "I cut off man from the face of the earth" (1:3b)? This dramatic beginning has a strong rhetorical effect in Zephaniah's preaching. The book's prophecy is dark, and this beginning prepares the hearer for the difficult words to come and inclines them to listen for hope. It is more than rhetorical, however, for it tells the truth about the horror that will indeed descend on the whole known earth. Babylon will obliterate the land.

Against Judah (1:4–13)

THESE VERSES DECLARE the offenses of Judah and especially Jerusalem, the capital city (1:4).[5] The long list addresses issues of worship and trust in wealth: Baal, idolatrous priests (1:4), worship of the starry host and Molech (1:5), turning back from Yahweh (1:6), corrupt government (1:8), violence and fraud (1:9), trust in commerce and wealth (1:10–11), and complacent wealthy believers (1:12–13).

I will stretch out my hand against all who live in Jerusalem (1:4–6). "I will stretch out my hand" is a Hebrew expression that indicates the use of power, usually to punish offenders by means of other governments (Isa. 14:26–27), but sometimes by natural events (Ex. 7:5). As the capital of Judah, Jerusalem in 640 B.C. represented the faith and trust of the whole country of Judah. Judah was already a remnant of Israel since the Assyrian wars that culminated in the loss of the ten northern tribes (722 B.C.). By this time Yahweh's people had experienced more than seventy years of prosperity, but a quiet corruption had taken hold. In 1:4–6 five offenses will be "cut off" by Yahweh:

1. "every remnant of Baal"
2. "pagan and . . . idolatrous priests"
3. "those who bow down on the roofs to worship the starry host"
4. "those who . . . swear by the LORD and . . . by Molech"
5. "those who turn back from following the LORD and neither seek the LORD nor inquire of him."

The list of offenses moves from the obvious worship of other gods (Baal, starry host) to syncretistic worship of Yahweh (with Molech), to the very heart of the matter, a lack of trust in and ignoring Yahweh.

Baal was a Canaanite household god of prosperity and fertility. The local Baals and the nationalized Baal were gods or a spirit that controlled the fertility of people, land, and animals. Good fertility of land and animals meant pros-

---

5. More offenses are listed in 3:1–4.

perity and wealth. Baal was incited to give the gifts of fertility and prosperity through ritualized public sexual acts. This worship of sexuality and wealth was a threat throughout Israel's history, beginning in Numbers 25:1–3.

The "pagan and idolatrous priests" are the Israelite *kohen* (Ex. 28:1), priests leading the people in worship of other things even as they worship Yahweh. These priests are syncretistic and corrupt (Zeph. 3:4), leading the people astray and confusing their pure worship of Yahweh.

"Those who bow down on the roofs to worship the starry host" followed the old mistake of worshiping a beautiful creation rather than the Creator. Worship of the stars occurred in Canaan, Babylon, Assyria, and Egypt. It was a prevalent and growing problem in Judah as well (Deut. 4:19; 2 Kings 21:3, 5; Jer. 8:2; 19:13; 44:17–25). Zephaniah includes them all with a generic description of their worship. No idols are used, but incense is burned and libations are poured out on the flat rooftops with the stars and moon in view. The biblical counter to these "starry hosts" is the claim that Yahweh is "the LORD of hosts" (2:9, 10, NRSV).

The fourth offense that will be cut off by Yahweh is "those who . . . swear by the LORD and . . . by Molech." Several variations of "Molech" are found in Scripture, including Milcom/Milcam/Malcam ("their king" or "their Molech").[6] The most heinous practice of the Molech cult was child sacrifice (prohibited in Lev. 18:21; 20:2–4; 1 Kings 11:7). Late in the monarchy, even in Israel people sacrificed a child as a means of securing their prosperity (1 Kings 11:5, 33; 2 Chron. 28:3; Jer. 49:1, 3). Jeremiah especially conveys Yahweh's condemnation of this practice, common in the Valley of Hinnom outside Jerusalem (Jer. 32:35). King Josiah in Zephaniah's day tried to put a stop to it physically (2 Kings 23:10, 13).

The final condemned offense is committed by "those who turn back from following the LORD and neither seek the LORD nor inquire of him." This is "practical atheism" by those who know Yahweh.[7] To follow Yahweh is to trust in him enough to seek his presence (Hos. 5:15; 10:12) and inquire of him concerning important life decisions (Amos 5:4, 14; "seek" and "inquire" are synonyms in Hebrew). In Zephaniah 1:6 Yahweh's desire to be in relationship to the created is heard, almost plaintively.

The list of offenses moved increasingly toward the average believer, from the chaff to the grain. It begins in the extreme with Baal worship and idolatrous priests (1:4) but ends with the same fate for those who simply do not bother

---

6. Scholars do not agree on the association of these gods. The correspondence of Molech with Milcam is implied in the NIV translation (Milcam=Molech). Both are called Ammonite gods in 1 Kings 11:5–7. See the variety of opinions in George Heider, "Molech," *ABD*, 4:895–98.

7. J. Alec Motyer, "Zephaniah," in *The Minor Prophets*, ed. Thomas McComisky (Grand Rapids: Baker, 1993), 3:913.

to inquire of Yahweh concerning their decisions. Yahweh will cut off all of them in Jerusalem (1:4) but calls for the humble to seek him (2:3).

The day of Yahweh's sacrifice (1:7–9). Verses 7–9 present an image that can cut in both directions. In verse 7 Zephaniah tells the people of Jerusalem to be silent (lit., "hush"; cf. Hab. 2:20) before Yahweh, "for the day of the LORD is near." This is the first mention of "the day of the LORD" and its nearness.[8] The people are not asked to prepare a sacrifice or to consecrate themselves because Yahweh himself has done these things. They are simply invited to participate. Yahweh speaks again in verses 8–9, however, revealing that the "sacrifice" that Zephaniah announces will be a sacrifice of Jerusalem's leaders.

This prophecy is made darker by the worship sacrifice context. It begins quite innocently with a call to worship before "the Sovereign LORD" (lit., "Lord Yahweh"), who has prepared the sacrifice and even consecrated those he has invited. This seems appropriate to the prophecy since the problem in 1:4–6 was one of false worship. Taken by itself, this verse would be innocuous, but in the context of 1:8–9, it is clear that the invited are consecrated as the sacrifice itself and not simply as the guests. The consecration of guests, also to be the sacrifice, occurs with the prophets of Baal (1 Kings 18:19–40; 2 Kings 10:20–27). The "guests" here, however, are the people of Jerusalem (1:4–6).

Especially mentioned among the guests-sacrifice are the wealthy duplicitous leaders of Jerusalem (1:8). Yahweh declares his punishment of the "princes" (probably officials and administrators of Assyria ruling in Jerusalem), "the king's sons," and "all those clad in foreign clothes." The mention of foreign clothes likely refers to those who have adopted the culture of Assyria, with whom Judah has been allied. Clothing was a symbol that people were adopting the cultural and religious values of Assyria at the expense of the worldview and faith revealed to them by the true God. The second group especially mentioned for punishment is "all who avoid stepping on the threshold, who fill the temple of their gods with violence and deceit" (1:9). Avoiding stepping on the threshold was a ritual custom of avoiding the power of a god that resides in the doorway (1 Sam. 5:4–5).

The intensity of Yahweh's desire for relationship with a faithfully worshiping people is demonstrated in his willingness to sacrifice even the beloved city of Jerusalem. In doing so, he shows that his kingdom is not a political kingdom but a kingdom of steadfast love and faithfulness between him and his created and delivered people.[9]

Those who trust in wealth (1:10–13). These verses continue the theme announced in 1:4: "I will stretch out my hand against Judah." Verses 4–6

---

8. For "the day of the LORD" in Zephaniah, see 1:18. For the concept of "nearness," see 3:15.

9. See the further reference to the "sacrifice" at 3:18, where Yahweh removes the sorrow over this "appointed time."

began with the issue of trust in and worship of things other than the Creator. Now Yahweh turns to secular kinds of trust and worship, especially images of material wealth: the Fish Gate, the New Quarter, "hills" (1:10), market district, merchants, silver trade (1:11), wine resting on its sediment (1:12), wealth, houses, and vineyards (1:13).

Verse 10 describes the sounds of the day of punishment. A "cry" for help "will go up" from the Fish Gate—the food market of Jerusalem. From the New Quarter will come "wailing"; this quarter was the newest neighborhood. The "loud crash" (lit., "breaking") from the hills is probably the sound of the destruction of the Baal pillars (see Deut. 12:2; 1 Kings 14:23; 2 Kings 17:10; Jer. 2:20). These idols were typically raised on the highest hill in or near a town. When people faced life decisions or uncertainties, they would take a small offering, climb the hill, pray, and leave the offering in hopes of a good outcome to their petition. The crash of these pillars sounds the dramatic end of the Baal's influence (*ba'al* means "master, owner"). These three sounds (cry, wail, crash) along with the "wail" of the market district (1:11) constitute a comprehensive representation of the whole city life: grocery source, neighborhood, hillside, and downtown businesses. The whole city, Yahweh says, will resound with their anguish.

Verse 11 takes up the theme of the security of wealth in earnest. The market district (called "the Mortar") with all its merchants and money market traders "will be ruined" (*karat*).[10] Yahweh calls on them to "wail" (*yalal*) in anticipation of the day of the Lord. The word *yalal* is usually used for (and sounds like) animals "howling." This kind of "wail" implies that these traders share some characteristics with animals. Merchants (same root as "Canaan") and money traders *in general* are not judged negatively, but those in Jerusalem *at that time* are condemned.

Yahweh says, "I will punish" three times in chapter 1 (1:8, 9, 12). Each time he moves closer to the average citizen. The first group mentioned for punishment includes the rulers who capitulated to Assyria (1:8). The second group includes those who entered into the violent and deceptive worship of false gods (1:9). The third group includes complacent believers, "who are like wine left on its dregs, who think, 'The LORD will do nothing, either good or bad'" (1:12b). The list moves from the most heinous offenders to believing Israelites who are simply "complacent."[11] Searching "with lamps" (1:12) means

---

10. This root (meaning "cut off") occurs seven times in Zephaniah: 1:3, 4, 11; 3:6, 7. In 2:5, 6 it constitutes the name Kerethite or Cretan.

11. This pattern repeats a similar progression in 1:4–6, which moves from the most heinous worship offenders to those who simply did not "seek the LORD nor inquire of him." The two sets of progressive judgments are separated by the central verse, "Be silent before the Sovereign LORD, for the day of the LORD is near" (1:7).

that no one will be able to hide in the darkness, including those who are complacent and even those who are religious (Amos 9:2).

"Who are like wine left on its dregs" (1:12) is a metaphor for complacency. The metaphor is of aging wine that must rest undisturbed in order to grow richer. The "dregs" or "lees" are the natural sediment that settles to the bottom during this process and must not be shaken up if the wine is to age well. The metaphor is neither positive nor negative until it is applied to the inactivity of a believer's faith. Inactivity is good for aging wine. For Yahweh's chosen, who in their fiscal security think that he will not act, inactivity is complacency.[12] It is particularly jolting to hear the Lord repeat the thoughts of the people. He knows that they have been thinking "the LORD will do nothing" (cf. Mal. 2:17).[13]

These complacent people have replaced their belief in an active Lord with a preference for the stability and security of their wealth. They have stopped believing Yahweh will act at all. Their wealth, the source of their complacency, "will be plundered, and their houses demolished" (1:13). Their attention and confidence have turned toward their own accomplishments—the building of houses and the planting of vineyards. These are the things that Yahweh will cut off. Verse 13 is the first indication that the coming judgment of "the day of the LORD" will take the form of military violence against Jerusalem ("plundered," "demolished"). This military action is confirmed in the verses that conclude the first chapter (1:14–18).

A Great Day of Darkness (1:14–18)

THE DESCRIPTION OF "the day of the LORD" as "great" (1:14) introduces the actual day that Judah is attacked by Babylon. The day is "great" in its intensity and extent. The sights and sounds described intensify the image of "the day" of the enemy warrior presence in Jerusalem: "near and coming quickly ... cry ... bitter ... shouting ... warrior" (1:14); "day of wrath ... distress ... anguish ... trouble ... ruin ... darkness ... gloom ... clouds ... blackness" (1:15); "trumpet and battle cry against the fortified cities ... corner towers" (1:16); "distress ... walk like blind men ... blood ... poured out like dust and entrails like filth" (1:17); "wrath ... fire ... consumed ... sudden end of all who live" (1:18).

This description leaves no doubt about the horror that will come to Jerusalem in 587 B.C. Verse 17 brings the day's description close to home. The physical suffering and death of the people during the Babylonian attack is

---

12. See Jer. 48:11 for an expanded use of the metaphor of "wine on its dregs."

13. Jeremiah spoke to the same problem and the same solution. Yahweh will bring Babylon to their door (Jer. 5:12–19).

described (compare with the description in Lamentations). On this day of clouds and blackness, the people "will walk like blind men" (1:15, 17). The civilian population will be dazed and shocked in their defeat, for they will lose their orientation to Yahweh (see Bridging Contexts section). The central phrase of the verse "because they have sinned against the LORD" leaves no doubt that the sins described in 1:4–13 are the cause of this devastation. The word for "sin" in 1:17 (*ḥata³*) means "to miss [God's] mark."

Anyone who truly believes this word from Yahweh will be very motivated to participate in Josiah's reform, in hope of avoiding its fury. This "great day of the LORD" is said to be "near and coming quickly."[14] The first wave of judgment came on Jerusalem in 597 B.C. If this prophecy was given in 630 B.C., Zephaniah's message was heard for about thirty years.

The themes of chapter 1 are summarized in 1:18:

> Neither their silver nor their gold
> will be able to save them
> on the day of the LORD's wrath.
> In the fire of his jealousy
> the whole world will be consumed,
> for he will make a sudden end
> of all who live in the earth.

The totality of the consuming fire (1:2–4), the theme of impotent trust in wealth (1:10–13), and the suddenness of the end (1:14–17) are each mentioned in this verse.

The offense of false worship (1:5–9) is gathered in the cryptic word "jealousy" (1:18b). In Scripture the jealousy of Yahweh is not simply an emotion but a comprehensive concept, focused on the Creator/creation and Deliverer/delivered relationships. The two main biblical settings for understanding God's jealousy are the first part of the Ten Commandments (Ex. 20:1–7) and the golden calf incident (read Ex. 32:7–8 with 34:5–9, 14). God's jealousy is easily misunderstood. God is "jealous" not because he is lacking in himself (a common human form of jealousy), but in the positive sense of being zealous for his precious creation that is in danger of corruption and death. When the human creation turns away from the source of its life (Creator/Deliverer), it is on a path toward death. God's "jealousy" is a prejudice *toward life* for his created and delivered people (see the introduction, "Jealousy and Wrath of Yahweh").[15]

God's jealous consuming of the "whole world" is for the expressed purpose of establishing a remnant of the faithful—in a sense to rescue or preserve the

---

14. "Near" also at 1:7; see the contrast of "nearness" in 3:15–17.
15. Yahweh's jealousy and wrath are mentioned in Zeph. 1:18; 2:1–3; 3:6–10.

faithful from the corruption of all life. This verse has in view the historical events of 587 B.C., when the whole world *was* "consumed" by the Babylonians. The Babylonians did "swallow up" everything for a time (612–539 B.C.; see the introduction, "Historical Context"). God's "jealousy" for a future remnant to live in the freedom, innocence, and justice of the world he intended required a cataclysmic act against his own people. The only hope for their rescue as a faithful people was in the suffering of exile and captivity (Isa. 37:32). It is this same "jealousy" or "zeal" (Heb. *qana'*) that leads to the announcement of a coming King who will be a "Wonderful Counselor, Mighty God, Everlasting Father, Prince of Peace," bringing an end to warfare (9:6–9).

"The day of the LORD" as a day of judgment is mentioned many times in Zephaniah (1:7, 8, 9, 10, 14, 15, 16, 18; 2:2, 3; 3:8). In Israel's early history, that "day" referred to Yahweh fighting with elements of creation against Israel's enemies (Ex. 14:20; Judg. 5:4–5; 1 Sam. 7:10). The historical referent in Zephaniah, however, is the destruction of Jerusalem by the Babylonians. For this reason Amos also said, "Woe to you who long for the day of the LORD" (Amos 5:18). The later prophets announced that Yahweh would use creation's forces and enemy forces against his own unfaithful people.

Zephaniah shares this tradition with Amos, Isaiah, Jeremiah, Ezekiel, and others. A biblical survey of the expression "day of the LORD" reveals consistent characteristics: The day is near, it is God's anger against the wicked, it is dark and gloomy, it is God's battle, but he uses real armies. It is a day of impotence and dismay for a rebellious nation. The day of the Lord is the day of God's search and destruction of enemies. In that day, wealth is useless to save and human pride is destroyed. Zephaniah stands squarely in this broader biblical tradition.[16]

At 3:9, however, Yahweh declares an important short expression with the word "then." After the word "then," the expression "the day" refers to "a new day." After that reference, the expression "that day/time" always refers to the return of the remnant to the city of Jerusalem (3:11, 16, 19, 20). It denotes significant hope for the humble remnant (described in 2:3, 7, 9; 3:12–13).

Bridging Contexts

ZEPHANIAH SPOKE DURING the reign of Judah's King Josiah, who tried to reform the extensive corruption in Jerusalem. His prophecy offered no hope that general reform would be successful, but it probably aided Josiah's national effort by drawing attention to the deep-

---

16. Elizabeth Achtemeier, *Nahum–Malachi* (Interpretation; Atlanta: Westminster John Knox, 1986), 66–67.

seated problems. The king's reforms, which were too little, too late, gave way to destruction within twelve years of his death (609/597 B.C.).

The seeds of Judah's self-serving religiosity and self-indulgence had already taken root. The people believed that catastrophe would not come near their door. Professing faith in God, they trusted in the things they made to secure their lives. Many also believed they were immune to destruction because of Yahweh's previous blessings and his dwelling in the temple. Zephaniah forms a warning, not just for Judah at the beginning of the sixth century but for any country at any time. He warns that cataclysmic destruction may come to any country that lives without reference to the God who has given it prosperity and success.

Future and eschatological (end-time) interpretations. Zephaniah has rightly been interpreted in historical "layers." The warning of the destruction it delivers is against Jerusalem at the end of the seventh century, but its significance did not end with the destruction of Jerusalem. Although this is its primary meaning, Zephaniah is open to a much wider application. Using Jerusalem as a paradigm, God will, by the end of time, expose all false gods and false hopes.[17] What was historically true for Judah is also universally true for every country and culture. They will be tested by fire and exposed.

Zephaniah suggests this broader application in several ways, beginning with universal language ("I will sweep away everything from the face of the earth," 1:2). Even though the book shows this to be hyperbole (since many in Judah do survive), the prophet begins with this comprehensive expression before moving to the specifics in Judah (1:4–18a). This progression opens the way for interpretations in later historical settings and for end-time interpretations. It has a worldwide range.[18]

Zephaniah also opens the way to wider interpretation by not mentioning which army God will use. Although we know from 2 Kings that it is the Babylonians, Zephaniah remarkably never mentions them by name. This leaves open the possibility of future applications. Chapter 1 ends with expansive language that continues to address the imagination of the reader: "The whole world will be consumed, for he will make a sudden end of all who live in the earth" (1:18b).

The fulfillment of the positive promises in Zephaniah's prophecy would have been expected by the postexilic community (see 3:9, 13, 20). They were disappointed that they did not live to see its fulfillment. At the time of Jesus (about six hundred years later), God's personal righteous judgment of the earth and the advent of the righteous remnant were still expected.

---

17. Motyer, "Zephaniah," 3:918.
18. Ibid., 3:922.

The prophetic texts had been discussed during these centuries to attempt to understand how and when God would intervene in the world political situation. The discussion led to a reinterpretation of these expectations toward a messianic hope. Jesus inaugurated the kingdom of God and extended, by his gospel, the offer of forgiveness for sin to all the cultures of the world.

Even Jesus did not, however, bring the day of wrath and final judgment to bear upon the world. He brought the good news of God's love in the flesh and died to accomplish the victory over sin, death, and the devil for all people. Yet he spoke of that final Day of Judgment, when eternal justice will be done for all (Matt. 24). The early church expected it to arrive soon (Acts 2:20; Rom. 2:2–9; 1 Cor. 5:5; 1 Thess. 5:2; 2 Thess. 2:2; 2 Peter 3:10; Rev. 6:17). Today Jews and Christians still look forward to the day when the Lord will fulfill his promise and establish purity of worship, heart, and speech, freedom from fear, and honor of God's people by all nations.

The New Testament uses the images of Zephaniah in an expansive way. Paul wrote to Christians in Rome concerning the day of the Lord's wrath using language similar to Zephaniah's warnings:

> Now we know that *God's judgment* against those who do such things is based on truth. So when you, a mere man, pass judgment on them and yet do the same things, do you think you will escape *God's judgment?* . . .
>
> But because of your stubbornness and your unrepentant heart, you are storing up *wrath against yourself for the day of God's wrath, when his righteous judgment will be revealed.* . . . For those who are self-seeking and who reject the truth and follow evil, there will be *wrath and anger.* There will be *trouble and distress* for every human being who does evil. (Rom. 2:2–3, 5, 8–9, italics added)

These conclusions of judgment are based on the exposure of sin in the previous chapter (Rom. 1:22–2:1). Paul lists the foolishness of serving created things, including sexuality and lust, greed, envy, murder, strife, deceit, malice, gossip, slander, atheism, insolence, arrogance, boasting, disobedience of parents, faithlessness, and heartlessness. He ends by adding those who also judge these sins. This list includes *everyone.* Who is free of every sin on this list?[19] Those who do these things will suffer the same fate as the people of Jerusalem in Zephaniah's day. They will experience the day of the Lord's wrath. No one will escape "the Day." The best one can hope for is shelter on that Day (Rom. 5:9).

---

19. Note how Paul's argument in Rom. 1–3 culminates in the well-known 3:23: "For all have sinned and fall short of the glory of God."

Zephaniah does not offer a way of escape from "the day of the LORD." He only offers the possibility of "shelter" by seeking Yahweh, gathering together in righteousness and humility (2:3). In the light of the resurrection and Jesus' teaching, the "escape" takes on eternal significance. Paul describes the possibility of eternal life through God's kindness, tolerance, and patience to those who repent and persist in doing good (Rom. 2:4–7). It is given not as a reward for faithfulness but as a gift of God's grace through faith in Jesus' sacrificial death ("they are justified freely by his grace" [3:24]).

It may be tempting, in light of this gift of redemption and forgiveness of sin, to dismiss the "day of wrath" as something in the future for "those outside the faith," but neither Zephaniah nor Paul allows this move. Both are writing to the insiders, the believers of their times. Both offer detailed lists of sins common to people "of faith." Believers are to be included among those who are at risk and threatened by the day of wrath in both Zephaniah and Romans. E. Achtemeier reminds us that "there is no guarantee that the cross will shield us from similar condemnation."[20] The warning is clear even to us, who claim the cross of Christ: If we persist in the actions and attitudes condemned by Paul and Zephaniah, we claim it falsely and share the syncretism of their days.

In the book of Hebrews, the Day of the Lord's wrathful judgment is also a subject for believers to consider (Heb. 10:19–31). The writer uses the shorthand "Day" in its full sense of the end of life and time, when all will be judged guilty except for those who trust in the mercy of God. Like Paul, he encourages and warns believers. The fear of that Day is not removed but shielded by faithfulness (cf. Zeph. 2:1). That Day itself will certainly be full of "fearful expectation of judgment and of raging fire.... For we know him who said, 'It is mine to avenge; I will repay,' and again, 'The Lord will judge his people.' It is a dreadful thing to fall into the hands of the living God" (Heb. 10:27, 30–31).

Hope is found in the shield we have in Christ's friendship, priesthood, and forgiveness. "'Their sins and lawless acts I will remember no more.'... We have confidence ... by the blood of Jesus, by a new and living way opened for us through ... his body" (Heb. 10:17, 19–20). The author of Hebrews then describes in detail how we may live freely in that grace, even though that fearful Day of death and destruction will come (10:22–25). Drawing near to God in Christ is possible because of Jesus' assurance given in the cleansing of our conscience and because of our participation in his death and resurrection through our baptism. "Let us draw near to God with a sincere heart in full assurance of faith" (10:22). Clinging to our hope of shelter in that

---

20. Achtemeier, *Nahum-Malachi*, 65.

Day, we are called by the preacher to encourage each other toward love, good deeds, and meeting in worship.[21]

The alternative to clinging to Christ, with the confidence and shelter that come from his forgiveness, is for the believer to disregard Jesus' blood and to insult the Spirit of grace. To neglect the One who has delivered and will deliver us is to abandon one's shelter. It is to trample the Son and to insult the Spirit. It will result in a more severe punishment for the believer (Heb. 10:29). As in Zephaniah, God's day of wrath will expose those who have and those who have not wholly trusted the Lord with their hearts and actions.

There is no escape or human shelter on the Day of Judgment. Total exposure and death are the unifying theme of Zephaniah 1 and of its New Testament eschatological applications. (1) Both Old and New Testaments (Zeph. 2:1–3; Rom. 1–3; Heb. 10) offer the possibility of God's shelter, but they do not offer escape from physical death. (2) The Day exposes the fallacy of home, savings, and business (career and commerce) as shelters against it. (3) The Day exposes the fallacy that all life ends with physical death. In each case, God is the unaccounted-for factor.

The Day will certainly come and bring exposure to death. Universally, it will expose the denial of our mortality. The great modern illusion is that we will not die, or perhaps that when the time comes, we will persist vaguely as spirits beyond the grave without any help from anywhere. "Who knows?" becomes "Who cares?" The Day of the Lord in Scripture confronts this attitude as fallacious. No one will be able to hide (1:12). Whether it was in Zephaniah's day, in the final judgment, or sometime between, death has and will have its day.

Many "days" of God's wrath have come and gone in the history of the world. The faithful in Jerusalem also died or were deported in 597/586 B.C. In A.D. 70, when the city fell to Rome, faithful people of God, including Christians, died. Many others have endured days of wrath faithfully in the conflicts of the twentieth and twenty-first centuries. The book of Revelation acknowledges the death of the saints in the days of God's wrath (Rev. 7:13–17). It is a necessity in every age to trust God when facing death. Every time someone dies of disease, violence, or failed flesh, it is an extension of God's judgment in Eden, removing humanity's access to the tree of life. Only a life lived in reconciliation with God can be sheltered in that day. Every day has a "small d" day of wrath. Zephaniah's call is for us to act on that reality before the Day arrives.

---

21. A similar theme of mutual encouragement against the day of the Lord in 1 Thess. 5:1–11 is read with Zeph. 1:12–18 in some lectionaries. Also read is the parable of the ten virgins (Matt. 25:1–13) concerning the uncertain timing of that day and the parable of the talents (Matt. 25:14–29) concerning the investment of time and resources while waiting for that day.

"The day of the LORD" in Zephaniah also exposes the fallacy of a career or commerce as shelter against it. Believers through the ages have often lived a "practical atheism" that acknowledges that God is in heaven "but not here in daily life." They think, "The LORD will do nothing, either good or bad" (1:12). The practical atheist-believer believes in the value of his bank balance, home, and employment above all.[22] The Day exposes the transience and insubstantiality of money and property (see Lev. 26:14–39; Deut. 28:15–68).

The Day also exposes the fallacy that life ends at death. The judgment of death is not the end for anyone. This is suggested in Zephaniah by God's promises to establish a pure remnant in Jerusalem, bringing them home from every land after sweeping everything away (3:9–20). Those who have entirely relied on Yahweh, seeking "righteousness and humility" (2:3), will also be revealed. In the New Testament it is those who have trusted the grace of Christ by drawing near through honoring his law and gospel who will be rescued at the judgment. Those who have drawn near to the God of history and those who have not both will be revealed.

The Day will also expose the guilty conscience and hidden deeds (Heb. 10:22, 26). Those who say, "The LORD will do nothing either good or bad" (Zeph. 1:12b), believing that there is no final consequence for their actions, will be exposed as "supreme" idolaters. This is the sin of the Garden of Eden.[23] They have made themselves gods by making themselves the judge of right and wrong. These believers live as though God sees nothing and does nothing (Ezek. 9:9), though they may not say it. The exposing universal Day described in Zephaniah ought to fill us with the fear of Yahweh. "For a church as conformed to the world as we are, that pronouncement from Zephaniah is a fearful and terrible word from God."[24] It ought to drive us to Christ and a life within his righteous mercies, for judgment begins with the household of God (1 Peter 4:17).

GOD'S ANGER. God sounds angry in Zephaniah 1:1–18. It is perhaps the most graphic description of his anger in the Bible. The intensity of language, its magnitude, and its detailed descriptions of Jerusalem's demise demonstrate that God is more than angry; he is enraged. The intensity of that anger is a measure of how much he cares about the human subject. In Zephaniah we encounter God's ultimate concern for us.

22. Moyter, "Zephaniah," 3:921.
23. Achtemeier, *Nahum-Malachi*, 69.
24. Ibid., 71.

Zephaniah 1 is specific about the source of his anger. It is not the outsider or unbeliever but the hypocrisies and betrayals of his own created, chosen, and redeemed people. The greatest intensity of his anger is reserved for those for whom he cares the most and for those in whom he has invested everything.

God is so angered by the sins of his created, redeemed, and prospering people that he is going to turn the creation on its head. He will reverse it (1:2–3). He is so angered by the sins of his people that his hand, which was often extended for their salvation, will be stretched out against his people for their destruction (1:4–6). He is so angered by the betrayal of his covenant people that he will turn the blessings of sacrifice on their head. His people will become the sacrifice (1:7–8). The Lord's fury is so great that he will reverse deliverance and redemption. The Day of Yahweh will not be a day of deliverance for his people but a Day when his people are delivered into bondage (1:9–18a). Creation, salvation, sacrifice, and deliverance all will be turned on their head.

That God has been consummately angered is also communicated by the sheer *weight* of the graphic language of chapter 1: "I will sweep away both men and animals . . . birds of the air and the fish of the sea. The wicked will have only heaps of rubble . . . cry will go up . . . wailing . . . a loud crash from the hills . . . wail . . . wiped out . . . ruined . . . I will search . . . with lamps and punish . . . their wealth will be plundered . . . houses demolished . . . Listen! The cry . . . will be bitter, the shouting of the warrior . . . a day of wrath . . . distress and anguish . . . trouble and ruin . . . darkness and gloom . . . clouds and blackness, a day of trumpet and battle cry . . . I will bring distress . . . they will walk like blind men . . . their blood will be poured out like dust and their entrails like filth."

Sources of God's anger. What makes God this angry? The source of that anger is the same today. It is the response of One who has cared, loved, and invested deeply in people who have prospered under his care but have turned away. His people have either rebelled or ignored the One who provided everything for them. His people and religious leaders have tried to combine lukewarm faithfulness to the Lord with allegiances to a variety of other created things.

(1) The first kind of turning away that is common among the redeemed who are prospering is a preoccupation with their general fertility and capacity for production. The misuse of sex and money angers the Lord. The acquisition of fertility was the object of Baal worship in the Old Testament. Fertility is a broad concept that means "production power."[25] People turn toward

---

25. This is Webster's definition.

whatever helps them produce power (usually money) and pleasure (usually sexuality). Preoccupation with fertility in our culture takes similar forms to those known in every age: the acquisition of wealth and sex.

When the pursuit of either of these forms the substance of the identity of a person or a culture, the Baals of old have returned. Sex and wealth have both been created, of course, by God for good purposes. That is part of the source of God's anger. When they are misused or treated as a fountain of life by his people, God's anger and jealously are kindled. Prosperity and sexuality, given by God, are meant to honor him, but too often they are used selfishly. This is the case in every age, including ours.

(2) The second source of God's anger is the combination of the worship of the Lord with the secular worship of created things, such as the "starry host" in the night sky (1:5). The starry host of our time is whatever is considered "awesome." In the present culture consider the everyday exaltation of vacation experiences, image-making cars, status clothing, or the latest technology. The worship status of these wonder-filled things can be measured by how much money is sacrificed to them. Preoccupation with any created thing may compete for the time and financial resources that the Creator has provided and expects to be used according to the system of values laid out in the commandments given at Sinai. These values are clarified in the teachings of Jesus on covetousness (cf. Mark 10:17–22).[26]

(3) The third source of God's anger toward the prospering redeemed is the neglect of child-raising. Believers combine a reliance on God with a reliance on the back-up plan of "doing whatever it takes" to secure one's wealth or career. This is the meaning of worshiping Molech alongside Yahweh (1:5). In order to secure one's position of safety or financial security, the ultimate (and appalling) sacrifice of a child's life was offered in ancient times. In our contemporary world, through major and minor neglects, children are still being sacrificed for the sake of parents' careers and security by God's people. In some cases, the unborn are destroyed. Whenever believers engage in unethical business practices or life-denying personal habits, they rouse the wrath of God described in Zephaniah 1:9.

(4) The fourth source of God's anger toward the prospering redeemed is that they do not speak to him concerning their daily lives (1:6). In Zephaniah, God targets complacent wealthy believers (1:12–13). These are sometimes called "practical atheists." They believe in God only abstractly but live without reference to his acts. God has sought and bought the redeemed,

---

26. See J. K. Bruckner, "On the One Hand . . . On the Other Hand: The Two-Fold Meaning of the Law Against Covetousness," in *Hear and Obey: Essays in Honor of Frederick Carlson Holmgren* (Chicago: Covenant, 1997), 97–118.

not with silver or gold but with his personal intervention. When God's people live as though they have not been sought and delivered by the Creator of the universe, and when they turn away to consult with themselves as if they were their own protectors, God becomes angry. He knows they have turned toward their own destruction and his good creation is lost. They have turned to their own counsel just as Eve and Adam did in the Garden. They have returned to the original sin of reaching and taking and eating, without reference to the words of God.

God's desire for us is not that we rest and get richer in peace (1:12–13). Of course, God is not against building homes or planting vines. He is not against wealth per se or against secure houses. He is against the complacent attitudes of those who are so fortunate, especially those whom he has blessed. Because of their complacency, the Israelites' wealth was not for retirement; it was "for plunder." Their homes were not for a legacy; they were for "devastation." They built but did not dwell; they planted vines but did not drink the wine.

God has clearly told his people that he wants his law honored with the blessings of wealth. He gives security and prosperity through the intelligence, opportunities, and energies he has given us, and he cares deeply how and with what motivations they are used. But achieving financial or career success all too often turns a believer away from God rather than in thanks to him. This phenomenon is warned against in Deuteronomy 8:10–14, 17–19:

> When you have eaten and are satisfied, praise the LORD your God for the good land he has given you. Be careful that you do not forget the LORD your God, failing to observe his commands, his laws and his decrees that I am giving you this day. Otherwise, when you eat and are satisfied, when you build fine houses and settle down, and when your herds and flocks grow large and your silver and gold increase and all you have is multiplied, then your heart will become proud and you will forget the LORD your God. . . . You may say to yourself, "My power and the strength of my hands have produced this wealth for me." But remember the LORD your God, for it is he who gives you the ability to produce wealth, and so confirms his covenant, which he swore to your forefathers, as it is today.
>
> If you ever forget the LORD your God and follow other gods and worship and bow down to them, I testify against you today that you will surely be destroyed.

At first, our turning away from God in our successes begins in slight ways: forgetting to thank God or not acknowledging, even to ourselves and those closest to us, that our opportunities, talents, and daily strength come from

God. The greater our security appears to be, the more our perspective becomes warped in relation to God. The greatest practical atheists are those who act as though they are "self-made" people. We may claim to believe in God, but the word "God" is often a cipher for "*my* luck," "*my* ingenuity," "*my* hard work," "*my* security," or "*my* successes." These "false gods" that we call "God" become obvious in mentoring. When we guide others toward their success by advising them how to be made in *our own* image, our true beliefs are exposed.

Repentance. This warped view of reality and the sources of our successes may be reformed through repentance and by returning to the biblical view of wealth presented in Deuteronomy 8. (1) Wealth is dangerous, even when it is a gift from God. God knows and wants us to know how vulnerable we are to following its power instead of his. Discipline is required to keep generations from believing in its lie of security. (2) The power and strength required to attain wealth (intelligence, opportunity, and daily energy) are directly from God. We are cautioned to remember this, as should be done in daily prayer. (3) God expects that wealth will be used according to his commands. Many of the commands of Sinai concern wealth, and many of Jesus' teachings address its use. Jesus vociferously reminds the religious people of his day not to neglect the tithe and to practice justice, mercy, and faithfulness (Matt. 23:23; Luke 11:42).

In Scripture, the phrase "justice and mercy" is an expression that means helping the poor and unfortunate. Some are poor through birth, lack of opportunity, guidance, lack of intelligence, or unpredictable circumstance. As Jesus reminds us, the poor are always with us. God expects, as a matter of our allegiance to him, that we will side with them. God gives some of us more than we need so that we can participate in giving to those who have less than they need. In this unnatural and uncommon discipline, we participate in God's work.

This may also serve to keep us from becoming practical atheists. God must find it frustrating to deal constantly with people who trust in him and acknowledge him and live by his word only until he blesses them with financial success or fame. His greatest successes become his worst failures because of their success! The fact is, as Zephaniah shows, nothing makes him angrier.

Zephaniah 2

¹ Gather together, gather together,
    O shameful nation,
² before the appointed time arrives
    and that day sweeps on like chaff,
 before the fierce anger of the LORD comes upon you,
    before the day of the LORD's wrath comes upon you.
³ Seek the LORD, all you humble of the land,
    you who do what he commands.
 Seek righteousness, seek humility;
    perhaps you will be sheltered
    on the day of the LORD's anger.

⁴ Gaza will be abandoned
    and Ashkelon left in ruins.
 At midday Ashdod will be emptied
    and Ekron uprooted.
⁵ Woe to you who live by the sea,
    O Kerethite people;
 the word of the LORD is against you,
    O Canaan, land of the Philistines.

 "I will destroy you,
    and none will be left."

⁶ The land by the sea, where the Kerethites dwell,
    will be a place for shepherds and sheep pens.
⁷ It will belong to the remnant of the house of Judah;
    there they will find pasture.
 In the evening they will lie down
    in the houses of Ashkelon.
 The LORD their God will care for them;
    he will restore their fortunes.

⁸ "I have heard the insults of Moab
    and the taunts of the Ammonites,
 who insulted my people
    and made threats against their land.
⁹ Therefore, as surely as I live,"
    declares the LORD Almighty, the God of Israel,

"surely Moab will become like Sodom,
    the Ammonites like Gomorrah—
a place of weeds and salt pits,
    a wasteland forever.
The remnant of my people will plunder them,
    the survivors of my nation will inherit their land."

[10] This is what they will get in return for their pride,
    for insulting and mocking the people of the LORD
        Almighty.
[11] The LORD will be awesome to them
    when he destroys all the gods of the land.
The nations on every shore will worship him,
    every one in its own land.

[12] "You too, O Cushites,
    will be slain by my sword."

[13] He will stretch out his hand against the north
    and destroy Assyria,
leaving Nineveh utterly desolate
    and dry as the desert.
[14] Flocks and herds will lie down there,
    creatures of every kind.
The desert owl and the screech owl
    will roost on her columns.
Their calls will echo through the windows,
    rubble will be in the doorways,
    the beams of cedar will be exposed.
[15] This is the carefree city
    that lived in safety.
She said to herself,
    "I am, and there is none besides me."
What a ruin she has become,
    a lair for wild beasts!
All who pass by her scoff
    and shake their fists.

THE THEME OF chapter 2 is the cleansing of other nations from the land so that it may be possessed in the future by the humble remnant of Judah. The chapter begins with the possibility that a remnant that seeks Yahweh will survive (2:1–3) and goes on to declare that survivors will live again in the land (2:6–7, 9b, 11; see also 3:9–10, 12–13). The prophet calls on the humble and obedient to seek Yahweh, in hope of protection in the Day of the Lord's wrath.

This clearing and cleansing of the land is described in the remainder of the chapter (2:4–15). The violent "day of the LORD" (a judgment against Judah in ch. 1) is against the others living in that land in chapter 2. Gaza and the Philistine cities (2:4–7) will be completely destroyed. Moab and Ammon (across the Jordan) will be plundered and possessed for their pride and taunts (2:8–11). Ethiopia (Cush) and Assyria will be turned into wild lands (2:12–15).

This clearing of the nations from the land prepares it for a new beginning. In the midst of the emptied land we see a future with the survivors in the pastures and meadows (2:6–7). In the north will be domestic herds, wild animals, and birds (2:14). The land, its animals, and a humble remnant will be renewed by God. The hope of this chapter is whispered in the possibility of surviving the Day, but also in the vision of a new beginning. For most people, however, the Day will mean an end to life in the land, a reality the Babylonians later accomplished.

Call for a Remnant to Seek Yahweh (2:1–3)

ZEPHANIAH 2 BEGINS with a call for the humble people in the nation of Judah to seek righteousness and humility in the hope that they will be sheltered on "the day of the LORD's anger." The prophet pleads for them to "gather together, gather together, O shameful nation." English does not communicate the deeply metaphoric reference of the word translated "gather together" (*qašaš*). This word means specifically to "gather stubble." The implication is that they are stubble, good only for a fire (or a broom), but are, nonetheless, called to gather and bind themselves together. Perhaps then the Day will not "sweep" or blow them away collectively (2:2). The violent day also plays this metaphor, for although they (the gathered stubble) may form a "broom," Yahweh will do the sweeping.

Zephaniah uses the term "nation" (*goy*) for Judah, an expression that is usually used for the Gentile nations. This may reflect how far they have fallen from faithful worship of Yahweh. It is not, however, simply a chastisement. It is the beginning of Zephaniah's call to the "humble of the land" (2:3) to seek

Yahweh. The prophet's preaching is part of the call to begin, or to participate in, the reform of King Josiah (see the introduction).

Judah's shame is that they no longer "long for" Yahweh. The word "shameful" (or "shamelessness") comes from the Hebrew root *kasap*, meaning "not to
long for." Biblical "shamefulness" means "not to long for [the LORD]" and "to
long for what is not [the LORD]." That kind of shamefulness is described in
1:4–13, which can be summarized by saying that the people have stopped
longing for the Lord in worship. They have not stopped worshiping (1:4–
9), but they have stopped worshiping their Creator and Deliverer. They
have also stopped longing for Yahweh's counsel in their business decisions
(1:10–13). They have not stopped longing for things (1:13, 18), but they
have stopped longing for the Creator of things.

Verse 2 expresses the urgency of the gathering by beginning each of
three phrases with the same word, "before" (*beterem*):[1]

> before the appointed time arrives and that day *sweeps on* [*'abar*] like chaff
> before the fierce *anger* [*'ap*] of the LORD comes upon you
> before the day of the LORD's *wrath* [*'ap*] comes upon you

Three separate Hebrew words are sometimes translated "wrath" in Zephaniah (*'abar*, *'ap*, and *za'am*). Two of these words are used in 2:2.[2] The word
root *'ap* is "wrath" in the sense of anger as someone's flaring response to sin,
insult, or injustice. It has a metaphorical reference to the nose and nostrils that
flare in anger. The word root *'abar* (NIV "sweeps on") is "wrath" in the sense
of "overflowing" fury, or in the case of chaff, "bursting out" in a gust of wind.

The wrath of Yahweh must be understood in biblical narrative context.[3]
God's love for his creation and covenant people does not allow a perversion
of that creation or covenant. He warned them for two hundred years through
the prophets. He warned them through the example of the destruction of the
northern ten tribes (722 B.C.). Yahweh even brought the Assyrian army to
besiege Jerusalem, delivering them at the last moment (701 B.C.). Despite
these dramatic warnings, the people preferred their own versions and per-
versions of the creation and covenant.

Finally, God's loving anger will lead him to destroy his own temple and
send his corrupt but beloved people to Babylon for years of captivity (587–
538 B.C.). This is also an expression of his love. This is not to say that the

---

1. For the expressions "the appointed time," "that day," and "the day of the LORD," see
comments on 1:14.

2. *'abar* is translated "wrath" by the NIV in 1:15, 18. The third word (*za'am*) is translated
"wrath" and has the sense of "indignation" (see comments on 3:8).

3. See the introduction, "Jealousy and Wrath of Yahweh." Yahweh's jealousy and wrath
are mentioned in 1:18; 2:1–3; 3:6–10.

Babylonian attack will not be horrific. People will die terrible deaths on the "day of the LORD's wrath." For some in Judah's day, the warning that this day is coming is enough *not* to believe in Yahweh. Others understand the reality of his love behind the wrath, for they understand the arrogance and injustice of their society. They are humble and obedient to the Sinai law and its insistence on compassion and justice (2:3a).

These few people are the ones whom Yahweh calls to gather together to "seek the LORD" (2:3a). In this single phrase the possibility of hope is offered. Until this word is spoken, only doom is heard. After it, the unconditional doom continues in the chapter, with only a few hints of hope (2:7, 9), until 3:9. This imperative to "seek" is a call to the remnant that will be described later (3:12–13). Here they are simply called "all you humble of the land [ʾereṣ], you who do what he commands." No promise of shelter is offered from "the day," only a "perhaps" (2:3b). Nonetheless, they are called to "seek righteousness, seek humility." These biblical virtues stand in contrast to the previously described sins: a corrupt relation to God and particularly a skewed relationship to wealth (1:4–13).

Zephaniah calls on the people three times to "seek" Yahweh and his way in 2:3. This minor key remnant stands over against the people of Jerusalem described in chapter 1: "those who bow down and swear by the LORD and who also swear by Molech" (1:5), "those who turn back from following the LORD and neither seek the LORD nor inquire of him" (1:6), and "those who are complacent ... who think, 'The LORD will do nothing, either good or bad'" (1:12). Neither their silver nor their gold will be able to save them (1:18).

The humble and those who keep the commands of Yahweh are called to seek him (2:3). The duplicitous (1:5), the quietly arrogant (1:6), the half-believing complacent (1:12), and those trusting in their own success are *not* called to seek Yahweh. Even for the humble it is rather late to find shelter from the coming storm. The "humble" (ʿani) does not denote simply people with a "good attitude." In its most basic original meanings, both the English and Hebrew words meant "poor, weak, afflicted." Those who see a need for Yahweh's shelter are by definition "humble."

Against the Philistines to the Southwest (2:4–7)

ABRUPTLY, ZEPHANIAH'S FOCUS shifts from Jerusalem to the Philistines (also called Kerethites). The cities, regions, and people of Philistia are declared forfeit. Zephaniah begins the oracle of "woe" against the nations with a single quote from Yahweh, "I will destroy you, and none will be left" (2:5). A surprise is announced in verses 6–7. "Shepherds and sheep pens" will exist there after the destruction. It is the first mention of Judah's remnant in the book (see a more complete description at 3:12–13). They will live with their flocks in Philistia and receive care and provision from their God.

The transition sentence "Gaza will be abandoned" (2:4) announces a shift in focus from the potentially humble remnant (2:1–3) to the longer oracle of "woe" against Judah's many neighbors (2:5–15).[4] In these verses the day of Yahweh spreads out beyond Jerusalem and Judah to consume the "whole world" (1:18).

The cities and regions named in this judgment of woe are Judah's nearest neighbors and enemies to the immediate west and southwest, on the coast of the Mediterranean. The name "Palestine" has been derived from the word "Philistine."[5] The Philistines were part of the sea peoples who immigrated to Canaan from the Aegean area in the thirteenth century B.C. They lost their autonomy to the Davidic monarchy but retained their cultural identity along the southern coast of Palestine. Five Philistine cities formed a confederacy that was frequently in competition with and antagonistic toward Jerusalem. "Canaan" means "merchant" (see 1:11), which is a reminder that the land is on a major trade route between the east and the Mediterranean.

Gaza was a major town of the Philistines on the southern coast (Josh. 13:3; Judg. 16:1; 1 Sam. 6:17). Ashkelon is another Philistine town along the coast, fifteen miles north of Gaza (Judg. 14:19; 1 Sam. 6:17). Fifteen miles further was Ashdod (1 Sam. 5:1; 2 Chron. 26:6). Ekron was a Philistine town thirty miles north of Ashdod in the coastal plain.[6] "Kerethite" means Cretan. The Kerethites originally entered Canaan from the sea (see 2:6a) and were thought to be from Crete.[7]

The names of two of the cities and the verbs used with them form similar sounds, forming wordplays that drew attention (in Heb.) to the subject matter. "Gaza" (*ʿazzah*) and "abandoned" (*ʿazubah*) sound alike, as do "Ekron" (*ʿeqron*) and "uprooted" (*[te]ʿaqer*). "Kerethite" may be a play on the Hebrew word root *karat*, meaning "cut off" (1:3, 4, 11; 3:6, 7).

"Woe to you" begins the description of the woes that Judah's neighbors will experience (2:5–15) when the "whole world" is consumed (1:18). This woe also functions, however, as an oracle of (limited) salvation for Judah.[8]

---

4. Some publishers include 2:4 with 2:1–3 as one paragraph. The NIV uses it as an introduction to the "woe." In either case it is a transition sentence. The "for" (*ki*) in Hebrew is adversative ("but") or asseverative ("surely") and not causal ("because").

5. From "Palestine" comes the name of the land's more recent Arabic residents, the Palestinians.

6. Gath is the only major Philistine city not mentioned here.

7. They also lived in the south of Palestine. Some Cretans/Kerethites joined David's mercenary troops (see 1 Sam. 30:14; 2 Sam. 8:18; 15:18; 20:7).

8. C. Westermann, cited in Smith, *Micah–Malachi*, 135.

The survival of shepherds and sheep pens in the southern coastal plain is the first word of certain hope in Zephaniah. The previous possibility of "shelter" in 2:1–3 was conditioned by a "perhaps" (2:3b). Now, in the midst of this woe to the Philistines, surviving shepherds and sheep are mentioned. Yahweh begins again with the poor of the countryside. Sheep and sheep pens were not the height of sophistication. The remnant (described more fully in 3:12–13) will be cared for by "the LORD their God." The word "God" is used here for the first time in the book. It means they will acknowledge Yahweh as *their* God.[9]

The remnant of humble survivors "will find pasture" (2:7). This metaphor refers to people as the sheep of God (Ps. 79:13; 95:7; 100:3; Ezek. 34:31; John 10:11–16). It is an image of humility before the Creator. The sheep of God do not arrogantly seek their own way but "follow ... seek ... and inquire of him" (1:6). The remnant will find pasture and lie down in houses built in Ashkelon. The arrogant of Judah built houses but did not live in them (1:13). Now Yahweh will provide houses built by another arrogant people. It means the humble remnant will daily understand that their homes are gifts provided to be enjoyed with reference to God and not enhancements of their own power. The remnant will relax and "lie down" to eat. God "will care for them; he will restore their fortunes" (2:7b).

Against Moab and Ammon to the East (2:8–11)

IN VERSES 8–9 Zephaniah turns his attention to Judah's traditionally antagonistic "cousins" on the east side of the Jordan River. Yahweh speaks directly, this time against the Moabites and Ammonites, who have insulted and threatened Judah with violence; he will make them like Sodom and Gomorrah. He mentions "the remnant" for a second time as "survivors ... [who] will inherit their land (2:9; the remnant is described at 3:12–13). Zephaniah declares a surprising secondary result with a broader hope: "Nations on every shore will worship him" (2:10–11).

Moabites and Ammonites were cousins to the Israelites through Abraham's nephew Lot and his daughters (Gen. 19:37–38). Yahweh had given them the territory east of the Jordan and protected them against Israel's expansion because of special familial relationships: Edom was protected because of Esau, and Moab and Ammon because of Lot (Deut. 2:8–9, 19). But the hundreds of years of history between these nations were filled with hostility (Num. 22:1–6; Judg. 3:12–14; 2 Sam. 10:1–4; 1 Kings 11:7–8). Judah was not permitted to attack them, but here God will use another nation to chastise them for their arrogant attacks on his beloved people.

---

9. The name *ʾelohim* occurs four times in Zephaniah: 2:7, 9; 3:2, 17.

The jealousy of "the LORD Almighty [*seba°ot*]"[10] surfaces again in reference to "my people" (2:8) and "my nation" (2:9). Zephaniah echoes his jealous commitment in a corresponding phrase, "the people of the LORD Almighty" (2:10). The crimes of Moab and Ammon are the cause. The God of Israel swears his ultimate oath in 2:9: "Therefore, as surely as I live." This name of God and this oath express Yahweh's passion for his unique people. Yahweh is the Creator and Master of all creation, not simply some local god. He is also the specific Creator of the sociality and uniqueness of Israel, whom he created to be a blessing (Gen. 12:1–3; 22:17–18), through his unique intervention in the Exodus, in giving the laws of Sinai, and by forming the people around that law in the desert. God further formed Israel by fighting for them in the conquest of the land of Canaan and in continuing to discipline them as a nation through their enemies and through prophets calling them to remain faithful in lifestyle and worship.

Judah belongs to "the LORD Almighty," and Yahweh declares that he will punish the neighboring people because of "insults ... taunts ... and ... threats" against God's people (2:8), summed up as "their pride" (2:10), even though his own people are so sinful that God himself has decided to destroy them. An insult or threat against God's chosen amounts to an insult and threat against God's integrity (the significance of "as surely as I live" in 2:9). These previously protected cousins will suffer the fate of Sodom and Gomorrah, notorious for their arrogance toward Yahweh and violence against visitors (Gen. 18–19). Through God's judgment of fire they became a place of "weeds and salt pits" as a warning against such sins. Like Moab and Ammon, they were on the east side of the Jordan.

The "remnant" is mentioned again in 2:9 (see 2:7; 3:12–13). They will scavenge the depopulated east bank, but the ancient reader would not have missed the caution against arrogance in the word "survivor": "The survivors of my nation will inherit their land" (2:9b). Judah will be destroyed and plundered as well. Only the humble remnant will survive. The reversal of fortune here is not simply that the people will inherit their enemies' lands. Rather, the proud of *every* nation, *including* Israel, will be plundered and dispossessed. The humble will inherit the land of the proud.

Verses 10–11 may be the most revealing expression of both Yahweh's complaint and desire for the nations. After reading verse 10 in this prophecy of doom, the listener would expect to hear another description of physical devastation and death (as in 1:9). Instead, Zephaniah speaks this amazing revelation: In place of pride, Yahweh will be "awesome to them," and "the nations

---

10. Sabaoth (common spelling for *seba°ot*) means of "hosts," a reference to the angelic hosts as well as the hosts of heaven or stars.

on every shore" will bow down in worship before the Creator "LORD Almighty." Yahweh's desire is not simply to eradicate arrogance but to replace it with true worship in every land. This theme is not developed in Zephaniah's short prophecy but is implied again in the final verse of the book (3:20, "honor and praise among all the peoples of the earth"). This larger goal waits in the background as Yahweh seeks first to establish a single people who will demonstrate faithfulness to him in every circumstance through many generations.

The destruction of "all the gods of the land" means the lands immediately to the east and west of the Jordan River, including Israel, the Philistine coast, Moab, and Ammon. The gods were the local symbols of security and power. The word for "destroy" (*razah*) means "famish" or "make lean." Through the Babylonians, Yahweh will make them thin, wasting away for lack of food. Babylonian practice was to take the gods of the people and put them in a kind of museum in Babylon, a symbol that these gods needed the care of their protectors, the Babylonians. The god of a defeated people was considered a weak god or no god at all.[11]

When Zephaniah speaks the surprisingly hopeful words, "nations on every shore will worship him, every one in its own land," he is not speaking of their "serving the LORD" (*cabad*). He used the Hebrew verb that means "bow down." That is, the nations will be so amazed by what God has done that they will prostrate themselves in recognition that Israel's God is superior to their defeated gods. Although this is not "conversion" in the fullest sense, it is a beginning of recognition in history that the Lord of Israel is not a "god of the land" (2:11), but the "Almighty" Creator of all that is, one day to be recognized by "nations on every shore."

Against Enemies to the North and South (2:12–15)

YAHWEH SPEAKS A single verse against Cush (Ethiopia) in 2:12. The "day of the LORD" will spread to the extreme southwest and to the political power of the extreme northeast (Nineveh)—the two extremes of the Fertile Crescent. The slaying of the Cushites is accomplished directly and personally by Yahweh ("my sword"). Cush is the edge of ancient Israel's "whole world" (1:18). Northeast Africa was a refuge for the peoples of Canaan during famine and a source of military power (it is mentioned again in 3:10). Worshipers will come from there (cf. 2:11).

Zephaniah then describes in greater detail Yahweh's hand stretching to the north to destroy Assyria (2:13–15). Assyrian power and cruelty were

---

11. The challenge of Isaiah's preaching to the exiles was for them to see their God's creating hand in creation, even as captives without a country or temple (see Isa. 40:12–31; 42:5–17).

legendary. No one could imagine the defeat that came swiftly in 612 B.C. at the hands of the Babylonians and Medes (see the introduction to Nahum). Nineveh will become "utterly desolate and dry as the desert" (2:13b). This desolation is masterfully described in both negative and positive ways in 2:14. Positively, when destroyed, Nineveh will becomes a home for all kinds of Yahweh's creatures. Negatively, it is dismantled as a human habitation. The "utterly desolate" refers especially to a deserted human habitation. No one will live there.

Zephaniah begins his figurative description at the top with the columns, where birds will roost. He moves down to the windows, where birds will call, and to the doorways, where rubble rests. Finally, the plaster falls off the cedar beams (plundered from the "cedars of Lebanon"), leaving their created glory visible. Only what is of Yahweh will remain.

The city will become a "ruin" of human habitation but a home for the animals. "Dry as the desert" does not mean uninhabitable for any life. The word for "desert" (*midbar*, sometimes translated "wilderness") means the semi-arid lands surrounding towns that were used seasonally for livestock (see 2:14). "Flocks and herds will lie down there, creatures of every kind. The desert owl and the screech owl will roost on her columns.... What a ruin she has become, a lair for wild beasts" (2:14, 15b). This proud place will become a home for a more humble creation. The place will not be inhospitable to all life, but only to people who were consumed with their own glory and arrogance.

Carefree safety can be good news or bad news (2:15a). "This is the carefree city that lived in safety. She said to herself, 'I am, and there is none besides me.'" Being "carefree" (*ʿallizah*) is good, meaning "jubilant." "Safety" (*beṭaḥ*) is also a simple good, meaning that she lived "trustingly." The second half of verse 15a, however, presents the bad news. Nineveh's jubilation and trust are in herself (lit., "in her own heart"). Trust in self was Zephaniah's indictment against Jerusalem as well (3:2). Nineveh's carefree safety was based in arrogance. Zephaniah declares these self-congratulations will be forfeited.

Bridging Contexts

GOD GIVES TWO responses in chapter 2 that correspond to two general human attitudes. The first, the more predominant one, is Yahweh's total opposition to human arrogance. The second response is heard as a whisper in 2:3, 11b, where God calls for the possibility of humility and obedient living from Judah and the surrounding cultures. The attitudes of human humility and arrogance and God's responses to them are as old as Genesis 2–3 and will endure until the end of time.

God's response to arrogance: total opposition. Yahweh is fiercely opposed to false pride (2:1b, 10, 15). From Eve and Adam's reaching to take what belonged only to God to the final arrogance of the nations in Revelation, the biblical witness declares that God is totally opposed to arrogance.

He speaks against the pride of "shameful" or "shameless" Judah (2:1–2) by comparing it to straw that is easily burned (Ex. 15:7; Isa. 5:24; 47:14; Joel 2:5) and chaff that is easily blown away (see comments on 2:1). These are common metaphors for what is worthless after the harvest. As grain grows, the stalk is an integral and necessary part of the plant. At the end of the life of the stalk of grain, however, it is separated from the grain proper and becomes worthless.

God's words against the cultures to Judah's north, south, east, and southwest are a result of their arrogance and taunts (2:8, 15). Assyria said to herself, for example, "*I am, and there is none besides me*" (2:15; cf. Isa. 45:5, 14, 18, 21). This is understood as blasphemy, since "I am" is the name of Yahweh spoken to Moses at Sinai (and claimed by Yahweh in Isa. 45:5–6).[12]

God's angry response to self-aggrandizing and self-promoting arrogance is summed up in the phrase, "the word of the LORD is against you" (2:5b). Self-pride is common to all humanity. It is known as the "original" sin of Eve and Adam—reaching up to take and eat the fruit in order to become wise like God (Gen. 3:5–6). A classic text of the Reformation reminds us of the ongoing struggle of God to reach human hearts so that we may learn to love the One who made us and can redeem us:

> The human heart either despises the judgment of God in its smugness, or in the midst of punishment it flees and hates his judgment. So it does not obey the first [of the Ten Commandments]. It is inherent in man to despise God and to doubt his Word with its threats and promises.[13]

Arrogance toward God stems from our natural tendency toward pride. It is the kind of pride that has become so much a part of a person's or society's life that it is assumed to be normal and healthy. This pride is "false" because it exists without a true reference to God, from whom come all power and strength. Conversely, a "true" pride does not lead to arrogance because it is, in every time and every place, related to the true Source of life. All people, regardless of weakness as the world measures it, may have true pride by their praise of the Creator, who gives whatever strength we have (cf. 2 Cor. 12:8–10).

---

12. When Jesus says the same thing, he is accused of blasphemy in John 8:58.

13. "Apology of the Augsburg Confession" in *The Book of Concord*, trans. and ed. by T. G. Tappert (Philadelphia: Fortress, 1959), 112.

God's use of nature and history. God uses natural means to oppose pride and arrogance in the world. The earliest example of his anger, experienced in a firestorm from the sky (falling comets or asteroids?), was the destruction of Sodom and Gomorrah.[14] Their destruction became a primary model for understanding how God works against arrogance in the world (Isa. 1:9; Jer. 50:40; Amos 4:10–11).[15]

God used storms and earthquakes, rivers and wind, the sun and wild animals, fire-fall and plagues to accomplish his purposes in opposing the arrogant. In the destruction of the northern ten tribes (by Assyria) and the fall of Jerusalem (to Babylon), he also declared by his prophets that these warring nations were a part of the creation. As God used nonhuman creation, so he also employed these violent warring nations to oppose his arrogant people. They were part of the natural created order used to curtail the falsely proud, both among his people and among the nations.

In Zephaniah the historical and the natural merge as simultaneous agents of God. The historical arrogance of nations is like a natural force in the world.[16] God acts against the land of the Philistines with a human army (2:4–5). The Cushites are killed with real swords (2:12). Assyria is destroyed by the Medes and Babylonians in 612 B.C., who are God's "servants" (Jer. 25:10–11). Yet he subsequently destroys the Babylonian army in 539 B.C. by the Persian army, which is also his servant (Jer. 25:12; Dan. 5:31). One commentator rightly notes that "the Day of the LORD is not an arbitrary infliction but coincides with the horrific climax of human mismanagement of world affairs."[17] The end of the world as we know it may begin in the same way. The forces of arrogant nations and the force of the atom irresponsibly employed will certainly lead to a gruesome end of humans, animals, birds, and fish.[18]

Whispers of hope of a new relationship. God's response to humility is a surprisingly positive note in the midst of this oracle of doom. After announcing the total destruction of the land, Yahweh suggests the possibility that he will leave a blessing and the hope of a renewed land, animals, and the remnant of his people. As in Joel 2:3, complete annihilation is followed by the slight possibility of renewed blessing (Joel 2:12–14).[19]

The core of hope for God's people is not in individual survival techniques but in gathering together in humility and worship. "Gather together . . .

---

14. Motyer, "Zephaniah," 3:934.

15. Yahweh's use of his own creation does not blunt his agency in destroying the arrogant.

16. God's actions are "firmly bedded in the historical process" (Motyer, "Zephaniah," 3:938).

17. Ibid., 3:938.

18. Noted in 1:2–3; cf. Achtemeier, *Nahum–Malachi*, 65.

19. Roberts, *Nahum, Habakkuk, and Zephaniah*, 189.

before the appointed time arrives and that day sweeps on like chaff" (2:1a, 2a). The images of the gathering and the sweeping away of the chaff imply that grain will fall into the keeper on the threshing floor. Grain is beaten and exposed to the wind for the purpose of gathering the grain. It settles and stays while the chaff blows away. This familiar image in the ancient agrarian world is difficult to apply to our time. In trial and tribulation the faith of the faithful is proven. The implied question is whether the faithful will be prepared to endure the beating, suffering, and dying that they will surely face when the society is punished by the attacking (Babylonian) army.[20] Will they be faithful even in their dying and be proven as true grain, or will they be blown away by the wind as inconsequential?

Additional whispers of hope are offered to the few who will survive and whose children will return (in 538 B.C.) to the land (2:7, 9, 14; see Contemporary Significance section). For those who will experience the devastating attack, however, the difference between the "grain" and the "chaff" is found in the test of their humility before God.

Like pride, humility may be true or it may be a "false" humility. True humility is present when a society or a person recognizes that the goodness of his or her life is a gift of grace from God. True humility also recognizes that unavoidable hardship may be borne by means of God's sustaining strength. False humility retreats from God's justice. It is present in enabling violent persons to prosper by capitulating to them when God's justice opposes them. It is also present in those refusing to use the gifts and strength, however limited, that God gives (like burying a talent in the sand, Matt. 25:18). God calls for humility before him, not humility before evil. True humility recognizes God's gifts and uses them to work for his kingdom.

Yahweh also mentions a positive future hope for the surrounding cultures ("nations") of the world. In the midst of describing the nations' destruction, a half verse of hope is offered before the oracle of doom continues: "The nations on every shore will worship him, every one in its own land" (2:11b).

Several important cues help the reader understand God's positive response to the nations in this chapter (even if they are only briefly positive).[21] These hints of God's grace may be better understood from the broader perspective of Scripture. God created these cultures, and they are loved as his creation (Gen. 9:18–10:32; Isa. 19:25). God's intention is to bring blessing to these cultures (Gen. 12:1–3; 22:17–18). The literary form of Zephaniah 2:5–15 is a lament over their destruction (the "woe" in 2:5 signals a lamenting or

---

20. The suffering they did endure is described in detail in the poetry of Lamentations. Jeremiah's faithful response in the midst of horrific suffering may be found in Lam. 3:18–26.
21. Robert Bennett, "The Book of Zephaniah" (*NIB*; Nashville: Abingdon, 1996), 7:692.

grieving of death). The short mention of the Cushites may also show us the prophet's personal grief, since his father ("Cushi" in 1:1) was likely part-Ethiopian (perhaps named so by an Ethiopian mother). Note that Cush had been his great, great grandfather Hezekiah's ally during his reign (Isa. 18:1).[22]

This half-verse concerning worship by the nations (2:11b) is a beacon of hope for the world. It is an enduring vision of hope for all the peoples of the world that is expanded in chapter 3 (see comments on 3:9, 20b). Yahweh will not only eradicate arrogance but will replace it with the true worship of people from every land (cf. Ps. 47:2; Isa. 19:21–25; 45:23). This theme endures in the New Testament in light of the resurrected Christ (Rom. 14:11; Phil. 2:10; Rev. 7:9–12). Yahweh's purpose is to establish a diverse human creation that is unified in true humility and worship of the Creator and Redeemer of the world.

Crossing over from the false to the true. How do God's people move from false pride and arrogance to true pride in the works of Yahweh? How do they move from a false humility that avoids participating in the purposes of God in the world to a true humility that engages God's gifts and accepts the accompanying hardships? The word describing this movement in chapter 2 is that the Day "sweeps on" (2:2). The original word (ʿabar) also means "crosses over." In the "sweeping" Yahweh causes the "crossing over" from the false to the true. The concept indicates a dramatic conversion.

When water flows over shallow and wide places in a river, it creates a ford (a crossing place). There the river can be "passed" (or crossed) safely (the root is used in this sense at 3:10). This means too that everything in the water can be seen easily. This image serves as a metaphor for the times in Israel's history when judgment was brought by Yahweh on unjust society. Everything passed close to the surface and was exposed at the place of the "passing over" (the same word is also translated "wrath"). A ford is also the place were trouble may come while crossing. It is the place in Scripture (and in Western movies) where boundaries are most heavily defended, since people are most vulnerable when crossing water (Josh. 2:23). The biblical image of crossing over is central to "crossing the Jordan River" into a new and promised land (Josh. 1:11; 3:14, 17). God's favor is needed especially there.

In the midst of sweeping away what is false, God prepares a new landing beyond the crossing for his faithful. Even in the midst of societal or personal disruptions, God has a word of hope for those who turn to him. At the end of life as well, Scripture insists that God has prepared a place to which his own may cross over. He is preparing a new earth with new heavens, where righteousness will rule.

---

22. Ibid., 7:692.

GOD'S OPPOSITION TO arrogance is clear. Any arrogant nation or culture of the world can and should take to heart Yahweh's words, "The word of the LORD is against you, O Canaan, land of the Philistines. 'I will destroy you, and none will be left.'" (2:5). The whole known world, from Nineveh to Ethiopia, was included in Zephaniah 2. As contemporary readers, we are invited by the text to think in comprehensive and global terms.

Yahweh's opposition to the arrogant has the purpose of (eventually) bringing hope. The thin signs of hope in the midst of God's strong language against arrogance hinge on four themes: a simple description of the mysterious remnant, a call to "seek the LORD," a test of faith in God's "perhaps," and promises for the future. God is still soundly against arrogance, but he calls us to seek him and to live by faith in the face of our own uncertain future. The surviving remnant is promised the provision of pasture, land inheritance, and the peace that comes with wild lands for animals. These thin hopes are "the central announcement of the book."[23] The one hope of salvation is to remove our self-reliance and pride and cast ourselves on the mercy of God. Perhaps we may also be part of a future faithful remnant.

Humble and obedient. The mysterious "remnant" are the "humble" (2:3; 3:12) who "do what he commands" (2:3). It is these meek ones who will inherit the earth (Zeph. 2:9b; Matt. 5:5). God's faithfulness to the humble assures their survival beyond the violence of the arrogant.

Humility is an attribute of the Bible's greatest figures. Moses, who talked with God in the "Tent of Meeting," was known as the most humble man who lived (Num. 12:3). His humility was in relation to those he led toward God. When God shaped his people through difficult times in the desert, he was seeking to create in their midst the excellence of humility in relationships (Deut. 8:2, 16). The healing of societies and communities comes through humbling ourselves before God (2 Chron. 7:14).

Biblical humility is not, however, simply a life of personal religious devotion. The purpose of humility is societal justice and service toward those in need. Humility is relational and brings saving help, such as Moses' helping his community to resolve their disputes by administering justice (Ex. 18:13–18). The great hymn of Christ's humility calls us to have a similar attitude, looking to serve the needs of others (Phil. 2:3–8). Christ did not cling to his equality with God but became a servant in human form. He humbled himself, obediently submitting to death on a cross for our sake. His humility

---

23. Achtemeier, *Nahum–Malachi*, 74.

was not abstract but led to the salvation of those in need. He even allowed himself to be deprived of justice in order to help us (Act 8:33). He calls us to walk with him in the miraculous "rest" of this kind of humility (Matt. 11:29).

The humble also show themselves to be "needy" in relation to God, acknowledging him in worship and obedience to his laws. They "do what he commands" (2:3). For Christians this means keeping Christ's law of love (John 13:34) and the basic Ten Commandments, endorsed as a baseline of behavior by Jesus (Matt. 19:17–19; Mark 10:17–19; Luke 18:18–20).[24] They do what God commands.

Seeking Yahweh when the word is against you. The word of the prophet is against the sin that has taken root in the lives of God's community of faith. Yahweh calls them to "seek" him, even though his word of judgment is against them and will surely result in destruction. Such is the case for all of God's faithful—and for all humanity. Those who seek Yahweh even when his prophecies are against them demonstrate that they are "grain" and not "chaff." This kind of seeking is called "the ethics of anticipation."[25] Our lives are present witnesses to what God will eventually bring to the world in the new creation.

This is sometimes called "proleptic eschatology," which means that the reality of the future is experienced and practiced before the future arrives (*proleptic* means "beforehand" or "anticipated"; *eschatology* is the study of the last things). We live now by the power of the risen Christ and his Spirit, as though the new creation were already here. We know that we will die, but we live knowing that we will be changed and be raised to new life. We know that our temptations to sin continue, but we live in the freedom of Christ's power over sin and forgiveness. We know that the enemy seeks to destroy our faith, but we live in the knowledge that he is defeated in Jesus' innocent suffering and death on the cross and his victory in the resurrection.

The judgment against Judah at the beginning of Zephaniah was that they did not seek Yahweh in their prosperity (1:6). How much more difficult it is to seek Yahweh when the word is against you! The remnant of the faithful is always small in times of persecution. In the days of oppression in the Soviet Union, faithful Christians were few and far between. Professing faith meant an end to opportunities for jobs and minimized educational opportunities for one's children. That kind of sacrifice is too much for most people to endure.

---

24. For the variety of Christian uses of the 613 Old Testament laws see J. K. Bruckner, "Ethics," in *Dictionary of the Old Testament: Pentateuch*, ed. David W. Baker (Downers Grove, Ill.: InterVarsity Press, 2002).

25. Brown, *Obadiah Through Malachi*, 108.

If we could imagine the grace and faith we would need in oppressive economic circumstances, we might be less cavalier about seeking Yahweh and serving others for his sake in prosperous times.

Amos dramatically sets prosperity and destruction side by side in his warning to prosperous people who think they are worshiping Yahweh. They act as though they do not know that their prospering business practices and worship of God are not related (Amos 8:3–7). Seeking Yahweh is more than Sunday worship. It means seeking him in every aspect of behavior, business, and relationships. Micah shines the spotlight on the same bifurcated piety in Judah (Mic. 6:6–13). In this context God does not call the prosperous to seek him through extravagant *religious* acts, but to seek him humbly through *economic justice and mercy* toward those who have little: "He has showed you, O man, what is good. And what does the LORD require of you? To act justly and to love mercy and to walk humbly with your God" (Mic. 6:8).

In 1 Corinthians 1:26–31, Paul likewise develops the theme of seeking Yahweh when his word is against you.[26] The gospel of Christ is first a word against us: against our presumed righteousness, holiness, and autonomy. Our culture's pride in independence and self-sufficiency is challenged by the claim that all we have is from God, fully revealed in Christ. He nullifies all autonomous claims to power. "He chose the lowly things of this world and the despised things—and the things that are not—to nullify the things that are, so that no one may boast before him" (1:28–29). Christ Jesus has become our wisdom, our righteousness, our holiness and redemption. So Paul admonishes us, "Let him who boasts, boast in the LORD" (1:31). In this way, we may seek him in great hope and expectation, even when world events turn against our cultural pride.

Living with "perhaps." Almost everyone wants to be a "survivor" or thinks that they will survive the challenges they may face. Almost everyone wants to be included in the humble obedient remnant who will survive, even in the Day of the Lord. The present "test" as to whether we will be able to survive is given in what we do with the words "perhaps you will be sheltered" (2:3b). The message of the whole book of Zephaniah hangs on the "perhaps." The prophet asks us to trust that the "perhaps" of God is surer than any security the world has to offer. With the total destruction of their society in view and no other hope beyond "perhaps," Zephaniah urges the people to gather together to seek Yahweh (2:1–2). "Perhaps" is what the Ninevites thought about their salvation when God's message to them was only destruction (Jonah 3:9, "Who knows?"; cf. Amos 5:15 and a statement contemporary to Zephaniah in Jer. 26:1–3).

---

26. Cf. Achtemeier, *Nahum-Malachi*, 76. Also see Matt. 5:1–12.

Where else may we turn than to Yahweh? If we are among those who believe that this world will end in destruction and that Yahweh is just in his wrath and judgment against an arrogant world, to what hope will we cling? Those who sought Yahweh in Zephaniah's day were able to cling in faith to the "perhaps" of God. In the disciples' witness to the death and resurrection of Jesus, we have more than a "perhaps." We have the face of God dying in love for us and rising to new life, the firstborn of the new creation. Yet the struggle of faith to believe the witnesses around us, the conflicting voices of our culture, and suffering in the world sometimes reduce even a Christian's confidence to "perhaps." When the judgment of war on a world scale begins, no individual is guaranteed shelter from physical suffering and death. Resilient faith is faith that clings to God even when the surety of hope is elusive.

Zephaniah preaches this possibility. He calls us to recognize that when we "gather together," we open ourselves to the possibility that that Lord will shelter us. Even if our faith is only as strong as believing in "perhaps," we may cling to him. Jesus' disciples were confused and challenged one day when the crowds turned and walked away. Jesus had asked them to believe something they could not possibly understand about eating his flesh. When Jesus asked the disciples if they too would leave him, they said, "To whom shall we go? You have the words of eternal life" (John 6:51–68).

Faith is resilient faith when it believes, not just in difficult times but especially in impossible times. Faith is resilient when it believes not simply what is hard to believe, but what seems unbelievable. Resilient faith believes not only in living, but in suffering and dying. That is Zephaniah's legacy, made explicit in the cross. Christ completes the divine order by turning the judgment of the cross to the blessing of new life and resurrection. The "perhaps" of the prophets has become the promise of Christ's presence.

Three promises of provision. Yahweh says he will provide for the humble and obedient remnant who seek him. Each provision involves a renewed and peaceful earth. It includes a place to live, abundant pasture for domestic flocks, and the peace that comes with wild lands for animals.

(1) God gives a place to live (2:7b, 9b). The "humble" are those who see their need for Yahweh's shelter. The power to own a house or land is a gift from God. God will take homes away from the arrogant who build them (1:13) and give them to the humble when the arrogant are destroyed. The wisdom gained by God's people after the Exile is that prosperity clouds a person's (and a society's) perceptions about the source of prosperity. To make matters worse, the prosperous, while confused about the source of wealth, think they see things more clearly. The humble inherit the land of the arrogant. The meek shall inherit the earth.

(2) Abundant pasture for domestic flocks (2:6–7a) is a picture of the blessing of domestic order and release from bondage. "He will restore their fortunes" (2:7) means that God will return his troubled remnant to their former security.[27] The emphasis in Zephaniah is not on "fortune" (as in great wealth) but on a restoration of the general order of life and strength after suffering loss in captivity. The key image is his picture of people as sheep being guided by God to lie down in good pastures after being scattered, as in the well-known psalm, "He makes me lie down in green pastures. . . . He restores my soul" (Ps. 23:2–3). The humble who seek him will find release from their bondage and be renewed according to the order God intends for his good creation. The image of abundant pasture for domestic flocks implies this double blessing.

(3) Yahweh also provides the peace that is available to us when we live near wild lands set aside for animals (2:13b–14). The natural environment endures as a witness to God's glory beyond human arrogance. The land and all nonhuman life in it are a witness to the Creator just by their existence as a pure creation. Only human creation rebels against God. Without humanity the creation is clean and a witness to the glory of God (Ps. 19:1–4a; cf. Job 38–41). The created environment does not indefinitely support sinful societies' rebellion against the creation (Isa. 5:5; 24:16–23). There are always environmental consequences to sin (Gen. 3:17–19; Lev. 26:21–22). "Creation always sides with its Creator against the rebel."[28] In Zephaniah the consequences are dramatic (1:2–3; 2:13b–14).

The provision of wild lands around Nineveh may not seem at first to be a gift to the remnant (2:13b–14). It could be understood only as the absence of the violent enemy, Assyria. The remaining emptiness of the land, however, is a gift. It means that armies will no longer threaten the remnant from that direction.

The presence of the open land also gathers the positive biblical attitude toward "desert." The biblical word "desert" does not mean sand dunes. It is more accurately translated "wilderness" (*midbar*). It is a place for herds to live contentedly (2:14) and for wild animals to live undisturbed by humanity. The so-called "desert" is a place where God can be encountered and heard more clearly. Israel was formed by God in the wilderness. It is a place where the temptations to uncritiqued wealth and comfort may be confronted. Elijah and John the Baptist lived there, and Jesus retreated there to pray. Hosea

---

27. The expression "restore their fortunes" is widely debated. Lit., it means "return captivity," but it has a broader sense of restoring former societal order (see Smith, *Micah-Malachi*, 136).

28. Motyer, "Zephaniah," 3:937.

prophesied that God's people would be renewed there (Hos. 2:14–15). God provides open lands for animals without people as part of his blessing of the remnant, for he knows they are essential to the life of the society.

These promises of provision are given as a future hope to a people under judgment. Hoping in this future is based on the word "perhaps," the test of faith. This is the word *against* us that is also *for* us. It calls us to live by faith in the mercies of God that we now enjoy, and it challenges us to consider our own sins of arrogance. It calls us to live with confidence in his good purpose for us, expressed most fully in the innocent and righteous death of Jesus. Though our sin has marred God's good creation, God calls us to live in hope of the new creation, even as we honor him in our use of this one. Living daily within the righteousness of Christ, we should have no room for arrogance or boasting, only humility and confession of his mercy.

Zephaniah 3

¹ Woe to the city of oppressors,
   rebellious and defiled!
² She obeys no one,
   she accepts no correction.
 She does not trust in the LORD,
   she does not draw near to her God.
³ Her officials are roaring lions,
   her rulers are evening wolves,
   who leave nothing for the morning.
⁴ Her prophets are arrogant;
   they are treacherous men.
 Her priests profane the sanctuary
   and do violence to the law.
⁵ The LORD within her is righteous;
   he does no wrong.
 Morning by morning he dispenses his justice,
   and every new day he does not fail,
   yet the unrighteous know no shame.

⁶ "I have cut off nations;
   their strongholds are demolished.
 I have left their street deserted,
   with no one passing through.
 Their cities are destroyed;
   no one will be left—no one at all.
⁷ I said to the city,
   'Surely you will fear me
   and accept correction!'
 Then her dwelling would not be cut off,
   nor all my punishments come upon her.
 But they were still eager
   to act corruptly in all they did.
⁸ Therefore wait for me," declares the LORD,
   "for the day I will stand up to testify.
 I have decided to assemble the nations,
   to gather the kingdoms
 and to pour out my wrath on them—
   all my fierce anger.

The whole world will be consumed
>by the fire of my jealous anger.

⁹ "Then will I purify the lips of the peoples,
>that all of them may call on the name of the LORD
>and serve him shoulder to shoulder.
¹⁰ From beyond the rivers of Cush
>my worshipers, my scattered people,
>will bring me offerings.
¹¹ On that day you will not be put to shame
>for all the wrongs you have done to me,
because I will remove from this city
>those who rejoice in their pride.
Never again will you be haughty
>on my holy hill.
¹² But I will leave within you
>the meek and humble,
>who trust in the name of the LORD.
¹³ The remnant of Israel will do no wrong;
>they will speak no lies,
>nor will deceit be found in their mouths.
They will eat and lie down
>and no one will make them afraid."

¹⁴ Sing, O Daughter of Zion;
>shout aloud, O Israel!
Be glad and rejoice with all your heart,
>O Daughter of Jerusalem!
¹⁵ The LORD has taken away your punishment,
>he has turned back your enemy.
The LORD, the King of Israel, is with you;
>never again will you fear any harm.
¹⁶ On that day they will say to Jerusalem,
>"Do not fear, O Zion;
>do not let your hands hang limp.
¹⁷ The LORD your God is with you,
>he is mighty to save.
He will take great delight in you,
>he will quiet you with his love,
>he will rejoice over you with singing."

¹⁸ "The sorrows for the appointed feasts
>I will remove from you;
>they are a burden and a reproach to you.

> [19] At that time I will deal
>>   with all who oppressed you;
> I will rescue the lame
>>   and gather those who have been scattered.
> I will give them praise and honor
>>   in every land where they were put to shame.
> [20] At that time I will gather you;
>>   at that time I will bring you home.
> I will give you honor and praise
>>   among all the peoples of the earth
> when I restore your fortunes
>>   before your very eyes,"
>
> says the LORD.

IN VERSE 1 the focus abruptly shifts from the nations back to Jerusalem, summarizing and expanding the themes of destruction and survival. This chapter begins with Jerusalem's judgment (3:1–8) and ends with her joy (3:9–20). The central verses (3:8–9) form a bridge, verse 8 speaking judgment and verse 9 announcing joy's beginning.[1]

The judgment of Jerusalem is divided into two parts. (1) The city's sins of arrogance and corruption are described (3:1–5), sins that are against both God and people. The sins continue, although Yahweh has been faithful. (2) Yahweh describes the futile warnings he has given (3:6–8), but Jerusalem will not accept correction; "therefore . . . the whole world will be consumed."

The joy of Jerusalem (3:9–20) may also be read in two parts. (1) In 3:9–13 God makes promises for the remnant. He will establish those who trust in his name in purity, humility, and safety. (2) The last verses (3:14–20) describe part of the day of joy in Jerusalem. They will sing in security because Yahweh will be near to them. Speaking directly ("I . . . you"), Yahweh makes seven direct promises to those who trust in his name.

This chapter contains many changes in voice. The subject of the verb shifts between "the LORD" and "I" (God speaking in the first person).[2] The object of the verb also abruptly shifts. Verses 1–10 are words of judgment spoken to the entire city of Jerusalem in the third person ("them"). Verses 11–20

---

1. Most translators divide the two sections between verses 7 and 8 at "therefore." I have divided it in the middle of the bridge, between verses 8 and 9, dividing the judgment ("consumed by fire") from the promise introduced by "then will I purify."

2. "The LORD" is a third person subject in 3:1–5, 14–17 and a first person subject in 3:6–10, 11–13, 18–20.

are a word of hope spoken to the remnant ("you"). This combination of the "I" and the "you" makes the last half of the last chapter of Zephaniah powerfully personal for the community of faith.

The City of Arrogance and Corruption (3:1–5)

AFTER THE WOE against Jerusalem's neighbors (2:5–15), Zephaniah's second "woe" is against Jerusalem. The change in subject from Assyria to Jerusalem is unannounced. It begins ambiguously, "Woe to the city of oppressors" and continues with a description of arrogance, "She obeys no one, she accepts no correction" (3:2). The original listener may have been confused as chapter 3 begins. Which city? The obvious first response might be "Nineveh" or one of the cities of the other nations mentioned in chapter 2. Slowly the city is revealed by implication, as Jerusalem and the listener are caught in the descriptive judgment. In this masterful way the reader is drawn into the "woe." Jerusalem is gradually recognized by the phrases: "does not trust in the LORD," "her God" (3:2), and "the LORD within her" (3:5). Everything else mentioned in these verses could have referred to Nineveh, and the comparison is not flattering.

The prophet presents Jerusalem's twelve sins in a list (3:1–4):

1. oppressors
2. rebellious
3. defiled
4. she obeys no one
5. she accepts no correction
6. she does not trust in the LORD
7. she does not draw near to her God
8. her officials are roaring lions
9. her rulers are evening wolves, who leave nothing for the morning
10. her prophets are arrogant; they are treacherous men
11. her priests profane the sanctuary
12. her priests do violence to the law

The first seven sins are sins against God. "Oppression" results in sin against the poor, but God always claims this as a personal offense (Ex. 22:21–27). These believers are also obstinate in their rebellion (Deut. 21:18; Ps. 78:8) and defiled by mixing worship of the Creator with the worship of created things (Isa. 59:3; Mal. 1:7; Neh. 7:64). Like Nineveh, "she obeys no one" (2:15), including the commands given at Mount Sinai. When God gives discipline and wisdom to correct their path, Jerusalem refuses it (Deut. 11:2–7; Prov. 1:2, 7; 15:33; 23:23). Not trusting in Yahweh meant that they trust in other things for their security and safety. As a result, they are not inclined to "draw near" in worship (Deut. 5:24–27).

The eighth and ninth sins are directed against the population. Her officials are roaring lions, like the Ninevites (see Nah. 2:11). "Officials" (*śarim*) is the same word translated "princes" in 1:8—a reference to those who govern and administrate (taxes) for Assyria.[3] The "rulers," who are like "evening wolves," are the court judges (*šopet*) who pervert justice for economic gain, devouring the resources of defenseless citizens.[4]

The last three sins of the believers in Jerusalem are against God and the people. The keeping of the sanctuary and the law have been commanded by God, but they are for the benefit of the people. False "prophets" at the temple were a constant problem in Israel; they were the preachers of that time, who used their position and preaching to secure their own power. "Arrogant" (*pahaz*) carries connotations of "wanton, haughty, extravagant, and reckless." Their treachery implies cloaked dealings (see also Hab. 1:13; 2:5).

Yahweh's "priests" are no better, polluting the sanctuary with their entwined worship of gods of prosperity (see comments on 1:4–5). They do this by misinterpreting Yahweh's word (*torah*). They are the scholars of the day, ruling on the interpretation of texts (Jer. 18:18; Ezek. 7:26; Mic. 3:11).[5] In this way they "do violence to the law."

These sins are against God and his people. Many of Jerusalem's sins are like Nineveh's in the same time period. Jerusalem was a vassal of Nineveh (see 1:8); she trusted in Assyria and fell soon after her (Babylon captured Nineveh in 612 B.C. and Jerusalem fifteen years later). In contrast, verse 5 describes the faithfulness and righteousness of Yahweh in two parallel phrases:

> The LORD within her is righteous; he does no wrong.
> Morning by morning he dispenses his justice, and every new day he does not fail.

Yahweh's faithfulness and righteousness are the people's only hope. Especially important in Zephaniah is the expression "within her" (*beqirbah*), referring again to the theme of Yahweh's "nearness." "Morning by morning" is the exact biblical expression used for God's gift of manna (Ex. 16:21), for Isaiah's daily inspiration (Isa. 50:4), and for the Levite's daily responsibility to stand and thank and praise God ("every morning"; 1 Chron. 23:30). The message is clear. Although the people have been thoroughly rebellious, Yahweh is present daily, is good, and does not fail. This is the center of any future hope.

---

3. English does not translate the Hebrew preposition "in her midst" (*beqirbah*). See the use of this word throughout Zephaniah, discussed in the Bridging Contexts section "Nearness."

4. Compare Hab. 1:8, where the Babylonians are "fiercer than wolves at dusk."

5. Berlin, *Zephaniah*, 129.

Futile Warnings (3:6–8)

THE SECOND PART of the "judgment of Jerusalem" describes Yahweh's futile warnings. Yahweh speaks directly ("I" in 3:6–10) of the strongholds and nations he has destroyed in Israel's past (e.g., Jericho and the conquest of Canaan) as an example of his power to his people (3:6). Still, Jerusalem refuses correction (3:7). As a result Yahweh has decided to gather all the nations and consume the whole world (including arrogant Jerusalem) in the "fire of my jealous anger" (3:8; cf. 1:18).

In 3:6, the dramatic language describes the absolute ending of peoples whom Yahweh has judged. The emptiness is expressed in many ways: "I have cut off nations . . . strongholds are demolished . . . streets deserted . . . no one passing through . . . cities are destroyed . . . no one will be left—no one at all." The once proud Egypt, the strongholds of Canaan before its conquest, and the glory of the northern kingdom of Israel have all passed into oblivion. Jerusalem has seen the defeat and end of many nations in her history.[6]

Over the years the prophets had delivered many warnings to Jerusalem. (In Zephaniah Jerusalem is still unnamed but is "the city.") "I said to the city, 'Surely you will fear me and accept correction!'" (3:7). Amos's warnings to Israel began around 750 B.C. He was joined by many other true prophets in the 130 years prior to the days of Zephaniah. By that time the northern ten tribes were gone, dispersed by Assyria, for one hundred years (722–622 B.C.). These displays of power shown to his people were in hope that they would fear God and accept correction (3:7), although they refused (3:2).

The result is a "visit" (*paqad*; NIV "punishments") from Yahweh (3:7b). The same word is translated "care for" in 2:7.[7] The original root word is value free, neither positive nor negative, meaning "attend to." It implies a relationship of responsibility between God and people. God cares for and blesses the creation. People are called to give praise and thanks and to obey. In 3:7, "attending to" means "punishment" only because the people have not "accepted correction" (3:7a) in God's previous "attention." God attends to his creation first by blessing them, then by correcting them, and if ignored, by

---

6. The NIV alone supplies the abrupt future tense in 3:6b. "No one *will be* left." The Heb. does not have a verb or tense change here. This insertion draws attention from Yahweh's destruction of nations *in the past*, to the destruction of nations prophesied *for the future* (2:4–15, Philistia, Moab, Ammon, Cush, and Assyria). The shift in tense may be warranted by the allusion to ch. 2 made in the phrase "streets deserted, with no one passing through" (3:6b). This reminds the reader of "utterly desolate" and the description of Nineveh's bird-echoing windows (2:14) and shifts the attention there.

7. The root occurs five times and is translated "punish" in 1:8, 9, 12; "care for" in 2:7; and "punishments" here.

"visiting" them in their rebellion. In spite of the warnings, they are "still eager to act corruptly" (cf. 1:4–13; 3:1–4). This visit is a nonnegotiable correction, but God's intention is more than "punishment." Its purpose is the same as that of the other "visits" of blessing and warning: to bring blessing to the whole earth through them.

In 3:8 God puts himself on the witness stand "to testify." He "will stand" (as in ancient courts) and testify that "they were still eager to act corruptly in all they did" (3:7b). He is also the judge, using courtroom language (*šapat*, "I have decided") to announce the assembling of nations and kingdoms. This consuming judgment is not just for Jerusalem but for "the whole world" (3:8–10; Ethiopia to Assyria, and everything in between, as in 2:4–15). No doubt is left concerning his anger or the comprehensive extent of the purging fire to come (cf. 1:18).[8] The purpose behind God's jealous anger is taken up in 3:9–20 (see also 1:18; 2:1–3; 3:6–10), announced by the "then" of 3:9 (see the introduction, "Jealousy and Wrath of Yahweh").

The immediate historical events for Zephaniah's audience would have been the demise of the Assyrian empire (beginning with Ashurbanipal's death in 628 B.C.) and the rise of the Babylonians (who captured Jerusalem in 597)—events that God's people watched with unease. Immediately, however, Yahweh announces the purpose for and outcome of this jealous fire: He will purify the remnant. Although the whole world will be consumed by "the fire of his jealous anger," the world does not simply end. All the peoples of the earth will survive the consuming anger, to give "honor and praise" to the remnant of God's people (3:20).

Promises for the Remnant (3:9–13)

IN THE FIRST part of the joy of Jerusalem (3:9–20), God makes promises concerning the remnant: "Then will I...." Yahweh continues speaking with a dramatic change to the first person "I" subject. He speaks about the purity and unity of the future remnant after the Babylonian devastation of the whole world: "Then will I purify the lips of the peoples" for worship (3:9); "I will remove" the haughty from Jerusalem (3:11); but "I will leave ... the humble, who trust in the name of the LORD" (3:12). The remnant is described as good, honest, and unafraid (3:13). God's speaking "then" in 3:9 explains the purpose and intention behind "the fire of my jealous anger" (3:8). After this word, the rest of the book is a series of promises.

Historically, this remnant returned to the land after about sixty years of exile in Babylon (597–538 B.C.). Others fled or were "scattered" (3:10) to slave

---

8. For the meaning of the "whole world," see comments on 1:2–3 and in the introduction. See 1:18 for comments on "jealous anger."

markets in other ancient Near Eastern countries. They understood them-selves to be a fulfillment of this prophecy.[9]

"I will purify" (3:9–10). Yahweh is still speaking to the people of Jerusalem in verses 9–10, but he is speaking about the future beyond their destruction. He offers a vision of hope for those who will listen. He offers a future promise of purity of lips, serving Yahweh, and bringing offerings. These are images of worship, and they are spoken concerning all peoples. (After this, the remaining promises are only to the remnant.)

The first promise is that he will purify the lips of the peoples for worship (Ps. 24:4; 15:2–3). Isaiah experienced the purification of his lips by Yahweh in order to speak God's word to the people, who also had unclean lips; the purity of lips signifies the forgiveness of sins (Isa. 6:5–8). The English "I will purify" does not communicate the power of the Hebrew verb (*hapak*), which means "overturn" the lips (3:9). Yahweh will cause a radical conversion of the speech of his people(s).[10]

The purpose of this conversion (overturning) to Yahweh is that they may "serve him shoulder to shoulder" (3:9b). The original word for "serve" (*'abad*) also means "worship." "Shoulder to shoulder" (*šekem*) is a wordplay on "eager" (*hišekem*, 3:7b), which means "to rise early to shoulder the load of the day." The two uses of the same root set up a contrast between being "eager to act corruptly" (3:7b) and "worshiping shoulder to shoulder." The shoul-der image is continued in 3:10 with "my scattered people will bring [*yabal*; bear] me offerings."

The future generation will carry the hope of the message home. From Africa (Cush) the exiles will return (see 2:12). They will be of the next gen-eration, suggested in Hebrew by the expression (lit.) "*daughter* of my scattered people" (NIV, "my scattered people"). "Scattered" is a reference to the "scat-tered flock" of the Exile, who will return to worship (2:7; cf. Jer. 10:21; Ezek. 34:6). The purpose behind the "fire of [God's] jealous anger" (Zeph. 3:8) is the future possibility of a worshiping people (3:9–10). These two verses are packed with worship images.

I will leave a remnant (3:11–13). "On that day you will not be put to shame." Until now (in ch. 3) Yahweh has been speaking about Jerusalem as "they" and "them." Now he speaks directly to the humble remnant with "you." The first time after 3:9 that the dreaded phrase "on that day" is spoken, it is no longer a day of doom. Rather, it is a day in which the remnant is restored from exile (see comments at 1:14–15).

---

9. The glowing terms describing their purity and unity, however, did not match their experience. See the Bridging Contexts section for a discussion of the fulfillment of this prophecy (see the book of Nehemiah).

10. See comments on the same root used in Jonah 3:4.

In 3:11, the purification of the lips by Yahweh includes the forgiveness of sins: "You will not be put to shame for all the wrongs you have done." This is a reversal of 3:7b: "still eager to act corruptly in all they did." Now they will be restored as God's grace meets their humility. The remnant trusting in Yahweh will be free of the taunts of their haughty brothers, who will not be present to shame them. "Those who rejoice in their pride" will not be present (3:2a, 4a, 7b, 11).

The meek and humble remnant that Yahweh will establish (lit., "I will remainder") is first hinted at in 2:1–3, directly mentioned in 2:7, 9, and now described by God: "But I will leave within you the meek and humble, who trust in the name of the LORD. The remnant of Israel will do no wrong; they will speak no lies, nor will deceit be found in their mouths" (3:12–13). The purity that Yahweh gives will be seen in their goodness ("no wrong," used also of Yahweh in 3:5).[11] Their honesty will also distinguish them. "No lies" is used especially in relation to false prophecy (3:4). "Deceit" is especially a crime of priests, who have made money promoting worthless gods (1:9). Above all, the remnant will trust in Yahweh. The concluding promise that they will "eat and lie down and no one will make them afraid" (3:13b) echoes Yahweh's promised provisions in chapter 2 (abundant pasture for domestic flocks, a place to live, and the peace that comes with wild lands for animals).[12]

This word of Yahweh is a promise to be kept in trust for the future of Zephaniah's original audience. The doom of chapters 1 and 2 is still to come on Zephaniah's Jerusalem, yet they are given this message in the second half of chapter 3 as a possibility of hope for their children.

A Day of Joy in Jerusalem (3:14–20)

IN THE SECOND part of the joy of Jerusalem (3:9–20), the day of joy is described. Zephaniah calls on the future remnant to "sing . . . shout aloud . . . and rejoice" (3:14). The prophet speaks directly to them, promising that Yahweh will remove all fear and be in their midst. He will "take great delight in" and "rejoice over" them with singing (3:15–17). Then Yahweh speaks concluding promises directly: "I will" lift burdens of the past (3:18), deal with oppressors, and rescue and honor those put to shame in the exile (3:19). He will restore their fortunes and bring the humble remnant home.

Yahweh is with you. In 3:14–17 Zephaniah presents a song, in escrow for the future remnant to sing. It begins with the typical call to "sing" (Ps. 33:1–3; 95:1–2; 96:1–3; Isa. 12:5–6). More than singing, he calls on them to exult

---

11. "No wrong" (*loʾ . . . ʿawlah*) means no unjust actions, usually in relation to care for the powerless.

12. See the Bridging Contexts section of ch. 2.

"with all [their] heart" (3:14). The call to the "Daughter of Zion" can mean simply God's people but can also signify that this future hope will be experienced not by the people of Zephaniah's Jerusalem but by their children.

This first half of the song (3:14–15) ends with four promises for the future community of faith. The "punishment" (lit., "verdict") of exile and the enemy are taken away. Yahweh's presence and freedom from fear are given.[13] The second half of the song (3:16–17) begins with the promise of future encouragement, for others will witness God's presence and his might to save them. The song ends with the community being taken into the life of Yahweh— into his delight, love, and rejoicing. This description approaches a beatific vision of the remnant and Yahweh. The words bridge the known world and the world for which the trusting humble hope.

This song is given for singing by the exiles who return from exile (c. 520 B.C.). Their enemies are still present (3:15), for God's people still need to defend themselves (3:16, "Do not let your hands hang limp," i.e., in weakness). Yahweh's might "to save" is still necessary (3:17). The exiles need to be active in rebuilding the city of Jerusalem. In Jeremiah 47:3, as here, "hang limp" is a figure of speech for the helplessness of terror or fear. The meek and humble remnant (3:12–13), however, will be free from fear, cared for and celebrated by Yahweh.

I will bring you home (3:18–20). The final words are grammatically the most intimate of the entire book. Yahweh speaks ("I") directly to the future remnant that trusts in him ("you"), promising them seven actions.

1. The sorrows for the appointed feasts I will remove from you (3:18).
2. I will deal with all who oppressed you (3:19a).
3. I will rescue the lame (3:19a).
4. I will give them praise and honor (3:19, 20).
5. I will gather you (3:19, 20).
6. I will bring you home (3:20).
7. I will restore your fortunes before your very eyes (3:20).

In these promises Yahweh announces more than a change in fortune for the remnant. The fourth promise declares a fundamental change in Israel's relationship to the nations.

These promises begin with "the sorrows for the appointed feasts I will remove from you; they are a burden and a reproach to you."[14] The phrase

---

13. "Punishment" is *mišpat*, a reference to Yahweh's earlier decision (also *mišpat*) in 3:8, "I have *decided* . . . to pour out my wrath." This decision (rather than "punishment") comes to an end for the remnant that trusts in Yahweh. It is a decision that leads to blessing.

14. Many English translations place the first half of v. 18 with the previous sentence, but the NIV rightly follows the Heb. verses.

"sorrows for the appointed feasts" is difficult for interpreters. Literally, it is "grieved over the appointed time." Most translators take "appointed time" to mean "festivals." While it can mean "festival" (it is a singular noun), in the context of Zephaniah "appointed time" has a specific meaning (see discussion of "Day of Yahweh" at 1:14). It is a reference to the day of Yahweh's "sacrifice" (1:7–18). This is the ironic festival of sacrifice, in which Jerusalem will be slaughtered. In 3:18 the "appointed feast(s)," the "sorrows," "burden," and "reproach" all refer to the devastation of Jerusalem.[15] Verse 19 confirms this translation, continuing to describe the reversal of the shame and injury done in the day of Yahweh's sacrifice of Jerusalem.

The promises continue in 3:19: "At that time I will deal with all who oppressed you; I will rescue the lame and gather those who have been scattered. I will give them praise and honor in every land where they were put to shame." The change in indirect object (from "you" to "them") in the middle of this verse seems odd, since 3:18–19a and 3:20 use the second person, "you." The change, however, is due to decree language. Note that the same idea is expressed in 3:20b in direct language: "I will give *you* honor and praise." In English the verbs are the same ("give"), but in Hebrew the first verb (3:19b *sum*) means "establish, ordain, set in place," whereas the verb in 3:20 (*natan*) means "give." In 3:19b Yahweh is "ordaining" a reversal for his people (from shame to honor) and speaks a decree about them to the world. In 3:20 he speaks similar content, but this time as a word of comfort and promise to them.

Verse 20 fills out the last four of the seven promises. "'At that time I will gather you; at that time I will bring you home. I will give you honor and praise among all the peoples of the earth when I restore your fortunes before your very eyes,' says the LORD." For an exiled people, no set of promises carries more hope (see Ps. 137). To be gathered home, to have what was lost restored, and to be honored by other peoples of the earth are the normalcy and health for which every culture longs. For believers in Zephaniah's Jerusalem, hearing the promise before any of this is lost will expand their view to the greater good God desires for them. Their culture will pass first through the great Babylonian crucible of purification. Then the people will understand that their previous cultural successes have come only through God, who gives all good things.

---

15. In the NIV this verse has a text note that says, "Or 'I will gather you who mourn for the appointed feasts; your reproach is a burden to you.'" This alternate reading better communicates the original context referent, but would be more accurate if "feasts" were singular ("feast"), as is the Heb.

SEVERAL IMPORTANT INNER-BIBLICAL interpretations have developed from Zephaniah's message of the surviving remnant (3:9–20) and the future worship and praise of other nations (3:9, 20). These later biblical interpretations echo Zephaniah's message in their own historical contexts. The three major interpretive contexts discussed here reveal the layered meaning of Zephaniah's text to us. The first context is the disappointment experienced after the remnant's return to Jerusalem (sixth century B.C.), with the messianic hopes that emerged from that struggle. The second is the understanding gained by the New Testament church in light of Jesus' presence and resurrection gifts. The third consists of the faith of later believers who read Zephaniah's hopeful words of peace, purity, and praise and wait for God's gathering home in the new creation.

These three layers of interpretation help us to see the trajectory of Zephaniah's words, from their original historical context through subsequent generations. The postexilic context of frustration and developing messianic hope, the New Testament resurrection perspective, and the future hope of the new heaven and new earth each are anchored in Zephaniah's eschatological vision. All of them are necessary for a full understanding of this living word of prophecy.

Postexilic frustration. The prophet said that God would bring destruction but that a faithful and humble remnant would survive and be restored to the land. Zephaniah's peers expected that they or their children would experience this fulfillment (see Original Meaning). They did experience it, though only in part. The survivors of the sixty-year Babylonian exile who returned to the land initially experienced the glowing promises of return with excitement (Ps. 126). This was soon replaced, however, by disappointment in the struggles and corruption that remained (see Nehemiah and Zechariah-Malachi). As their children and grandchildren wrestled with God's promises of a pure remnant, God-honoring Gentiles, and peace, the prophecy eventually became a messianic expectation, fortified with texts from Isaiah and with what became known as "messianic psalms."

In this first major context of meaning, the postexilic community of faith recognized that prophecy is a living word. While they rejoiced that God had restored them to Jerusalem, they looked for and expected a greater blessing: purity and peace in Jerusalem and the nations' praise abroad (3:12–20). The reality experienced by those who returned to a devastated homeland fell short of Zephaniah's description of the righteous remnant.

The nearness of Yahweh. Zephaniah's living word was also rediscovered in the aftermath of Jesus' resurrection and is recorded in the writings of the

New Testament. The writers saw that God's promise to be *with them* and *near them* in Zephaniah was fulfilled in Jesus' ministry and in the presence of the Holy Spirit in the life of Christians. The New Testament trajectory of Zephaniah's prophecy is a necessary layer of hope for Christians.

Twice in chapter 3 Zephaniah says to the remnant that "the LORD ... is with you" (3:15, 17). The word behind this expression (*qereb*) occurs frequently in Zephaniah and is translated in various ways (all of the italicized words in the following two paragraphs are translations of the Heb. *qereb*). This theme of the *nearness* of Yahweh is easily missed but represents the longing heart of God to be close to his people. The broader meaning of *qereb* is *near* or *midst*. Zephaniah's message began with the declaration that "the day of the LORD" is *"near"* (1:7, 14). This *nearness* is doom for those who experience his anger *with* them. In chapter 3 the absence of *nearness* is a key to understanding the problem and Yahweh's response to the community: "She does not trust in the LORD, she does not *draw near* to her God. Her officials [*within* her] are roaring lions, her rulers are evening wolves" (3:2–3).

In these verses we see the values of the community in regard to nearness. Yahweh, however, is not absent from his community, despite their choices. "The LORD *within* her is righteous, he does no wrong" (3:5). Yahweh takes responsibility for the problem of lack of nearness in his community. "I will remove from this city [*your midst*] those who rejoice in their pride. But I will leave *within* you the meek and humble who trust in the name of the LORD" (3:11–12). In this context of *nearness* in Zephaniah, the song for the remnant that trusts in Yahweh declares that "the LORD ... *is with* you" (3:15, 17). It is followed by the related theme of God's "gathering" the remnant "home" (see below).

The New Testament echoes and develops Zephaniah's theme of the nearness of God. Paul speaks of God who has drawn near in the person of Jesus (incarnation) and of his presence in the resurrection by the Spirit. This nearness of God is still near to us through faith:

> But the righteousness that is by faith says: "Do not say in your heart, 'Who will ascend into heaven?'" (that is, to bring Christ down) "or 'Who will descend into the deep?'" (that is, to bring Christ up from the dead). But what does it say? 'The word is *near you; it is in your mouth and in your heart*," that is, the word of faith we are proclaiming: That if you confess with your mouth, "Jesus is Lord," and believe in your heart that God raised him from the dead, you will be saved. (Rom. 10:6–9)[16]

The Gospel writers witness to Jesus as the very presence of the God of Israel. Zephaniah's central image of nearness is the forgiveness of sins and the

---

16. Paul quotes Deut. 30:12–14.

presence of God the King with the "Daughter of Zion" (a term of endearment in 3:14). "The LORD has taken away your punishment, he has turned back your enemy. The LORD, the King of Israel, is with you; never again will you fear any harm" (3:15). John describes the entrance of Jesus the King in the palm procession into Jerusalem in John 12:13–15 (cf. Zech. 9:9):

They took palm branches and went out to meet him, shouting,

"Hosanna!"
"Blessed is he who comes in the name of the Lord!"
"Blessed is the King of Israel!"

Jesus found a young donkey and sat upon it, as it is written,

"Do not be afraid, O Daughter of Zion;
see, your king is coming,
seated on a donkey's colt."

Jesus is also called "the King of Israel," a title of the expected messianic fulfillment, in mocking terms by the crowd as he is dying on the cross (Matt. 27:42; Mark 15:32).

The promise of God's nearness in Zephaniah is shared by Matthew's messianic reading of Isaiah 7:14: "The virgin will be with child and will give birth to a son, and they will call him 'Immanuel,' which means, 'God with us'" (Matt. 1:23). God has drawn near to humanity in the incarnation, life, and death of Jesus. The reality of this nearness is perpetuated in his resurrection and Jesus' gift of the Holy Spirit (John 14:16–30; 16:13–15; 20:19–22; Acts 2:1–4).

The theme of God's nearness begins the book of Hebrews. "In the past God spoke to our forefathers through the prophets at many times and in various ways, but in these last days he has spoken to us by his Son" (Heb. 1:1–2a). John's Gospel begins with a similar theme. "The Word became flesh and made his dwelling among us. We have seen his glory, the glory of the One and Only, who came from the Father, full of grace and truth" (John 1:14; see also 1 John 1:1–4). Paul's appeal to the Gentile Ephesians expresses a fulfillment of Zephaniah's vision (Zeph. 3:9) for the Gentile nations and peoples (Eph. 2:12–13):

Remember that at that time you were separate from Christ, excluded from citizenship in Israel and foreigners to the covenants of the promise, without hope and without God in the world. But now in Christ Jesus you who once were far away have been *brought near* through the blood of Christ.

Philip met a Cushite (Ethiopian) in a chariot who was a worshiper of Yahweh (Acts 8:27–38; echoing Zeph. 3:10). That meeting resulted in his baptism, after Philip explained the prophet Isaiah's messianic words that had been fulfilled recently in Christ (Isa. 53:7–8). The apostles experienced the nearness of the Lord in the flesh and in his resurrected body. That nearness transformed the world. The apostles' witness brought many diverse people near to the Lord Jesus, beginning with this Cushite, the first New Testament fulfillment of Zephaniah 3:9–10.

Non-Jews now have been brought near to the Lord. We are subject to the same scrutiny as Zephaniah's Jerusalem. From whom much has been given, much is required. The God who is near us in Christ sees our arrogance too. James reminds the early church that the God of Zephaniah still intensely desires honest and humble nearness (James 4:5–10):

> Or do you think Scripture says without reason that the Spirit he caused to live in us *envies* intensely? But he gives us more grace. That is why Scripture says:
>
>> "God opposes the proud
>> but gives grace to the *humble*."
>
> Submit yourselves, then, to God. Resist the devil, and he will flee from you. Come *near* to God and he will come *near* to you. Wash your hands, you sinners, and purify your hearts, you double-minded. Grieve, mourn and wail. Change your laughter to mourning and your joy to gloom. *Humble* yourselves before the Lord, and he will lift you up.

Christians are a remnant waiting to be gathered home. The third major element in Zephaniah's living word is yet to be fulfilled among us. It is Yahweh's promised gathering home (3:20). We too long to experience the purity of Yahweh's remnant that Zephaniah describes (3:12–13). We long for the nations to praise and honor God and for God's faithful and pure remnant (3:9, 19–20). We too long for the peace that God promised 2,600 years ago. People of faith believe the hopeful words of purity and praise and wait for Yahweh's gathering of the remnant peoples home. What is promised to Jerusalem cannot be fulfilled by any human devising. The promise points beyond us to our hope in Yahweh's re-creation of heaven and earth.

While the original audience may have looked for a close and complete fulfillment, the power of Zephaniah's vision (and other prophetic visions like it) has compelled Christians throughout history to live for, work toward, and wait for something that is to be established in our world. Isaiah, Jeremiah, and Zechariah add to this vision that endures in the imagination of people of faith today. In each case, Yahweh speaks the hopeful vision of the future directly. The gathering is more than a physical congregation of people. Gathering *to* Yahweh and *by* Yahweh implies the relationship of nearness and faithfulness.

"My house will be called
  a house of prayer for all nations."
The Sovereign LORD declares—
  he who gathers the exiles of Israel:
"I will gather still others to them
  besides those already gathered."
              (Isa. 56:7b–8; cf. 43:5–6; 54:7–8).

"I myself will gather the remnant of my flock out of all the countries where I have driven them and will bring them back to their pasture, where they will be fruitful and increase in number. I will place
shepherds over them who will tend them, and they will no longer be
afraid or terrified, nor will any be missing," declares the LORD. (Jer.
23:3; cf. Zech. 10:8–10)

Note how Jesus shared in God's longing to gather the people of Jerusalem
to himself:

"O Jerusalem, Jerusalem, you who kill the prophets and stone those
sent to you, how often I have longed to gather your children together,
as a hen gathers her chicks under her wings, but you were not willing."
(Matt. 23:37; Luke 13:34)

Jesus also prophesied a time of future gathering of his remnant in the tradition of the prophets.

"At that time the sign of the Son of Man will appear in the sky, and
all the nations of the earth will mourn. They will see the Son of Man
coming on the clouds of the sky, with power and great glory. And he
will send his angels with a loud trumpet call, and they will *gather his elect*
from the four winds, from one end of the heavens to the other." (Matt.
24:30–31).

Jesus enlarged Zephaniah's concept of the "home" to which God would
gather his remnant (3:20). When a disciple asked why Jesus did not unveil
his power to the whole world, Jesus suggested that the transformation of
the world began with a home created by love between the Lord and anyone
who would love and obey, not by a show of power (John 14:22–24). He
acknowledged that this home will one day also be established as a place
(14:1–4). Paul longed for that place in preference to the one he knew, since
it was a "home with the Lord" (2 Cor. 5:8). Peter also hoped for the new
Jerusalem in the new earth as a home of righteousness: "But in keeping with
his promise we are looking forward to a new heaven and a new earth, the
home of righteousness" (2 Peter 3:13).

Zephaniah's vision of a home created by Yahweh (3:20), where God's people are without lies or deceit (3:13), is an enduring vision with a trajectory in the New Testament. Jesus declared seeing this lack of deceit (prophesied by Zephaniah) when he met Nathaniel: "Here is a true Israelite, in whom there is nothing false" (John 1:47b). Jesus himself was also without deceit and without sin that we might die to sin and live for righteousness (Heb. 4:15; 1 Peter 2:22–25; cf. Isa. 53:9). His righteousness will also be found in those whose robes are washed in the blood of the Lamb at the judgment to come. Wrapped in the robes of Christ's righteousness, they are welcomed home. "No lie was found in their mouths; they are blameless" (Rev. 14:5).

HOPE IN THE **midst of judgment.** The world experiences God's judgment against sin daily, especially sins of human arrogance against God and his good creation. The violence of war maims children. Human pollution destroys soil and drinking water. Famine emaciates. Extramarital sexuality spreads dozens of debilitating diseases. Children suffer the sins of parents' uncommitted dalliances. Greed is eventually judged through calcified corruption that handcuffs economies and traps the populace in cycles of uncertainty and poverty. National corruption and the lies of government propaganda are judged through a populace's frustration, radicalization, or acts of terror. God's judgment of corruption in the world's societies is reported as news every day. These judgments are not the final judgment, but they are, nonetheless, real judgments in Zephaniah's tradition.

No one escapes God's judgment for arrogance. Zephaniah mentioned idolatry as the first problem among his people (1:4–6, 9) but quickly moved to the problem underlying it: the trust and worship of one's own opinions and desires. Our pride, arrogance, and trust in self and wealth are summed up in 3:5a: "The unrighteous know no shame." The church must listen to these words, first spoken to Jerusalem. "She obeys no one, she accepts no correction. She does not trust in the LORD, she does not draw near to her God" (3:2).

We are under judgment when see the negative effects on children exposed too early to violence and greed through the media in our homes. We recognize judgment when deep anxiety disrupts sanguine lives for no apparent reason. We are judged when substance abuse takes its vengeance on dear relationships. Human arrogance is judged when we live with the memory of violence past. Judgment reigns through the self-destructive tendencies of laziness and overwork, failure to worship and pious self-righteousness, habitual self-deprecation and smug satisfaction, and the hidden powers of sensuality and the pride of asceticism.

Our arrogance is not limited to personal and social realms. We are under God's judgment for contaminating air and thereby threatening public health, the fouling and mismanagement of soil and its threat to agriculture, and the pollution and waste of clean water. Individuals reap what businesses and nations sow in every aspect of God's creation.

Judgment denied is like alcoholism denied. Admitting our true situation and complicity with our inherited condition is the beginning of our only hope. Ignoring it doesn't make it go away but guarantees that it will kill again. Many societies since Zephaniah's oracle have suffered Jerusalem's fate. Some people in ancient Judah understood his warning and turned to Yahweh. They heard and saw the judgment before it arrived. As a result, they also heard and saw the hope that God offered.

Hope in God's personal promises. In the midst of the judgment against sin suffered in the world, God offers personal promises to break through to hope. Both judgment and hope are true. This is the enigmatic way of Yahweh.[17] The law and gospel are each present to us. Zephaniah insists that there is no escape from judgment but that those who trust in Yahweh will not be disappointed. "Wait for me," God says, to judge (3:8) and to purify (3:9). He will forgive: "On that day you will not be put to shame for all the wrongs you have done to me" (3:11a). He will restore: "I will leave within you the meek and humble, who trust in the name of the LORD" (3:12). He will take away their punishment (3:15). He will be with those who trust him to protect and save (3:15, 17). He will delight in, rejoice over, rescue, gather, give praise and honor to, and bring home those who trust him (3:17–20).

This is the good news at work in the midst of Old Testament judgment. This is the hope that is made explicit in the life and work of Jesus. Jesus purged the temple (judgment) and cured the blind and lame (good news) in the same afternoon (Matt. 21:12–14).[18] No one is beyond hope. No one was further from God's mercy than the people of Jerusalem who spurned his love, yet he offered it to them again and again. In Christ this love is offered to every culture. God makes promises to the hopeless that may still turn to him in trust and faith. Even those who suffer judgment for their actions may still turn to trust in Yahweh until their last breath (Luke 23:41–43; 1 Cor. 3:15).

These promises are far more than personal (or psychological) matters of individual faith. Zephaniah concludes the long list of God's promises (3:18–20) with the pledge that the world will see it and that those who trust will

---

17. Motyer, "Zephaniah," 3:945.

18. Brown, *Obadiah Through Malachi*, 116.

experience it ("before your eyes"). His promises are sealed with the pledge, "says the LORD" (3:20). These promises to the ancients are reiterated by Jesus for his followers. In Christ, God has made a commitment to the physical fulfillment of the new creation. Jesus is the firstborn of the new creation—eating, walking, talking, and touching his disciples in a resurrection body. He promises to come again, to receive us to a place with many rooms (John 14:1–6).

These kinds of divine promises invite us to a daily response of faith and obedience. Songwriter Lina Sandell expressed her hope in these promises in the words of a hymn:

> Day by day and with each passing moment,
> strength I find to meet my trials here;
> trusting in my Father's wise bestowment,
> I've no cause for worry or for fear.
> He whose heart is kind beyond all measure,
> gives unto each day what he deems best.
> Lovingly, it's part of pain and pleasure,
> mingling toil with peace and rest."

She concludes with hope, even in tribulation.

> Help me then in every tribulation
> so to trust thy promises O LORD;
> that I lose not faith's sweet consolation,
> offered me within thy Holy word.
> Help me LORD, when toil and trouble meeting,
> e'er to take, as from a father's hand,
> one by one, the days, the moments fleeting,
> 'til I reach the promised land."[19]

Hope in correction. Those who turn, acknowledging their guilt to the Lord, find hope and refuge in his correction of his people. The Lord has provided many reliable means of restoration and correction for those who want to return to a life of faith and trust. The law, the prophets, the natural order of creation, and the history of protection of God's people all witness to his way in the world and love for his people, even today.[20] Christians living by faith find hope in the law, especially in the words given from Mount Sinai and in Yahweh's command to love. The witness of the first five books of the Bible is set in a broad narrative that continues to shape the character of Christians who read it. God invites a return to his law: "Surely you will fear me and accept correction!" (3:7a). The prophets also provide a way of return.

---

19. *The Covenant Hymnal: A Worshipbook* (Chicago: Covenant Publications, 1966), #435. Used by permission.
20. Achtemeier, *Nahum-Malachi*, 81.

Zephaniah was one among many, during three hundred years, who spoke directly, amidst false prophecy (3:4), of Yahweh's passionate love for his people. These prophets still speak to us today.

The gift of the nonhuman creation is another witness to God's care. Daily strength, food, shelter, protection, and work are good gifts from God's hand. "Morning by morning" and "every new day" (3:5), God does not fail to provide.[21] Recognizing God's provision and its witness to his love for us is a discipline of correction against our arrogant assumption that we are self-sufficient. Our ability to do anything comes from Yahweh. This correction becomes a refuge of thanksgiving and joy for those who accept it too, as a gift.

Finally, Scripture and church history provide a rich witness to God's faithfulness, love, and correction in the historical process (3:6). He brings down the arrogant and sets captives free. The study of God's acts on behalf of his people is a resource of hope and a refuge of correction for those who trust in the Lord. God has been and is at work in creation, history, his law, and his prophets to provide broad opportunities of hope for those who seek his correction, that they may trust in him.

God's ultimate message of correction came to us in the redeeming work of Jesus. After pouring out his anger on Jerusalem, God charted a new course with humanity. His new strategy for communicating the hurt behind his anger was to absorb the destructive forces of sin into himself through the Son Jesus, this time publicly demonstrating the love behind the anger. The Word declares that God has rerouted his anger from his rebellious people toward himself. In that new word, he communicates and gives his "righteousness" (the Son) to humanity in place of his anger. This is the great exchange called redemption in the New Testament. We may be redeemed from an eternity of separation from a holy God through the gift of Jesus' righteousness. To refuse such a gift is to be judged truly lost.

Hope in cultural reconciliation. Zephaniah was keenly aware of tension between cultures and races. His grandmother was most likely Ethiopian (see comments on 1:1).[22] An important portion of Yahweh's word of hope to him concerned other cultures (Zephaniah uses the word "peoples" to denote the races and cultures of his world in 3:9, 20 and "nations" in 2:11). In the midst of judgment, God's created peoples are called to imagine and participate in a vision of the future reconciliation of all races.

If Jerusalem could be a city of peace between cultures and races even today, reconciliation would be possible for the whole world. People of many ethnic groups have immigrated to Israel. Other various cultures surround it.

---

21. Achtemeier rightly notes that "justice signifies God's order in the natural world" (ibid., 81).

22. See also the conflict over Moses' Ethiopian wife in Num. 12:1–10.

Nations throughout the world are affected by war and peace in the Middle East. The call to pray for Jerusalem's peace (Ps. 122:6) is a relevant call to pray for the reconciliation and unity of all cultures. Such peace would be a source of hope for unity everywhere.

Racism is still deeply embedded throughout the world. Justice and trust between people of different cultures are essential to real hope and peace. Zephaniah's reconciliation envisions an end to deceit and lies (3:13).[23] The holy mountain (which means Jerusalem, 3:11) will be a place where no one is afraid of anyone else (3:13). The lips of the peoples will be pure (3:9), and the peoples in every land will give God's humble remnant honor and praise (3:19–20). People freely give honor and praise to an honest and just people, out of trust and respect. In this vision, the cultures have been truly reconciled, and Jerusalem is the heart of this reconciliation.

What source could possibly deliver such unimaginable unity for us? The original division of races was a negative consequence of the sin of arrogance against God at Babel (Gen. 11:1–9). Zephaniah's vision is that humility in relation to God is the first step toward reconciliation and the restoration of his original intention for the unity of the human race. The heart of his vision is that all people will worship Yahweh shoulder to shoulder in Jerusalem (3:9) and in their own countries (2:11). They will call on his name and serve him. God is the source of this unity, and the humble of the earth will be his new community of faith.

Our vision of racial unity today is not limited to Zephaniah's few verses. Zephaniah was a forerunner of a more explicit action of God in Jesus and the Holy Spirit to reverse Babel and bring the diversity of his human creation to peace in the coming kingdom of God. Acts 2:9–11 records the presence of many peoples and nations on the day of Pentecost: Parthians, Medes, Elamites, Cretans, Arabs, and residents of Mesopotamia, Judea, Cappadocia, Pontus, Asia, Phrygia, Pamphylia, Egypt, Libya, and Rome. It is perhaps also no coincidence that the first two converts outside Jerusalem were an Ethiopian (Acts 8:27–39) and a Roman (the commanding officer Cornelius, ch. 10). The first general conference of the early church in Jerusalem concerned cultural relations and how these relations would influence the spread of the gospel of Jesus Christ (15:1–35; cf. 11:1–18). The gospel and God's vision of the future are not complete without our attention to breaking down the divisions and lies between cultures. The primary witness of the coming kingdom among us is unified worship and table fellowship.

God's joy. What could be greater than God's gladness? It indicates the longing of the Lord's heart. God will celebrate when we live the life of hope

---

23. Bennett, "The Book of Zephaniah," 7:700.

he has provided. God rejoices when our lives of arrogance are reversed and we begin living in hope of his coming kingdom.

The real reversal of our lives under the judgment of alienation from each other and from God is not based simply in admitting our sin but in truly repenting. True repentance means changed personal and social realities. Our relationship with God and with each other is transformed. When people humbly receive the gospel, God rejoices and sings (3:17). When diverse people call on the name of the Lord with one voice, God will delight (Isa. 62:1–5; 65:17–19). His rejoicing is like that of a father waiting for and rejoicing in the prodigal son who returns home (Luke 15:11–32). Even in a prophetic book known for its judgment, the heart of God longs to bring his people home (3:20). That is the purpose of the judgment. God longs to restore a good creation. All are invited to the party.

When anyone enters God's life of hope and reconciliation, the nonhuman creation also rejoices: "The creation waits in eager expectation for the sons of God to be revealed" (Rom. 8:19). It waits for the redemption of those who will live their lives with God in the new creation. When the prophets and psalmists envisioned the day of this renewal, they declared that the creation would also rejoice as the stars and angels did at the first creation (Job 38:7). The hills and rivers rejoice and the sea resounds with praise at God's salvation (Ps. 98:7–8). "All that lives in the earth, sky, and sea will rejoice when his salvation appears (96:11–13)."[24]

We are invited to join God and the rest of creation in rejoicing over our reconciliation with the Creator and Redeemer. Every Sunday is a reminder to rejoice in Christ's Easter victory over sin, death, and the evil one. God has, in Christ, secured our hope and our future. Even in the midst of hardship we may enter into the rejoicing of hope (Phil. 4:4–7). The fullness of joy is in our future, but it has already been fulfilled in Jesus, the firstborn of the new creation. In him our future joy may be fulfilled in the present.

After the Exile, Zechariah used Zephaniah's language to fill in the picture of the joy to come. "Rejoice greatly, O Daughter of Zion! Shout, Daughter of Jerusalem! See, your king comes to you, righteous and having salvation, gentle and riding on a donkey, on a colt, the foal of a donkey" (Zech. 9:9; cf. Zeph. 3:14; Matt. 21:5). In Jesus we have reason to sing Zephaniah's song of victory (Zeph. 3:14). We have the Lord in our midst (3:17) through the preached word and sacraments. Sorrows are removed (3:18) by his presence in prayer. The oppressions of sin and death (3:19) are relieved by the power of his forgiveness and resurrection from the dead. Our joy is future, but it is also present in the gifts of the Lord.

---

24. Achtemeier, *Nahum-Malachi*, 86.

Scripture Index

Genesis

1	30
1:2	72
1:9–10	156
1:15–19	247
1:20–27	276
2–3	311
2:15	284
3:5–6	312
3:12	217
3:17–19	320
4	128, 158
4:6–7	128
4:6	112
4:7	128, 227
4:8	128
4:16	128
4:24	135
8:10–11	41
9:18–10:32	314
11:1–9	342
12	23
12:1–3	23, 212, 309, 314
12:3b	118
12:10–20	23
15	23
15:1–6	23
15:4–6	212
15:6	91, 198, 238
15:12–20	24
17:1–21	23
17:5–8	212
17:17–18	24
18	155, 158, 198, 309
18:1–15	23
18:16–33	105
18:17–33	218
18:17–21	24
18:21	209
18:23–33	24
19	91, 105

19:9	105
19:21, 25, 29	105
19:37–38	308
20	47, 48
20:1–18	24
21:1–3	24
21:17–21	107
22:17–18	309, 314
28:13–22	176
32:24–32	176
37:35	74
49:24	217

Exodus

2:23	209
3	218
3:11–4:17	24, 102
4:24–26	24, 176
5:3	260
7:5	286
9:15	260
9:16	231
12:25–27	171
14–15	254, 255
14	257
14:20	292
14:31	104
15	156
15:2	259
15:3–12	252, 260
15:4–5	72
15:6	232
15:7	312
16:21	326
18:13–18	316
19:6	256
19:16–19	252, 260
20:1–7	291
20:2	75
20:5	146
21:23–25	126
22:21–27	325

22:21–24	155
22:23	209
22:26–27	110
23:16	113
24:18	90
28:1	287
32:7–10	99
32:7–8	291
32:8	276
32:14	99
34	147, 152, 153
34:5–9	291
34:5–6	133
34:6	147
34:6–7	99, 111, 152
34:6–7a	119, 274
34:7	147
34:7a	52
34:13	149
34:14	146, 291
34:22	113

Leviticus

3:6–11	78
5:7, 11	41
7:11–18	78
16	98
18:21	287
18:25, 28	77
19:18	158, 160
20:2–4	287
20.22	77
22:18–30	78
23:39–43	113
24:17–21	126
26:14–39	297
26:21–22	320
26:25	260
30:33	178

Numbers

12:1–10	341

12:3	316	32:12–13	268	23:3	217
13:25	90	32:15–18	217	30:14	307
14:17–25	245	32:21	75		
14:18	119	32:23	255	**2 Samuel**	
14:21	231	32:30–37	217	5	254
14:44	227	32:35	147, 154, 158	7:13, 16	212
15:27–31	33	33	257	8:18	307
16:30	50, 74, 84	33:29	268	10:1–4	308
21:9	73	34:1–4	262	12:22	100
22:1–6	308			12:30	287
22:22–33	122	**Joshua**		15:18	307
23:18–19	100	1:11	315	20:7	307
25:1–3	287	2:23	315	22:22–37	268
25:3–9	260	3	255	22:31	149
31:2	135	3:14, 17	315		
31:7	255	9:9	253	**1 Kings**	
35:33–34	246	13:3	307	2:45	212
		24:15	227	8:12–13	27
Deuteronomy				9:5	212
1:5	242	**Judges**		11:5–7	287
1:39	123	3:10	255	11:5	287
2:8–9, 19	308	3:12–14	308	11:7–8	308
4:19	287	5	254, 257	11:33	287
5:9	146	5:4–5	252, 260, 292	13:20–32	122
5:24–27	326	5:4	255	13:30	183
7:5	149	5:5	252, 260, 262	14:23	289
8	301	8:34	75	17:4–6	122
8:2, 16	316	14:19	307	18:19–40	288
8:3	267	16:1	307	18:27	247
8:10–14	300	16:5, 9, 19	212	19	260
8:12–19	243			19:1–18	102
8:17–19	300	**Ruth**		20:35–36	122
8:18	75	4:16	237		
11:2–7	325			**2 Kings**	
12:2	289	**1 Samuel**		2:23–25	122
12:3	149	2:2	217	5	52, 107
15:10–11	178	4	156	5:19	53
16:13–15	113	4:1–11	168	6:20–23	53
18:22a	52	5:1	307	8:9–15	107
20:19	166	5:4–5	288	8:12	186
21:18	325	6:17	307	9:7	135
23:5	106	7	254, 257	10:20	288
24:20a	169	7:3–11	95	14:23–27	25
26:1–11	259, 266	7:10	292	14:25–27	27
27:8	242	10	105	14:25	21, 25, 27, 31, 40, 60
28:15–68	297	14:24	135		
30:12–14	334	15:28–30	100	15	27
32:4	217	22:32	217	15:29	29
		22:47	217	17:10	289

18–19	27, 254, 277	27:1–6	83	25:8	132
18:10	29	30:2–23	215	27:5	217
18:13–19:35	173	31:6	215	28:1	217
19	29, 176	31:35	215	28:7	259
19:23	246	38–41	320	28:8	256
19:35–36	254	38:7	343	30	78
19:35	286	39:11	212	31	215, 217
21–23	202, 277	39:16	231	31:2–3	217
21:3, 5	287	40:5b	265	31:6–7	76
21:24–23:30	284	41:31–32	72	31:14	76
22	27, 209	42:7–8	215	32	78
22:20	284	42:8	83	33:1–3	330
23:10, 13	287			33:16–22	241
23:35–37	209	**Psalms**		34:7–8	149
24:10–25:21	173	3–7	215	35	172, 215, 217
25:1–13	210	3:8	76	35:15–17	162
		5:7	76	36:7	149
1 Chronicles		5:11–12	258	37:11	245
20:2	287	6:3	215	39	215
23:30	326	7:1	251	40:2	217
25:1	202	7:15–16	185	42–44	215
		9:9	149	42:9	217
2 Chronicles		10:1	215	44:3	232
7:14	97, 316	11:4	71, 247	44:17–26	160
26:6	307	13	86, 215	44:23–24	215
28:16, 20–21	183	13:1–4	162	46	217
30:9	119	13:1–2	86, 215	46:1	149
33:25–35:27	284	13:5–6	86, 258	47:1–4	259
		13:5	76	47:2	315
Ezra		15:2–3	329	51	215
8:21–23	95	16:5–11	258	54–57	215
		17	215	55:4–8	41
Nehemiah		17:7	232	55:16	76
3:16	289	18	78	57:1	149
7:64	325	18:2	217	58	172
9:17b	120	18:6–19	252, 260	59:10	259
		18:6	72	59:16	76
Esther		18:30	149	59:17	259
4	95	18:34	268	61:2	217
		19:1–4	259, 261	62:1–8	241
Job		19:1–4a	320	62:2–7	217
2:10	265	19:14	217	62:5–7	241
3	276	20:6	232	62:8	149
7:9	70	22	215	66	106
10:22	70	22:1	215	66:5–6	106
13:15	265	23:2–3	320	68:4–19	252, 260
24:8	199	24:4	329	69–71	215
26:6	84	25–28	215	69	172
26:12–13	256				

71:3	217	103:12	119	**Isaiah**	
72:10	43	104:16	246	1:5–10	246
73	268	104:35	131	1:9	313
74	215	105	171	5:5	320
74:1–10	162	105:41	217	5:8–25	243
74:11	215	106	171	5:24	312
74:12–14	256	106:12–15	241	5:29	170
75:8	186	107:24–26	73	6:5–8	329
76	215	109	172, 215	6:5	266
77	199, 215	109:4	76	7:14	335
77:11–20	255	111:4	119	8:1–4	242
77:16–18	255	114:8	217	9:6–9	292
78	171, 259	115:17	70	10:34	232, 246
78:8	325	118	78	11:9	231
78:20	217	118:14	259	12:2	259
79	215	119	76	12:5–6	330
79:5	215	120	215	13	139
79:13	308	122:6	342	13:1	144
80	215	126:1–6	333	13:5–9	265
81:16	217	127:1	245	13:16	186
83	172, 215	130	215	14:8	232, 246
86	215	136	111	14:26–27	286
86:15	120	137	172, 215, 244, 332	15	139
88	86, 215	138	78	15:1	144
88:3–7	74	139:7–12	84	17	139
88:5	70	139:7–10	54	17:1	144
88:10–12	70	139:8	70, 84	18:1	315
89:9–10	256	140–143	215	19	139
89:26	217	144:1	217	19:1	144
89:46	215	145	119	19:14	186
90	215	145:8–10	149	19:21–25	315
92	78	145:8	119	19:25	314
92:6–9	126			20:1–12	240
92:15	217	**Proverbs**		21:1–10	172
94:3	158	1–4	189	21:1	144
94:22	217	1:2, 7	325	21:3	240
95:1–2	330	1:12	50	21:4	240
95:1	217	7–9	189	21:8	241
95:5	46	13:21	132	21:9	241
95:7	308	15:11	70	23:1–14	43
96:1–3	330	15:33	325	23:1	144
96:8	178	16:32	111	24:16–23	320
96:11–13	343	23:23	325	27:1	256
98:7–8	343	25:21–22	160	28:4	77
100:3	308	30:5	149	28:7–8	228
102	215			29:14	104
103:2–4	74	**Ecclesiastes**		30:7–8	242
103:8	119	7:8–9	147	35:6	269

36–39	17	62:1–5	343	31:11	106
36:1–22	171	63:1	212	31:13	106, 132
37:24	246	63:10	192	31:20	70
37:32	292	63:15	70	32:35	287
37:36–37	173	65:1–2	234	33:10–11	149
38:14	41	65:17–19	343	36	214
38:17	74	66:19	43, 253	44:17–25	287
38:18	70			47:3	331
40:1–2	113	**Jeremiah**		48:11	290
40:1	99	1:10	149	49:1, 3	287
40:2	151	2:2	76	50:40	313
40:12–31	259, 310	2:20	289	51:34	77
40:12	254	4:23–28	276	51:58	245
40:16	246	5:12–19	290	52:14	149
40:28	254	6:23–24	265		
42:5–25	259	8:2	287	**Lamentations**	
42:5–17	310	10:21	329	2:11–12	173
42:5–9	254	12:1	158	2:13	173
42:6–7	118	13	192	2:20–22	173
43:1	254	13:14	139, 192	3	176
43:5–6	337	13:26	139	3:18–26	314
43:15–21	254	14	192	3:20–24	265
44:9–20	222, 247	14:12	260	3:21–26	149
44:12	212	14:19–20	162	3:21–24	87, 174
44:28–45:1	232	16:19	259	4:18–19	173, 257
45:5–6	312	17:15	227	5:3–4	173
45:5, 14, 18, 21	312	18	96	5:11–13	173
45:23	315	18:7–11	99	5:20–22	173
47:2–3	139, 192	18:7–10	96		
47:14	312	18:7	149	**Ezekiel**	
49:5	259	18:18	326	5:8	192
49:6	118	20:7–9	24, 102	5:13	135
50:4	326	20:14–18	25	5:16	255
51:9–10	256	21:4	210	7:26	326
51:17	186	21:5–6	192	9:9	297
52:7	152, 176	22:13–19	209, 214, 244	9:16b	192
53:7, 8	336	22:18–19	183	13:6–19	242
53:9	338	23:1–2	214	14:21	260
54:7–8	337	23:3	337	16:14–34	184
55:12	232, 246	23:9–11	214	16:37	139, 192
56:7b–8	337	25:5	97	16:39	149
57:1	76	25:10	313	18:4	131
58:2–10	98	25:12	313	18:31–32	162
58:4–7	97	26:1–3	318	18:32	99, 107
59:3	325	26:2–3	99	21:3	192
59:11	41	26:3–6	97	23:1–21	184
60:4	237	26:20–23	214	23:6	167
60:9	43	28:10–15	242	23:14–15	167

23:23	210	2:14	212	2:5	326
24:6, 9	183	4:10–11	313	2:20	288
26	172	5:4, 14	287		
26:9	149	5:15	318	**Zephaniah**	
27:12, 25	43	5:18–20	183	1:7	248
34:6	329	5:26	75	1:12	227
34:31	308	6:1–7	183	2:15	93
38:13	43	7:2, 5	123	3:12	245
		7:3–6	99		
Daniel		8:3–7	318	**Haggai**	
5:1–5	232	8:3	248	2:6–7	260
5:31	313	9:2–3	55	**Zechariah**	
8:6	212	9:2	70, 84, 290	9:9	335, 343
				10:8–10	337
Hosea		**Jonah**		14:2a	192
1:2	184	2	260	14:2	139
2:3	139	3	158	14:3–5	156
2:14–15	321	3:4	133, 137, 274, 329	14:16	113
3:1	111	3:6	169		
4:1–3	256, 276	3:9	318	**Malachi**	
4:12	75	3:10	134, 153	1:7	325
5:15	287	4	155	2:17	129, 290
6:4, 6	76	4:2	152	3:2	157
9:16	139	4:11	133, 155	3:10	179
10:10–15	192			3:13–15	129
10:12	287	**Micah**		3:14	112
10:14	139	1–4	260		
11:1–12	147	1:1	17, 27	**Matthew**	
11:5–9	125	2:1–4	183	1:21	85
11:8–9	100, 162	2:6–11	242	1:23	335
13:16	186, 192	3:9–12	245	2:16	189
		3:11	326	3:16	122
Joel		6:6–13	318	4:4	267
2:3	313	6:8	318	4:17	126
2:5	312	7:18–20	127	5:1–12	318
2:11–19	95	7:18	119	5:5	245, 316
2:12–14	101, 313	7:18b	109	5:44	53, 60, 138, 158, 160
2:13	99, 119				
3:16	149	**Nahum**		6:19–21	178
		1:1–3a	277	8:26–27	122
Amos		1:1a, 2	60	11:2–6	156
1:3–5	174	1:3	119	11:5	269
1:6–8	174	2:11	326	11:17	153
1:9–10	174	3:1	245	11:20	126
1:11–12	174	3:7, 19	310	11:29	317
1:13–15	174			12:38–40	56
2:1–3	174	**Habakkuk**		12:39–41	20, 22, 61, 83
2:4–5	174	1:8	326	12:39–40	62, 83
2:6–16	174	1:13	326	12:41	62, 98, 103, 177

16:4	56, 62	10:31–34	266	2:38	126
16:17	63	11:29–32	20, 22, 56, 62	7	259
17:7	266	11:29–30	83	8:27–39	342
17:8	266	11:32	98, 103	8:27–38	335
17:25–27	122	11:42	301	10	34
19:17–19	317	13:34–35	126	10:1–48	342
21:5	343	13:34	337	10:34–35	163
21:12–14	339	15:11–32	343	11:1–18	342
23:23	178, 301	18:18–20	317	13:37–41	220
23:37–39	126	19:40	243	15:1–35	342
23:37	337	19:41	116	19:18–20	190
24	155, 192, 294	19:44	192, 194	20	126
24:30–31	337	19:44a	194	20:35	179
25:1–13	296	21	192	21	126
25:14–29	296	23:41–43	339		
25:18	314	24:11	85	**Romans**	
27:42	335			1:15–17	238
27:46	215	**John**		1:17	198, 234, 237–39,
28:19	153	1:3	262		241
28:19a	60	1:14	335	1:19–20	259
		1:32	122	1:22–2:1	294
Mark		1:47b	338	1:26–31	296
1:10	122, 262	1:49	335	1:28b–29	62
1:13	90	3:16	107	2:2–9	294
1:15	241	3:19–20	190	3:21	238
3:20–30	156	6:51–58	319	3:23	294
4:35–41	67	8:58	312	3:25	98
4:39–41	122	9:1–3	162	4:3	238
9:2–8	262	10:11–16	308	5:9	294
10	239	11:50	63	6:1–7	97
10:17–22	299	11:51	153	7	59
10:17–19	317	12:13–15	335	7:22–26	59
10:21	178	13:34	317	8:9	343
10:32–34	266	14:1–6	340	8:18–25	241
10:38–39	195	14:1–4	337	8:31b	177
13	155, 192	14:3	241	8:35–39	84
13:32	241	14:16–30	335	8:36–39	175
15:32	335	14:22–24	337	9–11	62
16:8	127	16:13–15	335	9:19–24	215
		20:19–22	335	9:22–26	147
Luke				9:33	217
1:45–46	267	**Acts**		10:6–9	334
3:22	122	1:8b	60	10:14–15	176
4:18–21	156	1:13	53	10:15	152, 163
6:27–30	138	2:1–4	335	11:1–2a	62
6:38	178	2:9–11	342	11:17–18	62
7:22	269	2:14–42	63	11:20b	62
10:29–37	21	2:20	294	12:6–8	179

12:14–21	175	5:8–14	190
12:19–21	160	6:10–20	157
12:19	147, 154	6:11–12	175
13:12–14	190	6:14–15	163
13:14	98, 190	6:15	152
14:11	315		

Philippians

1 Corinthians

1:17–25	104	1:12–14	86
1:18–25	61	2:3–8	316
1:26–31	318	2:5–11	84
1:28–29	318	2:10	315
1:30	238	4:4–7	343
1:31	318		
2:3	25	**Colossians**	
3:15	339	2:8–15	157
5:5	294	2:13–15	175
10:4	217		
10:16	195	**1 Thessalonians**	
11:25	195	5:1–10	296
12:2	247	5:2	294
15:4	56		
15:43	25	**2 Thessalonians**	
		2:2	294

2 Corinthians

2 Timothy

4:6	245	4:2	63
5:1–9	86		
5:5	337	**Hebrews**	
9:6	179	1:1–2a	335
9:7	179	1:22–25	295
9:10–11	179	10	296
10:3–5	176	10:17–22	295
11:24–27	193	10:17–19	238
11:30	25	10:22	297
12:7–9	193	10:23	238
12:8–10	312	10:25–34	237
		10:26	297

Galatians

		10:27	295
3:6	238	10:29	296
3:8	153	10:30–31	295
3:11–12, 14	239	10:30	147, 154, 158
3:11	234, 237, 239, 241	10:35–39	237
4:2–5	241	10:37, 38	241
		10:38	227, 234, 237

Ephesians

James

1:10	241	4:5–10	336
2:12–13	335		
4:7–13	157	**1 Peter**	
4:10	84	2:22–25	338

3:18	238
3:22	175
4:17	297

2 Peter

3:3–9	120
3:3–4	227
3:9	131
3:10–13	275, 276
3:10	294
3:13	337

1 John

1:1–4	335
1:9	101
2:1	238
3:17–18	179

Revelation

3:14–19	190
6:8	260
6:10	193, 218
6:16–17	157, 162
6:17	294
7:9–12	315
7:13–17	296
8:1	248
9:20	194
14:5	338
14:10	186
15:4	153
16	275
16:19	186
17:1–2	194
17:3–6	184
18:23	194
19:11–21	157
19:15	186
22:2	153

Subject Index

anger, 18–20, 24, 32–33, 65, 79, 92, 99–101, 106–25, 128, 133, 135, 145–47, 152–63, 172, 195, 219, 246, 251, 255, 274–77, 285, 292, 294, 297–301, 304–5, 312–13, 327–29, 334, 341

arrogance, 62–64, 103, 120, 127–29, 152–53, 156–58, 161–62, 171–74, 228, 271–73, 285, 294, 306–21, 324–27, 336–43

Assyria, 17, 26–29, 32, 40–42, 60–61, 90, 93–96, 101–2, 118, 131–33, 136–37, 148, 151–57, 159–62, 166–76, 182–91, 194, 202, 211, 261, 271–72, 275–77, 284–90, 304–5, 310–13, 320, 325–28

Baal, 102, 247, 260, 271, 286–90

Babylon, 17, 26–29, 41 60, 77, 87, 120, 130, 133–38, 145, 154–55, 161, 166–73, 176–78, 186–94, 197–202, 208- 221, 225–38, 240–48, 251–61, 265–67, 272–77, 283–92, 304–6, 310–14, 326–28, 332–33

chiasmus, 71, 74

child sacrifice, 287

comfort, 83, 95, 99, 106, 116–18, 132–39, 145–47, 151–53, 157–58, 162, 177, 185, 192–93, 199, 213, 216, 242, 256, 320–32

compassion, 19, 32, 40–42, 47, 53, 69, 74, 83, 88–102, 107–20, 125–29, 134–37, 152–53, 162, 192, 218, 306

confidence, 79, 112, 120, 167, 175, 237–38, 264–69, 290, 295–96, 319, 321

consuming fire, 275, 285, 291

creation, 17, 20, 22, 30, 33, 49, 50, 54–55, 59, 72, 75–77, 90, 97, 101–4, 107–18, 121, 124–32, 136, 145, 148–50, 153–57, 160–61, 167, 175–

77, 194, 214, 217–19, 225–27, 231–34, 241, 245–47, 251–64, 275–76, 287, 291–92, 298–300, 305, 308–21, 327, 333, 336–43

Creator, 18–19, 46, 49, 59, 77, 96, 102–5, 113–19, 122, 127, 135–36, 145–49, 157, 161, 167, 177, 190, 194–95, 198, 215, 231–33, 246, 253–62, 275–77, 287–91, 299–300, 305, 308–12, 320, 325

Creator-Warrior, 253–59, 260, 262

cruelty, 28–29, 133–39, 145–50, 158–60, 169, 182, 183, 187, 310

Cush, 185, 272–75, 284, 285, 304, 310, 315, 323, 327–29

day of the LORD, 218, 271–72, 276, 283–84, 288–95, 304–6, 332–34

death, 18–19, 22–27, 31–33, 40–41, 44–50, 57–59, 63–66, 70, 74–75, 78, 82–87, 90, 97–100, 109, 115–22, 124–25, 128, 131–32, 136, 146, 154–57, 163, 173–77, 188–91, 194, 211, 215, 218–22, 228–29, 238, 241–44, 260–68, 277, 283, 290–97, 309, 315–21, 328, 335, 343

deliverance, 20–22, 33–34, 47, 49–50, 55, 57, 61, 64–70, 76–81, 84–86, 94–96, 99, 106, 114–18, 132, 146, 152, 157–59, 171–72, 217, 241–42, 253–54, 258–64, 269, 298

dominion, 247

dove, 41, 53, 122, 168

down, 18, 24, 41–44, 47–51, 55, 64, 69–73, 77, 80, 92–98, 105, 113–14, 125, 128, 149–50, 167, 177–78, 187, 200, 225–26, 232, 243–46, 254, 275–76, 286–87, 300, 306–11, 320, 330, 334, 341–42

expose, 45, 124, 182, 185, 188, 190–91, 198, 222, 228, 231–32, 246, 293–97 extortion, 198, 228–30, 242, 244

faith, 21, 30–31, 40–46, 49–51, 54–
57, 61–71, 76, 79, 82–87, 102–3,
110–15, 118–21, 125–26, 129, 157,
171–76, 192, 197–203, 212–21,
225–28, 234–40, 241–48, 252–54,
257–59, 261–69, 286–90, 293–95,
314–21, 325, 331–36, 339–42
fame, 198, 201, 251–53, 268, 301
fear, 20, 30, 42, 46–49, 52–53, 64, 72,
85, 128, 130, 136–38, 152, 163,
170, 194, 198, 240–41, 264–66,
272–74, 294–97, 322–23, 327,
330–31, 335, 340
fish, 17–22, 30–33, 40, 44, 47–51, 54–
59, 63, 66, 69–87, 90, 114, 118–24,
201, 214, 217–19, 272–76, 285,
298, 313
forgiveness, 22, 25–26, 32–34, 41, 47,
52–58, 61–63, 83, 89, 91–94, 98–
112, 115, 118–19, 121, 125–31,
154, 174, 191, 220, 238–40, 294–
96, 317, 329–30, 334, 343

glory, 97, 162, 169, 178, 198–200, 225,
230–32, 236, 245–46, 253–54,
261–62, 294, 311, 320, 327, 335–37
good news, 33–34, 51, 61, 85, 105,
151–53, 158, 162–65, 174–76, 192,
240, 294, 311, 339
gospel of peace, 152, 163, 175
grace, 20–24, 34, 50–51, 58–67, 74–
76, 79–80, 82, 85–87, 97, 104,
111–12, 118–21, 126–33, 147, 193,
237, 240–41, 264–66, 295–97, 314,
318, 330, 335–36
greed, 184, 244, 294, 338

hope, 19, 22, 25, 28, 58–62, 66, 73, 85,
87, 91–96, 104–6, 127, 132–33,
137–39, 147–49, 152, 157–58, 166,
171–75, 185, 188, 194–95, 199,
202, 213–20, 229, 235, 238, 241–
42, 246–48, 257–69, 272–74, 277,
284, 286, 291–95, 304–8, 313–21,
325–43

humility, 62, 84, 89, 93–94, 272–73,
276, 284–85, 295–97, 304–8, 311–
17, 321, 324, 330, 342
Husur River, 166, 168

idol, 74–81, 95, 137, 146, 185, 190,
198, 212, 225, 233, 242–44, 247,
255, 271, 287, 338
incarnate, 22, 63, 84, 111, 261–62,
334–35

jealous, 60–61, 135, 145–47, 271–72,
275–77, 283–85, 291–92, 305, 309,
327–29
Jeroboam II, 17, 27, 40, 41
Jerusalem, 17, 22, 27–29, 41, 60, 63,
77–79, 87, 90, 101, 113, 116, 120,
125–26, 136, 151, 166–68, 171–76,
183–84, 192–94, 202, 209–14,
216–20, 225, 229, 235, 243–47,
254, 271–77, 283–97, 305–7, 311–
13, 324–43
Jesus, 20–23, 50, 53, 56–67, 83–85,
97–98, 103–7, 111, 116, 122, 125–
29, 138, 153, 156–63, 175, 178–79,
189–95, 215, 220–21, 237–41, 245,
261–69, 293–99, 301, 312, 317–21,
333–43
Josiah, 27, 94, 202, 209, 272, 277, 283–
84, 287, 290–93, 305
joy, 69, 106, 115, 119, 132–34, 182,
198–200, 203, 213, 227–29, 257–
59, 264, 267–69, 271–73, 324,
328–30, 336, 341–43
Judah, 17, 25–28, 101, 112, 118, 133–
37, 145–63, 166–67, 174–76, 199–
202, 209–13, 216, 226, 235–36,
263, 271–72, 275–77, 283–93,
304–12, 317–18
judgment, 22, 28, 30–32, 41, 48, 51,
60–66, 77, 95–101, 117–21, 126,
129–30, 133, 136–39, 149, 155–58,
162, 174, 182, 184, 190–95, 201,
216–17, 236–38, 243, 246–48, 252,
260, 263–67, 271–77, 283–86,
290–97, 304, 307–9, 312, 315–28,
338–43

justice, 32–34, 83, 95–101, 106–11, 117–18, 121–22, 126–32, 139, 153, 156–62, 172, 178, 201, 209–11, 214–19, 226, 229, 233–36, 256–58, 265, 269, 273, 292–94, 301, 306, 314–18, 322, 326, 341

lament, 41, 86, 87, 134, 162, 173, 199, 209, 214–15, 229, 243, 248, 314
Lebanon, 148, 161, 201, 232–33, 246, 311
life, 18, 23–27, 30–34, 40–42, 44–48, 51–53, 60–66, 71, 74–77, 80–87, 91–92, 97, 102–5, 112–16, 120–29, 138, 156–59, 175–78, 188–91, 194, 198, 202, 209, 214–15, 218–21, 227–30, 233–40, 243–48, 261–62, 264–67, 287–92, 295–99, 304, 311–21, 331, 334–35, 339–43

mercy, 18, 41–42, 53, 56–61, 64–69, 91, 95, 98–99, 102, 106, 109, 112–13, 126–31, 139, 147, 160, 178, 190–92, 197, 201, 218, 247, 251–53, 295, 301, 316–18, 321, 339
Messiah, 156, 256, 263, 267, 294, 333–36
miracle, 20–22, 49, 55–58, 61, 69, 83, 89
mission, 19–20, 28, 31, 41, 50, 53, 56, 60–61, 64–66, 82–83, 89–90, 93, 102, 107, 116, 123
music, 74, 202, 209, 217, 251–59

naked, 180, 184–85, 190–91, 232, 246
nationalistic, 138, 156, 174, 192
nature, 17, 42, 59, 69, 86, 90, 103, 138, 146–47, 154, 157–58, 161, 184, 239, 254–55, 260–61, 313
Nebuchadnezzar, 210–12, 232
Nineveh, 17–22, 25–34, 40–50, 52, 56–64, 74–77, 79–87, 88–107, 108–39, 144–63, 165–79, 182–93, 211, 245, 274, 310–11, 316–20, 325–27
nonhuman creation, 17, 54, 77, 114, 118, 122, 168, 246, 310, 313, 341–43

oppressed, 26, 99, 130, 133–39, 152, 155–56, 159, 171–72, 213, 229, 254, 257, 271–73, 322–25, 330–32
oracle, 30, 60, 130, 134, 137–39, 145–49, 152, 160, 169–70, 183, 191, 199–200, 209, 214, 251, 275, 306–7, 313–14, 339
overturned, 19, 26, 30, 42, 90–91, 94–101, 131, 137–39, 274

Paul, 25, 42, 54, 59, 62, 67, 84, 85, 86, 97, 98, 126, 160, 161, 163, 175–79, 190–93, 220, 238–41, 294–95, 318, 334–337
Philistia, 95, 218, 253–54, 272, 304, 306–10, 313, 316, 327
piety, 31, 59, 76–83, 86–87, 107, 318
plunder, 29, 125, 137–38, 167–69, 173, 177, 180–86, 228–30, 233, 290, 298, 300, 304, 309, 311
poor, 103, 110, 174, 178, 214, 301, 306, 308, 325
postexilic, 26, 235, 293, 333
protest, 18, 20, 25, 31, 34, 52, 60–61, 65–66, 76, 81–83, 86–87, 94–95, 107, 112–13, 122, 130, 162, 215–18, 253
punishment, 47, 98, 101, 107, 118, 121, 125–28, 147, 152, 157, 192, 216, 243, 272–73, 288–89, 296, 312, 323, 327–28, 331, 335, 339

reconciliation, 22, 50, 56, 58, 63, 90, 102, 111, 116, 119, 131, 155, 296, 341–43
rejoice, 31, 76, 96, 106, 186, 197, 199–200, 252, 257–58, 263–67, 271, 273, 330–34, 339, 343
remember, 73–75, 80, 137, 171–73, 179, 186, 197–201, 236, 243, 245, 251–59, 263–65, 268, 295, 300–301
remnant, 28, 118, 127, 133, 146, 174, 219, 271–77, 281, 285–86, 290–93, 297, 304–9, 313, 316–21, 324–25, 328–37, 342
repent, 17–34, 40, 47–53, 55–58, 61–63, 66, 80–83, 89–107, 109–13,

117–37, 152–58, 162, 168–69, 174, 185, 190, 193–94, 241, 274, 284, 295, 301, 343

resurrection, 21–22, 57–58, 63–66, 85, 87, 97, 104, 111, 128, 156, 163, 175, 193–94, 220, 241, 247, 261, 268, 295, 317, 319, 333–40, 343

righteous, 34, 52, 59, 65–66, 76, 83, 99–101, 105, 111, 127, 131, 163, 175, 195, 197–202, 209–10, 213, 217, 225–29, 234–42, 256, 266–69, 273, 276, 293–97, 304–6, 315, 321–22, 325–26, 333–34, 337–38, 341–43

sacrifice, 18, 22, 40–43, 46, 49, 58, 75–80, 98–99, 105, 131–32, 195, 272, 283, 288, 298–99, 317, 332

salvation, 19, 22, 33, 51, 58, 65–66, 69, 74–77, 82–86, 93, 99, 103–4, 118–20, 124–25, 128–30, 158, 172, 175, 221, 231, 238, 259, 274, 298, 307, 316–18, 343

seeking, 26, 45, 51–55, 58, 83–85, 91, 98, 104–5, 117, 124, 154, 158, 162, 172, 184–88, 240, 246, 268, 271–73, 276, 286–90, 294–97, 304–8, 316–20, 341

selah, 252–53, 255–56

shelter, 113, 124, 199–200, 273, 294–97, 306–8, 319, 341

Sheol, 50, 70, 74

sign of Jonah, 56–58, 66, 83, 85

slowness to anger, 112, 129, 147, 153, 155, 157

Tarshish, 18–19, 23, 32, 41–42, 53–55, 58–61, 63, 73, 85, 91, 109–12, 118

temple, 17–18, 28, 42, 53–54, 58–60, 64, 71–76, 79–83, 137, 168, 184, 199–202, 209, 216–19, 225–29, 233–35, 247, 256, 262, 266, 288, 305, 310, 326, 339

terror of trees, 198, 231, 246

thanks, 18–20, 55–56, 69, 74, 77–83, 86–87, 118–21, 327

theophany, 148, 252, 260–61

three days, 21, 40, 49–50, 55–58, 62–63, 83, 90, 102

trust, 18, 53, 66–67, 76, 81, 86, 120–21, 133, 136, 145, 149, 153–54, 159–61, 173, 190, 213, 216, 220, 226–27, 233–39, 252, 258–59, 263–66, 271–73, 276, 283–91, 295–96, 301, 311, 318, 324–25, 328, 330, 334, 338–43

unbelief, 244, 266

upside down, 91, 94, 128

vengeance, 60, 95, 135, 145–47, 154–63, 172, 190, 193, 338

victim, 28–29, 52, 118, 121, 133–35, 138–39, 159, 169–72, 180–85, 198, 213, 228–29, 232, 244–48, 258

violence, 18, 22, 24–28, 42–44, 89, 92–97, 103, 107, 117, 123, 125, 128, 130–31, 135–38, 145, 152–61, 172–74, 182, 188–93, 200–203, 209–14, 218, 221–22, 229–36, 243–48, 271, 277, 281, 286–90, 296, 308, 309, 316, 322, 325–26, 338

wealth, 75, 99, 137–38, 168, 169, 172–74, 177–79, 184–87, 194–95, 221, 228–30, 240, 243–44, 271–73, 276, 283–92, 298–301, 306, 319–20, 338

woe, 182–83, 195–98, 214, 218, 225–35, 240–48, 258, 306–8, 325

wood, 173, 198, 230, 233–34, 244–45

worship, 18, 31, 40, 46–51, 54, 57–59, 64–65, 75, 82, 85–87, 93, 100, 113–19, 137, 178, 194–95, 201–2, 211–13, 217–22, 234–37, 240–44, 247–48, 254, 260, 268, 271–77, 283–92, 294–300, 304–5, 308–10, 313–18, 325–29, 333, 338, 342

wrath, 60, 100, 134–35, 145–48, 153, 156–62, 174, 182, 192–95, 197, 201, 251–53, 271–72, 276–77, 290–91, 294–99, 304–6, 315, 319, 322, 328–31

Yom Kippur, 97–98, 103, 127, 190

Bring ancient truth to modern life with the
NIV Application Commentary *series*

Covering both the Old and New Testaments, the **NIV Application Commentary** series is a staple reference for pastors seeking to bring the Bible's timeless message into a modern context. It explains not only what the Bible means but also how that meaning impacts the lives of believers today.

Genesis
This commentary demonstrates how the text charts a course of theological affirmation that results in a simple but majestic account of an ordered, purposeful cosmos with God at the helm, masterfully guiding it, and what this means to us today.

John H. Walton   ISBN: 0-310-206170

Exodus
The truth of Christ's resurrection and its resulting impact on our lives mean that to Christians, the application of Exodus is less about how to act than it is about what God has done and what it means to be his children.

Peter Enns   ISBN: 0-310-20607-3

Leviticus, Numbers
Roy Gane's commentary on Leviticus and Numbers helps readers understand how the message of these two books, which are replete with what seem to be archaic laws, can have a powerful impact on Christians today.

Roy Gane   ISBN: 0-310-21088-7

Judges, Ruth
This commentary helps readers learn how the messages of Judges and Ruth can have the same powerful impact today that they did when they were first written. Judges reveals a God who employs very human deliverers but refuses to gloss over their sins and the consequences of those sins. Ruth demonstrates the far-reaching impact of a righteous character.

K. Lawson Younger Jr.   ISBN: 0-310-20636-7

1 & 2 Samuel

In Samuel, we meet Saul, David, Goliath, Jonathan, Bathsheba, the witch of Endor, and other unforgettable characters. And we encounter ourselves. For while the culture and conditions of Israel under its first kings are vastly different from our own, the basic issues of humans in relation to God, the Great King, have not changed. Sin, repentance, forgiveness, adversity, prayer, faith, and the promises of God—these continue to play out in our lives today.

Bill T. Arnold
ISBN: 0-310-21086-0

1 & 2 Chronicles

First and Second Chronicles are a narrative steeped in the best and worst of the human heart—but they are also a revelation of Yahweh at work, forwarding his purposes in the midst of fallible people, but a people who trust in the Lord and his word through the prophets. God has a plan to which he is committed.

Andrew E. Hill
ISBN: 0-310-20610-3

Esther

Karen H. Jobes shows what a biblical narrative that never mentions God tells Christians about him today.

Karen H. Jobes
ISBN: 0-310-20672-3

Psalms Volume 1

Gerald Wilson examines Books 1 and 2 of the Psalter. His seminal work on the shaping of the Hebrew Psalter has opened a new avenue of psalms research by shifting focus from exclusive attention to individual psalms to the arrangement of the psalms into groups.

Gerald H. Wilson
ISBN: 0-310-20635-9

Proverbs

Few people can remember when they last heard a sermon from Proverbs or looked together at its chapters. In this NIV Application Commentary on Proverbs, Paul Koptak gives numerous aids to pastors and church leaders on how to study, reflect on, and apply this book on biblical wisdom as part of the educational ministry of their churches.

Paul Koptak
ISBN: 0-310-21852-7

Ecclesiastes, Song of Songs

Ecclesiastes and Songs of Songs have always presented particular challenges to their readers, especially if those readers are seeking to understand them as part of Christian Scripture. Revealing the links between the Scriptures and our own times, Iain Provan shows how these wisdom books speak to us today with relevance and conviction.

Iain Provan   ISBN: 0-310-21372-X

Isaiah

Isaiah wrestles with the realities of people who are not convicted by the truth but actually hardened by it, and with a God who sometimes seems unintelligible, or even worse, appears to be absent. Yet Isaiah penetrates beyond these experiences to an even greater reality, seeing God's rule over history and his capacity to use the worst human actions for good. He declares that even in the darkest hours, the Holy One of Israel is infinitely trustworthy.

John N. Oswalt   ISBN: 0-310-20613-8

Jeremiah/Lamentations

These two books cannot be separated from the political conditions of ancient Judah. Beginning with the time of King Josiah, who introduced religious reform, Jeremiah reflects the close link between spiritual and political prosperity or disaster for the nation as a whole.

J. Andrew Dearman   ISBN: 0-310-20616-2

Ezekiel

Discover how, properly understood, this mysterious book with its obscure images offers profound comfort to us today.

Iain M. Duguid   ISBN: 0-310-21047-X

Daniel

Tremper Longman III reveals how the practical stories and spellbinding apocalyptic imagery of Daniel contain principles that are as relevant now as they were in the days of the Babylonian Captivity.

Tremper Longman III   ISBN: 0-310-20608-1

Hosea, Amos, Micah

Scratch beneath the surface of today's culture and you'll find we're not so different from ancient Israel. Revealing the links between Israel eight centuries B.C. and our own times, Gary V. Smith shows how the prophetic writings of Hosea, Amos, and Micah speak to us today with relevance and conviction.

Gary V. Smith   ISBN: 0-310-20614-6

Jonah, Nahum, Habakkuk, Zephaniah

James Bruckner shows how the messages of these four Old Testament prophets, who lived during some of Israel and Judah's most turbulent times, are as powerful in today's turbulent times as when first written.

James Bruckner   ISBN: 0-310-20637-5

Joel, Obadiah, Malachi

David Baker shows how these three short prophetic books contain both a message of impending judgment (for Israel's enemies and for Israel herself) and a message of great hope — of the outpouring of God's Spirit, of restoration and renewal, and of a coming Messiah. We need to hear that same message today.

David W. Baker   ISBN: 0-310-20723-1

Haggai, Zechariah

This commentary on Haggai and Zechariah helps readers learn how the message of these two prophets who challenged and encouraged the people of God after the return from Babylon can have the same powerful impact on the community of faith today.

Mark J. Boda   ISBN: 0-310-20615-4

Matthew

Matthew helps readers learn how the message of Matthew's gospel can have the same powerful impact today that it did when the author first wrote it.

Michael J. Wilkins   ISBN: 0-310-49310-2

Mark

Learn how the challenging gospel of Mark can leave recipients with the same powerful questions and answers it did when it was written.

David E. Garland   ISBN: 0-310-49350-1

Luke

Focus on the most important application of all: "the person of Jesus and the nature of God's work through him to deliver humanity."

Darrell L. Bock   ISBN: 0-310-49330-7

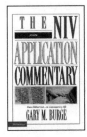

John

Learn both halves of the interpretive task. Gary M. Burge shows readers how to bring the ancient message of John into a modern context. He also explains not only what the book of John meant to its original readers but also how it can speak powerfully today.

Gary M. Burge   ISBN: 0-310-49750-7

Acts

Study the first portraits of the church in action around the world with someone whose ministry mirrors many of the events in Acts. Biblical scholar and worldwide evangelist Ajith Fernando applies the story of the church's early development to the global mission of believers today.

Ajith Fernando   ISBN: 0-310-49410-9

Romans

Paul's letter to the Romans remains one of the most important expressions of Christian truth ever written. Douglas Moo comments on the text and then explores issues in Paul's culture and in ours that help us understand the ultimate meaning of each paragraph.

Douglas J. Moo

ISBN: 0-310-49400-1

1 Corinthians

Is your church struggling with the problem of divisiveness and fragmentation? See the solution Paul gave the Corinthian Christians over 2,000 years ago. It still works today!

Craig Blomberg

ISBN: 0-310-48490-1

2 Corinthians

Often recognized as the most difficult of Paul's letters to understand, 2 Corinthians can have the same powerful impact today that it did when it was first written.

Scott J. Hafemann

ISBN: 0-310-49420-6

Galatians

A pastor's message is true not because of his preaching or people-management skills, but because of Christ. Learn how to apply Paul's example of visionary church leadership to your own congregation.

Scot McKnight

ISBN: 0-310-48470-7

Ephesians

Explore what the author calls "a surprisingly comprehensive statement about God and his work, about Christ and the gospel, about life with God's Spirit, and about the right way to live."

Klyne Snodgrass

ISBN: 0-310-49340-4

Philippians
The best lesson Philippians provides is how to encourage people who actually are doing quite well. Learn why not all the New Testament letters are reactions to theological crises.

Frank Thielman   ISBN: 0-310-49300-5

Colossians/Philemon
The temptation to trust in the wrong things has always been strong. Use this commentary to learn the importance of trusting only in Jesus, God's Son, in whom all the fullness of God lives. No message is more important for our postmodern culture.

David E. Garland   ISBN: 0-310-48480-4

1&2 Thessalonians
Paul's letters to the Thessalonians say as much to us today about Christ's return and our resurrection as they did in the early church. This volume skillfully reveals Paul's answers to these questions and how they address the needs of contemporary Christians.

Michael W. Holmes   ISBN: 0-310-49380-3

1&2 Timothy, Titus
Reveals the context and meanings of Paul's letters to two leaders in the early Christian Church and explores their present-day implications to help you to accurately apply the principles they contain to contemporary issues.

Walter L. Liefeld   ISBN: 0-310-50110-5

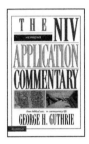

Hebrews
The message of Hebrews can be summed up in a single phrase: "God speaks effectively to us through Jesus." Unpack the theological meaning of those seven words and learn why the gospel still demands a hearing today.

George H. Guthrie   ISBN: 0-310-49390-0

James

Give your church the best antidote for a culture of people who say they believe one thing but act in ways that either ignore or contradict their belief. More than just saying, "Practice what you preach," James gives solid reasons why faith and action must coexist.

David P. Nystrom   ISBN: 0-310-49360-9

1 Peter

The issue of the church's relationship to the state hits the news media in some form nearly every day. Learn how Peter answered the question for Christians surviving under Roman rule and how it applies similarly to believers living amid the secular institutions of the modern world.

Scot McKnight   ISBN: 0-310-49290-4

2 Peter, Jude

Introduce your modern audience to letters they may not be familiar with and show why they'll want to get to know them.

Douglas J. Moo   ISBN: 0-310-20104-7

Letters of John

Like the community in John's time, which faced disputes over erroneous "secret knowledge," today's church needs discernment in affirming new ideas supported by Scripture and weeding out harmful notions. This volume will help you show today's Christians how to use John's example.

Gary M. Burge   ISBN: 0-310-48620-3

Revelation

Craig Keener offers a "new" approach to the book of Revelation by focusing on the "old." He stresses the need for believers to prepare for the possibility of suffering for the sake of Jesus.

Craig S. Keener   ISBN: 0-310-23192-2

Praise for the NIV Application Commentary Series

This series promises to become an indispensable tool for every pastor and teacher who seeks to make the Bible's timeless message speak to this generation."
—Billy Graham

"It is encouraging to find a commentary that is not only biblically trustworthy but also contemporary in its application. **The NIV Application Commentary** series will prove to be a helpful tool in the pastor's sermon preparation. I use it and recommend it."
—Charles F. Stanley, Pastor, First Baptist Church of Atlanta

"**The NIV Application Commentary** is an outstanding resource for pastors and anyone else who is serious about developing 'doers of the Word.'"
—Rick Warren, Pastor, Saddleback Community Church, Author, *The Purpose-Driven Church*

"**The NIV Application Commentary** series shares the same goal that has been the passion of my own ministry—communicating God's Word to a contemporary audience so that they feel the full impact of its message."
—Bill Hybels, Willow Creek Community Church

"**The NIV Application Commentary** series helps pastors and other Bible teachers with one of the most neglected elements in good preaching—accurate, useful application. Most commentaries tell you a few things that are helpful and much that you do not need to know. By dealing with the original meaning and contemporary significance of each passage, **The NIV Application Commentary** series promises to be helpful all the way around."
—Dr. James Montgomery Boice, Tenth Presbyterian Church

"If you want to avoid hanging applicational elephants from interpretive threads, then **The NIV Application Commentary** is for you! This series excels at both original meaning and contemporary signficance. I support it 100 percent."
—Howard G. Hendricks, Dallas Theological Seminary

"**The NIV Application Commentary** series doesn't fool around: It gets right down to business, bringing this ancient and powerful Word of God into the present so that it can be heard and delivered with all the freshness of a new day, with all the immediacy of a friend's embrace."
—Eugene H. Peterson, Regent College

"This series dares to go where few scholars have gone before—into the real world of biblical application faced by pastors and teachers every day. This is everything a good commentary series should be."
—Leith Anderson, Pastor, Wooddale Church

"This is THE pulpit commentary for the 21st century."
—George K. Brushaber, President, Bethel College & Seminary

"Here, at last, is a commentary that makes the proper circuit from the biblical world to main street. **The NIV Application Commentary** is a magnificent gift to the church."
—R. Kent Hughes, Pastor, College Church, Wheaton, IL

Look for the NIV Application Commentary at your local Christian bookstore

ZONDERVAN®

GRAND RAPIDS, MICHIGAN 49530 USA

We want to hear from you. Please send your comments about this book to us in care of zreview@zondervan.com. Thank you.

GRAND RAPIDS, MICHIGAN 49530 USA

ZONDERVAN.COM/
AUTHOR**TRACKER**